BURYING THE ENEMY

BURYING THE ENEMY

The Story of Those Who Cared for the
Dead in Two World Wars

TIM GRADY

YALE UNIVERSITY PRESS
NEW HAVEN AND LONDON

For information about this and other Yale University Press publications, please contact:
U.S. Office: sales.press@yale.edu yalebooks.com
Europe Office: sales@yaleup.co.uk yalebooks.co.uk

Set in Adobe Garamond Pro by IDSUK (DataConnection) Ltd
Printed and Bound in the UK using 100% Renewable Electricity at CPI Group (UK) Ltd

Library of Congress Control Number: 2024949499
A catalogue record for this book is available from the British Library.
Authorized Representative in the EU: Easy Access System Europe, Mustamäe tee 50, 10621 Tallinn, Estonia, gpsr.requests@easproject.com

ISBN 978-0-300-27397-7

10 9 8 7 6 5 4 3 2 1

CONTENTS

ILLUSTRATIONS AND MAPS

Illustrations

Maps

ABBREVIATIONS

BArch Berlin	Bundesarchiv, Berlin
BEF	British Expeditionary Force
BRIXMIS	British Commanders'-in-Chief Mission to the Soviet Forces in Germany
CWGC	Commonwealth War Graves Commission
GDR	German Democratic Republic
GEC	General Electric Company
IBCC	International Bomber Command Centre
IWGC	Imperial War Graves Commission
IWM	Imperial War Museum Archive, London
MRES	Missing Research and Enquiry Service
NATO	North Atlantic Treaty Organization
NMA	National Memorial Arboretum
PA-AA	Auswärtiges Amt – Politisches Archiv, Berlin
POW	Prisoner of War
RAF	Royal Air Force
ReK	Reich Association of Former Prisoners of War (Reichsvereinigung ehemaliger Kriegsgefangener)
SED	Socialist Unity Party (Sozialistische Einheitspartei Deutschlands)
StAHH	Staatsarchiv Hamburg
TNA	The National Archives, Kew

VdH	Association of Returnees, Prisoners of War and Relatives of the Missing (Verband der Heimkehrer, Kriegsgefangenen und Vermisstenangehörigen)
VDK	Volksbund Deutsche Kriegsgräberfürsorge
WASt	Wehrmacht Information Office for War Casualties and Prisoners of War (Wehrmachtauskunftstelle für Kriegerverluste und Kriegsgefangene; later Deutsche Dienststelle)
ZAK	Central Information Office for War Casualties and War Graves (Zentralnachweiseamt für Kriegsverluste und Kriegergräber)

ACKNOWLEDGEMENTS

There are a whole host of people that I would like to thank for helping me to write this book, but I must begin with Victoria and our children, Orla and Frieda. I want to thank them for their love, patience and continual support. But I also need to offer them an apology for turning so many family days out into site visits. As I began to research this book, I was amazed to discover just how many communities in Britain and in Germany had once held enemy graves. This realisation was very convenient for me. It meant that every outing, family visit and even holiday offered the potential for a quick research trip, which is perhaps something my children did not always appreciate, particularly in the rain.

I have resisted taking the other historians at the University of Chester on too many field trips, although my students have got to know Chester's Overleigh Cemetery very well over the past few years! Nonetheless, my colleagues have been extremely generous with their time and advice in many different ways. I'm particularly grateful to Kara Critchell, Hannah Ewence and Howard Williams who kindly commented on early chapters of the book. But I must also thank Paul Bissell and the wider research team for supporting this project, providing funds for archival visits, and crucially for backing a successful Leverhulme Trust Research Fellowship. The Leverhulme's very generous funding award gave me the time and space to write, and also provided me with the opportunity to take up a Simone Veil Fellowship at the

LMU's Project House Europe. Thank you to Kiran Patel, Lisbeth Matzer and Thomas Süsler-Rohringer for making it such an enjoyable and productive stay in Munich.

Over the course of the project, I have become deeply indebted to Roland Clark and Caroline Sharples, who have not only been wonderful friends but have also gone above and beyond by reading, and commenting on, every draft chapter. I was really pleased, therefore, that they were both able to join me in London in 2023 for the Royal Historical Society's inaugural book workshop. A full day dedicated to the book manuscript seemed incredibly indulgent, but it was so helpful. I am incredibly grateful to Lucy Noakes, Panikos Panayi, Layla Renshaw and Matthew Stibbe, who also took time out of their busy schedules and brought so much to the workshop discussions.

I have tried to minimise my environmental impact in researching this book, travelling almost exclusively by rail on my many research trips from home on the Wirral to Germany. If nothing else, the train journeys themselves and the inevitable delays provided me with plenty of time to ponder the sources and my approach to the book. In criss-crossing Germany, I spent a lot of time in many smaller communal archives far removed from the Bundesarchiv in Berlin, although I was there too of course. Wherever I ended up, though, the archivists were unfailingly helpful and always keen to share their material. But special thanks must go to Peter Päßler in Kassel, who went out of his way to find me every conceivable source on the war dead, and also to Falk Bachter in Oberschleißheim for taking me on a personal tour of local cemeteries. Closer to home, Anne Buckley and Richard Millington very kindly passed my way obscure sources that they uncovered on their own travels.

The book has definitely been shaped by the many conversations I've enjoyed with friends, colleagues and editors over the years. At Yale, I must thank Jo Godfrey, Rachael Lonsdale and Katie Urquhart for their absolutely brilliant advice and very wise words on all aspects of the book. Thank you! Neil Gregor, Stefan Manz, Mathias Seiter, Gavin Schaffer have always been on hand to offer help and to talk through the broader history, as well as to discuss the immense challenges of the current environment in higher education. At Chester, Katharine Wilson and Tom

ACKNOWLEDGEMENTS

Pickles are always happy to discuss all things research, which is an absolute comfort. The regulars at the RKEI writing café have been brilliant too; it's been so nice to see everyone else's projects develop with every meeting. Finally, a big thanks to the Bebington 'history' circle for being such a great source of friendship.

Cemeteries
First World War ■
Post-War (Interwar) ◆
Second World War ●
Post-War (after 1945) ▲

—— Pre-Second World War frontiers
----- East Germany and Poland from 1945

1 Becklingen War Cemetery ●
2 Berlin 1939–1945 Cemetery ● ▲
3 Berlin Olympische Strasse Cemetery ● ▲
4 Berlin Stahnsdorf (Südwestfriedhof) ■
5 Celle War Cemetery ●
6 Cologne (Südfriedhof) ■ ◆ ● ▲
7 Dürnbach War Cemetery ●
8 Hamburg (Ohlsdorf) ■ ● ▲
9 Hanover Military Cemetery ▲
10 Hanover War Cemetery ●
11 Kassel (Niederzwehren) ■

12 Kiel (Nordfriedhof) ●
13 Münster Lauheide
     (Waldfriedhof) ● ▲
14 Oppeln/Opole (Alter Friedhof) ◆
15 Reichswald Forest War Cemetery ●
16 Rheinberg War Cemetery ●
17 Rheindahlen Military Cemetery ▲
18 Sage War Cemetery ●
19 Wiesbaden (Südfriedhof) ◆
20 Worms (Hochheimer Höhe) ■
21 Zehrensdorf Indian Cemetery ■

Map 1. Location of the main British war cemeteries in Germany.

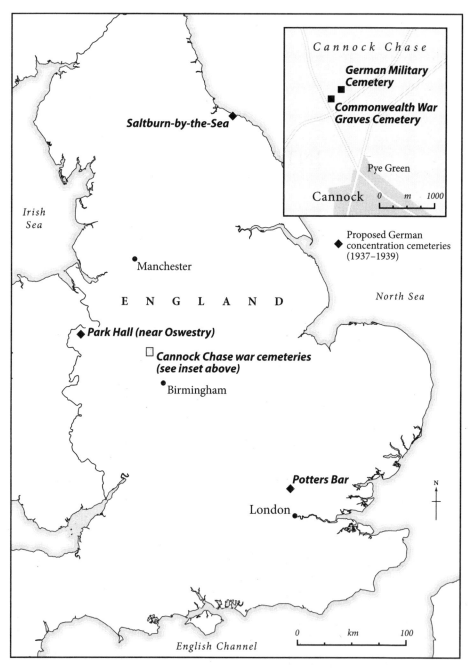

Map 2. Location of the actual, and proposed, German war cemeteries in the United Kingdom.

INTRODUCTION

St Cyrus, a small Aberdeenshire village, just north of Montrose, sports a wonderful sandy beach that curves for miles along the North Sea coast. On a summer's evening, as the sun sets over the horizon, the sky sometimes glows a light orange to match the colour of the sands below. In July 1941, long after the Battle of Britain had petered out, the serenity of this scene was briefly disrupted by a Junkers Ju 88 bomber of the German Luftwaffe. The powerful twin-engine aircraft had already been hit and was clearly in trouble. It stuttered its way through the clouds, before smashing into the ground just beyond the costal dunes, scattering aircraft parts, oil and human lives in its wake (see image 1). Little could be done for the four-man crew. One man managed to scramble free but died soon after in hospital, while the other three airmen were killed at the scene as flames quickly engulfed the wreckage.

All four Germans were very young. Eduard Becker, nicknamed Eddy by his friends, who served as the aeroplane's observer, was just 21, and had only completed his A-levels (*Abitur*) shortly before the outbreak of war.[1] Hans Steggemann, a mere three years older than Becker, but already married and father to little Edelgard, found himself in the strange position of being the senior crew member.[2] Steggemann, Becker and their fellow crew members were among a total of some 4,500 Germans to lose their lives on British soil during the course of the

1

1. The smouldering remains of a Junkers Ju 88 bomber, shot down over the east coast of Scotland in July 1941. Three German airmen died at the scene; the fourth succumbed to his injuries soon after in hospital.

Second World War. They died not on some distant battlefield or in international waters, but breathed their last in and around civilian communities, ordinary homes, schools and workplaces.

Once peace came, these very visible deaths gradually became invisible. There is, for example, no memorial to Becker, Steggemann and the Junkers crew in St Cyrus or in Montrose. This, though, should really come as no surprise. Unlike in Belgium or France, where memorials to foreign soldiers abound, the British have largely limited their remembrance efforts to their own military dead. Even their fellow Allies, whether Poles or colonial soldiers, have struggled to secure a place in Britain's memory culture.[3] The same is true of the civilian victims of the bombing raids, whose presence in narratives of the air war has largely served to confirm the mythologised 'Blitz spirit'.[4] The enemy may well have left a mark as their aircraft hurtled into the ground and bodies smashed into British soil with a fatal thud, but in today's Britain few signs of these deaths remain.

The primacy of one's own war dead over the enemy is of course not a uniquely British phenomenon. It reflects the stark difference between 'grievable and ungrievable lives', as Judith Butler once put it.[5] During the Second World War, some 26,500 military personnel from Britain and its empire died in Germany fighting the Nazi regime. The majority lost their lives in the air war over urban centres, but others died on the ground, fighting during the final months of the conflict, or in captivity, sometimes even from wilful neglect.[6] Just as in Britain, however, there are very few traces of these wartime deaths today. For a long time, at least until the mid-1960s, many Germans were too engrossed in their own suffering to pay much attention to anyone else, even the actual victims of Nazi genocide struggled to get much of a voice.[7] Instead, people told themselves 'war stories' about missing prisoners in the East, bombed-out civilians at home and the plight of expellees who had fled the Russian advance.[8] As was the case in Britain, the enemy gradually faded to the margins, leaving behind few signs that they too had died throughout Germany in the conflict.

There was nothing particularly new about this process. During the Great War of 1914–1918, the enemy also died in their thousands on the home front; they too have largely vanished from sight. Clearly the earlier war was a very different conflict to the Second World War. It was never merely a forerunner of Hitler's genocidal campaigns, just with a different set of leaders at the helm. Ideological fervour, genocide and an annihilationist war in the East set the two firmly apart.[9] Nonetheless, when it comes to the enemy war dead, there are some striking similarities, which makes it pertinent for this book to explore these seemingly separate histories together.

In public narratives, the home front in the Great War was about volunteering, labour disputes and food shortages; it was certainly not about German or British bodies piling high, even though some 2,700 Germans expired on British soil and over 6,500 men from Britain and its empire died in wartime Germany.[10] Some of this number arrived in Britain and Germany already sporting battle wounds that they then succumbed to in hospitals on the home front. The vast majority of deaths, however, occurred behind the barbed wire of internment camps. Illness and disease, particularly the influenza pandemic of 1918–1919, were the biggest killers, sweeping quickly through the confined spaces of camp barracks, while other men died from neglect or even took their own lives, ground down by the monotony of life in captivity. Some prisoners of war (POWs) managed to escape the confines of the internment camps on work duties, only to die in accidents, falling down quarries or being flattened by goods trains.[11]

It is clear then that the enemy dead are largely a blank spot in both Britain and Germany's 'collective remembrance' of the two world wars.[12] With this in mind, this book sets out to return the two countries' wartime foe to the history of twentieth-century conflict. No narrative of the world wars should be complete without recognising the extent of death, mutilation and mutual destruction, which embraced friend and enemy alike. At the same time, the book also decentres the geography of the world wars, moving such deadly encounters from distant battlefields to the home fronts.[13] Whether in St Cyrus or in Hamburg or Berlin, the death of the enemy at home was hard to hide during the war itself. Local people were often witnesses to death; aeroplanes spiralled down into villages and towns or POW workers fell ill in the midst of otherwise fairly serene communities.

British and German civilians did not just passively observe such losses, they also frequently ended up nursing the enemy in their dying moments or at least clearing away the corpses that remained.[14] Such moments of care, even tenderness, were very different to the 'brutalizing effect' of war on the frontlines, where enemy bodies were often mistreated.[15] On the home front, people took the responsibilities of burial, funerals and mortuary care much more seriously. In most cases, the enemy was buried close to where they died. The local authorities, for example, gave Becker and the other crew members a lavish public funeral in Montrose. The four coffins, bedecked with Nazi swastika flags, were carried through the town to the main municipal burial ground, the enchantingly named Sleepyhillock Cemetery.[16]

This practice of making use of existing municipal cemeteries and parish churchyards was repeated time and again throughout the two world wars. The wartime foe, therefore, ended up having much more of a local than a national presence. The number of cemeteries containing enemy graves was staggering. By 1948, around 700 separate cemeteries in Britain, Northern Ireland, the Isle of Man and the Channel Islands contained German graves from the two conflicts. In Germany, the figures were even higher, with over 600 cemeteries used in the First World War and an unspecified, though surely much larger, number in the Second.[17]

The interment of the enemy in parish churchyards and small municipal cemeteries, such as the one in Montrose, helped to create a diverse community of the dead. German airmen were interspersed with British sailors, Canadian pilots and other members of the opposing forces. These different groups of military dead all had to share the cemetery space with local civilians – aunts, uncles, grandparents and other family members – who had passed away in the normal rhythms of life. With the enemy dead lying in the heart of local communities, they proved very hard to ignore. Even when the fighting had stopped, the bodies of the former enemy remained, forever reminding people that friend and foe alike had died in conflict. Cemeteries across both Britain and Germany, therefore, were never singular spaces where only one's own dead rested, but were rather sites where two different histories of conflict came together. Within the constraints of these confined spaces, the former enemies had little option but to negotiate some form of shared presence.[18]

Montrose again offers a striking illustration of the ways in which seemingly competing memories of conflict ended up coexisting. At the war's end, Eddy Becker's mother, Agathe, was determined to fulfil her husband's dying wish to bring the body home. After years of exchanging letters with the town clerk, she finally managed to make the journey to her son's grave in 1954. Agathe, an older fairly subdued lady with a mass of grey hair stuffed into a bun, arrived in Montrose to be greeted by the clerk who immediately took her to lunch.[19] The pair then visited the graves, which she found to be 'so well cared for and beautifully set out'. It then suddenly dawned on Agathe that she 'couldn't disturb her son's sleep' and take him home. She eventually returned to Cologne empty-handed, but was reassured by the idea that her son's presence in Montrose was helping to heal everything that 'the war had destroyed'.[20]

Agathe Becker's experience of Montrose goes to the very heart of the book's opening argument, which is covered in the first half of the study. It maintains that tentative local discussions about the care of the enemy war dead were crucial for reconciliation between the former foes. While diplomats and politicians sitting in Berlin, Bonn or London eyed their opposite numbers with suspicion, communities that ended up with the enemy dead in their midst often gradually reached out to the bereaved overseas.[21] Cemeteries in both Britain and Germany, therefore, acted as significant 'zones of contact' for rebuilding the British–German relationship, for bringing the British and German people together.[22] This was reconciliation work from below, driven by humanitarian concern, rather than diplomatic calculation.

At its core, then, this is a history of emotions, of bereaved, distraught families seeking comfort for their pain. This emotional labour often fell on women who pushed through gendered social conventions to fight for the rights of their dead sons or husbands.[23] What was remarkable, however, was that in these particular circumstances, the process of working through grief and the legacies of wartime loss had to occur in partnership with their old foes.[24] Just as Agathe Becker had done in Montrose, thousands of other families embarked on their own emotional journey. They tentatively reached out to the former enemy, sometimes with a deep sense of bitterness, but always determined to discover more about their loved one's final resting place. As a result, letters flew back and forth between the people of Chingford and Worms, Koblenz and Oswestry, Datteln and Widnes, and many more besides.

Over time, as trust and understanding grew, local British and German communities fulfilled a string of requests from the bereaved, laying flowers, tidying headstones or sending on photographs of the graves. On many occasions, locals were also instrumental in helping relatives to plan pilgrimages to far-flung parts of Britain or Germany.[25] One of these trips ended in Castle Donington, where in a 'touching scene' German families and local residents came together around the POW graves.[26] Similar scenes played out in German communities, as bereaved British relatives arrived to pay their own respects. The 'work of the dead', it seems, particularly when the British and Germans were buried together, often did far more to unite than to divide.[27]

Yet, just as it seemed that the dead could help to bring the former foes together, all of this organic work of reconciliation came to a shuddering halt. The reason for this, quite simply, was that the enemy dead were no longer there. Both the British and the Germans made separate decisions to strip out their national remains and to concentrate them instead into large military cemeteries. The British had already set the exhumation ball rolling in the mid-1920s. Teams from the then Imperial War Graves Commission (IWGC) criss-crossed defeated Germany on a mission to concentrate the dead into four national cemeteries in Kassel, Hamburg Ohlsdorf, Cologne and Berlin Stahnsdorf. After the Second World War, the British repeated this feat, moving thousands of bodies to an additional eleven cemeteries.[28] As the vanquished power, Germany's own war graves commission (Volksbund Deutsche Kriegsgräberfürsorge, VDK) had to wait until 1959 until it could do the same.[29] However, once the digging started, the VDK made quick work of things, moving almost 5,000 bodies from across Britain, including Becker and his comrades, to Cannock Chase in Staffordshire in only twelve months.[30]

Disinterring bodies from local cemeteries, many of whom had lain undisturbed for decades, was a massive undertaking. Yet, these exhumation operations have rarely been discussed.[31] It has proved much easier, it seems, to focus on the finished military cemeteries with their neatly lined headstones than to delve into the unearthing of bones, flesh and personal artefacts.[32] This book reverses this oversight. It demonstrates that the exhumation and movement of thousands of enemy corpses was a fundamental part of the history of war and remembrance.[33] Military corpses, at least those classified as such, were rarely stationary; they were buried, exhumed and moved, sometimes on numerous occasions.

Moving many thousands of bodies was not without consequence. If the first part of the book argues that the presence of the enemy dead helped to bring the British and German populations together, then the second half of the book focuses on the breakdown of these very same relations. The mass exhumation of the dead had a devastating effect on the British–German relationship, not quite setting off a new 'antagonism', but certainly pushing constructive discussions on the ground back into the political arena.[34] The unmaking of these fragile local relations encompassed three entangled themes which are explored in depth across chapters 7 to 11.

At the centre of the first theme is the destruction of the tentative and often still raw relations between local communities and their former enemy. These relationships had been built on the tangible presence of the dead, not on their absence. After all, there was no longer much of a reason for German families to visit Montrose or any other British town if the graves had been moved to Cannock Chase. Equally, British relatives could bypass the smaller German communities that had once been the custodians of their loved ones' remains and instead head straight for the large war cemeteries. The VDK even facilitated relatives in this endeavour by laying on special tours to the German graves on Cannock Chase.[35]

All of this may have been immensely practical for the casual traveller, but the move to military cemeteries, known as concentration cemeteries, created new voids, which is the focus of the second theme. Where friend and foe had once lain together in local burial grounds, they now found themselves interred in sober national spaces that stand as small islands of Britishness or Germanness in each country. Architectural historians like to emphasise the apparent national differences in the design of the British and German cemeteries, but far from being in opposition, they are actually very similar.[36] These concentration cemeteries, where white soldiers from the Dominions lie alongside the British, are relics from an earlier age of colonialism and national expansion, a final 'enclave' of empire in a rapidly changing world.[37] Cannock Chase also reflects multiple incarnations of the German nation. First World War dead from far-flung corners of Austria, Alsace-Lorraine and Poland rest in one area, while Nazi war criminals rest incongruously alongside persecuted refugees in the 1939–1945 section.

Collective remembrance of the world wars in the wake of the mass exhumations of the enemy is the subject of the third theme. While the original burial grounds, with their central position in community life, had encouraged raw, sometimes even lively, discussions between the British and German publics, this was never the case with the new national cemeteries, which have sometimes done more to divide than to unite. They have been the setting for ritualised gatherings between diplomats and politicians of course, but the enemy cemeteries remain out of sight and out of mind for most people.[38] The ending of shared remembrance cultures, which quickly faded with the mass exhumations, meant that neither the British nor the Germans were constrained by the presence of the enemy dead. Their bodies no longer worked to remind people that the two world wars had been global conflicts with casualties on both sides.

Once freed from the duty to remember the enemy dead, there was nothing to stop people telling themselves more comforting stories about their own country's wartime exploits. The history became one of heroic national sacrifice, rather than of shared loss in a world war. It was the German Right in the interwar years that initially perfected the art of propagating their own simple, but satisfying, 'myth of the war experience'.[39] The absence of the British dead, secreted away to very separate spaces, made it much easier for dangerous myths about the war to form.

The defeat of the Nazi regime and the slow process of coming to terms with Germany's genocidal past (*Vergangenheitsbewältigung*) helped to rein in such narratives after 1945.[40] Britain's memory culture, in contrast, increasingly moved in the very opposite direction. Powered by a 'culture of victory' and with the enemy dead absent, the British have managed to concentrate almost solely on their own wartime sacrifices.[41] Stories of bravery and selfishness in the muddy trenches of the Great War or the bombed-out cities of the later conflict have seeped into the national consciousness. The dominant place that the two world wars enjoy in the country's post-industrial heritage industry, in particular, has helped to turn war and remembrance into a national past time that can be visited, enjoyed and consumed.[42]

The National Memorial Arboretum (NMA) in Staffordshire and the International Bomber Command Centre (IBCC) in Lincolnshire – two sprawling sites of national remembrance – are perhaps the most striking examples of remembrance as heritage. Both sites appear in tourist brochures and travel guides, places for a day trip to soak up the British national story, while enjoying refreshments in the café and souvenirs from the gift shop.[43] The two attractions ostensibly honour the dead, but neither are actual wartime sites, nor are they cemeteries; they are recent constructs, which means that the dead, and in particular the enemy dead, have no real role to play.

Far more visitors flock into the grounds of the NMA and IBCC than the formal war cemeteries in Germany or Britain. The dominance of these new sites, as this book makes clear, stems from the extraction of enemy bodies from scattered graveyards to large national cemeteries. In Montrose's Sleepyhillock Cemetery today, there is no sign that the German aircrew had ever been there. The site where Agathe Becker made the painful decision to let her son 'stay [. . .] undisturbed', was now empty, the headstones were gone and even the information board from the Commonwealth War Graves Commission (CWGC), as the IWGC has been known since the 1960s, mentions only the Allied dead.[44] In the public records of both the VDK and the CWGC, the German aircrew are listed simply as buried on 'Cannock Chase'.[45] This is certainly a statement of fact. But if the history of the enemy war dead only starts from where the bodies are currently buried, then the wider context of death, burial, reconciliation and exhumation is entirely 'lost to us'.[46]

1

LOCATING

In 1909, a group of more than 200 German politicians, industrialists and state officials arrived in the English port of Harwich on a journey of discovery and learning. As enthusiastic members of the Gartenstadt-Gesellschaft, Germany's version of the garden city movement, they were determined to learn how the British had created new towns that meshed urban housing with countryside living. After taking in workers' quarters in York and Manchester, the group arrived in the village of Port Sunlight, a sea of urban tranquillity, in the heart of England's industrial north. Rising out of the boggy plains of the River Mersey, Port Sunlight offered everything the group was after. Not only was every little cluster of houses its own 'work of art', the German visitors purred, but the village was also awash with green spaces that had been carefully designed for both the living and the dead. As the group wandered around, they discovered a school, parks, sports pitches and even a small cemetery enveloping the recently built church. 'It is not possible to think of a more beautiful garden city,' one of the delegates eulogised after a day spent exploring.[1]

The British residents of Port Sunlight seemed equally excited at the sight of the German delegation. People opened the doors to their homes to allow the Germans a peek inside, a group of schoolchildren welcomed the visitors with a maypole dance and William Lever, the soap magnate and founder of the village, also put on a special luncheon for the guests. Under the flags of Imperial Germany and the United Kingdom, the

German visitors and their British hosts dined and chatted, before Lever took to the stage to give a rousing speech. As a veteran of many such gatherings, Lever knew how to get his audience on side, praising the Germans' 'beautiful country', before going on to expound about his own personal architectural values. Veering off topic somewhat, Lever ended with a little spiel about the importance of imperialism. The 'German race and the English race', he declared, are jointly 'teaching a higher form of life to other races'.[2] Similar exchanges to this interlude by the Mersey were repeated across Britain and Germany in the decade before the First World War. Business trips, cultural exchanges and even shared ventures in colonial Africa, as Lever hinted, often made the British–German relationship one of deep and meaningful entanglements.[3]

However, a few none too subtle remarks in Lever's talk also pointed to a more familiar 'Anglo-German antagonism'. Several times, he referred to the German visitors as being part of an 'invasion' of England, albeit a 'peaceful' one; 'laughter and cheers' was reportedly the German delegate's polite response.[4] Lever's rather awkward attempt at joviality was a clear sign of Britain's growing nervousness at Wilhelmine Germany's global ambitions or a wish for its own 'place in the sun', as Bernhard von Bülow, the later chancellor, so memorably phrased it.[5] The visit of the Gartenstadt-Gesellschaft, therefore, encapsulated the two sides of the British–German relationship. For the most part, there were shared goals, mutual respect and even deep admiration for one another. But under-pinning this warmth was also a nagging fear of hostile competition or even a full-on invasion. By 1914, and again in 1939, the pendulum had clearly swung towards antagonism, severing any previous bonds. Yet, even then, it proved impossible to separate the two populations entirely. The living and, in particular, the dead were already too deeply entangled for all relations to end.

Finding the Foe

Shakespearean tragedies generally come to a climax with vengeful murder, a poisoned chalice or blinded grief, but most relationships tend to fizzle out in a less dramatic fashion. More commonly, fric-tions and grumbles mount over the years before couples eventually drift apart.[6] In the decades before the world wars, the British–German relationship followed this more familiar path of ups and downs before the pair descended into the horrors of full-blown conflict. Clashes over colonial ambitions, naval power and diplomatic alliances in the early twentieth century all served to stoke antagonism. Yet, at the same time, there were also plenty of moments of togetherness, as Lever's hosting of the German urban planners had shown. Twenty-five years later, by which time Hitler was sitting supreme as German chancellor, relations were again particularly tetchy, but then the Nazis' brutal suppression of their political opponents, wanton violence and casual disregard of international treaties was hardly the best recipe for a firm friendship.

What was important about the wax and wane of international relations in the run-up to the two world wars was that they left a deep mark on the wider public. As Edward VII and Kaiser Wilhelm II squabbled over the size of their battleships or Hitler and Chamberlain bickered about the future of Czechoslovakia, the British and German people also started to learn the same language of hostility and enmity. One housewife living in deepest Warwickshire, for example, appeared at first glance to be fairly cocooned from the mêlée of British–German tensions. On one cool November morning in 1937, she was preparing tea with a friend, 'adding meat, flour and [. . .] stock to vegetables' to the pan, with the wireless playing the annual Armistice Day service in the background. All was well, as the verses of 'O God Our Help in Ages Past' came through the airwaves, but then suddenly a German voice broke the peace. Compared to the 'calm' British demeanour, the sound of the Germans came across as 'shouting, harsh and militaristic, [so] full of hatred', her companion complained.[7] Such comments were certainly never confined to one small corner of Warwickshire. In the years preceding the world wars, both the British and German people increasingly viewed their opposite number not just as a rival on the world stage, but also as a genuine danger.

Journalists and writers proved to be most adept when it came to helping their readers to locate the enemy. In the decade before the First World War, the German press went through various waves of bitterness when they managed to paint the British as being at fault for almost everything. Take the Agadir crisis of 1911, for example. The whole incident had mainly been a spat between Paris and Berlin over the future of Morocco, but then the British waded in. Determined to keep German colonial ambitions in check, the Chancellor of the Exchequer, David Lloyd George, fired off a thinly veiled warning to Berlin, stressing that the British would not stand by and suffer a 'humiliation'.[8] The thought of the British bossing them around, however, caused much consternation in the German press. Even the popular satirical magazine *Simplicissimus*, often fairly liberal in its content, took to the barricades. Against the backdrop of an ornate Moroccan mosque, three athletes – a muscular German, a scrawny Spaniard and a rather effeminate Frenchman – lined up to race (see image 2). But before the German could claim his rightful prize, a dour-faced Lloyd George brought the competition to an abrupt halt, shouting: 'Stop! The German can't take part; he might actually win!'[9]

Britain had its own breed of popular writers, who, like the cartoonists at *Simplicissimus*, managed to point their readers in the direction of an emerging overseas rival. Leaning more heavily on sensationalism than reality, some British journalists found the time to invent their own imagined scenarios about a rampant enemy, none of which seemed likely to improve British–German relationship. One of the most dramatic examples of the genre came strolling through central London in late spring 1906. By all accounts, it had been a rather 'fine day' on Oxford Street, already the capital's main retail destination, when a line of soldiers dressed in 'spiked helmets and Prussian-blue uniforms' descended on shoppers. As they 'parad[ed] moodily' past the bustling shops, each soldier carried a weighty sandwich board over his shoulders advertising the latest novel from William Le Queux – *The Invasion of 1910* – that was being serialised in the *Daily Mail*.[10]

Le Queux, a moustachioed Anglo-French journalist with a withering view of continental Europe, established himself as the master of invasion literature. The genre had first emerged in the 1870s, after the unification of Germany, when a British army officer wrote a popular novel about fighting a marauding enemy at *The Battle of Dorking*.[11] Other books came and went, but it was Le Queux who ran the furthest with the concept.[12] In *The Invasion of 1910*, he depicted German troops storming through innocent British villages on their way to capture London. After first passing through Chelmsford, the fighting in Le

2. The 1911 Agadir crisis started as a race for European supremacy in Morocco, but ended with a noticeable souring of British–German relations, after Berlin's colonial advances were rebuffed. Here, the satirical magazine, *Simplicissimus*, complains that David Lloyd George, then Chancellor of the Exchequer, used unsporting tactics to stop Germany from claiming its rightful prize.

Queux's imaginary war then moved further into Essex. 'The hamlet of Howe Street was in flames and burning furiously', while the surrounding countryside, 'a perfect maze of trees and hedgerows', was torn apart by 'bursting projectiles'.[13] Such vivid descriptions of destruction, coupled with the sight of Prussian soldiers marching down Oxford Street, meant the German threat suddenly became very real. To help cement such fears in the minds of the public, the *Daily Mail* also published detailed invasion maps based on Le Queux's story, making it clear to readers that their village might well be next in the firing line.[14]

Some thirty years later, two London-based journalists, Roy Connolly and Frank McIlraith, the latter a 'medium height, tanned, quizzical-eyed' Australian, tried to step into Le Queux's sizeable shoes.[15] By now, the threat was no longer the Kaiser's army charging through Essex, but rather Hitler's Germany launching an *Invasion from the Air*. Clearly inspired by Stanley Baldwin's oft-repeated quip that the 'bomber will always get through', Connolly and McIlraith tried to demonstrate the destructive potential of a future air war. The resulting novel, which captures eleven days of London life, was entirely bleak. On only the 'Second Day', the British government ended up joining with the French in a new European war against Nazi Germany. Thereafter, the remaining nine days of the novel are nothing but page after page of death and destruction. German bombing raids prove impossible to stop. 'No matter how many machines were brought down,' the authors complain, 'more and still more were coming.' On the ground, amidst burning buildings, 'bodies were charred beyond recognition' and simply 'laid in long lines in open spaces'. Meanwhile, the living, desperate for food, 'swept in a riotous mass', ransacking hotels and shops for anything they could grab.[16]

Much of the power of Le Queux's earlier novel had come from its vivid maps and illustrations that helped readers to imagine the horrors of a German invasion. Connolly and McIlraith digested this lesson too, commissioning James Boswell, a left-wing New Zealand illustrator, to visualise what a German *Invasion from the Air* might actually look like. Boswell was an accomplished artist with a generally cheery demeanour who knocked out a stream of illustrations for books and company advertisements, but when it came to imagining a future air war, he was overwhelmed by dark foreboding.[17] In a series of prophetic lithographs, Boswell took recognisable London landmarks and then rendered them as bombed-out warzones. Waterloo station, the grand terminus for services from the south-west, was turned into a world of shadows and danger. A signal tilted at an ungainly angle, while the sole train hung from the tracks on the left (see image 3). The message from both the illustrations and the novel was clear: Nazi Germany not only was a genuine enemy, but also posed a very real threat to Britain's future security.[18]

3. Fearing the deadly potential of a future bombing war, the New Zealand artist, James Boswell, imagined how London's landmarks would look in the wake of a German attack. This lithograph captures a dark and destroyed Waterloo station with derailed carriages and smashed platforms.

It was not quite on the same level as Le Queux's band of uniformed Prussian soldiers but, to mark the publication of Connolly and McIlraith's book, their publisher sent a postcard to every serving Member of Parliament containing the single question: 'What is your solution to invasion from the air?'[19] The answer Connolly and McIlraith were after was appeasement, rather than mutual destruction in a future conflict. For much of the 1930s, this was a sentiment that the German public could easily share. The British may have increasingly loomed large as a potential enemy power, but this did not mean there was a rush to war. Life for many Germans, so long as they were firmly within the Nazis' racial 'people's community' (*Volksgemeinschaft*), was looking up. Thanks to a growing economy, opportunities for people from all social classes started to open up, allowing Germans to dream of a better future.[20] The prospect of swapping this for another conflict was never really at the top of many people's wish lists. Indeed, during the 1938 Munich crisis, some factory workers simply downed tools and went to local taverns. They could see that Hitler's manoeuvres in Czechoslovakia risked war and so they decided they may as well get drunk, rather than readying themselves to fight.[21]

In both the 1910s and the 1930s, years of niggles and complaints had certainly led many people in Britain and Germany to recognise the other as a potential enemy, but not necessarily one they particularly wanted to fight. This situation only really started to change as war suddenly drifted into sight. In 1914, it was the assassination of Archduke Franz Ferdinand, heir to the Austro-Hungarian throne, and his wife Sophie, that shifted the diplomatic dial, if not domestic opinion. As tensions rose in cabinet offices and embassies across Europe, most people continued with their daily lives somewhat oblivious of the dangers ahead. The only fight that seemed to interest the London press was that between Georges Carpentier, the 'Adonis of the boxing world', and Edward 'Gunboat' Smith live from Olympia.[22] By the end of July, however, as one country after another entered the fray, ignorance was no longer an option. After German troops marched into neutral Belgium, public opinion started to change and the British eventually joined the fight on 4 August.[23] 'Enemies [are] all around [now],' sighed one Rhineland mother, seemingly resigned to her country's new relationship with Britain.[24]

In 1939, the atmosphere also started to change as the world hurtled towards war. Going back on assurances given in Munich just six months earlier, Hitler sent troops into the Czech provinces of Bohemia and Moravia in March, before setting his sights on Poland. Still in shock at this betrayal, the British prime minister, Neville Chamberlain, issued a grave warning to the German people. 'This is a great and powerful nation', he declared, speaking of Britain. 'In the end she [the Germans] will bitterly regret what her Government has done.' Unfortunately, nobody was really listening. The German press quietly dismissed Chamberlain's warning as being full of 'spurious accusations and suspicions', while on the streets, small children started to mock the British prime minister for his silly walk and umbrella.[25] As exchanges heated up through the summer, the two populations seemed increasingly resigned to conflict. 'Everyone could see it coming,' noted one middle-aged man in Schwäbisch Gmünd with no particular enthusiasm. In similarly glum tones, a young man living in rural Essex simply wanted to 'get it over with', as everyone knew it was 'going to come some time'.[26]

Hitler's decision to invade Poland at the start of September 1939 left Chamberlain with few options. The British government issued an ultimatum demanding the withdrawal of German troops, but this went unanswered. On 3 September, therefore, Chamberlain followed in the footsteps of H.H. Asquith who had made a similar pronouncement from the same spot a quarter of a century earlier, and announced to a tense House of Commons that 'this country is at war with Germany'.[27] Across in Berlin, there were also echoes of August 1914 as Hitler responded to Chamberlain's declaration with a characteristically wordy statement. 'The British government is wrong about one thing,' he boasted. 'The Germany of 1939 is no longer the Germany of 1914.'[28] From this point on, there could no longer be any doubts in the minds of the British and German people: the enemy had now finally been located, lurking somewhere on the other side of the North Sea. The task of both government and people quickly became one of defence, ensuring civilian life on the home front was protected. In a short space of time, the British–German relationship had been reduced to one of barricades and borders, physically fighting to keep the new enemy at bay.

The Enemy at Home

As soon as the fighting started in earnest in August 1914, British and German artists went into overdrive, pumping out a stream of post-cards and posters, all clearly identifying their country's new wartime enemy. One early British postcard, for example, humorously depicted the Kaiser tucked up in his gilded bed, replete with miniature eagles on the bedstead. Unfortunately for him, the panic sets in when he starts dreaming of the mighty Royal Navy storming into battle. Another sleepless night quickly turns into 'The Kaiser's Nightmare' (see image 4). This postcard was fairly typical of many propaganda efforts of this time that tried to draw a clear line between a country's own strong army and the enemy, who was either depicted as weak and broken or as brutal and depraved depending on circumstances. The problem for both the British and Germans, however, was that it was very easy to paint an exaggerated image of their wartime foe, but in real life, the newly created enemy looked very different. They wore suits, were married with children and in fact had often lived in Britain or Germany for years, even decades. Sealing the borders to the military was one thing; dealing with an enemy who was already 'in our midst' was quite another.[29]

The largest influx of German migrants into Britain occurred during the latter half of the nineteenth century, raising the country's German population to over 50,000. For many of these migrants, industrialised Britain was the great lure. Secure employment, better working conditions and greater political freedoms certainly drove many of the first German dockworkers, labourers, hairdressers and waiters across the North Sea.[30] Other migrants, though, saw in Britain an opportunity to start their own businesses or to innovate with more advanced technologies. Ludwig Mond, a trained scientist with a notoriously short temper and a penchant for strong cigars, first made the journey across in the 1860s. Raised in a German-Jewish family in the commercial city of Kassel, the young Mond ended up settling in the slightly less dynamic surroundings of rural Cheshire. What the county's flat plains lacked in urban flair, they made up for in an abundance of natural resources. Within two decades, Mond and his business partner, John Brunner,

The Kaiser's Nightmare.

4. During the First World War, many artists in both Britain and Germany produced propaganda material to support their respective countries' war efforts. In this widely distributed postcard, the overwhelming strength of the Royal Navy proves to be a nightmare for the Kaiser.

had revolutionised the British chemicals industry and made their fortune in the process.[31]

In the 1880s, Mond and his German-born wife, Frida, became naturalised British citizens, although they retained a very strong bond to Kassel and Germany. Mond himself reportedly never 'master[ed] the

English "w's" and "th's" ' when speaking, while the family's home was
something akin to a German-speaking enclave, and included a governess
from Bremen for the two children.[32] Like the Monds, other migrants
from continental Europe developed their own transnational worlds in
pre-war Britain, marrying, raising families, building their own futures.
Ludwig Trapp, whose finances were in a very different league to those
of his namesake from Kassel, had moved from Württemberg to the
Yorkshire spa town of Harrogate at the turn of the twentieth century.
The owners of the town's grand Prospect Hotel took a chance on the
young Trapp, employing him as a gardener and general groundsman.
By 1907, he had married a Yorkshire woman, Florence Smith, and
taken a better paid job in the coastal town of Grange-over-Sands, which
is where the couple also welcomed their first child to the world.[33]

The flow of intrepid travellers in the opposite direction was never as
strong, but nonetheless some 9,000 or so British citizens found themselves in Germany on the eve of the First World War. The country's elite
universities, such as Heidelberg, had long been a magnet for wealthy
British students keen to build European connections before embarking
on a diplomatic or industrial career.[34] John Masterman, a colourful
Oxford academic and prodigious sportsman, arrived in Germany in
1913 under slightly different circumstances. His Oxford college had
sent him to Freiburg for a year 'to learn something of German methods
and German university teaching'. Other than falling asleep during
a seminar led by the great intellectual historian, Friedrich Meinecke,
Masterman's academic achievements in Freiburg were extremely slim.
His energy and success, however, lay in other more corporeal areas.
Hours spent playing lawn tennis, walking in the Black Forest or
drinking in Freiburg's many taverns all helped Masterman to ingratiate
himself with the locals. Even when he reigned supreme in the university's tennis championship, there were no complaints. 'All seemed to
have been friendly to me,' he later recalled.[35]

The interwar years never witnessed the same level of cosy interde-
pendence. Masterman built up his academic career in Oxford rather
than in Freiburg, while Ludwig and Florence Trapp divorced and went
their own separate ways.[36] Any hope of rebuilding the earlier intimacy
of British–German relations in the wake of conflict also foundered,

quickly scuppered on the rocks of government legislation designed to protect each country's borders from seemingly unwanted immigrants. In Britain, the 1919 Aliens Restriction Act, for example, allowed for the deportation of former enemy civilians resident in the country, and therefore condemned Trapp and thousands of other Germans to a life beyond Britain's shores.[37] This was devastating for families whose lives had once straddled the British–German divide. Indeed, in Liverpool, 60-year-old Ferdinand Mittelsteiner, owner of a laundry business, was so broken by the developments that he took his own life rather than be driven away from his British-born wife and son. 'All they will take is my dead body,' he reportedly told an acquaintance, before his lifeless corpse was found stone cold at his home.[38]

From this nadir in the British–German relationship, there was a gradual reacquaintance of the old wartime foe during the late 1920s. Tourism was one of the key drivers of this renaissance, even if this remained something of the reserve of the more adventurous traveller. One of the barriers for German visitors to Britain, explained one experienced youth group leader, was not only that food and accommodation were 'difficult to find and expensive', but the British people themselves 'show no real interest in foreigners and can only speak English'.[39] A Mrs E.A. Critchley from Chesterfield seemed unperturbed by such concerns and bravely headed off in the opposite direction to embark on a walking tour through the Black Forest. Her days of walking were as much about soaking in the outdoors as rekindling forgotten relations. She spent a day in Freiburg taking in the university, where fifteen years earlier Masterman had once studied, and in the small villages en route, locals welcomed her in. 'At one little place', Critchley explained, the landlord's wife came out with a 'huge teapot in the English style'. The woman had worked as a housemaid in Brighton before the Great War and had apparently 'never forgot[ten] how to make English tea'.

After a 'fortnight or three weeks of the simple life', Critchley returned home to Chesterfield and its famously crooked church spire.[40] A small number of visitors, however, managed to stay overseas much longer. Little groups of German students popped up again in Britain's historic university towns. In Birmingham's iconic Golden Eagle pub, once a huge art deco venue in the heart of the city, a 'row of young men' seemed happy enough with their lot, singing away in German at the back of the public bar.[41] Christabel Burton, a privately educated young woman with aspirations to become a singer, also ended up savouring the delights of student life, when she exchanged suburban Hertfordshire for the port city of Hamburg in 1932. She had not necessarily planned on staying permanently in Germany, but she met a 'very good looking' trainee lawyer, Peter Bielenberg. The pair married sometime later amidst the 'usual turnout of top hats, morning coats, picture hats and messages of goodwill'.[42]

The Bielenbergs' timing was anything but auspicious. Married life in Hamburg started in autumn 1934, by which time the young Nazi government already seemed unassailable. 'In Hamburg, they were [all] falling into line with the Nazis,' lamented Peter Bielenberg.[43] However, not everyone was so pessimistic. Others saw in Nazism a promise of a new British–German relationship based on a shared fascist future. Even Adolf Hitler himself was at first relatively open to some form of alliance with Germany's former enemy. After all, Britain's global empire, deep-rooted military traditions and a confident adherence to ideas of racial difference all sat well with Hitler and his entourage in the new Nazi regime.[44] There were certainly moments of genuine British–German exchange during the 1930s. The British Union of Fascists under Oswald Mosley, for example, took plenty of its violent inspiration from its larger and more successful continental cousins, even if its roots were firmly at home.[45] In a slightly more genteel fashion, there was also a coming together of Britain's own elitist education system and a new breed of German public schools, the Nationalpolitische Erziehungsanstalten or Napolas. For a brief period in the mid-1930s, pupils crossed between the schools, learning from one another, all in the spirit of British–German understanding.[46]

The Nazis' sentimental wooing of Britain and its institutions, however, never provided a basis for a sustainable relationship. Hitler, whose vague thoughts could quickly drift in a different direction depending on his mood, soon lost interest, deciding instead that Britain would have to be destroyed in a future war.[47] As the Nazi hierarchy stormed off, like jilted lovers, some people in both countries, mainly from the social elites, tried to keep the flames of their romance alive. They established friendship groups, gave heartfelt lectures and undertook tours of each other's countries. Keith Norman Hillson, a Cambridge scholar, lawyer and sometime journalist, embarked on his own private journey around Germany to prove that 'friendship' with Nazi Germany was desirable. Turning rather a blind eye to Jewish suffering and a violent dictatorship, Hillson discovered a 'new Germany' where the people had apparently 're-found their self-respect and pride of spirit'.[48] Even though Hillson's dreams of unity between Britain and Nazi Germany faded, other relations persisted. Just as in 1914, many people from Britain and Germany continued to travel, work and even live together. Governments could easily talk of keeping the enemy at bay, but often their new foe was already well over the border.

Internment

When war was finally declared in 1914 and 1939, people ended up looking in two directions. There was a very real threat from above of Zeppelin airships in the Great War or deadly bombers in the second global conflict. In one small English village, in scenes that were repeated across Europe in late summer 1939, the noise of an approaching aircraft coming 'over very low' set hearts racing. '[I] thought it was going to drop a bomb,' one young woman recalled still in some panic.[49] Yet, while some people scanned the skies above for any potential threat, others looked inwards to what was happening on the ground. The British communities in Germany and their German counterparts in Britain may have both been long established, but with war none of this mattered. Overnight, the young English students at German universities no longer seemed quite so friendly and the old work colleague in London, who just happened to have been born in Munich, suddenly came under suspicion.

For populations that had dined for years on a diet of spy books and invasion literature, it was no surprise that people started to find the enemy lurking behind every corner. Friedrich Stampfer, a prominent social democratic politician and journalist, was lucky enough to observe a crowd unmasking a 'Russian spy' in the very centre of Berlin during the first days of the Great War. After chasing him down the streets, the police finally intervened, only to discover that the 'spy' was in fact a rather

shaken Bavarian army officer.[50] At much the same time in the historic
city of Chester, John Thomas 'of no fixed address' had been enjoying a
few too many drinks. Before he knew it, a crowd had also started following
him through the city, allegedly 'because he was speaking German and
had maps'. The police made short work of their investigation, discovering that Thomas was in fact a Welshman who had been singing away
in drunken Welsh. 'I am simply a Taffy gentleman,' he assured the
officers.[51] What led to such confusion on the streets was not just public
nerves and recklessness, but also the fact that spies were hard to spot.
Clueless as to where spies were actually operating, the public took matters
into their own hands and decided to hunt out the enemy themselves.

The 'Russian spy' in Berlin and the 'German' spy in Chester turned
out not even to be foreigners, yet they still faced a torrent of verbal and
physical abuse. For immigrant communities branded as 'enemy aliens',
the situation was clearly far worse. Overnight many of the fixed certain-
ties of life came to an end, as friends faded away and careers stuttered
to a halt. In Freiburg, John Masterman lost not only his academic existence at the university, but also his lodgings. He returned to his room
one summer's day in August 1914 to find a note from his landlady
stuffed under the door. 'Given the war with England, I am requesting
that you vacate my house 3 o'clock this afternoon,' she wrote bluntly.[52]
As a young single man, Masterman only really had his own fate to
ponder. The situation was far more complex for Ludwig Trapp, who
had been enjoying life and work in north-west England with his young
family. But with war, everything suddenly became far more precarious.
Some villagers ran to the police accusing the family of spying for the
enemy and at school his daughter was bullied relentlessly: 'German
pig,' the other pupils shouted.[53]

The ostracisation of the Trapps and Masterman was merely a foretaste
of the violence that was to come. When news of Britain's declaration of
war reached the baroque city of Dresden in early August 1914, small
groups of locals decided to smash up anything foreign in celebration.
The windows of the British Consulate were the target for some well-
aimed missiles, while a mob surrounded the home of the resident British
diplomat, hurling insults and rocks at the building until the police called
them off. It was not just the new enemy's official representatives that

came under attack.[54] Small business owners along the city's normally bustling Prager Strasse, who were more used to dealing with flocks of foreign tourists, suddenly found themselves facing off against a crowd of angry locals. On the hunt for anything or anyone foreign, people chucked advertising boards into the street and tried to tear down shop signs.[55]

The worst attacks, however, occurred in wartime Britain. A wave of anti-German riots took place through late 1914 and then again in May 1915 after a German torpedo had sent the luxury liner *Lusitania* plummeting to the seabed. In the railway town of Crewe, the Gronbach brothers found themselves on the wrong side of this violence. For years, they had been the familiar face of all pork products in the town, but as German immigrants nobody was interested in paying for their wares once war started; they were happy to rob them instead. One Saturday night in October 1914, a crowd, reported to be in the thousands, gathered on the streets in front of the Gronbachs' shop. Using a pickaxe, one of this number eased up a paving slab and hurled it through the shop's 'large plate-glass windows'. After that, 'men and women' stormed in, grabbing 'hams and strings of sausages, whilst others ran off with sides of bacon'. Even this haul failed to sate everyone's appetite; some people then ran off to smash up other German businesses in Crewe.[56]

The wartime states created the conditions that allowed such abuse to flourish. In 1914 and again in 1939, both the British and the German governments brought in measures designed to curtail the freedoms of 'enemy aliens', thereby marking them out as somehow different to the majority population. Britain's Aliens Restriction Act, introduced at the start of the Great War, confined Trapp, the Gronbachs and other Germans to within a small radius of their homes. Equivalent moves in Germany meant that British civilians like Masterman also lost all travel rights.[57] In the Second World War, the two countries again sought to isolate 'enemy aliens', just the pace was very different. The Nazi regime, already well-versed in registering and persecuting individuals, quickly brought its experience to bear on British civilians. With the start of hostilities, the authorities demanded all 'enemy' aliens register with the police; they were then subsequently arrested. The British, meanwhile, played the long game, choosing to round up just a handful of enemy civilians at first, leaving the vast majority free.[58]

Yet, their liberty proved to be short-lived. In both conflicts, the British and Germans rapidly moved to a system of complete internment, at least for male civilians. The respective governments probably would have found their way to this destination on their own, but anxious politicians and a vehement press helped to accelerate the process. 'Our people over there are treated like pariahs', one Cologne newspaper observed in 1914, demanding action be taken against British civilians apparently still living 'fresh and free' in Germany.[59] The British tabloid press in the Second World War issued their own stream of lurid headlines about 'Dangerous Aliens' who should be locked away.[60] The result in both instances was wholesale internment. The German authorities arrested all British males in November 1914, with the British, who had already been interning thousands of civilians on an ad hoc basis, following suit in May 1915. Twenty-five years later, in May 1940, full internment was again on the menu; the fall of France forced a panicked British government into action.[61]

Make sure they take 'their cats and dogs too', one person helpfully commented as the last of the German citizens were rounded up in 1940.[62] Ludwig Trapp and the Gronbachs certainly did not have any pets in tow when they ended up in internment camps during the Great War. Instead, both left behind young, often scared, families, stranded on the other side of the wire. Trapp's wife, Florence, tried to hide the shame of her husband's internment. 'If anyone asks about your father', she instructed their young daughter, '[tell them] he's died of a heart attack.'[63] Most of the civilian internees only spent a few months in camps on the mainland before the authorities shipped them off to larger facilities on the Isle of Man, which became the centrepiece of Britain's internment system.[64] The British must have been fairly satisfied with these arrangements because, during the Second World War, the Isle of Man again came into its own as an internment hub. By August 1940, 14,000 'enemy aliens' had taken the boat across the Irish Sea, not as holidaymakers, but as captives forced to enjoy the island's seaside delights from behind barbed wire.

With internment, Masterman's relationship to Germany also came to an unhappy end. After a brief sojourn in Plötzensee prison, Masterman arrived at Ruhleben, one of Berlin's premier racecourses, in late

November 1914. Sadly, he was not there to watch any of the racing action, as the military had already sent the horses packing. Instead, Masterman and the other 4,000 or so British civilians herded into Ruhleben had to find space in the newly vacated stable blocks, where the amenities were something of a bring-your-own affair. 'The arrested British', wrote the authorities generously, 'are allowed to bring a sheet, a pillowcase and two single blankets so long as they fit in a case.'[65] Unsurprisingly, for Masterman, therefore, his 'abiding impressions' of internment were mainly of 'cold and over-crowding'.[66] Whether it was Ruhleben in the First World War or the Isle of Man in both conflicts, civilian internment camps seemed to signify the final destruction of the British–German relationship. After the two countries' borders had been sealed and internal enemies safely held behind barbed wire, the British and Germans were instead free to concentrate on fighting their former neighbours.

The Ever-Present Dead

What nobody had cared to consider when locking away the enemy was that the British–German relationship had never been solely built on the living; it was also predicated on the dead. Relations between the British and German people may have descended into ever deepening antagonism, but the same was never true for the dead. One of the most ostentatious signs of this mortuary union was visible for all to see in London's St Pancras Cemetery. A four-pillared structure, modelled on the ancient Greek Temple of Nemesis, dominated the surrounding graves. The inclusion of the name 'MOND' in large writing above two bronze doors revealed who owned this imposing structure. Ludwig Mond, the great German-British industrialist, took his place in the family mausoleum in 1909 after dying aged 70. The Jewish funeral, a grand society affair, saw a 'string of carriages', reportedly stretching 'over half a mile or so in length' down the road.[67] The guests being transported to the cemetery included family, friends, notable scientists and industrialists from both Britain and Germany. Indeed, back in his birthplace, the press mourned the passing of a great 'German scientist', while the Rhenania student fraternity at Heidelberg University, Mond's old alma mater, marked his passing with their own short obituary.[68]

Very few individuals could match the grandiosity of Mond's final resting place; nonetheless, a wealth of British graves across Germany at least helped to make a similar point about deathly relations. The death of John Thelwall on the operating table of a Berlin hospital in May 1934 seemed to strike a particularly sad note in the Nazi capital. Thelwall was certainly no celebrity or high society figure; instead, he was an unassuming diplomat stationed at the British embassy. What gave him a certain prominence, however, was that his carefully crafted economic reports won the respect of British and German civil servants alike. His funeral, held in the British church of St George, which once stood in the heart of Berlin, attracted both British and German mourners who looked on as Thelwall's coffin, draped in the Union Jack, was carried to the grave. 'He will always be held in honoured remembrance,' the Berlin press proclaimed.[69]

Thelwall's funeral was a dignified affair, with the focus firmly on the loss of a clearly well-respected man, rather than on diplomatic point-scoring. Both the British and German governments, though, were acutely aware that dealing with the dead could also provide the perfect opportunity to boost their image abroad and even to calm international tensions. In the mid-1930s, few relationships needed more of a boost than the flagging British–German one. Leopold von Hoesch, the German ambassador to the United Kingdom since November 1932, did his best to ingratiate himself with the British public. He was very active on the London society scene and, in a rather light-hearted interview with the populist *John Bull* newspaper, came across as a 'staunch friend' of Britain. Indeed, Hoesch's 'faultless English and his unobtrusive dress', crowed the newspaper, 'might lead a stranger to think at first he was meeting an Englishman'. Helping to cement his place in British hearts, Hoesch was also a self-proclaimed 'dog-lover', who liked nothing more than to take his 'two four-footed companions' on a morning walk.[70]

This canine diplomacy appeared to have come to an unfortunate end in early 1934 when Hoesch's trusty terrier, Giro, bit through an electrical cable in the embassy garden. Hoesch had a small headstone placed over Giro's grave with the poignant words: 'A faithful companion!'[71] Little more than two years later, Hoesch himself followed Giro to the grave. Aged only 54, Hoesch had gone through his usual morning routine, taking breakfast and reading the first editions of the newspapers. He then readied himself for the day ahead, putting on one of his dapper suits and straightening his tie. But when Hoesch, who was apparently the embodiment of 'Prussian punctuality', failed to appear at his desk, his private secretary went up to his room, only to find him slumped over, cold and lifeless, after suffering a fatal heart attack.[72]

The timing of Hoesch's death was convenient for all concerned. Just five weeks earlier, Hitler had caused a diplomatic storm by sending his troops into the demilitarised Rhineland. Indeed, Anthony Eden, the recently appointed Foreign Secretary, had summoned the German ambassador to Whitehall to register his government's concerns.[73] But at this point, the British also wanted to keep the Germans close, which is where Hoesch again came in. His funeral offered the perfect vehicle for smoothing strained international relations. Pulling out all the stops, three Cabinet members and a range of international dignitaries joined the funeral cortège as Hoesch departed the German embassy for the final time (see image 5). A contingent of Grenadier Guardsmen, splendid in their bearskin caps, marched the swastika-draped coffin solemnly to London Victoria railway station. A waiting train then took the coffin to Dover, from where a British naval destroyer carried Hoesch back home to Germany. With a final nod to British sentimentality, the press reported that Hoesch's new dog, Martin, was 'utterly disconsolate' at the loss of his master and had had to be comforted in the embassy on the day of the funeral.[74]

Once on home soil, Hoesch's body was taken to Dresden for final interment in the family vault. The funeral took place on a bitterly cold spring day in April 1936; the crowds on the streets were 'blue with cold', noted the British ambassador, Eric Phipps, who had joined proceedings and was probably freezing himself.[75] The icy chill was rather ominous, for as the dignitaries gathered to mark one British-German death, news of further losses was just starting to break. Some 600 kilometres south-east near Freiburg, five London grammar schoolboys, aged only 12 to 14, lost their lives on a snowy mountainside in the Black Forest. The group had been on a school hiking trip led by their inexperienced and rather reckless teacher, Kenneth Keast. Ill-equipped

5. Leopold von Hoesch, the German ambassador to the United Kingdom, suffered a fatal heart attack in April 1936. Hoping to improve relations with Nazi Germany, the British staged a lavish ceremony to mark the return of Hoesch's body. Cabinet ministers and members of the Grenadier Guards walked alongside the swastika-draped coffin as it made its way slowly to London Victoria station.

and wearing shorts, sandals and only thin coats, Keast and his group, quickly became disorientated as snow started to fall and the weather closed in. Frozen, lost and exhausted, the young schoolboys started to drop like flies on the side of the Schauinsland mountain, as their school trip turned from adventure to disaster.[76]

Back in Dresden, Phipps wondered whether the Nazi regime had put on their own 'elaborate funeral' for Hoesch so as 'not [to] be outdone by His Majesty's Government'.[77] Phipps was possibly looking in the wrong direction as it was in Freiburg rather than in Dresden that the Nazis recognised the power of mortuary diplomacy for improving British–German relations. In Freiburg, the regime arranged a grand send-off for the victims. Five small coffins containing the bodies of the schoolboys were lined up in the city's Old Catholic community church under the swastika and Union Jack flags. Amidst a swathe of wreaths and floral tributes, brown-shirted members of the Hitler Youth kept a guard of honour for their British peers.[78] After two days, they could finally stand down as the coffins were loaded onto a train for the long journey back to Britain. However, the Nazi regime clearly decided that there was still more propaganda mileage to be had from the tragedy. To mark the apparent 'comradeship between the youth of two nations', it arranged for the construction of a large stone memorial on the mountain. The names of the five British boys appeared on one of the pillars under the more dominant inscription of the Nazis' eagle.[79]

Moving beyond the Nazi regime's performative commemorations, the bereaved families erected two subtler memorials for their children, which together hinted at a deeper, more genuine, British–German relationship. A small stone cross from the father of one of the boys marked the exact spot where his son had died, while a metal plaque in the nearby Catholic church of Saint Laurentius thanked villagers for their help rescuing the boys as the mountain tragedy unfurled. These two personal tributes withstood the period of Nazi rule unscathed and indeed continued to be maintained by locals after 1945.[80] There was nothing particularly unusual in such scenes. The same was true in north London, where Ludwig Mond's family mausoleum continued to stand silently throughout the two world wars, even as the British–German relationship, which he had so embodied, collapsed. Unlike the living who bore the brunt of wartime hostility, the dead, it seems, enjoyed a certain immunity, left to rest in peace as conflict raged around them.[81]

The policy of interning 'enemy aliens' along with military POWs was supposed to have secured the two countries' borders, stopping the perceived threat from within posed by spies or dangerous saboteurs. Locking up the enemy in secure camps also seemed to mark a symbolic break in the British–German relationship; the peacetime world of international friendships, mixed marriages and business dealings was replaced almost entirely by separation and division. The barriers that shot up in wartime certainly destroyed many of these existing relations. Masterman, whose academic studies in Freiburg abruptly ended in an internment camp, experienced this separation to the full, as did the Trapps, whose family life in northern

England was torn asunder by the outbreak of the First World War. Yet, in their determination to divide friend from foe, the two states completely ignored the dead. While they quickly locked up the living, the remains of the enemy who had already expired were left as before in cemeteries and churchyards. This was entirely understandable. After all, skeletal corpses were never going to spy on the living or launch an invasion from within. There was something almost poetic, therefore, in the fact that while British–German relations reached a new nadir in conflict, it was the dead that continued to offer a fragile thread silently linking the two countries together.

2

DYING

The waters off the North Kent coast provided rich pickings for Britain's fisherman during the two world wars. With the late summer sun beating down on their backs, two local men set out from Herne Bay in 1942 hoping to pull in a good catch on the rising tide. Once the pair had manoeuvred their trawler into position, they readied themselves to drop their nets, when they suddenly noticed something floating in the water ahead of them. On closer inspection, it turned out to be a corpse bobbing up and down on the waves. Between them, they attempted to haul the body on board, but it was bloated and too heavy, so they threw a rope around the corpse and tied it to the stern of the boat. After gathering in their nets, they headed back to shore with the body dragging along behind; every time the boat sped up, they could see the 'legs floating up' above the waves. Once on dry land, it was clear that the body belonged to an airman, who had presumably been shot out of the sky as there was 'a line of bullets across his back'. The coastguards identified the remains to be German, one of some 2,500 men killed in the Nazi air war against Britain.[1]

The body was most likely that of Henry Starke, a German Messerschmidt pilot, who had been shot down off the French coast in February 1942. His corpse had then spent almost seven months drifting out at sea before it was finally recovered off the Kent coast. Given the intensity of aquatic decomposition, driven by salt water, tidal currents and algae, Starke's body would have made for an uncomfortable sight when finally hauled ashore.[2] The fishermen's apparent calm in the face of such discomfort, as they casually dealt with the corpse, must suggest that discovering the human and material remains of the air war was not an isolated incident.[3] Indeed, it is well known that during the two world wars, British and German civilians frequently encountered death, whether in bombed-out buildings after air raids or through funerals held for the military dead.[4] What gets far less of a mention, though, is the fact that these bodies, as was the case off Herne Bay, were just as likely to belong to the wartime foe as to one's own side.

Not all enemy deaths, of course, were quite as gruesome as the one that befell Starke. There is maybe never anything akin to a 'good death' in wartime, but Georg Michael Geislinger's final hours were at the very least comfortable.[5] Geislinger, who worked as a baker in Bow, London, was already in his sixties when the war started. Born and raised in south-west Germany, he was arrested as an 'enemy alien' and interned in the Knockaloe camp on the Isle of Man. At around the same time, his son went in the opposite direction, and volunteered to serve in the British army. Suffering from severe constipation and 'senile decay', the older Geislinger quickly came to the attention of Knockaloe's civilian doctor, who kept him under observation in the camp hospital. He generally took 'his food fairly well and sometimes got out into the open air', the doctor reported. However, Geislinger's health rapidly deteriorated. The doctor wrapped his chest in cotton wool, gave him 'brandy and milk', but pneumonia set in, and he died in November 1915.[6]

Kent and the Isle of Man were obviously a long way from the fighting front in both world wars. Yet, the residents of these regions still encountered the dead or dying enemy. The same was equally true for civilians in Bath or Berlin, Liverpool or Leipzig; death occurred in close proximity to the usual rhythms of daily life. People continued to work and play; fishermen cast their nets; and children still traipsed to school for their daily lessons. Civilian encounters with enemy deaths took many forms, from the farmer watching a troubled aircraft come smashing to the ground through to the nurse tending the enemy in his dying moments. Whether people even witnessed the actual moment of death was not the point; it was the simple fact that the enemy died – sometimes violently – in their midst that was most important. Once the enemy had been unfortunate enough to die in communities across Britain and Germany, then people had to broaden their perception of wartime death. Acknowledging the sacrifice of one's own military was relatively straightforward; it was much trickier to be confronted with the expunged lives of those on the opposing side.

Death Spirals

A large proportion of enemy deaths in the Second World War, and a much smaller number in the Great War, occurred in the air, as marauding aircraft were shot out of the sky over Britain and Germany. These dramatic deaths seemed to linger much longer in the local imagination than stories of POWs dying in more mundane circumstances, through accidents or sickness. It was not just the spectacular intensity of combat that helped to etch these losses into people's minds, it was also the fact that the enemy had been killed in their midst. Places that had once been familiar and comforting, whether bustling urban streets or the relative calm of pastoral landscapes, were suddenly sullied, not just by war and death, but by enemy bodies.

Even though the Zeppelin raids over First World War Britain brought death and destruction to urban areas, they also proved to be a source of considerable fascination for those gazing up from below. During one attack on London, onlookers reportedly jostled for the best spot, wanting 'to see as much of the show as possible'.[7] The excitement ratcheted up a further notch whenever one of the giant airships was hit and in obvious trouble. In June 1917, a Zeppelin had been attempting to return home after an aborted raid; it had travelled as far as the Suffolk coast when the winds picked up and its engines started to fail. As it drifted slowly downwards, waiting fighter aircraft found easy pickings. With the airship's hull ablaze, 'hundreds of people left their beds', remembered one local resident, 'to watch and cheer the fateful descent'.[8] Standing on the moonlit streets, these local people ended up witnessing the physical destruction of their wartime foe. Just a few days earlier, German fixed-wing bombers had launched a deadly raid over East London, killing eighteen young pupils in a Poplar school, which perhaps explains why there were more cheers than tears that night.[9]

People had less appetite to stand around and observe similar scenes during the Second World War; the dangers were by now far too great. Yet, from a safe distance, those on the ground did sometimes manage to trace their attacker's final moments. One German schoolboy caught sight of a Royal Air Force (RAF) bomber 'held for some time in searchlights' over Cologne. The twin-engine bomber did not escape the deadly glare of the lights and was easily picked off by anti-aircraft fire from below; it lost height and hit the ground near the city of Mülheim. Sometimes people never saw the impact, but just heard an explosion followed by a long silence, all too aware that the crew entombed inside the doomed craft were never going to survive.[10]

The danger did not suddenly pass just because an enemy craft was floundering. An out-of-control bomber that was rapidly losing altitude had to hit the ground somewhere. The residents of Trebbin, just south of Berlin, had a lucky escape when a Lancaster bomber broke up over a small housing district. A part of the tail struck the side of one house; a machine gun fell into someone's kitchen and a bouncing wheel collided with another property (see image 6). While the locals escaped unscathed, the eight-man crew was less fortunate. All were killed outright, leaving a collection of mangled body parts behind, right in the middle of a residential street.[11]

A similar, but even more violent, incident occurred in the small village of Dunnington just outside York in March 1945. The Moll family had already retired to their beds when there was a terrific bang; a stricken Junkers Ju 88 aircraft struck an oak tree before smashing through the side of the Moll's farmhouse and bursting into flames. Richard and Ellen Moll died at the scene, while their 28-year-old daughter-in-law, who had tried to rescue the older couple, succumbed to her injuries soon after. There was no escaping the impact of the air war on this quiet corner of Yorkshire. A farmhouse had been peeled open, torn metal from an aircraft covered the ground, and four German airmen and three British civilians lay dead.[12]

Once an enemy aircraft had finally come to a halt, then the fear from those on the ground quickly dissipated. Local people often surged towards the wreckage, hoping to catch a glimpse of their helpless enemy or to secure a few war trophies to show their friends. As soon as the

6. In December 1943, a German fighter attacked and downed an RAF
Lancaster bomber south of Berlin. The stricken aircraft came down in a
semi-urban area, leaving debris as well the remains of the eight-man crew
scattered through the residential streets.

Zeppelin had touched the ground in Theberton, Suffolk, in June 1917,
'crowds of people from all around [. . .] started walking to see the crashed
airship'. One of this number, still just a child, later recalled his mother
grabbing a pushchair and then trekking with him for over three miles
until they reached the crash site.[13] It was a similar picture during the
later war, where local people also headed up the hunt for doomed
aircraft. Sixteen-year-old Peter Lyons watched as a stricken Heinkel
bomber came down on wasteland 'a few hundred yards' from his family's home in Widnes. It was 'quite an exciting thing really', he later
recalled. Together with some friends, Lyons rushed over to the aeroplane
and managed to grab 'bits of Perspex' and other parts from the wreck.[14]

Racing to the crash site could provide some material rewards, even if
these were just shards of Perspex. However, at the same time, it also
placed civilians face to face with the brutal effects of war. Lyons managed

to gloss over the fact in his later recollections, but mangled within the prized wreckage must have been the remains of two airmen who perished in the crash. The first civilians to reach the smouldering remains of the crashed Zeppelin in Theberton were also met by a grisly scene. The remains of one of the crew members, who must have jumped from a great height in a vain attempt to cling to life, lay smashed in the field. 'He was an awful sight,' recalled one local, the body 'literally fell to pieces'. After the flames had abated, the military took control of the site and managed to recover the bodies of the remaining Germans, charred beyond recognition.[15]

During the Second World War, when high-speed crashes were more common, often only body parts remained. In Cologne, which came under heavy bombardment during the Allied air war, a chief medical officer was supposed to record all military deaths. The details provided for the RAF crews killed over the city were generally cursory at best, with the word 'unknown' (*unbekannt*) occupying much of the form. This partly reflected indifference to the fate of the enemy, but it also hinted at the intensity of the aircrews' deaths. Where details were added, then phrases like 'severe burns' or 'partial disintegration of the body' dominated the page. The use of bureaucratised language may have spared people from the full horrors, but the trauma that occurred to the bodies can easily be read between the lines.[16] The equivalent British reports tended to reach for a similar set of formulaic phrases. The body of one German airman found on the Sussex Downs, for example, was 'in a very broken condition', while three others pulled from a 'burnt out machine' were registered simply as 'not identifiable'.[17]

These airmen lost their lives with civilians looking on, or at the very least aware of their demise. Not all deaths, however, were quite so visible. Often, people stumbled across the bodies of undiscovered enemy servicemen long after they had drawn their last breath. The two fishermen working their nets off the Kent coast had found the body of a German airmen floating in the water of course. However, the most common location for these encounters was on the beach, where the detritus of battle frequently washed up. Germany's North Frisian Islands, long a draw for local tourists, attracted a different set of visitors during the Second World War. Throughout the conflict, a steady trickle of

Allied bodies landed on the sandy beaches, some were from naval ships, but the majority were airmen whose aircraft had plummeted into the dark waters of the North Sea.[18]

Discovering the remains of the enemy out in the wilds of a North Sea island or on the rolling Sussex Downs had a chilling effect. The body clearly did not belong in these rural locations. It was an interloper whose very presence not only brought the violence of a military conflict closer to home, but also jarred badly with the wider landscape. The once sparsely populated Monach Islands in the Outer Hebrides are a case in point. As a haven for wildlife, the tiny islands normally witness little more than the comings and goings of thousands of grey seals that seek out the white sands for breeding. Yet, in summer 1918, the peace was briefly disturbed when the remains of Otto Schatt, an engineer on the German submarine, U-110, suddenly washed up. The U-boat had gone down months earlier off the coast of Ireland, after being attacked by two British naval destroyers. When Schatt's remains eventually resurfaced on a pristine Scottish beach, all that identified him was a gold ring, inscribed with the words 'M. Jessen', his mother's maiden name.[19]

The ring on Schatt's long-dead body gave life to death, helping to connect the decaying remains to a family and to a time before war. With the fighting ongoing, though, there was little space for sentimentality. The lifeless corpse that had once come to kill had now been subdued. The very presence of enemy bodies on the British home front was a grim reminder that in the two world wars military combat was not confined to some distant battlefield. Fighting and the resultant violent deaths also occurred within both Britain and Germany. Local communities, therefore, became reluctant witnesses to the dying enemy who all too often expired in their midst.

Killings

Dying in combat was an inherent risk for those wearing military uniform in wartime. However, to be deliberately shot while a prisoner was not something most soldiers had signed up for. After all, international law was clear that prisoners were to be protected and certainly not to be killed.[20] It was something of a shock, therefore, when British troops shot dead six internees in the Douglas camp on the Isle of Man during the early weeks of the First World War.[21] In the days leading up to the shootings, prisoner complaints about the quality and variety of food had been gaining momentum. The menu apparently changed very little from day to day, with 'a lot of porridge' and 'a few weevils' nestled in the bowls. On one Thursday in mid-November 1914, lunch was served in the dining room as usual, but at the end of the sitting, the prisoners decided to vent their frustrations. Several men threw their crockery at the walls; someone picked up a chair and smashed it through a closed window and 'boos' echoed through the building. Finding themselves in 'lethal' danger as a tsunami of 'knives, forks, plates, cups, and saucers' rained down on them, the guards opened fire.[22] Some of the men later claimed to have fired into the air, but as the officer in charge commented, the guards would have been 'perfectly justified' to have 'fired every shot into the crowd'.[23]

Some 400 kilometres away in London, the British military was also busy shooting the enemy. The circumstances of these deaths, though, were very different to the killings on the Isle of Man, for this group of men were deliberately executed having been classed as enemy spies. The first, and most prominent, of these men was Carl Hans Lody, a 39-year-old naval reservist from Berlin. Lody had spent the first months of the war traipsing around the country picking up useless trivia about British military manoeuvres that he then forwarded home. The police eventually tracked Lody down to a Dublin hotel, where they arrested him on suspicion of espionage. As they were already aware of his recent activities, Lody's trial in London turned into an open-and-shut case. Lody must have known this too, for when he was asked whether he wanted to make a statement in his defence, he shook his head forlornly and muttered the words 'No, Sir'. A few days later, Lody was marched to a small hut alongside the Tower of London, where eight men raised their rifles, took aim, then shot him dead.[24]

As the Germans had proved themselves to be so incompetent at spying, their espionage missions quickly fizzled out. Ludovico Hurwitz Zender, who faced the firing squad in April 1916, was the last of twelve enemy spies to be killed.[25] Thereafter, a dearth of enemy agents left the British with no one else to execute. However, more ad hoc shootings of internees, mainly by nervous guards with twitchy trigger fingers, continued throughout the war and even beyond the November 1918 armistice.[26] Wilhelm Schmidt, aged 22, was 'accident[ally]' shot in Handforth for getting too close to the wire; in Dorchester, Franz Radojewski, a soldier originally from Posen, was half under the perimeter fence when two bullets struck him in the back; further north, in the Park Hall camp, Willy Oster, who had not yet turned 20, was shot in the head during a stand-off between guards and the POWs.[27] Seen in the context of the grinding misery of the battlefield, such incidents appeared relatively minor. Yet, their significance lay not so much in the number of deaths, but rather that, on the edge of towns and villages, as people went about their daily business, the wartime enemy was shot and killed.

Surely the most egregious shooting incidents occurred at Scapa Flow, off the Orkney Islands, where the German High Seas Fleet had been laid up since the war's end. Aggrieved at the Allies' treatment of defeated Germany, Admiral von Reuter, the fleet's commander, managed to commit one of the largest mass-sinkings in history. On the morning of 21 June 1919, he ordered the skeleton crews manning his seventy-four ships to open the seacocks, sending their vessels slowly and unceremoniously to the seabed. Watching their war booty sinking before their eyes, the British sailors raced on board the ships to try and salvage what they could. In the ensuing mêlée, shots rang out and nine Germans died.[28] Another German sailor, Kuno Eversberg, followed them to the grave just over one week later. Unlike his comrades, Eversberg was already in captivity on a British ship when he died in rather hazy circumstances. He had been making his way to the toilet, when a shot rang out, striking him in the side. The German press rightly labelled it a 'murder', although the killer was never prosecuted.[29] A British sailor, who had allegedly always wanted 'to shoot a German', was later put on trial, but after twenty minutes of deliberations the jury somehow managed to return a verdict of 'not proven'.[30]

Random shootings or targeted executions of enemy prisoners in British hands were much rarer during the Second World War, but nonetheless the enemy continued to die in captivity.[31] The British decision to send civilian and military prisoners to camps in Canada, for example, proved fatal for some internees. The danger here was the Atlantic crossing, moving people safely through the stormy, submarine-filled waters separating the internment camps in Britain from those in Canada. The most well-known, and also the most shocking incident, occurred in July 1940, when a German U-boat torpedoed the former luxury liner, *Arandora Star*, which had been requisitioned for war purposes. Filled to the portholes with Italian and German civilian and military internees, the ship was only a day into its voyage when the torpedo struck, plunging at least 800 of the prisoners to their deaths. Although the British tried to play down their own culpability in the incident, the physical remains proved harder to ignore. For weeks after the sinking, people living on the north coast of Ireland, where the ship went down, and on the west coast of Scotland, found the bodies of German and Italian internees, as well as those of the British crew members, washed up on the foreshore.[32]

Drowning in the cold Atlantic waters was not the only danger facing the wartime prisoners; a spate of murders also occurred in the internment camps. Admittedly, being stuck in close proximity to complete strangers had tested the patience of people during the previous conflict. On the Isle of Man, one prisoner had even smashed a broom over another German internee's head, killing him instantly. The subsequent trial tried to get to the bottom of the incident, and in doing so ended up revealing much about the pettiness of camp life. There was apparently one new broom and an old one in the hut; the two men came to blows over the use of the better brush. I only 'made a dab at him', claimed the accused, before 'accidentally hit[ting] him on the head'.[33] This seemed to have been more about vexed personal relationships than an actual concern for the cleanliness of their living space. 'Trapped in a cramped hut for more than 3 years with 90 other men', as another internee complained, 'is enough to sink even the strongest of men.'[34]

Some twenty-five years later, POWs still found ways to kill one another. The trigger, though, was often more about ideological differences than personal irritations. In theory, the British interrogated all POWs to determine their loyalties, before sending the most ideologically committed Nazis in one direction and all others to different camps.[35] But this did not always happen. When these different factions came into contact, violent, occasionally deadly, clashes occurred.

Wolfgang Rosterg, a sergeant in his early thirties, found himself on the wrong end of these categorisations in late 1944. Some of the hardcore Nazi POWs in the Scottish Comrie camp, where Rosterg was held, believed he had betrayed an earlier escape attempt. Once the group had reached this conclusion, Rosterg's fate was sealed. The Nazi contingent staged their own mock trial, found Rosterg guilty, then proceeded to beat him with an iron bar, before hanging his battered body from pipes in the toilet block. Five of the murderers were themselves found guilty by a British military court and later hanged in Pentonville prison.[36]

The brutal murder of Rosterg and the subsequent execution of his assassins added a further six enemy deaths to Britain's wartime tally.[37] Yet, while the death rate ticked ever upwards in Britain, it was always much higher in Germany. There was a familiar pattern to this. In the early months of the two conflicts, the German authorities made some attempt to treat Western POWs – although never their Russian and then Soviet allies – according to international norms.[38] As the conflicts dragged on, however, this consensus started to break down. Severe food shortages at home, particularly during the First World War, and the impact of urban bombing raids during the second conflict, destroyed any public sympathies that Germans may have had for the interned enemy. Increasing violence, neglect and even deliberate killings became part of daily life for the British and Commonwealth prisoners confined to the German camp system.[39]

During the First World War, British newspapers were awash with stories of German atrocities. 'Prison Camp Horrors' screamed one head-line; 'Savage Dogs in German Camp' exclaimed another.[40] Attempting to cut through this emotional anger, the War Office in London concentrated its fire on irrefutable examples of unlawful killing. The death of Able Seaman John Genower fitted the brief perfectly. Genower, a tall, thin man with deep, penetrating eyes and a protruding chin, had survived the sinking of his ship, HMS *Nestor*, at the Battle of Jutland unscathed.[41] His subsequent internment in the large Brandenburg POW camp, however, proved more of a challenge. Genower had only been in the camp for a matter of months when he was placed in the prison cells for an act of apparent insubordination. In March 1917, the long wooden prison hut somehow caught alight, possibly from a discarded cigarette or from the heat of a neighbouring workshop. Regardless of the cause, it was at this point that the story turned from an accidental fire into one of manslaughter. The guards could see the flames, feel the heat and hear the screams, yet did nothing to free the prisoners. Genower, who clearly had no wish to burn to death, tried to smash his way out through a window, but was bayonetted in the chest for his troubles and was sent 'reeling back into the fire'.[42]

German excuses for the death of Genower and the six other POWs killed ranged from a misplaced door key through to the absence of senior officers. The 'Dynamic of Destruction' during the Second World War, when the Nazi regime killed some 3.2 million Soviet prisoners, was even greater and could hardly be blamed on simple administrative errors.[43] POWs from Britain and its empire were treated much better than their Soviet allies, but were never immune to moments of Nazi brutality. The execution of fifty airmen, who had escaped the Stalag Luft III camp, had been etched into British popular memory even before the 1963 American film, *The Great Escape*, brought the episode to an even wider audience.[44] Yet, there were countless other examples of unlawful killings in Nazi Germany's dense network of POW camps. One man was shot on the spot for refusing to push a heavy wheelbarrow, while in Oflag 79 camp, near Braunschweig, an Indian Officer, Jhuthar Mal, was enjoying a game of tennikoit when he was fatally shot. Mal had wandered over in the direction of the perimeter fence to retrieve an errant quoit. As he stooped down, a shot rang out, leaving his head 'half blown off' and his sporting opponent 'splashed by his blood'.[45]

The Oflag 79 camp, where Jhuthar Mal's life ended, was situated in a fairly secluded spot alongside the Querumer Forest, just north of the centre of Braunschweig. A wave of other killings of Allied airmen, however, occurred in far more public locations. As the bombing war intensified, the Nazi regime did its best to deflect public anger away from its own failings and towards the crews whose aircraft increasingly filled the night skies. German satirical magazines, such as the weekly *Kladderadatsch*, pointed the finger of blame squarely at the individual airmen.[46] One sketch depicted the exaggerated frame of an Allied flyer, with menacing animalistic features, angrily tossing down a bowling ball-shaped bomb. The innocent silhouette of Cologne's cathedral sits peacefully on the Rhine, apparently representing a more benign form of Christianity, while an English bishop sings the command: 'Onward, Christian Soldiers' (see image 7). Once British claims to moral leadership had been weakened, all Joseph Goebbels and other high-ranking Nazis had to do was to light the fuse. As ever, the propaganda chief had a cynical way with words. It would be understandable if these 'child murderers' were 'beaten to death by a beleaguered public', he casually suggested.[47]

7. As German public anger at the Allied bombing war grew, Joseph Goebbels and his propaganda machine openly blamed the Allied aircrews for the death and destruction. For its July 1943 cover, the satirical magazine, *Kladderadatsch*, depicted an airman looming menacingly in the skies over the peaceful silhouette of Cologne below.

Cyril Sibley, nicknamed 'Lofty' because of his height, was one of several hundred British airmen to suffer the full wrath evoked by Goebbels' murderous language.[48] In February 1945, Sibley had been sitting as the rear gunner at the back of a Halifax bomber on a raid over Germany. Before the aircraft could reach its target in Worms, an enemy fighter attacked, forcing the bomber to the ground near the sleepy village of Dirmstein. Sibley managed to jump from the stricken craft, opened his parachute and floated down, landing virtually unscathed in the back garden of a local woman, Frau Gassner. However, this is where his luck ran out. Three members of the Nazis' ad hoc Volkssturm militia got hold of Sibley and led him down the darkened streets of Dirmstein to the village's old railway station. Shielded by the gloom of the building, one of the Volksturm members fired two shots at Sibley, 'once in the head and once into the chest'. As he fell to the ground, a second man then fired a second bullet into Sibley's lifeless body.[49]

The killing of Cyril Sibley added another name to a long list of enemy soldiers and civilians shot in wartime Britain and Germany. This, though, is where the similarity ends. Although those killed all died in captivity, the circumstances were always unique. The shooting of Schmidt in First World War Handforth or of Radojewski in Dorchester were very different from Nazi Germany's state-sanctioned murder of unarmed airmen in a genocidal war. Nonetheless, there was some commonality. In all cases, the enemy was killed at home, in the midst of local communities. Often civilians living close by witnessed the actual killing or, at the very least, learnt of it soon after the event. In Dirmstein, for example, Frau Gassner could hear the shots from her garden as Sibley was murdered in cold blood. Another local, a teenager at the time, later recalled seeing Sibley being marched away and then hearing 'several shots' ring out.[50] In Dirmstein and elsewhere, the familiar landscapes of daily life had turned into places in which the enemy was intentionally killed.

Breathing Their Last

Violent deaths, where enemy soldiers were killed in direct combat or accidentally shot, garnered most of the headlines. Yet, POWs and civilian internees were far more likely to lose their lives quietly, through disease, accidents or even suicide. The renowned British novelist, Hall Caine, was clearly aware of this fact when, in 1923, he wrote his own novel about internment on the Isle of Man: *The Woman of Knockaloe*. In a nod to the great literary genre of forbidden love, Caine's two protagonists, a German internee named Oskar and a young farmgirl, Mona, are publicly shunned by those on the island.[51] 'The traitor!', the locals shout. 'It's an ill bird that fouls its own nest,' retorts another. The planned repatriation of the internees in 1919 proves to be the final straw for the young lovers. Distraught and broken, Oskar and Mona take themselves to the island's highest cliff and sit on the edge. The next morning, when 'the sun rises above the horizon in a blaze of glory', Hall reveals that 'the cliff head is empty'. *The Woman of Knockaloe*, while of course a work of fiction, does a wonderful job of highlighting not only the banality of many enemy deaths, but also their very visibility. After all, Oskar and Mona die in the open countryside, and in Caine's telling, it is local fishermen that later discover their bodies.[52]

New dangers emerged as soon as POWs left the relative safety of the internment camp for the civilian world surrounding them. Even the act of travel could prove deadly. During, and immediately after, the Second World War, the Aberdeenshire village of Fyvie saw a regular coming and going of POWs who laboured on the local farms. One unfortunate German was quietly 'riding a pedal cycle' on his way back from work in Aberdeenshire when he collided with a local servant girl who had been walking along the road. The German prisoner went flying to the ground, suffering a 'fractured skull and probably fractured cervical spine'. He died on the spot with the bruised pedestrian and other locals looking on.[53] Lorries, which were more regularly deployed to transport POWs, proved no safer than the humble bicycle. In County Armagh, two Germans died after being thrown from the back of a lorry; another two POWs were killed when their lorry struck a telegraph pole on a Derbyshire street, while in Norfolk two lorries carrying POWs back to their internment camp collided, killing five of them as a result.[54]

What all these accidents had in common was that POWs died not behind the wire of the internment camp, but in very public spaces. It often fell to civilians, therefore, to administer first aid to their mortally injured foes. In 1947 and again in 1948, local residents were first on the scene to crashes on railway level crossings involving lorries transporting German prisoners. These men represented the final remnants of an ever-shrinking POW system, retained by the British as a source of cheap labour, even though hostilities had long ceased.

The first accident involving the Germans occurred in Burton Agnes, just west of Bridlington. A passenger train ploughed right through a lorry heavily laden with POWs, leaving a pile of tangled wreckage, ten Germans and two British guards dead. The stationmaster's wife and the daughter of the signalman heard a 'terrible' scream then saw 'bodies lying all along the line'. Grabbing sheets and blankets, they rushed to the tracks, wrapped some of the men up, applied tourniquets where they could.[55] A similar incident occurred the following year in Conington, near Peterborough, when a light engine collided with a lorry, killing six of the German POWs on board. Mrs Parker, who lived nearby, responded fastest. She turned her 'cottage [. . .] into a hospital', laying out the injured and dying on her 'best carpet' in the living room. While she bathed their injuries, her husband gave the Germans the 'last of the brandy' for medicinal purposes.[56]

If POWs survived the journey to work unscathed, then the work-place itself could often be just as lethal. The various iterations of the Hague Convention and the much stronger stipulations of the 1929 Geneva Convention provided a regulatory framework to ensure POW safety, but for all their legal power, the conventions still relied on individuals on the ground abiding by the provisions. What POWs in both wars quickly discovered was that their chances of injury and death were far greater while labouring in dark mines than out in the fresh air of farms. Unfortunately for them, there was not always much choice in the matter. During the Second World War, the Nazi regime set some 4,000 British prisoners to work in Upper Silesia's coal and salt mines, where they laboured away in often appalling conditions. With poor food rations, inadequate clothing and lax safety standards, it is little surprise that injuries and fatal accidents were common.[57]

Thirty years earlier, mines had also proved to be dangerous spaces for POWs forced to labour away in them. When Farnham-born James Christie had first enrolled in the Royal Navy, he surely imagined a life on the high seas, rather than in the dingy depths of a German mine. Unfortunately for Christie, he was captured in Antwerp in the early weeks of the Great War, and from there eventually ended up in a POW camp in Cottbus. Christie was soon set to work in an opencast mine in landlocked Brandenburg, but after months of labouring away in grim conditions, his luck finally ran out in April 1917. He had been travelling on a mine wagon loaded full of coal, when it suddenly jumped the tracks and toppled over, leaving him crushed beneath. Evincing remarkably little sympathy, the Foreign Office in Berlin suggested that Christie only had himself to blame. He 'stood with both hands in his trouser pockets', rather than holding firmly to the guardrail 'as repeatedly instructed', they reported, thereby abrogating themselves from any responsibility in his death.[58]

While Christie died alone in the dusty gloom of a German coalmine, other work fatalities occurred far more in the public eye. POWs in both Britain and Germany often laboured for private firms or worked along-side civilians in very public places. Twenty-year-old Wilhelm Schönhert was captured at the Battle of Passchendaele in 1917 with a gunshot wound to his foot. After being treated at a military hospital, he was set to work, eventually ending up labouring in a British shipyard alongside civilian workers. On an early spring day in 1919, by which point he was no doubt ready for home, Schönhert and one of his British co-workers both died in an industrial accident. A ship's mast that was being lowered slowly into place suddenly fell, fatally crushing the pair beneath.[59] After surviving the Western Front and a severe gunshot wound, losing his life in peacetime Gloucestershire was unfortunate to say the least.

A British decision to retain its POWs at the end of hostilities in both 1918 and 1945 prompted a further spate of very public deaths.[60] Stranded far from friends and families, the German POWs had only 'one desire', reported a Swiss observer, 'to be sent home'.[61] During this long period of peacetime captivity, a steady line of frustrated German prisoners took their own lives. Such was the frequency of these deaths that one concerned Nottingham resident even put pen to paper urging that something be done. 'Another German prisoner recently committed suicide,' they wrote. 'We can hardly wonder at it', they continued, '[as] nothing is more demoralising than to be parted for a long while from a loved one.'[62] The death of Georg Zarembowicz was typical of many of these prisoner suicides. Zarembowicz had been billeted to an isolated farm near the village of Dalry in Ayrshire. One day in mid-April, he suddenly disappeared, leaving only a note behind for his employer in which he explained he wanted to end his life. Two days later, an off-duty naval officer was strolling through the woods near the farm, when he noticed an 'object hanging from a pine tree'. On closer inspection, it turned out to be a body, later identified as Zarembowicz.[63]

Trying to find ways to pass the time before eventual repatriation could itself prove to be a deadly sport for some of the younger German POWs. The Teddesley camp, based in a fine Georgian country house in Staffordshire, was the scene of two such post-war accidents. With several large expanses of water in the grounds, a legacy of Teddesley Hall's aristocratic owners, the POWs had plenty of opportunities to let off steam while dreaming of home. In July 1946, Henrick Koehler, still only 21 years old, charged into one of the pools, throwing himself headfirst into the cold water. Koehler hit the bottom, broke his neck and died some days later.[64] The following year, another German, Paul Hermann Schilling, was bathing in the murky waters when his feet became entangled in the vegetation. His friends tried to pull him free from the weeds, but were becoming trapped themselves, and could then only watch as Schilling slipped below the water.[65]

Across the Channel, it was the euphoria of victory that provided the backdrop to the deaths of further British servicemen in interwar Germany. Ostensibly stationed around Cologne to ensure Germany's commitment to the Treaty of Versailles, the British occupiers also spent a good portion of their time soaking in their surroundings. It was during these moments of relaxation that the death toll steadily rose. Traffic accidents, the strong currents of the Rhine or even altercations with local Germans precipitated deaths.[66] One of the more unusual military deaths occurred on a 'tropically hot' day in Bonn. During the army's 'Skills-at-all-Sports' competition, a team from the Royal Field Artillery squared up against the Welsh Regiment in a tense round of tug of war. The men pulled and puffed when suddenly one of the Welsh contingent collapsed. All attempts at resuscitation failed and the man died at the scene, which had the effect of 'marring the proceedings to a great effect'.[67] Enemy deaths, as the examples from Cologne, Staffordshire or Scotland demonstrate, were sometimes fairly mundane. Accidents or misadventure might have lacked the drama of a dogfight in the skies, but the results were similar: the enemy had once again died in the midst of local communities.

Nursing the Enemy

When Henrick Koehler dived into the shallow waters of a Staffordshire pool and broke his neck, he was taken not to a military hospital but rather to the Staffordshire General Infirmary. In the austere surroundings of Stafford's main hospital, Koehler rapidly succumbed to his injuries and died far from home with only civilian medics for company.[68] In Germany, the situation was very similar. Sick and dying British POWs frequently spent their final hours laid up in civilian hospitals alongside other patients. During the First World War, for example, a sad procession of British POWs passed through the heavy doors of the Eppendorf Hospital in northern Hamburg. Despite a reported severe shortage of food and medicines, recovery was more common than death. Those men that did die in Eppendorf, such as severely wounded Londoner Percy Allam, slipped away with only doctors and nurses for company.[69]

At the start of hostilities in 1914 and 1939, the British and German authorities had been under no illusions that they would need to care for the sick, injured and wounded from both sides. Their ideal solution was to treat the enemy away from prying eyes within the internment camps themselves, which generally contained some form of medical facility.[70] These sickbays or basic hospitals might have been locked away behind wire, but they still relied on outside help to function. The British camp hospitals of the First World War, in particular, seemed to be a constant hive of activity. Doctors from neighbouring towns ended up incorporating POW patients into their rounds, visiting them several times per week.[71] Thomas Hardy, whose imagined Wessex landscape was home to several internment camps, was even a regular visitor to the camp hospital in Dorchester. During these sojourns, he witnessed the wounded, sick and dying enemy. 'Prussian, in much pain died whilst I was with him,' he noted after one visit. Recognising the man's suffering, Hardy added that his death was both 'to my great relief, and his own'.[72]

Treating the POWs within the camps had the advantage of restricting contact between the interned enemy and the civilian population, but as a practice it was never entirely sustainable. The limited size of camp medical facilities relative to the number of prisoners meant that hospitals were often quickly overwhelmed. The German internment system of the First World War experienced this to devastating effect when typhus swept through the Wittenberg camp. Consisting of some fifty wooden huts positioned 'in a very unattractive spot', as the American ambassador put it, the infected lice had little trouble spreading through the tightly packed accommodation.[73] Panicked at the rapidly deteriorating situation, the camp commandant quarantined the entire site and then effectively left the POWs to deal with the epidemic themselves. By March 1915, there were over a thousand active typhus cases and at least fifty new ones per day. One British doctor tried to brush some dust from a man's arm, only to discover it was actually 'a moving mass of lice'. The epidemic finally started to ease in the spring, by which time sixty British prisoners, and even more French and Russians, had died.[74]

After the 'horrors of Wittenberg', which preceded a smaller, but still deadly, epidemic at Gardelegen camp near Stendal, the German authorities made an effort to improve the hygiene and cleanliness of the internment sites. The Wittenberg incident also illustrated why the camp hospitals needed to work in conjunction with external facilities, which became standard practice the longer the war went on. The larger military hospitals in Britain generally had separate wards for treating sick and wounded enemy patients. At the Dartford War Hospital in Kent, for example, thirty wards were set aside for German patients, which were easily connected by a covered walkway to the British military hospital on the same site.[75] In Berlin, British civilians held in the Ruhleben internment camp in the west of the city were sent to the intriguingly named Dr Weiler's Sanatorium. Patients had the option of paying Weiler a fee for a supposedly better-quality room or, as one former internee put it: 'extortionate fees for a minimum of comfort'.[76] The situation was similar in Nazi Germany. Allied POWs were treated principally in the camps themselves, but for more serious complaints, they were sometimes transferred to local civilian or military hospitals.[77]

Civilian facilities also played a role in housing, and sometimes treating, the large number of POWs and internees suffering from poor mental health. Swiss physician Adolf Vischer was struck by the large number of prisoners suffering from extreme lethargy and melancholy behaviour. Placing the blame squarely on the toll of internment, he labelled these cases 'barbed-wire disease' (*Stacheldrahtkrankheit*).[78] An inspection of the Knockaloe civilian camp on the Isle of Man certainly brought the psychological impact of internment into sharp relief. Bearing in mind that the inspectors found the camp to be generally well run, it was striking how many men were 'suffering from a distorted conception of their surroundings'. 'Many will never get better,' the inspectors lamented. 'They will end their lives in a lunatic asylum.'[79] The situation was little better during the Second World War. One soldier held as a prisoner in Nazi Germany recalled the many examples of 'mental break-downs' among his comrades who could no longer cope with the igno-miny of internment.[80] Whether in Britain or Germany, the camp commandants generally sought the easiest solution, which was to offload their sick internees to local asylums for some form of treatment.[81]

Once prisoners suffering from physical and mental illnesses were treated in civilian hospitals, then it follows that some of this number also died in these facilities. Frederick Martin was already in his mid-sixties when he was taken to Macclesfield's asylum suffering from 'senile dementia'. Not showing any great sympathy with his new patient, the doctor admitting Martin scribbled a note about his 'stupid appearance'. Yet, the grey-haired man with a neatly trimmed beard who stood before him had actually enjoyed a rich life (see image 8). Originally from Hamburg, Martin had ended up in England, married a local woman and then worked as a docker in Liverpool for years. Once in the asylum, Martin did not last long. He died alone from 'colitis' in March 1917, still registered as an 'enemy alien'.[82]

Many enemy deaths occurred in waves. The 1918 influenza epidemic, for example, which killed upwards of 30 million people across the globe, also saw large numbers of British and German POWs admitted to hospital, from where some never returned.[83] In Essex,

8. The only surviving photograph of Frederick Martin, a German 'enemy alien' who died in Macclesfield's Parkside Asylum during the First World War.

German prisoners from several small working camps were taken to Colchester for treatment, where twenty-four men died in November alone.[84] Further east across the North Sea and into Hamburg, influenza was also hitting British POWs hard. In the city's overfilled Eppendorf hospital, James Pollock, an Irishman from Cork, followed Martin Allan from Dundee and 29-year-old Philip Flower to an early grave.[85] Other big spikes in hospital admissions occurred during moments of increased military activity. The intensification of the Allied air war over Nazi Germany in 1942 or the advance onto German territory during the latter stages of the conflict led to an increase in POWs, many of whom were wounded or dying.

Whenever British or German internees died in enemy hospitals, suspicions were immediately raised by those at home. During the First World War, both sides were quick to accuse their opponents of medical mistreatment, sometimes with very good reason. The neglect of James Spensley, a lieutenant in the Royal Army Medical Corps, is a case in point. The Germans captured Spensley, who had been wounded in the stomach, at the Battle of Loos. By the time he arrived at a hospital in Mainz, he was already in a bad way; in great pain, and 'often delirious', he eventually passed away in November 1915. The British complained of 'gross medical neglect' on two counts. First, the German doctor waited four weeks before operating on Spensley and, second, in another 'act of carelessness', the patient was given solid foods despite having a gaping stomach wound.[86] Slightly less convincingly, the German authorities responded with their own litany of complaints about the quality of care received in Britain. In the Dartford War Hospital, there are the 'most unbelievable conditions', alleged one German POW. Surgical instruments went unsterilised; sometimes the same scalpel was used multiple times, he claimed, leading to many unnecessary deaths.[87] Swiss inspectors, however, stepped in to defend the hospital from such attacks, adding emphatically that it was 'as good as one can wish a hospital to be'.[88]

In both world wars, it proved easy to find instances of deliberate medical neglect that contributed to further suffering and death. Yet, while these were the focus of claim and counterclaim, more frequent examples of fair, equitable treatment often went unnoticed. Understandably, doctors and nurses were not always particularly pleased to find the usual rhythms of the hospital environment disturbed by the arrival of the sick and dying enemy. Fear and uncertainty of coming face to face with the enemy marked many of the early encounters. When a wounded German solider was brought to a hospital in Britain in late 1914, the duty nurse's immediate response was one of alarm: 'Shall I be left alone with him?' she cried. The sister reassured her that a sentry would keep guard in the corridor.[89] Sometimes the patients themselves did little to ease tensions. In one Plymouth naval hospital, a few staunch Nazis spent most of their time trying to annoy their captors, hurling abuse and throwing sick bowls at the nurses who were trying to treat them.[90]

Once the initial shock of the enemy's presence had passed, though, most medical staff concentrated not on nationality, but rather on the 'suffering body to be nursed'.[91] The British nurse who had been so wary when a German soldier was first admitted to her ward in 1914 soon started to treat him like any other patient. However, her caring role proved short-lived. After initially making promising progress, a tetanus infection took hold. She tried to 'relieve him', but his condition rapidly deteriorated. 'The hand that still held mine grew colder,' she sadly recalled, 'the breathing stopped, and I knew that my prisoner had been released.' The gentle touch between the dying German soldier and British nurse erased the wartime barriers separating friend and foe.[92] In such moments, comfort and human support took precedence over national animosities. At London's Royal Herbert Hospital, which had a dedicated German ward during the Second World War, the nursing staff followed the same tentative steps of their forebears. The sister in charge of the ward later recalled 'the calm dignity' of the German fighter pilot, Hasso von Perthes, who slowly died of his wounds in September 1940. 'His plight so moved one of the nurses', the ward sister recalled, 'that she vowed to write to his [mother] when the war was over.'[93]

In wartime Germany, similar encounters occurred, but there tended to be a much greater distinction between those prisoners treated within the camps and those who entered civilian facilities. G. Purves, a captain in the Royal Scots Fusiliers, apparently died peacefully in a Cologne hospital in November 1915. A fellow officer even commended the 'kind and attentive' German doctors, although his fulsome praise may have been as much to comfort Purves's grieving parents as a genuine reflection of standards.[94] Yet, at the same time, other British prisoners were dying in camp hospitals from neglect. The sixty British POWs who died from typhus in the 'horrors of Wittenberg' camp that same year, for example, would surely have had a very different take on the levels of German medical care.

There was, then, no single unifying experience of wartime medical regimes or, indeed, of death. In both world wars, the enemy lost their lives in a whole host of very different ways. Combat, disease or even shootings could be the catalyst, but so too could suicide or an accident. Despite these huge differences, there were also common threads. The belligerent powers, whether Nazi Germany or imperial Britain, of course, only wanted the more positive reports of the care they had provided to their POWs to surface. There was certainly no reason to draw attention to instances of mistreatment, neglect or unlawful killings, which were an all too frequent occurrence under the Nazi regime. Instead, as a British coroner's inquest into two German deaths in 1918 made clear: 'the public should know that they were properly treated'.[95] This was, therefore, a question of reciprocity. Each side needed to stress good treatment, in the hope that their opponent would act in the same way.

The coroner's remarks, though, also emphasised that the public had a knowledge of enemy deaths. It would certainly have been more convenient for the authorities if the enemy had chosen to expire quietly away from prying eyes. But this was rarely the case. Civilians often looked on as attacking aeroplanes came plummeting to the ground or they were there when POWs came to grief at work or at play. Local people, then, were not just aware that the enemy was dying around them; they were active participants in these deadly encounters, tending the injured, collecting the remains or even providing comfort as their foe drew his dying breath.

3

BURYING

Bernard Murphy, a 30-year-old Dubliner, had been a long-serving solider in the Royal Irish Regiment when Europe plunged into war in August 1914. Leaving his wife Bridget behind in Ireland, Murphy soon saw action as part of the small British Expeditionary Force (BEF), which had been sent to Belgium and France to help stem the early German advance. The freshly arrived members of the BEF first encountered the German troops just north of the Belgian city of Mons in late August. Murphy's involvement, however, proved to be as short-lived as the BEF's own defensive stand at Mons. Wounded in the foot, he was captured by the Germans and taken 300 kilometres further east to a Dortmund hospital where his condition rapidly deteriorated. A bout of pneumonia took hold in his lungs and Murphy died far from family and friends in early September 1914.[1]

In the midst of an escalating European conflict, it was clearly impossible for Murphy's parents, Emily and Patrick, to travel all the way from Dublin to Dortmund to collect their son's body. If the family was unable to take possession of the remains and the British authorities were also in no position to repatriate, then the Germans had little option but to do something with the corpse themselves. The issue of how and where to dispose of the deceased enemy was one that came up repeatedly in both conflicts. The most practical solution, which was also what happened in Dortmund with Murphy's remains, was simply to bury the enemy in the closest municipal or parish cemetery. After all, there seemed little point in traipsing the body around the country to a different cemetery when a burial spot lay close at hand. In Dortmund, therefore, local gravediggers excavated a hole ready for Murphy in the city's large South-Western Cemetery (Südwestfriedhof). Three days later, members of a Dortmund war veterans' organisation, whose ageing members had fought in the 1870–1871 Franco-Prussian War, then – somewhat unusually – gathered in the cemetery to accompany his coffin to the grave.[2]

In both world wars, similar funerals occurred, albeit generally with far less pomp. Dortmund's veterans may have wanted to show respect to their vanquished foe, but they were also very aware that a 'reverential' funeral should be reported abroad, and in particular in Britain, which was a point they also made to the Foreign Office in Berlin.[3] This was seemingly the group's own small attempt to promote German civility and culture in the face of international shouts of barbarism after the German army had barged its way through Belgium, leaving a trail of pillaged homes, destroyed lives and death in its wake.[4] The enemy corpse, therefore, was never a neutral object; it was a political being. Funerals, headstones and graves all combined to enhance the 'symbolic effectiveness' of the enemy dead during wartime.[5]

The grandeur of Murphy's funeral was rarely repeated elsewhere during either conflict, particularly in the latter stages of the two wars as resources became stretched, but the policy of burying the enemy in the heart of local communities most certainly was. Throughout both conflicts, cemeteries in villages, towns and cities across Britain and Germany became repositories for the enemy dead as well as for those killed from one's own side. When faced with the prospect of receiving the remains of their enemy, not all communities were quite as gracious as the Dortmunders. Local complaints, protests and obfuscation could just as easily accompany the enemy to the grave. Nonetheless, whether the public liked it or not, once the enemy had been buried in their midst, then the living and the dead, friend and foe, were tied together in a communal embrace. British–German relations may have been at their lowest ebb, but the presence of the remains of individual lives extinguished too soon went some way to ensuring some contacts survived.

Identifying

During the First World War and for much of the second conflict too, the enemy generally died in large numbers safely away from the British and German civilians curled up in the comfort of their homes. As enemy soldiers were mown down in a hail of bullets on the Western Front or drowned on a North Atlantic convoy, nobody showed any particular concern back in Schwerin or Stafford, Nuremberg or Norwich. In a war between us and them, the death of the enemy was generally out of sight and out of mind. Blanking out the death of the wartime foe when they breathed their last back at home, however, was not quite as straightforward. There was no distance to death; the remains lay within the confines of civilian life. And with a corpse came responsibilities. International law, in the form of the 1907 Hague Convention, stipulated that the 'same rules' for burying 'soldiers of the national army' applied to POWs. By the start of the Second World War, the Geneva Convention on Prisoners of War had added further clarity, stressing unambiguously that 'belligerents shall see that prisoners of war dying in captivity are honourably buried'.[6]

The enemy corpse stranded on the home front was someone's father, brother, son or lover back in Britain or Germany. On both a humanitarian and legal level, families had to be informed that their relative was no more. In both world wars, this process of knowledge exchange happened as a basic transaction, and involved various agencies. Emil Gruss, a 28-year-old lance corporal (*Unteroffizier*) from Hanover who drowned in September 1918, provides just one of many examples of this process in action. At the time of his death, Gruss had been with a small group of German POWs being taken by boat to their place of work. The boat suddenly capsized sending Gruss into the muddy waters of the River Teme in Worcestershire. There had been some suggestion that Gruss had managed to escape, but three months later his body was fished from the water, offering conclusive proof of his death. At this point, the International Committee of the Red Cross, which held records for all internees, then notified the German authorities of Gruss's fate, before the Prisoners of War Information Bureau finally contacted the family in Hanover in July 1919 to confirm his death.[7]

The British and the Germans agreed a very similar system in the early weeks of the Second World War, with the International Committee of the Red Cross in Geneva again acting as the intermediary.[8] The death of Andrew Bain, an RAF sergeant on a mission over Berlin in August 1943, illustrates how the bureaucratic cogs slowly moved into gear when the enemy died on the home front. Bain's wife, Isabel, first knew something was amiss when she received an urgent telegram from the RAF informing her with 'deep [. . .] regret' that Andrew had 'failed to return from operations'. A few weeks later, the Air Ministry's Casualty Branch listed Bain as missing, but stressed that this did not 'necessarily mean that he is killed or wounded'. Admittedly, all the signs pointed in this direction, but the RAF wanted to avoid declaring him dead until official confirmation came through from the Red Cross. Eventually, they must have received news from Geneva, as in November 1943, some ten weeks after his bomber had disappeared over Germany, the Air Ministry and then the Red Cross wrote to Isabel separately confirming rather matter-of-factly that her husband had 'lost his life as the result of Air Operations'.[9]

Just getting to this stage forced the British and German authorities to become more familiar with their recently deceased enemy. If they were going to communicate news of a death to the opposing side, then the body had first to be given a name, identity and a biography. When deaths occurred within the confines of the internment camp, this was a relatively straightforward process; both the camp authorities and the Red Cross generally held accurate records for each prisoner. In the event of an individual death, all they had to do was to thumb through the record cards and transmit the information home.

Deaths in aerial combat during the Second World War, by contrast, proved much harder to identify. The intensity of a crash or mid-air explosion often tore bodies apart, which of course did little to aid identification. The dog tags worn by British airmen were also flammable, which was again not ideal when dealing with bodies wedged in the wreck of a burnt-out aircraft.[10] Above all, though, there had to be a willingness to investigate carefully what human remains did survive. In Nazi Germany, particularly in the latter stages of the war, it was hard to find much enthusiasm for such a gruesome task, meaning that individual identities could be quickly lost. This was the case with the seven-man crew of a Lancaster bomber that 'dived to the earth in flames' somewhere outside the western German town of Kempen in December 1944. The day after the crash, local farmers were given the unenviable task of collecting the 'small pieces' of the bodies and placing them in a mass grave. A simple wooden cross inscribed with the single word – *Unbekannt* ('unknown') – was all that indicated the jumbled remains below.[11]

Had the farmers been more inclined to sift through the wreckage, they would no doubt have discovered further clues to the Lancaster crew's former lives. They may well have learnt that Julian Veglio, the navigator, was married to Dawn Ryan, or that the young pilot, Arthur Kennedy, was originally from New Zealand's North Island. Such details often came from scraps of uniform or from good luck charms that both British and German airmen often carried.[12] On other occasions, such items had helped rescuers to build a fuller picture of the enemy. When the body of Herbert Panzlaff was plucked from a Northumberland beach in early 1940, for example, his pockets contained a personal photograph, an Iron Cross and a lock of hair. On his finger was a gold wedding ring inscribed simply 'T.Z. 24/12/38', hinting at Panzlaff's now vanished life back in Germany.[13] The bodies of Allied airmen shot down over Germany threw up a similar list of possessions. One body fished from the North Sea provided two photographs, a medal ribbon, as well as one silver and one gold chain, while another body had a pocket watch, a medal ribbon and a bracelet inscribed with the name 'Marjorie'.[14] These last vestiges of life went some way to rehumanising the enemy. No longer was he part of a dangerous mass; instead, he was an individual who had once lived and loved, but whose life had expired within civilian communities at war.

A sense of common humanity came through particularly strongly in the medical setting. When a patient died, the hospital, even in wartime, had a responsibility to report this fact, filling in a death certificate for each corpse. In First World War Britain, medics generally appended a more complex form specifically designed for enemy patients. On a hectic ward, there must have been a temptation to get the administration out of the way quickly and to move on. Certainly, on many of these forms the comments were often curt and to the point. 'Did he leave any message?' the form asked. 'No,' was the answer. Sometimes, however, the medic went much further, as if they had connected to their recently deceased foe and were even looking to comfort his family back in Germany. 'The prisoner of war did not suffer much' was a common refrain, even when the evidence suggested quite the opposite. 'Gunshot wound: left hand and back (penetrating spine) [. . .] septic spinal meningitis' did not really suggest a lack of suffering. Telling the bereaved that their loved one died free from pain and sending 'greetings to his family' as he expired shows the dead breaching the wartime barriers that separated the British and Germans.[15]

In Britain, where the Home Office asked coroners to hold inquests into German prisoners' deaths, it did not take long for biographical details of individual enemy lives to circulate. When Walter Sick, an interned 'enemy alien', died from appendicitis in Chester, for example, the coroner was called to the city's main infirmary to investigate. During his enquiries, he confirmed Sick's age, 23 years old; his occupation, a hotel chef; and his familial status, married to an Englishwoman since 1913 with one new baby. The coroner also uncovered other details about Sick's short life, from his father's career as a master confectioner in Baden through to Sick's earlier travels through France, Switzerland and the Canary Islands. Once the coroner had concluded that Sick had died from 'natural causes', a summary of his enquiry then appeared in the Cheshire press.[16] In this way, Sick's identity and fate became public knowledge, which allowed local communities to discover much more about the life of their wartime enemy, soon to be buried in their midst.

Contested Ground

At home during both wars, the vast majority of the enemy dead received a proper burial. This was very different to the battlegrounds, where burial tended to be a luxury, not a right. During the fighting on the Western Front during the Great War, bodies ended up being used to patch up trench walls or they floated away during heavy rain. If people were fortunate enough to receive a proper burial, then these were often hasty affairs, a shallow grave and a rough bit of wood with a scrawled name being all that marked the spot.[17] On the battlefield, fighting the living, not burying the dead, generally took priority.

Even with greater time and space at home, there were still occasional instances where corpses were lost or never recovered at all. In his short story, 'Mary Postgate', Rudyard Kipling runs with this idea, seemingly fantasising around the thought of abandoning a German corpse to the elements. Postgate, a 'colourless' companion to a wealthy lady, discovers a dying German airman propped up against a tree at the back of the garden. 'His head moved ceaselessly from side to side', but the poor man's body was 'still as the tree's trunk', wrote Kipling. The German was clearly on the verge of death, not that this particularly concerned Postgate, who did her best to ignore his final groans. Once life had drained from the enemy, she simply left the body, went back to the house and took a 'luxurious hot bath before tea'. Kipling, whose only son, John, had gone missing on the Western Front, could perhaps take some comfort in this atrocious end.[18]

During the Battle of Britain, when the country's skies were lit up with searchlights, tracer rounds and burning fighter planes, it proved even easier to mislay an enemy body. Indeed, this was particularly the case when enemy aircraft came down with such force that they embedded both the machine and the crew deep into the ground. One airman to suffer this fate in October 1940 was newly married Werner Knittel, whose Messerschmidt 109 fighter nosedived into the soft earth of Romney Marsh on England's south coast. As most of the wreckage as well as Knittel's remains were below the surface, nobody bothered to excavate the field; daily life for everyone, bar Knittel, simply carried on as before.[19] Over in Germany, too, bodies were sometimes left in the wreckage of smashed British aircraft, only emerging years later as official investigators and amateur hunters combed deep into forests or dived into murky lakes. From the depths of the beautiful Walchensee, an idyllic Bavarian alpine lake, for example, the remains of two British airmen emerged in the 1950s; they had lain undisturbed in the waters since their Lancaster bomber had splashed down there in 1943.[20]

Leaving the enemy dead submerged in fields or lakes may have been a practical convenience in the mêlée of war, but it did rather overlook the requirement for a burial stipulated in international law. To meet these obligations and also in the hope of ensuring reciprocity, the British and Germans did generally manage to find some form of grave for the

enemy corpses at home. When local authorities or POW camp commandants needed to dispose of a body, there seemed little point in creating
a new cemetery for the occasion. Instead, it was much easier to make
use of existing facilities, and to bury the enemy in the closest churchyard or municipal cemetery that had space. In Kent, during the Battle
of Britain, for example, there was no time to find the perfect location
for the enemy dead, so German bodies were simply 'buried in any
graves that happened to be open'.[21]

There was, therefore, always a close physical connection between the
burial site and the original place of death. In Long Riston, a one-street
village in rural Yorkshire, for example, a single German grave lay in St
Margaret's churchyard. The body of Bruno Schakat had arrived in this
seemingly incongruent location in May 1941, when his Heinkel
bomber came under fire and crashed in a field just north of the churchyard, killing Schakat as it hit the ground. What was true for wartime
Britain was also true of Second World War Germany. In the tiny north
German village of Lehmke, deep in the wilds of the Lüneburg Heath,
there was a lone British grave. This belonged to Lincolnshire-born
Alwyn Patrick, who had been part of the Allied airborne forces fighting
their way into Nazi Germany in the final weeks of the Second World
War. Patrick's involvement came to a premature end when he was fatally
shot on the edge of Lehmke and then buried around the corner in the
village cemetery.[22]

Not everyone proved to be so taken with these mortuary entanglements, however. The residents of the Scottish port of Ullapool, not
known as a hotbed of twentieth-century protest, seemed taken aback
when a local POW camp commandant tried to leave the body of a
German influenza victim in the main cemetery. After being denied a
burial plot, and with the number of corpses rapidly mounting as the
1918 influenza pandemic swept through his camp, the commandant
pondered simply dumping the bodies at sea. Fortunately, the dead
Germans, whose numbers had by now risen to seven, avoided this fate
when space was found in the town's Old Mill Street Cemetery where
the enemy bodies could finally be laid to rest.[23]

Attempts to bury the German war dead during the Second World
War sometimes provoked a very similar response. In the railway town

of Derby, which itself came under air attack during the conflict, one local objected strongly to the presence of the German dead. 'There is no space for Germans,' the man complained. 'They should be buried in a communal grave [. . .] away from where some of our loved ones lie.'[24] Residents of the Channel Islands had similar objections to the new German graves as their compatriots did in Derby, but with one key difference. As the Nazi regime occupied the islands from 1940 onwards, it proved a little trickier for them to complain. The Feldkommandant, effectively the islands' German governor, initially requisitioned a portion of St Brelade's cemetery on Jersey for his war dead. As the number of casualties continued to rise, the occupiers simply increased their share of the cemetery, taking a chunk of the vicar's garden and even moving an errant British grave from the Great War to the other side of the island.[25]

In wartime Britain and the Channel Islands, any concerns about enemy burials paled in comparison to some of the violent responses to the British dead in Nazi Germany. From a long list of reported incidents, one in Schlalach, a tiny community south of Potsdam, stands out. In September 1943, a Lancaster bomber on a bombing raid over Berlin hit the ground near the village in flames. From the burnt-out wreckage, the German authorities eventually recovered the badly charred bodies of the seven-man crew. The corpses were then taken to the village cemetery, where they were chucked into a roughly dug pit and covered with earth, but not before some locals allegedly kicked and trampled the remains. The local mayor, seemingly little troubled by the responsibilities of his position, apparently looked on as the bodies were desecrated.[26]

In a small number of cases, local resistance to enemy burials led to the creation of brand-new cemeteries. In Britain, only the POW camps at Park Hall in Shropshire and Stobs in the Scottish borders received their own separate cemeteries. On both occasions, this was pitched as a practical solution to spatial constraints in the existing burial grounds. However, dig below the surface of the local exchanges and it becomes clear that space was a relatively minor issue. The landowners in Kirkton, who controlled the churchyard nearest to the Stobs camp, accepted a single German body in May 1915, before declaring themselves full and, for good measure, insisting that any 'future provision for burials of this nature' needed to be 'made elsewhere'.[27] In Oswestry, the main settlement near the Park Hall camp, similar animosities surfaced. With no other solutions open to them, the commandants of the two camps had to arrange for the construction of their own POW cemeteries.

There was perhaps greater justification to this approach in First World War Germany, where the death rates were much higher and consequently more burial space was required. Of course, having a genuine need for cemetery space was never a positive; it was a sign of mismanagement and a failure of adequate care. In the Wittenberg camp, for example, some 450 Russian, British, French and Belgian POWs succumbed to typhus during the 1915 outbreak. The town's existing cemeteries lacked the capacity to take in such a large influx of bodies. Yet the dead had to go somewhere. Following the same path taken in Stobs and Oswestry, the German commandant ended up organising the construction of a new POW cemetery situated just across the road from the camp.[28] Further east in Germany's Zehrensdorf camps, the prompt for a new burial ground had less to do with space and far more to do with religious belief. When the two Zehrensdorf camps were constructed in late 1914, they were designed to house mainly Muslim, Hindu and Sikh prisoners from the Allies' African and Asian colonies. Always with a ready eye for the propaganda value of Zehrensdorf, which was also home to the country's first mosque, the German authorities established a separate camp cemetery where they made some attempt to adhere to the different religious beliefs of those who had died.[29]

Securing cemetery space for the burial of the enemy dead did not necessarily mean that they were going to be given a generously sized plot. When burying the enemy, it was easy to dispense with such luxuries. The city council in Worms initially developed rather grandiose plans for its Hochheimer Höhe cemetery, with separate sections neatly laid out for both the German and the Allied dead. However, these schemes were quickly derailed by events on the ground; a lack of food, poor sanitation and rising prisoner numbers saw the death rate rocket. In 1918, the enemy dead, including 117 British prisoners, were simply buried in hastily dug mass graves.[30] During the Great War, the British authorities too were never averse to packing several German bodies into a single grave. Admittedly, the administrators of the Dartford War Hospital faced the conundrum of having large numbers of dead POWs and only a small on-site cemetery in which to bury them. Their solution was at least practical, even if the maths did not fully add up. They placed the 280 German bodies, six at a time, into forty-eight separate graves that stretched out in two parallel rows.[31]

The use of shared graves in Dartford followed a pattern that was also familiar from civilian life. The more powerful an individual, the more likely they were to receive a decent burial. Wounded, isolated and alone, the German patients in Dartford, most of them fresh from the front, were anything but powerful, and could therefore be quite easily confined to a shared grave if they died. In a similar fashion, when the enemy ended up spending their dying days in large civilian asylums, whether this was the so-called Stone Mental Hospital in Aylesbury or the Neuruppin asylum in Brandenburg, their final resting place also tended to be a mass grave. Poor Gustav Erich Piotrowski, a married man from West Prussia, had been sentenced to eighteen months' imprisonment in Walton Jail, Liverpool, for attempting to escape from the Knockaloe internment camp on the Isle of Man. Distressed at the sentence and unable to reconcile himself to confinement, he took his own life in March 1916; the same day his remains were committed, without ceremony, to the Walton Park Cemetery across the road.[32] While the British and Germans generally ensured that their wartime enemy received a burial plot, there was no equality when it came to the actual form of the grave. In these cases, death was certainly not the great leveller.

Staging the Funeral

In the early twentieth century, funerals not only marked the departure of a loved one to the grave, but also brought friends, family, colleagues and neighbours together, helping them to face the 'reality of death'.[33] Like thousands of other wartime widows stranded at home, Sibylle Neuenhöfer missed this entire layer of mourning. Her husband, Christian, and his fellow crew members had failed to return from a bombing raid over Britain in July 1941. She must have presumed the worst, but official confirmation of his death only reached the family home in Bonn the following summer. At the same time, she also learnt that his remains had been buried in Southend-on-Sea. Even had she known these details earlier, there was no way she could have been at the funeral to stand at the grave and say her final goodbyes. War rendered such conventions obsolete. What she could do, however, was to gather with their young son, Ulli, and other family members in the Catholic Church of St Remigus in Bonn for a memorial service, allowing them to start grieving their loss from home.[34]

It is unclear whether Neuenhöfer received much in the way of a funeral in Essex; often the dead were quietly dispatched with little ceremony. This was certainly the case in Nazi Germany, where Allied airmen shot down over Nazi Germany, particularly in the final stages of the conflict, were sometimes lucky even to get a proper grave. In Münster, the bodies of three RAF airmen eventually made it to a cemetery, but there was no sign of a funeral and no hint of dignity either. A member of the Flak battery who had shot down the men's Lancaster bomber in March 1945 later recalled that the bodies 'lay on the ground for some days'. Eventually, 'some Russians' took them to a nearby cemetery, where the corpses were thrown into a hole, covered 'first with straw and then with soil'.[35]

Yet, while many of the downed airmen disappeared silently into the ground, the Allied POWs from the Western nations, though certainly not those from the Soviet Union, who died in captivity often received something of a rousing send-off. It might seem rather a paradox, but some of the grandest funerals were actually held in German POW camps. With one hand, the camp guards sometimes deliberately killed POWs, but then with the other, they also provided space for proper burials. Funerals held for POWs from the Stalag IXC camp in Bad Sulza or from its associated hospital were designed to leave an impression. Representatives from the British camp population, along with detachments of German guards, accompanied the coffin to the grave. A sea of cut flowers, oversized wreaths and long flowing ribbons containing messages and insignia then topped the grave, almost as if attempting to bury the reasons for the death in the first place (see image 9). Of course, this was one of the benefits for the Nazi regime. Spectacular funerals highlighted to the outside world not only the regime's apparent benevolence, but also its respect for military sacrifice. Given that the Allies also

9. The grave of a captured British soldier covered in floral tributes with wreaths containing messages in both English and German. During the early years of the Second World War at least, Nazi officials were keen to highlight their apparent care of the enemy war dead.

held thousands of German POWs, highlighting such values was clearly of great import.

There was, however, nothing particularly new in such scenes. First World War funerals in both countries had also provided an opportunity for the belligerents to project humanitarian values to those watching on from abroad. Cologne's Southern Cemetery (Südfriedhof) on a crisp spring morning in April 1916 might not have been the most obvious place to stumble upon Paul von Hindenburg, Germany's most prominent wartime general. However, the moustachioed figure of a high-ranking officer, with a striking resemblance to the great general, is clear to see amidst the mourners attending a large public funeral (see image 10). Hindenburg or perhaps just his Doppelgänger had congregated in the cemetery not for the funeral of a high-flying German officer, but rather for Wilfred Birt Beckett, an inconsequential British captain, who had died from wounds in one of the city's hospitals. What the incident reveals is that in the First World War, just as in the later conflict, funerals provided each side with an opportunity to present a positive image to the outside world. The local press in Cologne did not hesitate to seize the opportunity, publishing their own eulogistic accounts of Beckett's funeral emphasising how his death 'had touched the hearts of friend and foe' alike.[36]

10. During the First World War, the German authorities sometimes put on substantial funerals for their vanquished foe, such as in this scene, which captures the burial of Captain Wilfred Birt Beckett in Cologne in April 1916.

Like the vast majority of burial grounds used for interring the enemy dead, Cologne's Southern Cemetery was a public, not a private, space. During the world wars, and also during the British occupation of the city in the 1920s and after 1945, Allied war dead joined the bodies of local residents in the cemetery's woodland grounds. The urban location of the Southern Cemetery, and similar burial grounds in Britain and Germany, also helped to make enemy deaths visible. Somehow the coffins had to be transported from the site of death to the intended burial place. When the cemetery happened to be contained within a POW camp or in hospital grounds, as was the case in Wittenberg or Dartford, then the body could be transported to the grave with ease and discretion. However, as soon as greater distances were involved, the actual act of moving the body again became much more of a public affair.

In Handforth, where both civilian and military prisoners died during the Great War, the distance from the camp gates to the burial ground in neighbouring Wilmslow was a good 2 kilometres. The town cemetery in Hohenfels, Bavaria, used for Second World War British and Allied dead, was even further away, some 5 kilometres from the large Stalag 383 camp. The commandants of the two camps both allowed a select group of POWs to accompany the coffin to the grave, a practice that was generally repeated in other camps too. George Soane, a British POW in Hohenfels, remembered the funerals as 'quite something to see'. The coffin, bedecked with a Union Jack, was marched along, while a lone Scottish piper stood at the front playing a lament.[37] German POWs in Handforth were less fulsome in their praise than Soane, but nonetheless their own funeral cortèges were also grand affairs. With the Imperial German flag draped over the coffin, a group of uniformed POWs, sometimes numbering over a hundred, marching alongside and a camp band following on behind, the funerals must have made for a visual and aural spectacle.[38]

As POWs marched down urban streets on their way to the burial ground, local people often gathered to watch. While simple curiosity or even an urge to soak in the spectacle was the main draw, occasionally anger and hostility boiled over. In Potters Bar, where the crew of a downed German airship were to be buried in September 1916, the Metropolitan Police came prepared for trouble. Three hundred special constables were drafted in to control the 'very large crowd', which spread through the town and up to the cemetery entrance. Even with this level of security, one woman still managed to step out to throw a 'stale egg' at one of the coffins. The vicar officiating at the funeral also came under attack, receiving a barrage of critical letters for giving a 'Christian burial' to the 'German murderers'.[39] One year earlier, in the town of Sangerhausen, west of Leipzig, a much smaller, but even more aggressive crowd, reportedly mocked the burial of John Sullivan, a private in the Irish Guards. As Sullivan was carried to the grave, 'loud roars of laughter' could be heard from some of the locals gathered, which added little to the solemnity of the occasion.[40]

However, it was during the Second World War that debates were at their fiercest. In October 1939, the British recovered the bodies of two German airmen, Kurt Seydel and August Schleicher, from the cold waters of the Firth of Forth. The pair had been killed in one of Nazi Germany's very first air raids over Britain, which turned them into something akin to celebrity casualties. The authorities brought the bodies to Edinburgh, placed them in wooden coffins and then left them to rest ceremoniously in a local church before the funeral. The presence of three uniformed policemen wearing regulation helmets, who had been tasked with guarding the swastika-clad coffins, further added to the incongruity of the occasion (see image 11). The following day, the coffins of Seydel and Schleicher, still draped in swastika flags, were taken through crowd-lined streets to Portobello Cemetery, east of Edinburgh, for final burial. Locals may have turned out, but sections of the press were not so pleased, urging people in the future to do no more than 'honour [the enemy] dead quietly'.[41]

It may have been the novelty of the situation that brought people out in Edinburgh, but this quickly passed. At the funeral of another three German airmen the following February, public anger was even more palpable. Events played out in the Northumberland village of Chevington, near where the German airmen had originally been killed. Following the Edinburgh example, the military authorities again covered the coffins with the swastika flag for the procession to the grave. But if the presence of Nazi insignia was not bad enough, the appearance of uniformed RAF personnel, some with their own wreaths, was deemed a step too far. 'It fills me with disgust to read of the military

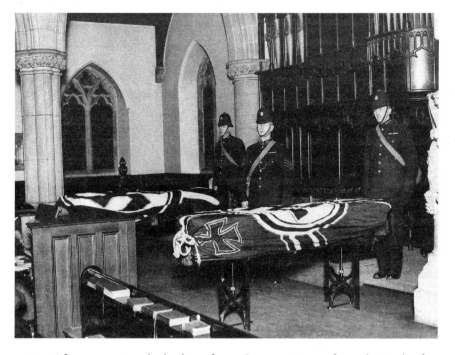

11. After recovering the bodies of two German airmen from the Firth of Forth in October 1939, the British saw fit to give them a full military funeral. Before being taken to Edinburgh's Portobello Cemetery, the wooden coffins replete with swastika flags were lined up in a local church on public display.

honours given to the three German airmen,' complained one local resident. 'It is time we treated these men as what they are, as cold blooded murderers,' another added. 'Give them a decent burial, yes, but no honours!'[42]

In an attempt to placate public anger, the British authorities went back through their earlier playbook and pointed out that it was simply a question of reciprocity. If the Nazis were giving 'full military honours' to the British dead, then they needed to follow suit, even though 'Hun airmen' were 'bombing [British] women and children'.[43] An awareness that the enemy also held their own soldiers as prisoners overseas had helped to keep crowds in check during the First World War too. Few people, though, expressed this thought with as much cynicism as a Dorset woman interviewed in autumn 1915. As a funeral cortège passed through the streets of Dorchester taking a German body to the grave, she shouted out that she hoped the Germans 'treat our men as well and pay as much respect to those [British prisoners] who die'.[44]

Yet, it was never just self-interest that held the curious crowds in check. The funerals themselves might have been for the enemy, but many of the symbols, rituals and procedures on display were extremely familiar. Locals watching the German POW burial in Dorchester, for example, would have heard the faint sound of Handel's 'Death March' in *Saul* floating freely from the town's German POW camp. The classical score regularly featured in German military funerals, such as the one in Dorset, but it also had a place in British culture, having featured in Horatio Nelson's funeral in 1806.[45] Much further north, in Inverness, local people gathering for another German funeral would have found much to enjoy in the music. Pipers playing a Highland lament led the coffin into the city's Tomnahurich Cemetery, while German POWs followed on behind.[46]

The liturgy and prayers that accompanied most enemy funerals provided another point of contact for any local onlookers. In First World War Berlin, German clergymen, from either the Jewish or Christian communities, were generally on hand to conduct funerals for the British civilian internees who died in the city's Ruhleben internment camp, bringing a certain familiarity to anyone viewing the services in Spandau, Hasenheide or Hoppegarten.[47] There could be no denying that this was still the enemy, but the familiarity of public funerals and a shared concern for the dead did at least help to soften any public hostility.[48]

Marking the Ground

A striking cortège, followed by a well-attended funeral, gave the enemy dead a fleeting moment in the public eye. Once the crowds had dispersed, though, and the soil had been piled back over the grave, the individual lives lost could quickly fade from memory. In Sangerhausen, where locals laughed and mocked the burial of John Sullivan, the authorities did their best to accelerate this process of forgetting. His grave was placed 'in a far away corner' of the cemetery, complained one fellow British POW, 'full of rubbish, broken glasses [and] decayed wreaths'.[49] This was certainly a case of out of sight, out of mind. If the enemy were to maintain a presence in the civilian landscape, then their graves had to be recognisable as such. Proper headstones or collective memorials for the dead not only made the enemy visible, but also forced local people to engage with these other graves that had been deposited into the heart of their communities.

In theory, all enemy graves, just as with civilian ones, should have had some form of grave marker placed above them as a matter of course. Again, this was a requirement in international law. Neither the British nor the Germans, though, had any intention of spending excessive time, money or materials on this task. Instead, they went for the bare minimum. The War Office in London insisted on nothing more than a 'simple wooden cross' for the graves of German First World War POWs, a policy that continued into the second conflict too.[50] Taking a very similar line, the German authorities also opted for simplicity, requiring a 'plain' wooden cross for the Allied war dead.[51] In First World War Cologne, the cemetery workers took these instructions a stage further, and managed to combine both simplicity and practicality in one go. Salvaging the wooden propellors of crashed aircraft, they placed these above the graves of British airmen, a practice that was also fairly common on the Western Front.[52]

The picture that emerges from the use of wooden grave markers was again one of reciprocity. Both sides were content to place a simple cross above the grave, safe in the knowledge that their wartime opponent was acting in exactly the same way. However, there seemed little point in going to such trouble, unless the other side was also fully aware of their efforts. The two wartime foes, therefore, put plans in place to publicise the work they were doing to care for the enemy dead. To the frustration of the British, it was actually the Nazi regime that took the lead on this during the early months of the Second World War. The German military started bombarding London not just with bombs, but also with 'very elaborate photographs' of British war graves. Under pressure to reciprocate by sending 'equally good photographs in return', but at the same time reluctant to spend 'public funds', the War Office delegated the task to the Red Cross, whose members ended up criss-crossing the country taking pictures of the German graves.[53]

The Red Cross teams took their duties incredibly seriously. If the aim was to give reassurance to the bereaved, then it was clearly crucial that the pictures captured British respect for the enemy dead. Before travelling to the different burial sites, therefore, they tried to make sure that the name on the grave matched other records. The Red Cross had already had their fingers burnt on several occasions when they had visited a grave, secured a photograph, and then only later discovered a glaring error. In Kent, for example, the Red Cross had commissioned a local journalist to collect the images. He diligently went around German graves in Chatham, Dartford, Gillingham and Shorncliffe, then sent his finished images to the Red Cross, who were unfortunately far from impressed with the results. The photographs are 'unsatisfactory'; they have 'evidently' been taken in a 'slap dash manner', they complained.[54] Such incidents made the Red Cross put more effort into first dressing the graves before photographing them. In Wrexham, they took this a bit far, demanding the cemetery superintendent dig up the turf around the German graves and plant flowers before the photographer was let loose.[55]

Unsurprisingly, the Nazi regime showed far less enthusiasm when it came to photographing the graves of the POWs it had murdered. After all, if the exercise was about encouraging reciprocal treatment, there was no point in drawing attention to its own criminal acts. Unlike the regular POW graves, which were dressed up smartly for the cameras, the small number of British soldiers and civilians to die in the Nazi concentration camp system often had no known grave and certainly no headstone. By far the most prominent of these victims was 22-year-old Keith Mayor from Preston, whose death received considerable press coverage during the post-war Bergen-Belsen War Crimes Trial.[56] Since Preston, Mayor had been on quite a journey. Captured in Norway on a Royal Navy Commando raid, the Germans had first taken him to Sachsenhausen for interrogation before dumping him in the Bergen-Belsen concentration camp in early 1945. He had not been in Belsen for long, when a French prisoner discovered his emaciated body with 'a small hole in the centre of his forehead'.[57] Without ceremony and certainly without a headstone, Mayor's remains then disappeared into a sea of corpses, human misery and death that swept through Bergen-Belsen during the camp's final weeks.[58]

The non-remembrance of Mayor and other British prisoners in Nazi Germany drew a distinction between the 'deserving' military dead and those murdered or killed who were lined up to be forgotten. Even in Britain, the dead were unofficially categorised, and this determined whether their presence was to live on through a proper grave marker. The graves of enemy civilians, whether in Britain or Germany, never featured that prominently in either conflict, presumably because they lacked the allure of a military, uniformed death. When asked about the graves of civilian internees in 1941, the British authorities rather flippantly dismissed these as 'not our concern at present'.[59] The spies of the Great War, shot in the Tower of London, and any German POWs tried and executed in Britain for crimes, such as the Nazi prisoners who had murdered Wolfgang Rosterg in 1944, also lacked proper gravestones. A visitor to London's Plaistow Cemetery in 1924, attempting to find the final resting spot of the German spies, discovered the graves 'very much overgrown', with no headstones and covered only with 'weeds'.[60]

While these unmarked, uncared for and largely neglected graves were in danger of quickly fading into obscurity, the regular military burials, in stark contrast, enjoyed a much grander presence. The difference was a simple one. Whereas the spies and Nazis tried for murder were executed outside a fixed community that may have advocated on their behalf, the military POWs generally died as part of a camp society. The bonds of the POW camp system, pitched in terms of comradeship and military loyalty, proved crucial in ensuring the enemy dead received not only funerals, but also adequate grave markers and memorials too. The German officers interned in Skipton's First World War POW camp expressed this belief most succinctly in their post-war memoir of life behind the wire in Yorkshire. 'For us it was a sacred duty', they wrote, 'to erect a memorial for our dead at their place of rest in a foreign land.'[61]

The thought of the enemy erecting permanent structures in the heart of their communities, however, was not always particularly welcomed by local residents, who generally viewed the POWs as a fleeting phenomenon. In most people's minds, the prisoners arrived, were interned and then were destined to depart at the war's end. It was something of a conceptual struggle, therefore, to conceive of the POWs leaving a memento of their stay behind. In Castle Donington, where thirty-nine Germans died, mainly during the 1918 influenza outbreak, one local penned an angry letter, rejecting plans for any form of permanent memorial. 'A small cross or stone to mark each grave', she suggested begrudgingly, 'would be quite a sufficient memorial.'[62]

Despite such objections, a range of memorials sprang up in the cemeteries surrounding many of the British and German internment camps. One of the most striking to appear was erected in 1919 in the Fordington parish churchyard on the southern fringes of Dorchester. With its squat rectangular tower, long nave and village green setting, the church appeared, and in fact still appears, as the epitome of the English rural idyll. It might have seemed rather an incongruous setting for a German war memorial, but this was also the final resting place for forty-five POWs who had died in Dorchester's large First World War internment camp. The memorial was all the more powerful for its location, particularly as it jarred ever so slightly with the lichen-covered Victorian headstones that otherwise filled the cemetery. Designed by one of the camp's more artistically inclined prisoners, the memorial made no attempt to hide its Germanness. The large stone structure depicted in sharp relief the figure of a kneeling German soldier (see image 12). The soldier's standard issue steel helmet, as well as the German language inscription at the base of the relief, made clear that this was a site of German remembrance, even though it was situated in the heart of an English parish churchyard.

The British authorities consented to POW memorials being built, albeit sometimes reluctantly, but the driving force behind them was always the prisoners themselves. After all, it was their friends and comrades who had died in captivity; consequently, it made sense that they would also be the ones pushing to mark their losses. In Germany, the process was very similar to Britain, although with a wider range of nationalities interned, the resulting memorials tended to have a more international flavour. Funding generally came from subscriptions that all POWs paid into. Everyone, therefore, wanted to see a reward for their spending, which is presumably why many memorials were inscribed in multiple languages.[63] One of the few memorials erected solely for the British dead stood in the large Parchim camp. The

12. Shortly before returning to Germany in 1919, some of the POWs held in Dorchester erected their own stone memorial. It stands over the graves of the forty-five Germans who remained behind in Dorset.

British contingent erected their own memorial plaque 'in loving memory of' their twenty-seven dead. Their marble slab, 'Laid by Comrades in Captivity', sat on a plinth in front of the camp's main memorial, dedicated to all POWs who had died in Parchim.[64]

During the Second World War, the enemy again died at home, graves once more needed to be dug and headstones erected, but these practices were always far more muted than had been the case in the earlier conflict. The POWs, in particular, seemed far less inclined to replicate the large war memorials of their predecessors. They were not alone in this; there was a more general aversion to the grandiose remembrance practices so beloved of the Great War generation, which, after all, had only led to further conflict.[65] One notable exception to this rule occurred in Sagan, a small town hidden away in a rural part of Lower Silesia, but better known as the home of Stalag Luft III, site of the 1944

'Great Escape'. Of the seventy-three POWs to break out, only three reached safety. The Nazis recaptured the remainder, executing fifty of them in a brutal act of revenge. The first that the POWs back in Stalag Luft III knew of their escaped comrades' fate was when 'little bronze caskets' filled with ashes arrived in Sagan. Cremation, as the prisoners knew, was 'ominous', as reducing the corpses to ashes clearly helped the Nazis to hide the evidence of their crimes. Nevertheless, the POWs remained determined to mark their losses. The German guards, somewhat chastened by events, gave permission for the construction of a memorial vault listing the names of the dead, to be located just outside the camp boundary.[66]

The surviving POWs who had been closest to the fifty killed carried out the work of designing the vault, clearing the site, which was in itself 'quite a big job', and building the memorial structure. In this way, the physical act of construction became a vehicle for their individual grief. However, this was never the only draw. Whenever POWs managed to bury their dead, mark the grave or even construct a memorial, as was the case in Sagan, they were also ensuring a presence in the wider landscape. Cemeteries that had once been the domain of local communities now gained structures for the enemy war dead, physical reminders that the enemy had also died in conflict. The little parish churchyard of Kirk St Patrick on the Isle of Man witnessed one of the greatest wartime transformations. Situated at the bottom of the long path leading up to the huge Knockaloe internment camp, the churchyard gradually filled with enemy headstones during the Great War. By the time of the camp's closure in 1919, row after row of 'inscriptions in German, Turkish, and Hebrew' stood alongside the older 'pious memorials [. . .] sculptured in English and Manx'. These observations from a Manxman passing through St Patrick were not made in malice, but were rather a comment on the silent legacies of war.[67]

The Isle of Man may have been at the 'centre of the whole [British internment] system' in both world wars, but small signs of the enemy war dead also appeared in hundreds of small communities across Britain and Germany.[68] A stone headstone for a member of the West Yorkshire Regiment in Mensfelden in the west of Germany, or a single wooden cross over a German grave in Bramley, Hampshire, marked individual deaths, while newly built POW memorials in Dorchester and Sagan bespoke larger losses. Local communities had certainly not always been that pleased to inherit enemy bodies and graves, but they had little choice in the matter. The priority during the war years was simply to dispose of the remains; with the fighting ongoing, there was little time to worry about local sensibilities.

Despite occasional complaints, a sign of wartime animosities, for the most part, local communities generally accepted the new graves. In Quedlinburg and Stendal, sites of two First World War POW camps, local dignitaries even turned out for the dedication of the prisoners' own war memorials.[69] Not all of the dead enjoyed such attention of course; many enemy bodies slipped quietly into the ground with little ceremony and nothing to mark the grave either. Irrespective of the initial response, if indeed there was one, once the enemy dead had gained a place in local communities, these mortuary interlopers proved very hard to ignore.

4

TENDING

After sometimes years of captivity in British and German camps, most POWs were desperate to be free. Unfortunately for them, they often had a long wait. In November 1918, the armistice came and went, but little changed for most POWs. The British in Germany spent a few weeks 'just lulling about', as one POW put it, until they could get home, while the Germans had to wait even longer, often not being repatriated until late 1919.[1] However, long before the big day, preparations for departure were generally in full swing. In Scotland's Stobs camp, the prisoners were busy discarding 'superfluous wooden shoes, boots, shirts, coats [. . .] and trousers', while the library had already 'dispose[d] of damaged and unusable books'.[2] The story was similar further south, where German officers in the Skipton camp made 'trunks and packing cases' as they readied themselves to leave, what was for many, their 'hated exile'.[3] The POWs may have been able to clear the camps and to neatly pack their belongings, but one area over which they had no control were the graves and memorials of their long-departed countrymen. These were destined to remain. Often the prisoners paid one final visit to the cemeteries to lay wreaths and 'to say goodbye', before they finally left for their homeland.[4]

There must have been some concern as to what would happen to the graves, as sometimes the departing POWs insisted on leaving money with local communities to help with the upkeep of the burial grounds.[5] On the Isle of Man, civilian internees from the huge Knockaloe internment camp diverted some of the profits from their canteen into a hefty maintenance fund. This was to pay for the upkeep of the graves of their fellow captives who had not survived but lay buried in the churchyard of Patrick parish church, over the road from the camp. The vicar and churchwardens must have seen this as a fair exchange. They might have inherited over 200 graves, but they received the princely sum of £500 in return to pay for their continuing upkeep. In Aachen, meanwhile, a group of Canadian POWs had similar concerns to the Germans across the Channel. Before leaving on the long trek home, they were determined to erect their own headstone over any unmarked graves in the Carolingian city. They never achieved their aim while stranded in Germany, so they later sent on the design and 40 Florins to pay for the work.[6]

The departure of POWs, whether from Britain or from Germany, caused a massive shift in the care of the enemy dead. After all, it had largely been the POWs themselves who had tended the graves, built the memorials and sometimes even returned for remembrance services. Once the original custodians had left, responsibility for the thousands of graves that remained ended up being transferred to the British and German populations living near the cemeteries. This was always going to be a difficult transition, for the people living near the cemeteries lacked the same deep emotional bond to the enemy bodies that lay in their midst. However, it was not just the dead that local communities found themselves dealing with, it was also the living. In the wake of war, the bereaved gradually started to discover their loved ones' graves for themselves. Places that had for so long been out of reach for relatives, started to open up. Small cemeteries and burial grounds scattered across the two countries, therefore, started to play a new role in post-conflict reconciliation, becoming a place for the British and Germans to meet.

Searching for the Dead

Once hostilities had come to an end in 1918 and 1945 respectively, the majority of the two countries' military personnel could easily be located. Some were still in uniform or in the process of being demobilised; others were languishing in POW camps or lying deep underground, dead. What complicated these neat categories somewhat was the large group of the missing, soldiers who had seemingly vanished without trace in the mêlée of war. These numbers were certainly at their highest in East Central Europe after the Second World War, where over 3 million members of the Wehrmacht had ended up in Soviet captivity, but beyond the brutality of the Eastern Front there were also plenty of absences; wherever the wars had been fought, people had disappeared. The task in the immediate post-war years, therefore, was to try to hunt for the missing, to provide some certainty as to whether individuals were 'alive, or long since dead'.[7]

With Britain and Germany no longer at war, the two home fronts suddenly appeared more accessible to families desperate for news about their missing loved ones. The authorities, though, saw the situation differently and were fairly insistent that they would be the ones to lead these searches, and not the relatives. There was a certain logic to their stance. After all, representatives of the state not only had the contacts and resources, they also had a collective responsibility for everyone that was missing. In the German case, the embassy in London acted as a conduit for multiple queries about individuals who had disappeared in wartime captivity. The parents of one soldier had lost contact with him towards the end of the First World War and wanted news, while the family of a submariner continued to hold out hope that he was still alive somewhere. After conducting its own enquiries, the embassy determined that the naval man was definitely deceased; any question mark over his fate was due to the lack of a body and not because there was any chance that he might have survived.[8]

The British faced an even greater task in the two post-war Germanys. This was partly a question of numbers, with far more Allied POWs held in Germany than the other way around, but it also reflected the Germans' rather haphazard record keeping in both conflicts too. During, and immediately after the First World War, members of Britain's Directorate of Graves Registration and Enquiries spent considerable time registering details of the missing and the graves of the dead.[9] Adelaide Livingstone, an American married to a British officer, became one of the directorate's leading lights. Highly educated, and clearly extremely determined, Livingstone found her calling during the war itself, when she worked both to protect the interests of 'enemy aliens' at home and British POWs overseas. With such a depth of experience on her side, the War Office recruited her in 1919 for a 'special mission to the Continent' to 'trace the missing'. It did not take long before Livingstone popped up in Berlin, requesting access to military records and the former POW camps.[10]

Livingstone was still going strong in the 1940s, but by then her attention had turned from missing soldiers to leading international efforts for peace. New agencies emerged to fill the void she left behind, with the RAF's Missing Research and Enquiry Service (MRES) being the most significant. The RAF had been busy throughout the war trying to keep track of bomber crews that never returned home or airmen who had vanished somewhere on operations. The scale of the task was enormous, with somewhere in the region of 40,000 airmen missing in Europe, the Middle East and the Far East, plus thousands more graves that needed to be formally identified. In an attempt to bring order to this chaos, the RAF established the MRES in summer 1945 with a clear remit of identifying and locating its dead. Staffed by RAF officers, many of whom were veterans of the recent conflict, the MRES started to scour Germany soon after the fighting had stopped.[11]

The personnel may have been slightly different, but the general procedure remained the same. After both wars, the starting point for the search teams was the written record. The laborious task of thumbing through captured German documents shed some light on the fate of the missing, but this work could never provide all the answers. Investigators, therefore, had to use other techniques, visiting German hospitals, so-called lunatic asylums and finally traipsing in person from one mayor's office to the next in the hunt for information.[12] Even then, not all of the missing could be found. Private Matthew Adam of the Royal Scots Fusiliers, for example, had been captured in 1918 and possibly taken to Germany. All of Livingstone's enquiries drew a blank. 'I regret the enquiry must therefore be considered closed, untraced,' she concluded regretfully.[13]

For the British–German relationship, it was not the outcome of such investigations that was important, but rather the process itself. In trying to locate the missing and the dead, officials from one side had to make direct contact with their recent enemy. The experience rarely proved positive, with the populations of both countries appearing to resent any intrusion. The German embassy complained that its enquiries to local parishes often went unanswered or met with resistance, while the MRES teams working in occupied Germany in the late 1940s were rarely greeted with open arms when they turned up in towns and villages with a page of awkward questions for local residents. 'Having had a few thousand tons [of bombs] rained down' on them, joked one MRES officer, 'it was hardly like that one would be welcomed with open arms!'[14]

For the families desperate for news, the whole process of hunting for the missing was too slow and too painful. The frustrations of one Cheshire family awaiting any news of their RAF son who had vanished over Germany reflected the thoughts of many. 'The majority of us <u>know</u> that the "missing" will not return now, but this is not sufficient,' they complained. 'We want to know what was their [actual] fate.'[15] Fed up with being stuck in emotional limbo, some families decided to take matters into their own hands. Bypassing the official channels, they started to approach the former enemy themselves. These unofficial, uncoordinated and largely unsuccessful interventions did at least force the British and Germans into direct contact.

Often families had very little to go on; they knew their loved one was missing and had possibly been taken prisoner, but that was about it. In these circumstances, the foreign press seemed to be the best chance of making progress. The parents of a British army officer captured in 1918 were sure that he was still in Germany somewhere. Out of desperation, and with few options available to them, they arranged for advertisements to be placed in German newspapers asking for news.[16] Erna Pancke, a mother of two from Hanover, found herself in a similar situation some thirty years later. Her son, Karl-Heinz had apparently been captured in 1944 and taken to a POW camp somewhere in Britain. The British and German authorities believed that Pancke was probably long dead, but they failed to convince his mother, who was sure that he was still alive, living dazed and confused far from home. She put notices in British newspapers and travelled the length of the country looking for clues. 'I beg you, please, help me,' she continued to plead, long after the war had ended.[17]

Pancke never did find Karl-Heinz, but the search itself did at least seem to provide her with a focus for her grief. Crucially, her efforts also garnered considerable sympathy from the local people she met who could relate to this human side of wartime loss – far more than was the case when uniformed state officials turned up and asked the questions. On one occasion, she sat down with a family living on the Welsh Marches who heard her tale of heartbreak and invited her in to 'enjoy a cup of English hospitality'; on another visit, a 'housewife' from Newcastle was so taken by Pancke's quest that she dedicated two years of her own time searching for Karl-Heinz.[18]

Surely the most emotionally draining journey, although one that also resulted in tentative discussions between the British and Germans, was taken by Ernest Barr, a pharmacist from Northern Ireland. Unlike Pancke, when Barr set out on his own 'little mission', he was already fairly certain that his son, Mackenzie, was dead. In January 1945, Mackenzie had been serving as an air gunner on a Halifax bomber on a mission over Hanau in the west of Germany, but the aircraft had failed to return. As the squadron commander reported at the time, since the raid 'nothing has been heard'. By the year's end, some news did start to filter back to the families. The bomber had apparently exploded in mid-air, killing six of the crew outright. However, there was still no sign of Mackenzie Barr. The wife of the flight engineer tried to keep the older Barr going. 'Please don't give up hope yet,' she urged, '[at least] until you get definite information.'[19]

Ernest Barr, himself a veteran of the Great War, was not the type of person to sit at home quietly waiting for snippets of news to reach him. Instead, he decided that he was going to search for his son himself, which was no easy task as travel to occupied Germany was severely restricted. By speaking to old contacts and calling in a lot of favours, Barr eventually got as far as Paris, where American officials granted him permission to travel on a secure train into Germany. This was not only a physically difficult and tiring journey through the ruins of bombed-out cities, but also an extremely lonely one. Barr had no company, and only some crude German translations scrawled on a piece of paper as his guide. Nonetheless, 'Wo ist die Bürgermeisterei?' and other essential phrases must have had some effect, as he eventually found his way to

Großauheim, a sleepy suburb of Hanau, largely untouched by the air war. There a local woman recalled an aircraft crashing the previous year, and the bodies of the crew being buried in the town's cemetery. The authorities allowed one of the recent, unmarked graves to be exhumed, which is where Barr found Mackenzie, 'identifying him by his hair, his teeth, and the shape of his head'.[20]

At the end of his mission, Barr was finally able to stand over the grave of his son in Großauheim. A tall, gleaming white crucifix loomed over the figure of the elderly war veteran, as he stared down at the ground below that held his son's remains (see image 13). For Barr, this long and arduous journey had never been about reconciliation; it was purely about finding out what had happened to Mackenzie. Yet, his travels had forced him to engage with the German people he met en route; he needed their help as he hunted for any clues that might shed

13. This is the extremely sad image of Ernest Barr standing over the grave of his son, Mackenzie, who had been killed in a bombing raid over Germany in January 1945. Immediately after the conflict ended, Barr senior travelled to Germany to look for his son's grave, eventually finding it in Großauheim, Hanau.

light on what had happened to the doomed bomber. For several years after the visit, he exchanged letters with residents of Großauheim, sharing photographs and discussing the care of the Allied graves in the town. In the most emotionally draining of circumstances, the presence of the enemy dead had started to draw the living together.

Securing the Grave

Ernest Barr was able to return to his home in Northern Ireland not only with definite news about his son's fate, but also safe in the knowledge that the grave was secure. His arduous journey had allowed him to see and touch the soil in which his son rested, while the photograph of the burial site ensured the memories of this moment would remain alive. After the world wars, thousands of people were also desperate for similar reassurance, simply to know that their loved one's grave was safe. However, very few people had the luxury of being able to travel in person to either Britain or Germany. In these circumstances, the only option that seemed open was to reach out directly to their former enemy and to make contact with the local communities holding the grave. Recent conflict, therefore, did not always lead to a brutalisation of international relations and local politics, as has often been claimed; it could also bring strangers together.[21]

George Dutton, a chief clerk to a London-based leather goods manufacturer, was one of many people to develop new relations through personal grief. In the wake of the First World War, Dutton sent out a very tentative letter to one of his firm's old contacts in Worms, Leo Grünfeld. He explained that his 'poor boy', Frederick, had died as a POW in the ancient Rhineland city. Making contact with the recently vanquished enemy in this way cannot have been easy for Dutton, but he was anxious for news. What he really wanted to know was whether 'his [son's] grave is marked and can be identified'. He hoped one day to be able to come over to Worms with his wife, but worried dearly that they would turn up to discover nothing but a void. 'It would break her heart to travel all those miles and then not be able to find his grave,' Dutton explained.[22]

Grünfeld, who was Dutton's only link to Worms, immediately stepped into action. He visited the cemetery in the north of the city, looked through the burial registers, checked the grave and reported back on its condition. He then promised to return at midday the following Sunday to lay a wreath on Frederick's grave. At this moment, he suggested, 'you may think of your son and this will perhaps be a holiday [comfort] for [you] both.' What seemed to provide the Duttons with the greatest solace, however, was the fact that Grünfeld also provided them with a photograph of the cemetery. 'I want to give you an idea of where your poor son is buried,' he added. As they were unable to get to Worms themselves, to be able to visualise the gravesite was incredibly important for the family.

These exchanges revealed both an emotional connection and a shared understanding of the depths of individual loss. Grünfeld recognised the importance of helping the Duttons to master their grief, seeing it as a 'duty of humanity to help one another'.[23] In Shropshire, some thirty years later, another family – the Steffens from Koblenz – also reached across the wartime divide. Their son, Hans, had died as a POW in 1945 and had been buried in Oswestry. With Hans's mother gravely ill and almost housebound, the family were desperate to learn anything they could of the grave. 'Is [it] still there; is it being taken care of; [. . .] and how long [will] the grave remain there?' they asked in desperation. Again, local people stepped in to fill in the gaps and to provide the bereaved with some emotional relief. A town councillor personally visited the grave and found it 'well kept'. He too promised to return at a later date to take a photograph for the family. In slightly broken English, the Steffens responded with 'heartiest thanks' and considerable gratitude for the 'kind efforts'.[24]

In some respects, the Duttons and Steffens were in a privileged position. From their conversations with the local custodians, they knew that the graves were safe, secure and cared for. Photographs of their sons' final resting places then provided visual reassurance, allowing the families to at least get close to the grave from afar. Other families were not quite so fortunate. In the 1940s, for example, the Prisoners of War Information Bureau in London received a string of requests for photographs of the German graves. Working with the Red Cross, they managed to send hundreds of images out, but not every application could be immediately realised. In Clacton, the graves were marked 'unknown' even though the names were available, while in Harlow the German spellings were completely wrong. Worse occurred in Thetford; a photographer turned up in the cemetery only to discover there was 'nothing to indicate the grave', which was certainly not going to provide the family with the solace they so craved.[25]

Understandably, relatives who discovered that a grave marker was lost, damaged or missing wanted the issue quickly rectified. Even when the grave had a marker in place, perhaps a temporary wooden stake or rudimentary cross, many families also wanted to secure a permanent headstone, something more fitting for their loved one. This reflected everyday cultural practices from civilian life. When people passed away in more gentle surroundings, the bereaved generally chose some form of headstone to mark their loved one's final resting place, thereby creating a new relationship with the recently deceased. The circumstances may have been very different, but the same also applied in the case of the war dead buried far from home.[26]

The family of Aubrey Fraser wasted no time in tidying up their son's grave in Cologne. Fraser had been just 18 years old when he was captured by the Germans in France and transported to a hospital in Cologne. His stay in the Rhineland was very brief, as he quickly succumbed to his wounds, dying on a mid-summer's day in July 1916. When it came to erecting a memorial over the grave, Aubrey's parents, Israel and Fanny, had the advantage that they had already had some contact from Cologne at the time of their son's death. Ludwig Rosenthal, a rabbi in the city, had written to them during the war to offer his condolences and to reassure them that Aubrey had been buried with 'military honours' in Cologne's oldest Jewish cemetery in Deutz.[27] These earlier contacts no doubt helped the parents to arrange for their own headstone – a tall urn-shaped slab with intricate detailing – to be placed above the grave, inscribed 'in ever devoted memory' of their 'second son'.[28] With a permanent headstone in place and Cologne's Jewish community on hand to care for the grave, the Frasers could be content that they had done everything possible for him.

Other families enjoyed their own successes and also managed to erect permanent headstones over their relatives' graves. In 1921, the Stephens family from Essex commissioned a 1-metre-high granite memorial to mark the grave of their son, Donald, who was lying in a cemetery in southern Bavaria. Donald had died three years earlier in a POW camp in Landshut, also aged just 18.[29] After the Second World War, the mother of George Warren, an RAF navigator killed on a bombing raid in March 1945, achieved something similar for her son. Warren's mother was desperate to see her son's grave in the Franconian village of Burgoberbach, properly marked. She was helped in this endeavour by one of her son's university friends who at the time was working as a translator for the Nuremberg War Crimes Trials, just down the road from the village. During a break in proceedings, she managed to speak directly with the parish priest, who promised to arrange for a permanent headstone. The priest kept his word, and by the time of her next visit, a glistening white headstone topped with a crucifix marked the grave.[30]

The flurry of private headstones that appeared in cemeteries from rural Franconia through to the Somerset Levels clearly provided the bereaved with considerable solace. Beyond the personal, though, there were also two significant consequences for the nascent British–German relationship. First, the use of foreign words, phrases and idioms on the headstones helped to sew the enemy dead to existing Christian cultures. George Warren's headstone, for example, marked the final resting place of an RAF 'Flying Officer' born in 'Birmingham, England', while the gravestone that Stephens' parents erected in Landshut was 'In Loving Memory' of their son. In Britain, visitors to local cemeteries would have been confronted with a similar sight, only in German. The gravestone of the Great War POW, Franz Zielinski, in King's Lynn contained the German words, 'Ruhe sanft im fremder Erde' ('Sleep Gently in Foreign Soil'). Further south in the Somerset town of Bridgwater, the joint grave of Fritz Klemm and Heinz Schier, both killed in 1941, had its own private headstone. Erected by Schier's mother and brother, the inscription read simply: 'Hier ruhen in Gott' ('Here Lie with God').[31]

A second consequence of the mini-boom in private headstones was that it threw the former foes into conversation. Nobody could erect a grave marker or alter a burial plot without acquiring the requisite permissions and the services of a stonemason. Every contact, every conversation between the British and Germans, even when it was in such painful circumstances, helped to chip away at the barriers separating the two sides. Once a contact between the families and local communities had been established, relations tended to strengthen rather than to fade anew. This was certainly the case in Burgoberbach. The priest who had helped to make arrangements for George Warren's headstone kept his mother updated on the grave, even inviting her to visit the village in the 1950s.[32] The emotions were still too raw to label this a reconciliation, but the increasing permanence of the enemy dead certainly provided a platform for further discussions, and a potential path towards some form of future relationship.

Diplomacy and the War Graves

The difficulty after the two world wars was that not everyone could follow in the footsteps of the Frasers in Cologne, the Warrens in Burgoberbach or the Schiers in Bridgwater. Erecting a private headstone over the grave required time, money and also the emotional resilience to build relations with those on the other side. If the bereaved were unable, sometimes even unwilling, to care for the dead, then the question that kept arising was who exactly was going to maintain the thousands of enemy graves scattered across Britain and Germany. A solution to this problem emerged not on the ground in the cemeteries themselves, but rather in the more serene surroundings of the Palace of Versailles outside Paris. Louis XIV's grand residence was of course the setting for the peace negotiations that followed the end of the First World War. Politicians, diplomats and leaders from around the world may have gathered in France to debate the future shape of Europe, but creeping into their discussions was also the thorny issue of the war dead. As there were somewhere in the region of 9 million to 10 million military deaths, this was a topic that undoubtedly concerned all the belligerent powers.[33]

When the final text of the peace treaty surfaced after months of often heated discussion, however, nobody was really jumping for joy. Crowds of Germans gathered in front of the Reichstag in Berlin to express their disgust. Even sections of the British public were dismayed at the terms, seeing the final treaty as either too harsh or too lenient, depending on their own political beliefs.[34] Two short articles dealing with the war graves also failed to muster much in the way of enthusiasm. It was hard to disagree with the sentiment of Article 226, which stated that the graves of POWs and civilian internees who had 'died in captivity shall be properly maintained'.

Article 225, however, proved a little more controversial. It stipulated that each signatory would maintain the graves, whether friend or enemy, 'in their respective territories'. With one stroke of the pen, the Germans lost control of their war dead overseas, while suddenly the Allies inherited the additional financial burden of maintaining thousands more graves. The outcome pleased no one. Looking on from just across the border, one Austrian journalist viewed the Allies' attempts to protect the war graves as nothing more than 'loathsome cynicism'.[35] There was talk of an international body to care for the graves, which many Germans favoured, but these ideas never got off the ground.[36] For want of a better solution, the same principle of territorial responsibility not only stayed in place through the interwar years, but was also loosely followed after the Second World War.[37]

Discussions in Paris had an immediate effect on British–German relations. Under the terms of the treaty, if the Germans wanted their graves in Edinburgh or Exeter to be made good, then this was not their responsibility, but rather that of the British authorities. The same, of course, applied to the graves of those men killed from Britain and its then empire, whose care now came under the jurisdiction of the newly formed democratic Weimar Republic. Just in case anyone thought differently, the British warned people against stepping in and doing any maintenance of the graves themselves. 'That would probably result in the Germans at once washing their hands of all responsibility for our graves,' the official remarked with some scepticism.[38] The two sides, therefore, found themselves locked together, needing to act at home to ensure that their own war dead were going to be looked after abroad.

This sense of reciprocity provoked a wave of activity in the post-war cemeteries. The new Weimar government, keen to make a good impression on the Allies and to re-establish itself on the world stage, pushed the German regional authorities to finish tidying their local POW graves. This work 'is of the utmost importance', it insisted, 'for the care of the German graves abroad'.[39] The government's talk of reciprocity seemed to have the desired effect. Any British graves still languishing away unkempt in cemeteries were gradually put in order, with new wooden crosses erected and much-needed maintenance completed.[40] After the Second World War, the picture was strikingly similar. In the Rhineland city of Wiesbaden, most famous for its thermal baths, the cemetery authorities were quick to place new white wooden crosses over the graves of nineteen British and seven Canadian airmen during the first post-war winter. As impressive as these efforts were, their alacrity had more to do with a surprise visit by a British officer who gave the Germans three weeks 'to bring the gravesites up to scratch' than any particular desire to prioritise the Allied war dead.[41]

In Britain, there was initially some confusion as to how to proceed. With so many of its own graves to make good, the German dead were something of an additional burden. Understandably, some officials clung to the idea that the Germans might deal with their own dead themselves regardless of what had been agreed in the peace treaties. Such faint hopes, though, were quickly quashed, when the legal advice came in. It is '[our] opinion that the British Government is responsible for the maintenance' was the final judgment on the matter.[42] Once the reality of the situation had dawned on them, the British, to their credit, did start to set out systematic plans for the German war graves. The Office of Works, an ancient government department responsible for the built environment, set the ball in motion. It started to draw up maintenance agreements with hundreds of local cemetery authorities across the country, promising a small annual payment in exchange for the upkeep of any German graves on their land. In Fovant in Wiltshire, for example, the local vicar was offered 2/6 to care for one First World War POW grave, while in Dorchester a much heftier fee of 5/- per grave was offered.[43]

Even though they had managed to negotiate a considerably better deal for themselves than the unfortunate vicar of Fovant, the burial committee in Dorchester was never wholly satisfied with the arrangement. The main sticking point, which admittedly was hard to avoid, stemmed from the fact that they had to maintain enemy graves. The burial committee in Dorchester sought reassurance that the German government is giving 'similar concessions' for the British graves in

Germany, as its members 'have no desire to favour the German Government'. The Office of Works explained patiently that the Treaty of Versailles included reciprocal clauses giving each country a 'solemn obligation' to maintain each other's war graves. To press home the point, it added that the Germans were undertaking their work 'with great thoroughness'.[44] Whether or not this was always the case was not the main issue, such comments were designed to quell any criticism at home by reassuring the public that the British graves were safe in German hands.

Similarly warm words were uttered after the Second World War. Again the line was that the British war dead had 'received much care and attention' from the German people who, according to a letter in the *Daily Telegraph*, were ensuring a 'common form of bereavement'. The comments in the *Telegraph* were based on a British army officer's visit to a host of small communities – 'Brunen [sic], Borken, Heiden, Gr. Reken, Gemen and Marl' – in the west of occupied Germany. Suddenly, these small towns and villages, which would have meant little to most British readers, were being discussed in the national press simply because they contained some of the British war dead.[45] Consequently, the drive to tidy up the enemy graves had the effect of internationalising the local.

The same was true of Britain. Not many people outside Norfolk, and surely even fewer from Germany, had probably ever given much thought to Kenninghall. The tiny village of less than a thousand inhabitants had last played a role on the world stage in 1066 when William the Conqueror gave the Kenninghall estate to the Chief Butler of England. However, the deaths of two German POWs, Otto Kohnert and Ludwig Wingert, in 1918, put the village back on the map. With both soldiers buried in the parish churchyard, the families of Kohnert and Wingert had little choice but to discover the name of Kenninghall for themselves. And when a 'commission from Germany' visited the graves as part of a nationwide tour in the early 1920s, the village seemed to have found its way into the centre of international affairs.[46]

Building on the Foundations

The earliest encounters with the enemy war dead had all occurred amidst the economic, political and social upheaval of the immediate post-war years. Germans had to deal with revolution as well as soaring inflation after 1918, then, following the total defeat of the Nazi regime, division and occupation as the victorious allies – Britain, France, the United States and the Soviet Union – each administered their own zone of the country. In comparison, the British, slightly cushioned by a 'culture of victory', had it much easier, but even then, they still faced strikes and rioting in 1919 and resentments over housing and the pace of demobilisation after 1945.[47] With so many domestic issues occupying their time, the initial interventions from the bereaved and state agencies had really just been about identifying and securing the graves. However, as the immediacy of conflict passed, the presence of the enemy dead started to play an even greater role in reinvigorating the shattered British–German relationship.

The process of local rapprochement, however, was never entirely straightforward. One notable row broke out in the well-heeled Hampshire village of King's Somborne. Local people, it seemed, had very little wish to be reminded of the crash of a German bomber in 1940, particularly as the bodies of the four crewmen had, rather strangely, never been seen again.[48] When one local resident, Charles Bowyer, himself a veteran of the Great War, proposed erecting a new memorial to the German dead, there was considerable anger. 'These Germans had best be forgotten,' argued one villager, while another resident made the point that a German memorial would be 'an insult' to the British dead. 'I hate the Germans,' she added for good measure.[49] Bowyer's plan never saw the light of day, although some years later a small, unobtrusive memorial stone, was placed down a quiet country lane, hidden away, out of sight and out of mind. It was the fact that the King's Somborne memorial was to be a new structure that provoked much of the controversy.[50] The message was clear: it was one thing to inherit enemy graves, headstones and memorials; it was quite another to put up new monuments in their memory.

The original wartime gravesites, by contrast, appeared to pose much less of a threat. This was partly a question of time. The changing of the seasons helped to soften the raw edges of grave markers, leaving the graves to sink slowly into their surroundings. But the bereaved also played a role in this process of familiarisation. The greater the contact between the British and the Germans, the more accepting people came to be of the enemy dead in their midst. These exchanges could take many forms. Sometimes local people initiated relations, writing to the bereaved with regular updates on their relative's grave. This was the case in the rural of community of Rüthen, east of Dortmund. One local farmer promised to keep in touch with the parents of William Read, who had died on his farm during the 1918 influenza pandemic, adding that he would also keep the grave 'in proper condition'.[51]

Across in Staffordshire, the Reverend R.A. Jones performed a very similar role only on a much larger scale, as he kept an eye on not one, but 222 German graves in his parish. Like Read, the majority of those buried locally had died from influenza in the final stages of the Great War, while being held in the large Brocton POW camp. Since the war's end, Jones had been a regular visitor to the graves, 'placing wreaths [. . .] taking photos & other mementos' for the relatives. It was a 'way of showing sympathy', as he put it. Jones's involvement must have made things much easier for the bereaved. Rather than having to wade through the administrative bureaucracy of death, they had a personal conduit through which they could direct their questions, queries and concerns.[52]

Such close personal relations, where the survivors and local communities built up a degree of mutual trust, also made it easier for the bereaved to make emotional trips to the graveside. One such visit occurred under the Reverend R.A Jones's watch in Staffordshire. On a 'sunny day' in early spring, a chauffeur-driven car pulled up outside the Great War cemetery on Cannock Chase. A 'thick-set, elderly gentleman' stepped out of the car and slowly walked up to the cemetery gates. He then carefully made his way through the German POW graves, looked at each headstone before suddenly stopping and falling 'down upon his knees'. He eventually got back to his feet, laid a wreath of white lilies and with 'tear-dimmed eyes' turned to exit. As he got back to his car, the old man whispered to no one in particular: 'He was my only son.'[53]

During the interwar years, in particular, Germans started to become something of a familiar sight in British churchyards and cemeteries. Although their visits were only ever for a fleeting moment, their very presence invariably led to new contacts and conversations between people from the two countries. Often it was the bereaved themselves who found their way to small towns and villages to view the graves. One of these pilgrims was Hedwig Sopkowiak whose destination – Ilford on the eastern fringes of London – was rather more of an urban setting. The object of her visit in autumn 1934 was the grave of her brother, Paul, an airman who had died on a mission over the capital in the final year of the Great War. When Sopkowiak found her brother's final resting place for the first time, 'much to [her] joy, a bunch of fresh flowers lay on the grave'. Apparently young women had been coming to lay flowers ever week, but despite asking around, she never managed to find out who exactly was behind the gesture so as to express her deep thanks.[54]

On other occasions, it was the former POWs who made the difficult journey back to their wartime places of internment, hoping not only to reawaken fading memories, but also to pay their respects to the dead. One German war veteran stumbled out of a train that had briefly paused at the Park Hall Halt in 1934. A few 'pairs of puzzled eyes' looked on with bewilderment as he made his way down the isolated platform. The veteran was looking to retrace his brother's wartime experiences of internment in Shropshire and to find the German war cemetery, where over a hundred German POWs lay buried. This was no easy task, as the cemetery was even more hidden than the tiny railway halt. A passing postman guided the German visitor part of the way, before a 'friendly' local pointed him in the right direction, 'through a field, then along a railway embankment' to the burial ground. After hours of walking, he discovered a fairly bleak site, stranded among farmers' fields and seemingly bereft of regular visitors.[55]

The situation was very different elsewhere. When Christel Eulen, a redoubtable figure in the German War Graves Commission, conducted her own tour across Britain in 1956, she frequently came across wreaths or freshly cut flowers on some of the graves. In Sevenoaks, Kent, she reached the grave of seven German airmen, killed between 1940 and 1943, and stood for a while gazing at the floral offering that someone had placed against the grave marker (see image 14). Eulen surmised that the grave 'had been visited by relatives', but in most cases, it was actually not the bereaved, but local people who provided the flowers. Had she travelled a little further south to West Hoathly, she might have seen the regular displays of 'nasturtiums, heather and wild violets' on two German graves; travelling north to Boldon, near Newcastle, Eulen

14. In 1956, Christel Eulen of the VDK undertook a tour of German
war graves in the United Kingdom. In Sevenoaks, she discovered a
plot containing the remains of seven German airmen. Note the wreath
and floral tribute to the left of the grave.

would have seen flowers over a German grave left anonymously by
those living close by.[56]

It is difficult to unpick people's precise motives for laying flowers or
tidying the enemy graves, but a sense of shared humanitarianism seems
to have been a common theme. Muriel Wright, a butcher's assistant in
Bishop's Stortford, and her mother, Ivy Coppen, may not have expressed
their care for fifteen German graves in such terms, but a deep concern
for the bereaved was certainly a key driver. Defying the 'angry glances
and sarcastic comments' from others less sympathetic to the enemy's

presence, the pair regularly laid fresh flowers on the graves, even decorating them with holly wreaths each Christmas. Wright explained that she had first started to take an interest in the German war dead when she was asked to do so by one of the German POWs. He was finally returning to his family and home in 1948 and, before leaving, wanted to ask if she could keep an eye on his friend's grave.[57]

Wright and Coppen ended up doing more than just keeping a close watch over the graves and laying the occasional flowers. As was the case in other local communities, they also reached out to the bereaved back in Germany. The War Office, with clearly few qualms about sharing personal information, provided the two women with the home addresses of the war dead, which allowed them then to write to the families in Germany directly. From this foundation, a voluminous exchange of letters occurred with some of the families, which even led to invitations for the pair to visit their erstwhile enemy in Germany. Coppen explained that her efforts were about trying to repair the deep bonds between the mothers and their children. As such she was the 'appointed representative of the mothers who are mourning their dead from home'.[58] For the younger Wright, caring for the enemy dead in Bishop's Stortford gradually became something of a duty. 'It is my greatest pleasure in life to go and look after the graves,' she explained emphatically.[59]

Elsewhere, it was often war veterans who were the driving force behind such reconciliation efforts. The main focus of an ex-servicemen's group in Lamplugh, a tiny Cumbrian community nestled in the shadow of the grassy Knock Murton Fell, was on the thirty men listed on the village's gleaming white war memorial, where they conducted annual remembrance ceremonies. Yet, the veterans also found time for seven German POWs buried in the churchyard. Each year, the men gently bowed their heads over the enemy graves and remembered their dead enemy too. There was little chance of reconciliation, though, unless the German people also learnt of events in distant Lamplugh. The veterans, therefore, contacted the German consul urging him to publicise their care of the graves and their work for 'eternal peace'. The veterans' plea had some effect, as one German ex-servicemen's newspaper picked up the story, dedicating a full page to events in Lamplugh.[60]

Regardless of what was driving people's interest in the enemy graves, the narrative that came through was one of an ever-deepening British–German relationship, particularly in Britain, where the graves rested in the same spot for much longer. In some towns, relations strengthened to such an extent that they even started to shape wider national and international discussions. This was the case in Birmingham, where, for a brief period in the 1920s, city dignitaries, German diplomats and the international press descended on the Lodge Hill Cemetery and its fourteen enemy graves. What brought Birmingham this renown was the decision of Harry Cohen, Superintendent of the Shenley Fields Children's Homes, to integrate the German dead into the orphanage's annual Armistice Day 'Pilgrimage'. In Cohen's view, after the war, 'death the leveller should soften all animosities' between former foes. The German ambassador in London clearly saw something in Cohen's approach. He ordered a wreath from 'Messrs. Perkins' florists and dispatched the Counsellor of Legation, Otto Meynen, to the Midlands to take part in the ceremony.[61] Meynen, with his head bowed in respect, stood solemnly alongside a war orphan to lay his wreath (see image 15). His efforts clearly had the desired effect. British newspapers filed reports, Pathé news beamed a film of the ceremony to hundreds of cinemas and even the German press ran the story, praising it for 'encouraging understanding between the nations'.[62]

During the Second World War, three more Germans, this time all airmen, were buried in Lodge Hill alongside the POWs from the earlier conflict. After 1945, there was no Harry Cohen on hand to draw the British and German dead together. While that moment may have passed in Birmingham, buried in the urban destruction of the bombing war, offshoots of his efforts flourished elsewhere. In the northern manufacturing town of Widnes, the beating heart of Britain's chemical industry, another community managed to place the enemy war dead on the international stage. On this occasion, a local retiree, James Dolan, proved the driving force. Dolan, who lived close to the site where a German bomber had crashed in 1941, killing two crew members, made a great effort to track down the bereaved back in Germany. His persistence bore fruit, and by the late 1950s, a lively exchange had developed between the towns of Widnes and Datteln in Germany's industrial

England ehrt die gefallenen Deutschen
Auf einem Friedhof der in englischer Kriegsgefangenschaft verstorbenen deutschen Soldaten legte am Waffenstillstandstage ein Waisenkind einen Kranz nieder

15. To mark Armistice Day in 1926, Otto Meynen (left) from the German embassy and Lilly Keylock, herself a war orphan, lay wreaths on both the British and German war graves in Birmingham's Lodge Hill Cemetery.

Ruhr district, and home to one of the killed airmen. School visits, letters and presents flowed across the divide; the mayor of Datteln gifted a plate, which prompted Widnes Borough Council to send a 'magnificent silver inkstand' in return.[63]

Dolan rightly received praise for creating a 'bond of [British–German] friendship between two towns' that had once been divided by conflict.[64] What had made this possible was the fact that enemy dead had remained exactly where they had first been buried. Almost every other trace of the wartime foe had gone. The living had of course long returned home; even the vast infrastructure of the internment camp systems was quickly dismantled. In Dorchester in 1920, for example, people had a chance to buy the 'fixtures, fittings and surplus material' from the closed POW camp, with the opportunity to pick up '30-gallon portable boilers' or 'double-oven ranges' at bargain prices.[65] The war graves, however, could not be sold off quite so easily. And if the dead were to stay, then something had to happen to the bodies, which was a point also recognised in the Treaty of Versailles.

The bereaved themselves clearly had the strongest emotional connection to the dead. Their main concern was to ensure that their loved one's final resting place was properly marked and that someone was caring for the grave. These might have been very practical questions but to achieve them the bereaved needed to open up some form of dialogue with communities located on the other side of the wartime divide. From these often-painful conversations, more encouraging exchanges gradually emerged through shared visits, letters and photographs. The presence of the war dead, therefore, repeatedly worked to shape the lives of the living, helping to stimulate conversations, bring people together and, crucially, rejuvenate an international relationship that had been broken by war, death and destruction.

5

CONTROLLING

It was a warm weekend in early 1921 when a small group of American soldiers arrived in the Rhineland city of Worms. While most Germans were busy navigating their ways through the early days of the new Weimar Republic, the Americans had a far more pressing task. They were on the hunt for the body of Private Axel Larson, a Swedish-American, who had died from dysentery ten days after the signing of the November 1918 armistice. Once the fighting had stopped, the American government had given families a choice. They could either leave their loved ones buried overseas or they could request their repatriation back to the United States. Larson's brother, who like him had emigrated from Sweden to Iowa, opted for the second option. His decision to have the remains returned set a bureaucratic train in motion, which eventually led the American soldiers to Worms ready to reclaim Larson's body.[1]

Getting to Worms was the easy part for the American team, actually finding Larson proved much trickier. The city authorities had already warned them that the body was probably in a mass grave with thirty-two other POWs, which in their view made it impossible to 'find the American soldier with any certainty'. Undeterred, the team opened the large grave and dug throughout the weekend. Marks on the coffins, clothing fragments and distinguishing features on the bodies all helped the Americans to put names to the corpses. Eventually, they managed to identify the bodies of nineteen Russians, seven Italians, five British soldiers and one Frenchman. By the Monday, after three days of digging and sorting, the Americans were confident that they had found their man. They packed Larson's remains into a fresh coffin ready for transportation across the Atlantic and then returned the remaining bodies to the original grave.[2]

Sometime later, a French exhumation team arrived in Worms, reopened the grave and dug out the remains of 35-year-old Armand Lelievre, who was also returned home.[3] This then left the bodies of the British, Italians and Russians in Worms. Given that the remains of the five British servicemen had been disturbed on several occasions, it might have seemed the ideal moment to repatriate them to their families too. However, this never happened. The British authorities, directed by the newly formed IWGC, decided that the future of their war dead was to be in Germany and not back home in Britain or elsewhere in the then empire for that matter. This decision made it clear that it was no longer the bereaved, nor local custodians who controlled the war dead; it was the IWGC.

As the vanquished power in the two world wars, the Germans found it much harder to seize control of their war dead in the same way. But gradually, the state authorities, and increasingly the German War Graves Commission (VDK), managed to gain a similar hold over the German bodies lying on British soil. Following in the footsteps of their former foe, the VDK and the German state, whether this was the Weimar Republic, Nazi Germany or one of the two post-war Germanys, also did their best to ensure their war dead remained overseas, rather than being returned home to the families. As the remit of the two war graves commissions grew, so the influence of local communities and the bereaved over the dead declined, and tentative British–German relations started to fade before they had even had a chance fully to bloom.

Bring Them Home

Any families harbouring a deep wish to repatriate their loved one's remains would have found much succour in the terms of the Treaty of Versailles. Besides requiring the Allies and Germans to maintain war graves on their territory, Article 225 also instructed the signatories to allow 'requests that the bodies of their soldiers and sailors may be transferred to their own country'. The German population might generally have found little to rejoice over in the treaty, but the possibility of recovering their dead from Britain and elsewhere was surely one small positive. Even the German delegation in Paris found little reason to object when this line appeared in the draft text.[4] For British families, the peace seemed to open new opportunities too. In earlier conflicts, the dead had been lucky just to have a grave; now relatives wanted to go several stages further and have the bodies repatriated.[5] Several weeks after the signing of the treaty, Winston Churchill, then Secretary of State for War, appeared to confirm this option. Asked directly in the House of Commons whether the war dead in Germany 'may be brought home at the wish of the relatives', Churchill replied that 'every reasonable facility shall be provided for the removal of the bodies'.[6]

The general tenor of Versailles provided a much-needed fillip for the bereaved, whether in Britain or Germany, who had often been longing for the day when they could finally bring their loved ones home. None were keener, perhaps, than the parents of Otto Günther, who had already started to make their own arrangements before the First World War had ended. Their 21-year-old-son had died from typhoid fever in the Leigh POW camp, west of Manchester, in October 1916. Soon after his death, Günther's parents managed to get a message to the British Foreign Office through an American intermediary, requesting that his corpse be placed in a zinc-lined coffin 'to make it easier to repatriate the body after the war'. Somewhat remarkably, given the military circumstances, the British responded with words of reassurance, confirming that Günther's body had been placed in a 'polished oak coffin bearing an inscription plate' and that any request for repatriation after the war would be 'favourably considered'.[7]

As soon as the war had ended and talk had turned to the possibility of repatriating the dead, Günther's parents put in a formal request to bring him home from Leigh. There was good reason for their haste. Troubled by the thought that they could receive the wrong body by mistake, they asked that two of Günther's fellow POWs, both still interned in Leigh, be present at the exhumation to identify the body. Whether the pair had volunteered for this grisly task is unclear, but the parents seemed desperate for any reassurance they could get.[8] Elsewhere, other German families started to issue their own repatriation requests in the hope of bringing loved ones back home. This raised the possibility of a vast criss-crossing of bodies, from Powick to Breslau, Frinsted to Frankfurt or even Greenwich to Hamburg.[9]

There was perhaps even greater demand in the other direction, from defeated Germany to Britain. No doubt encouraged by Churchill's statement in the House of Commons, more than 150 requests rolled in from families wanting to bring bodies from Germany back home.[10] One of these came from the parents and sister of London-born Alexander Smith. His death had occurred not in the Great War itself, but in March 1919, when he was serving as part of the British occupation forces around Cologne, which is also where he had been buried. In their quest to have the body returned, the family exchanged a series of letters with the War Office in Whitehall and with leading politicians. Although none of this correspondence had an immediate effect, it did provide them with some reassurance that Smith's remains would soon be returned. The Foreign Secretary himself urged them not to 'be too impatient', as 'we have had a definite undertaking from the War Office that he will be brought home'.[11] With support at the very highest level, the family must have believed it was only a matter of time before the body was repatriated.

The main driver behind the Smiths' request and those of other families was one of emotional need. With the body and grave overseas, people often felt disconnected from their loved ones, which even a post-war obsession with spiritualism was never going to resolve. Families were unable to visit the grave, lay flowers or simply touch the headstone, all common elements of the grieving process. The only solution was to bring the body home. A Frau Stein, from Breslau, expressed this view most succinctly when she fought to return the body of her 27-year-old son, Kurt. The younger Stein had died during the 1918 influenza pandemic as a prisoner in Staffordshire, a long way from the Silesian capital of his birth. 'My only wish', his mother pleaded, is 'to know that my child is near me.'[12]

Stein's heartfelt wish to have her son's grave close was one that united the bereaved in Britain and Germany, and across the two conflicts too.

The Second World War may have been a very different type of conflict, with urban areas laid waste and far higher numbers of civilian casualties too, but the one constant was this desire to bring the bodies of the dead back to the families. Home, for the Beudel family, was the village of Schottwien, set in a deep valley some 80 kilometres south of the Austrian capital, Vienna. Moriz and Valerie Beudel's only child, Erich, however, lay in a very different landscape. Killed in the Battle of Britain while piloting a Messerschmidt fighter, Erich's remains ended up in the flat pastoral landscapes of Burstow in Surrey, just east of Gatwick airport. Valerie, in particular, was desperate to have her son close and led the family's efforts to return his body to Austria. She negotiated with the British authorities, recruited a firm of undertakers to carry out the exhumation and even purchased a new grave in Schottwien, where the body would receive 'tender care' in perpetuity.[13]

Like Valerie Beudel, many bereaved families on the Allied side also wanted to bring their sons and brothers home after the Second World War. Edward Sabarsky's pained request to retrieve his son's body from Hanover, though, was more emotionally charged than most. Serving in the Royal Armoured Corps and going by the name of Harry Sayers, his son had been killed in April 1945, a few weeks before Nazi Germany's unconditional surrender. As Sabarsky later explained, Sayers had managed to flee Austria after the Nazis' 1938 *Anschluss* of the country and had eventually ended up in Britain, where he then joined the British army. While his son stayed in Europe, Sabarsky himself managed to cross the Atlantic and rebuilt his own life in New York, establishing a successful lingerie business. For Sabarsky, bringing his son's body to the United States did not just allow him to have the grave placed in a Jewish cemetery, but also enabled him to rescue everything that was dear from the death zones of Europe.[14]

Stemming the Flow

In the immediate post-war years, the bereaved were clearly worried about their relatives' remains lying far from home on enemy soil. But any dismay was tempered by the thought that the dead would soon be transported back to the families in Britain and Germany. Yet, in the vast majority of cases, such optimism was quickly dashed, and the dead remained exactly where they were. Harry Sayers or Sabarsky, whose body left Hanover in the 1950s for the Beth David Cemetery in Elton, New York, was one of the few exceptions. It was not any particular sympathy for the family's status as Holocaust survivors that led to his exhumation, but rather the fact that Sayers was eventually designated as an American and therefore was eligible for return. Few families enjoyed a similar outcome. What brought the repatriation plans of the bereaved to a largely disappointing halt was the efforts of the British and German authorities to regain control of their war graves. The Treaty of Versailles may have made an allowance for the repatriation of the dead, but it became increasingly clear that neither the British, nor the Germans, saw any reason to take advantage of these provisions.

German families who hoped to repatriate a body were not helped in their endeavour by the fact that they had to wade through a whole range of different agencies. On paper, the Central Information Office for War Casualties and War Graves (Zentralnachweiseamt für Kriegsverluste und Kriegergräber, ZAK), which had been formed in 1919 to register all German war graves, was also responsible for matters of exhumation and repatriation. After the Second World War, the ZAK was joined by the equally wordy, Wehrmacht Information Office for War Casualties and Prisoners of War (Wehrmachtauskunftstelle für Kriegerverluste und Kriegsgefangene, WASt), later shortened to Deutsche Dienststelle, WASt, which concerned itself mainly with the dead of the most recent conflict. If this was not complicated enough, a range of other groups also wanted their own say. The German Foreign Office (Auswärtiges Amt) took a keen interest in the German dead in Britain, as did the German embassy in London, which ended up leading a lot of the negotiations on the ground.[15]

However, the organisation that held the greatest sway in the end was the German War Graves Commission, the VDK. Rising above this bureaucratic fog, the VDK positioned itself as the only group able to care for the German graves at home and abroad. Unlike the other bodies involved in dealing with the German war dead, the VDK was a private, rather than a state, organisation. It had been founded in late 1919, largely thanks to the tenacious efforts of Siegfried Emmo Eulen, a former military officer who had a deeply held belief in the conservative values of 'honour, freedom and fatherland'. Eulen cleverly pitched the VDK as a politically neutral body that wanted nothing more than to ensure the future care of the war dead. The organisation's monthly newsletter, *Kriegsgräberfürsorge*, provided a visual representation of this mission, with each edition invariably opening to a scene of German war graves innocently resting in a variety of rural settings (see image 16). Eulen's approach quickly bore fruit. By the 1920s, the VDK could count 100,000 members in a network of local groups; a further 300,000 had joined by the eve of the Second World War.[16]

Despite enjoying such levels of support, the VDK never showed much enthusiasm at the thought of returning the war dead from abroad, preferring instead to concentrate its efforts on the care of the graves overseas. It followed the state's line, therefore, which was to try to discourage the bereaved from pushing for the return of the dead. The government had formalised this policy when it issued its own blanket ban on any repatriations in summer 1920. With the new Weimar Republic attempting to ease itself out of the triple challenges of war, revolution and defeat, the last thing it needed was thousands of corpses being sent around the country. 'Considering the transport difficulties that would be caused by the expected large number [. . .] of bodies,' the government explained, 'the ZAK has thus [. . .] for now rejected all applications.'[17] There may have been practical reasons for the government's approach, but that was of little comfort for the bereaved who cared little for post-war Germany's logistical failings. As one conservative politician forcibly explained: 'The attitude of the Reich government has caused deep outrage amongst the families of the war dead.'[18]

Faced with complaints from relatives and politicians, it did not take long for the German government to crack under the pressure. Given its ongoing efforts to return the country to a peacetime state, presumably the government had more pressing issues to deal with than to expend political capital defending its stance on the war dead. By the end of 1921, therefore, the ZAK permitted relatives to bring back bodies from abroad so long as they met a near impossible list of stipulations. The bereaved had to cover all costs; no other bodies could be disturbed

16. A striking image of the German military cemetery in Merano, South Tyrol, which adorned the title page of the VDK's newsletter in July 1921.

during an exhumation; transporting bodies home by rail was outlawed; and so the list went on. This was not a particularly enticing offer for relatives. It was clear that while they could bring the remains of their loved ones back to Germany, the state would still rather they let them be.[19] The VDK spelt this out even more bluntly to relatives, explaining that it was best 'not to transfer the fallen back home'. The war cemeteries had been set out 'in a lovely way' and it would be wrong to 'disturb the sleeping dead', it added for good measure.[20]

With so many hurdles blocking their path, it must have taken particular emotional strength to complete all of the administrative procedures and actually get a body returned from Britain to Germany. However, a small number of families did succeed, largely thanks to the persistence of female relatives who steadfastly battled the authorities. One of these was Frau Stein, who had been so desperate to bring her son Kurt back home to Breslau from Staffordshire. She had originally hoped, somewhat optimistically, that the British would cover the repatriation costs. Even when this proved to be false, she persevered and Stein's body arrived safely back in Breslau in 1925.[21] Of the handful of other families who managed to repeat this feat, the majority had a much longer wait, with the remains of one German officer only making it home to Düsseldorf a few months before the outbreak of the Second World War. The dead man's sister, who had travelled to Berkshire for the exhumation, 'wept bitterly' as his body was dug up and then sealed into an 'ornamental coffin' ready for the long journey back to Germany.[22]

The relatives of these two men were certainly in a minority. Many other families hoped to repatriate their loved ones' remains, but often failed to realise their goal. The parents of Otto Günther, the POW interred in Leigh, fell into this category. Despite years of discussions with both the British and German authorities, stretching all the way back to the time of Günther's death in 1916, the family had apparently 'relinquished the idea' by 1928. It is unclear what exactly led them to make this decision. The level of bureaucracy involved in any repatriation along with the ZAK's strict requirements was presumably a factor. The fact that Günther lay in a grave with five other German POWs was an added hurdle. In such situations, the ZAK required that the relatives of all five men must give their permission before the grave could be opened. The financial costs of repatriation may also have played a role in the family's thinking, particularly as the German economy stuttered along in the late 1920s before finally collapsing in the Great Depression. For example, another German family, who hoped to exhume their son from Greenwich, abandoned their plans due to the costs involved, or, as the German embassy put it, 'owing to pressure of [the] bad economic circumstances'.[23]

In the wake of the Second World War, some twenty years after the Günthers had reluctantly abandoned their own repatriation plans, the situation proved remarkably similar for a new generation of bereaved. Many Germans whose loved ones were buried on British soil were again keen to bring the bodies to a new cemetery much closer to where they lived. But the same bureaucratic and financial barriers continued to prove the major stumbling block. Amidst the turmoil of post-war Europe, neither the British nor the German authorities saw any need to encourage the repatriation of thousands of bodies from the former frontlines, which would have only added further stress to Germany's war-damaged infrastructure. Indeed, the War Office in Whitehall made it clear from the start that it did not want to see any of the German war dead removed from Britain, stating unequivocally that 'the repatriation to Germany of casualties [. . .] cannot be allowed'.[24]

As had been the case after the First World War, it was clear that all sides would prefer for the bodies to stay exactly where they were, rather than being repatriated from abroad. Valerie Beudel's hopes of bringing her son, Erich, from Surrey back to Austria also collided head on with the tough bureaucratic reality. By the mid-1950s, after years of planning, she seemed to be on the verge of realising her goal. Even the Home Office was ready to explain to her its 'normal requirements' for an exhumation, but then a further set of administrative hurdles were raised for transporting a body overseas. It can only be presumed that these new conditions proved too much, as Valerie Beudel's correspondence then dried up, the discussions ended and Beudel seemed destined to remain forever in a boggy churchyard in Surrey.[25]

Despite such personal setbacks, the occasional corpse did make it through the bureaucratic minefield, which must surely have given other families a small glimmer of hope that they too could exhume their loved ones' remains. Every successful exhumation, though, seemed to rely on a great deal of chance. The parents of Heinrich Meier, who managed to bring the body of their son back to their village in Lower Saxony, had simply been in the right place at the right time. Meier had been killed in August 1940, when his Junkers Ju 88 aircraft had come under attack off the Yorkshire coast. He died in the aircraft itself, while the other crew members survived the crashlanding as POWs. Meier's father had long been pushing for the return of his 'only son' from Britain 'to be re-interred in [a] family grave in Germany'. But all his enquiries to both the British and German authorities, as well as to the Red Cross had failed to give him the outcome he so desired.[26]

Clearly frustrated at the lack of progress, the parents decided to take matters into their own hands and travelled in person to the gravesite in the Yorkshire town of Thornaby. They visited their son's grave, spoke to local officials and again sought permission to exhume the body, all to no avail. It was only when they decided to stay in Thornaby to put pressure on the authorities that the bureaucratic cogs began to turn. Local people, hearing of their plight, started to rally behind their cause. The Town Clerk of Thornaby, along with a local firm of under-takers, wrote to the Home Office urging them to expedite the case. Taking a far more emotional line, a member of the British Legion's women's section even begged 'in all humanity's sake' that the authorities 'attend to this [case] immediately'.[27] These combined pleas eventually paid off. In August 1954, several weeks after the parents had first arrived, Meier's body was exhumed, cremated, then finally shipped back to Germany.

Taking Charge

It later emerged that the IWGC's own rules and regulations had played a significant role in the delayed exhumation of Meier and non-repatriation of Beudel. Fabian Ware, a 'tall and broadshouldered' former newspaper editor and imperial administrator, had founded the commission during the First World War and then served as its vice-chair for three decades until poor health forced him into well-earned retirement in 1948.[28] Under Ware's forceful leadership, the IWGC had shown great determination to record and mark the graves of Britain's war dead from the two world wars scattered across the globe. Its remit also stretched to those killed fighting from Britain's then empire, although when it came to commemorating black soldiers from the colonies its efforts proved far patchier, with graves lost, neglected or even wilfully abandoned.[29] By contrast, the IWGC found it much harder simply to ignore the German war dead actually buried on British soil, who, thanks to the terms of the Treaty of Versailles, had also become its responsibility.

When relatives of the former enemy dead planned to repatriate bodies from Britain, the IWGC understandably also wanted to have some say in the matter. With Meier and Beudel, it was never the case that the commission had any specific interest in the two bodies or that it wanted to cause the bereaved any further pain. Instead, its concern was more about aesthetics. Meier's body, for example, lay in a plot with another ninety-four British and German dead. If his body were to be exhumed from Thornaby, then it would have left a conspicuous gap in row of carefully aligned crosses. In the end, the IWGC had to admit that the loss of Meier's grave, being positioned as it was at the end of a row, would not be too disturbing on the eye (see image 17). The IWGC dragged its heels for as long as possible but, with the parents exerting pressure on the ground, it saw little option but for Meier's remains 'exceptionally, and somewhat reluctantly' to be returned to Germany.[30]

There was, however, a much deeper reason for the IWGC's reluctance to see Meier, Beudel and any other enemy bodies depart, which went to the very heart of its practice. In 1919, the IWGC had made permanent a wartime ban on the repatriation of its own war dead, a principle it then reaffirmed after the Second World War. Of course, some bodies could have been returned, but as far as Ware was concerned, it was a question of equality. Either all the dead had to come home, or they all had to stay. He was determined to avoid a situation where

17. In Yorkshire's Thornaby Cemetery, the German graves – all marked by wooden crosses – lie behind a row of headstones for the British and Commonwealth war dead. The empty spot at the far left of the second row is where one German airman was exhumed in August 1954.

wealthy relatives could buy themselves a mortuary advantage, leaving the poorer dead behind. However, the decision to leave the bodies of the dead overseas was highly controversial, provoking much debate in the immediate post-war years that played out particularly fiercely in the press. Reflecting one of the strongest lines of opposition, *The Times* argued that it was 'surely repugnant to British feeling that [. . .] the family should surrender all rights over the individual to the state'.[31]

Ware did his best to navigate the IWGC through these thorny debates; he either maintained a dignified silence or did his best to lobby the right politicians for support. Yet, for all his dogmatism, Ware was perceptive enough to know that he needed to keep the public on side. This is where Rudyard Kipling, a man with far more literary flair than Ware, came in. Kipling was charged with making an unpopular decision more palatable. In a pamphlet especially produced for the purpose, Kipling explained that 'to allow exhumation and removal' would be a 'violation [. . .] of the dead themselves'.[32] The problem for the IWGC, therefore, was simply one of reciprocity. To allow Beudel or Meier – the former enemy – to return, while imposing a 'ban on the repatriation of British war dead' would have been 'of some embarrassment', it admitted.[33]

What surely had the potential for even greater embarrassment was the fact that neither Ware nor the IWGC more generally had ever been entirely comfortable at the thought of the British and empire dead staying in enemy soil. After the two world wars, the IWGC demonstrated steadfast certainty that the dead would remain overseas in Allied countries, whether in Belgium, France or Singapore. Leaving the war dead in Germany, though, proved a far more contentious issue. Some families were understandably angry at the thought that their loved ones would not only remain far from home, but that they would be left on enemy territory too. The father of a private in the Yorkshire Dragoons Yeomanry, whose son had died a few months after the 1918 armistice in occupied Cologne, was livid that 'the graves of our brave boys' were to be 'left to the tender mercies of the Huns'.[34] It was this apparent incongruity that a second bereaved generation also emphasised after 1945. A letter in the London *Times* reflected the views of many, when the writer complained that 'England allows them [the heroic dead] to lie in enemy territory'.[35]

Although he would never have expressed this view publicly, Ware had every sympathy for the relatives' complaints, particularly after the brutality of the Nazi era. There was something deeply uncomfortable, he acknowledged, about having to leave British bodies on 'so-called "putrid" German soil'. Ware's colleague in the War Office, Brigadier John McNair, himself an old soldier of the Great War, tried to place himself in the metaphorical shoes of those who had been killed. He did not need to picture the scene for too long, before he reached the same conclusion as Ware: 'Personally, [I] would hate the idea of being buried in Germany,' he shuddered.[36]

Both the public and the bereaved seemed to favour repatriation, while the leading lights in the IWGC and the War Office found it unpalatable to leave the war dead on German soil. But despite the weight of evidence pushing towards repatriation of those killed, one thing kept niggling away at the members of the IWGC. If they allowed the dead to be removed from German territory to cemeteries in either Belgium or France, then relatives would surely demand that, once exhumed, the bodies be transported all the way back home to Britain or elsewhere. The worry was that this would be the thin edge of the wedge. 'If it were necessary to exhume and move the bodies at all,' Ware imagined relatives asking, '[then] why should they not be brought to their own countries[?]' This was a 'very difficult argument to answer', he admitted. Almost twenty-five years later the IWGC faced exactly the same conundrum. 'Once you began to move bodies for anything but necessity no-one could say where it would end,' feared one long-standing member. The end point did not bear thinking about. Relatives would start to demand the return of bodies from all over, and very quickly the argument so carefully built by the IWGC would come tumbling down.[37]

The IWGC actually decided very quickly, therefore, that the war dead had to stay in Germany; it just found it very difficult to tell relatives and the wider public of the plan. As a result, the IWGC's official policy towards the war graves on enemy territory ended up being cloaked in unnecessary ambiguity and secrecy. It was for this reason that Churchill could boldly stand up in the House of Commons in 1919 and declare that relatives could bring home their loved ones' remains from Germany. A quarter of a century later, politicians continued to offer their own vague interpretations as to what was to happen to the British war dead in Germany, leaving one Conservative MP to declare that there was 'some obscurity about the future treatment of the bodies', and demanding that the Secretary of State for War get the 'matter cleared up'.[38]

In the end, the IWGC proved much better at facing these realities after the Second World War than it had in the wake of the Great War. Presumably, the lessons of the earlier conflict were still live, and the commission's leaders recognised that they needed to act more decisively, both for the sake of the bereaved and for the IWGC's own reputation. Before they could go public with their non-repatriation plan, they first needed government approval. Clement Attlee's Cabinet gathered in early September 1945 to discuss epidemics, house prices and the ongoing issue of 'war graves on German soil'. The IWGC had already prepared a memorandum in which it recommended 'refusing requests from next-of-kin that bodies of officers and men' be returned from Germany.[39] With little fuss, the Cabinet fully approved the proposals, leaving the IWGC free to go public with its plans. When a statement finally appeared in the national press in October 1945, *The Times* framed it in clear and unambiguous terms: 'War Dead Not Being Brought Home'.[40] There was certainly plenty of upset at the decision. The problem, as one army officer put it, was that the decision 'may be good', but 'the public at present has no means of appreciating' how it was made.[41]

Despite such mutterings, the IWGC eventually did manage to draw up a clear policy for its graves in defeated Germany, and later in 1945 also informed the public unambiguously that the dead would remain overseas. Unfortunately, this was never the case after the First World War. For a long time, the IWGC worked to keep the war dead in Germany, but without ever fully admitting to the bereaved that this was its actual aim. Fearing the wrath of families with loved ones buried in Germany, the IWGC seemed content to keep matters this way for as long as possible. Three years after the fighting had stopped, leading voices in the IWGC still 'thought it inadvisable to make any public statement' on the enemy dead in Germany, as it 'would at once arouse opposition'.[42]

It was all very well for the IWGC to remain silent on the issue, but this of course meant that the bereaved were left entirely in the dark.

Margaret Staveley, a recent widow from Lancashire, wrote to the IWGC in early summer 1920 about her husband, Arthur. He had died just a few months earlier as an officer in the occupation army around Cologne. 'I should be most grateful', she politely wrote, 'if you would tell me any time there is a chance of my being allowed to bring my husband home.' In a later exchange, she added that her husband had always 'expressed a special wish that he should not be buried in Germany'. Rather than being the bearer of bad news, the IWGC's Permanent Assistant Secretary gave a more upbeat assessment. 'The whole question of the British war graves in Germany is at the present moment being discussed,' he assured Staveley. 'It is as yet impossible to say what arrangements can be made for the removal of the bodies from Germany.' The tone of the letter seemed to imply that in time the dead would be repatriated to Britain, even if the reality was very different.[43]

With a sense of increasing helplessness, other families kept writing to the IWGC pleading for a date for the repatriations to begin. 'I am compelled to again write and ask whether there will ever be a possibility of [. . .] getting my late son's remains removed to England,' one father from Essex asked. Seeing the Americans and the French exhume their dead from Germany, while the British bodies were left behind, only added to these frustrations. With a biting mixture of scorn and anger, the father pointed out that of course as 'the Americans won the war', they should be able to remove their own war dead. However, he added, 'British boys did something towards the victory', so perhaps 'their parents should have some consideration' too.[44] It must have been slowly dawning on this poor father, and on other bereaved families, that their loved ones were never going to return. They needed, though, to wait another few months before the IWGC finally acknowledged publicly that its non-repatriation policy also applied to the dead buried on enemy territory.

Fighting for Control

Once the enemy bodies were stranded in either Britain or Germany with little chance of return, relatives had few options. In the 1940s, one entrepreneurial family sought a legal means to challenge the

IWGC's non-repatriation policy. Their solicitors went straight to the source of the issue and demanded the IWGC justify its stance: 'We are instructed by a Client to ask you if you can give us the Authority under which the Government of the United Kingdom made such a decision.' Confirmation that it was a Cabinet decision was not enough to mollify the solicitors who concluded that there was actually 'no statutory authority' to refuse the return of the war dead. The War Office, which by now had also been forced to consider the legalities of non-repatriation, admitted internally that the government had no 'power to prevent a person bringing into this country the body of a deceased relative'. However, whether 'he could get hold of the body in the foreign territory [was] another matter', the War Office concluded with some confidence.[45] After the Great War, some families had indeed travelled to France hoping secretly to exhume their loved ones' remains. To do the same from occupied Germany after the Second World War would clearly have been an almost insurmountable challenge.[46]

The legal case for leaving the war dead on enemy soil may not have been entirely watertight, but in the end this did not really matter. The British and German authorities, and their respective war graves commissions, had effectively taken full control of the war dead, and it was clear that they had little desire to see the bodies returned. Just because they could not get hold of the bodies, however, did not mean the bereaved also forfeited their interest in caring for the graves. Many people had already started to arrange for a personal headstone to be erected above their loved one's grave, liaising with local communities to get a marker in place. This desire to beautify the graves did not suddenly end when control of the bodies was lost. After all, if the bodies were to remain on enemy soil, then the bereaved wanted to do everything they could to ensure their husband, brother or son was resting peacefully. William Robertson, a wealthy Londoner, barrister and an alumnus of the fee-paying Westminster School, was clearly someone who liked order, clarity and for affairs to be conducted correctly. After the fighting on the frontlines had ceased in November 1918, Robertson dedicated considerable time to honouring his two younger brothers – Laurance and Norman – who had never returned from the war.[47] His main concern to start with was that his siblings were properly buried and that their graves were marked. There was little that he could do immediately for Laurance, who went missing during the Battle of the Somme, but the grave of his middle brother, Norman, who had died in a German hospital, was a different matter. Driven by 'a solemn duty' to put his brother's grave in Hanover into a 'finished and proper condition', Robertson decided that he was going to travel to Germany himself, where he would then arrange for a 'suitable memorial' to be placed over the grave. Being the methodical and meticulous person he was, Robertson wrote to the IWGC before departing, outlining his plans and adding that in the future the IWGC would no longer need to 'concern itself in this case'.[48]

Robertson's attention to detail, however, seemed to be his undoing. The IWGC, which had its own very different ideas for the war graves, reacted to Robertson's headstone plans not with the gratitude he had expected, but rather with deep dismay. It first attempted to stall Robertson by deploying its full powers of persuasion. The IWGC 'intend[s] to erect memorials in Germany', the commission reassured him. 'I assume, therefore, that under these circumstances you would prefer to have a headstone erected over your brother's grave similar to those erected over all other war graves in Germany.' When this line of argument failed to pacify Robertson, the IWGC then took a more hard-line approach. It informed him that it was 'unable to permit' a private headstone to be set over the grave as this would be 'out of keeping with [the] general scheme which is based on the principle of equality'. Given that Robertson, unlike many of the bereaved, had the financial means to pay for a headstone, this seemed to be a fair point, not that he necessarily saw it this way. The IWGC's stance 'came as a surprise', Robertson complained, and for good measure added that he had great 'difficulty in understanding [its] position'.[49]

It may well have been hard for Robertson to grasp the IWGC's approach to the British graves in Germany, principally because the commission never fully publicised it, but the realities on the ground were much clearer. The commission was very aware that many relatives, like Robertson, were already busy liaising with local German communities, making plans to erect headstones or even arranging to have the body repatriated. For this reason, the IWGC decided it needed to act quickly to dampen such enthusiasm. Behind the scenes, it cautioned the German authorities against having anything to do with the bereaved. The ZAK passed this message onto the regional states who, up until this point, had been happily working with bereaved British families. 'Representatives of the British war graves commission have requested that [. . .] until further notice all requests from relatives of the British dead to erect their own headstones [. . .] are to be declined,' the ZAK explained.[50]

In Britain, by contrast, there were fewer formal restrictions in place for German relatives looking to erect their own headstones over graves. Nonetheless, the VDK also did its best to discourage relatives from taking such a course of action. Following the IWGC's initial tactic of gentle persuasion, it tried to reassure the bereaved that the graves were already being cared for. The POW graves in Sutton Veny, for example, were apparently 'in good condition and regularly maintained', while in Great Burstead the Zeppelin graves were 'repaired in the spring' and the 'grave mounds reseeded' in the autumn.[51] For readers of its newsletter, the message was clear: there was no need for them to go to the trouble of erecting their own headstones as the graves were already in safe hands.

British families seemed to be more put out than their opposite numbers in Germany by their loss of control. This partly reflected a difference in the outcome of the two conflicts, with those on the victorious side expecting to have a greater say over the care of their dead, but it was also a sign of the IWGC's stronger restrictions. William Robertson, for example, was particularly aggrieved that by 1922 – five years after his brother's death as a POW in Hanover – there was still no permanent headstone over the grave. 'Your department does nothing,' he complained to the IWGC, 'and objects to my doing anything.'[52] Robertson never gave up on his fight to commemorate his two brothers. In later life, when drawing up his will, he left most of his money to the National Trust on condition they purchase property and land, 'preferably within easy access of London', as a memorial. Sutton House in Hackney and eight parcels of land that his will funded all contain a metal plaque inscribed: 'In Memory of his Brothers Norman Cairns Robertson [. . .] who died 20th June 1917 at Hanover Germany and of

Laurance Grant Robertson [. . .]' (see image 18). Unable to control the grave itself, Robertson clearly decided to set his own agenda by creating living memorials within Britain.[53]

18. The Robertson memorial at Highcomb, Beacon Hill, Surrey. One of nine National Trust memorials erected in memory of Norman Cairn Robertson, who died in German captivity in 1917, and of his brother, killed on the Western Front the previous year.

Very few families had the money to follow Robertson's lead. If they were upset at the IWGC's approach to the war graves in Germany, people had to find different means of making their discontent felt. One outlet came in the form of the British War Graves Association. Formed in Yorkshire in 1919 by Sarah Ann Smith, the association campaigned for the return of the war dead from abroad, therefore placing itself in direct opposition to the IWGC's non-repatriation policy. Smith herself was a remarkable person with a steely determination. Driven no doubt by the loss of her 19-year-old son, Frederick, she provided a voice for other mothers who had been forced to grieve without a body or a grave. Edward Windsor, the then Prince of Wales, was one of the first to experience Smith's tenacity, when he received a petition demanding a reversal of the decision 'prohibiting the removal of the remains of the fallen to this country'.[54] Unsurprisingly perhaps, the prince failed to get behind Smith's campaign, but for her this was only the start. By the early 1920s, the British War Graves Association had over 3,000 members, all of whom were guided by the ever-energetic Smith as treasurer, secretary and lead campaigner.[55]

Most of the British War Graves Association's energies focused on the largest collection of bodies lying in Belgium or France, which is where Smith's own son was also buried. Yet, some of the members' loved ones had also died in wartime Germany. The petition did not discriminate between the place of death; the unifying factor was that the body was still overseas. Therefore, families whose relatives lay buried in different German towns and cities added their signatures to the long list of the enraged bereaved. John Clemenson from Cross Lane in Wakefield, a road of coalminers' houses, scrawled his name on the list in dark black ink, then for good measure added the name of his daughter – Ivy – in the line below. In their thoughts was 21-year-old Edward Clemenson, who had been captured on the Western Front in 1918 and had died of a lung infection in Recklinghausen, which is where he had then been laid to rest. Like many, all his family wanted was for Clemenson's body to be returned from enemy territory back home.[56]

Reflecting its members' concerns, the association raised the issue of the British dead in Germany on numerous occasions. The French government's decision to exhume and repatriate its own dead from German soil hit a particular nerve. 'I take it that relatives may remove their dead from [. . .] Germany (at their own expense) if they wish,' Smith suggested to the War Office with a heavy dose of sarcasm. The officials in Whitehall not only failed to see the joke, but also refused to engage with Smith at all, instructing the IWGC to respond instead: 'The Secretary of State [for War] is not interested in this Association or in the writer,' was their rather curt message.[57] The IWGC also failed to subdue Smith and her members, who continued to fight its policies, repeatedly pointing at the apparent indignity of leaving the war dead on what had been enemy territory. If 'our own soldiers buried in Germany' are not returned, the association argued time and again, 'it would be a grave injustice both to our glorious dead and their relatives'.[58]

Smith died in June 1936 and never achieved her goal of having the war dead returned to Britain. She must surely have been proud, though, of her movement and of the years of tenacious campaigning. Even the IWGC, for so long her major rival in war graves' matters, sent a note of condolence when it learnt of Smith's death, praising her 'cordial and friendly' exchanges.[59] After Smith's passing, the British War Graves Association was a shadow of its former self and the organisation eventually folded in the late 1940s.

In the wake of the Second World War, there was again plenty of heated debate over the future of the British war graves in Germany. As had been the case earlier, some of the bereaved wanted to see the dead returned, while the IWGC again did its best to maintain full control over the bodies. With the British War Graves Association no longer a force, the bereaved needed a new spokesperson to lead any protests. The long-established British Legion with its large veteran membership seemed like the ideal candidate to fill this void. And for a short period at least, the Welsh branch of the legion spoke out with some horror at the IWGC's plans to leave the British war dead on German soil. The legion argued that the dead should be exhumed and brought home to Wales or, as a bare minimum, to a cemetery outside Germany. Framing the issue in terms of national loyalties, the regional chairman insisted that the 'Welsh nation' would prefer its dead laid to rest 'in the lands they sought to save', meaning France, Belgium or the Netherlands.

The alternative, he argued, was for them to be stuck 'in the midst of the race who [. . .] brought about their untimely deaths'.[60]

As the British Legion's campaign gathered momentum, they managed to recruit the Cardiff Labour MP, George Thomas, to their cause. Thomas made a personal plea to the Secretary of State for War, calling for the return of the Welsh soldiers killed in Germany, pointing out that the Americans were repatriating their own dead, which demonstrated that it was certainly possible to return the dead.[61] Despite a string of similar appeals, the IWGC proved to be as resolute in its position as it had been when Smith had pursued her own campaign a quarter of a century earlier. Where possible, it avoided engaging with complaints at all, for fear of 'provok[ing] further correspondence', and simply reminded relatives that it was merely following a government decision.[62]

The IWGC may not have spelt it out directly, but the implication of its exchanges was that the future of the British war dead lying on enemy territory was a state, rather than a private, matter. Neither the bereaved relatives, nor the local communities in whose midst they lay, therefore, needed to concern themselves any longer with the care of these graves. It was clear to all concerned that the IWGC had taken full control of the British dead in Germany, and that the VDK sought a similar level of control over their soldiers and civilians buried in Britain. What the war graves commissions intended to do with their hard-won power, however, remained an open question.

6

CONCENTRATING

In October 1959, John Profumo, then better known for being Minister of State for Foreign Affairs rather than for a scandalous affair with the 19-year-old Christine Keeler, invited Joachim Friedrich Ritter from the West German embassy to his Whitehall office. After exchanging the usual diplomatic pleasantries, the pair picked up their pens and affixed their signatures to a major international treaty between the United Kingdom and the Federal Republic of Germany. The 'Agreement [. . .] regarding German War Graves', to use the treaty's formal title, gave the VDK, as representatives of the West German state, the power to decide the future of the German dead of the two world wars buried on British soil.[1] Ritter's visit to the Foreign Office, and indeed the treaty itself, initially went almost entirely unnoticed. There was no flying of flags, singing of national anthems or even an official press release to mark the occasion. However, the *Birmingham Post* had its finger on the pulse, finding the space to dedicate a single sentence to this new international treaty: 'An agreement between the British Government and the Federal German Government providing for the care of German war graves in Britain was signed at the Foreign Office yesterday.'[2]

Although this British–German meeting seemed to pass most people by completely, given its significance for British–German relations it was surely worthy of much greater attention. On one level, the treaty was a further sign that the Federal Republic was gradually returning to the international stage. Indeed, in 1955 it had already made great strides in this direction, regaining sovereignty from the American, British and French occupiers, establishing its own army, the Bundeswehr, and joining the North Atlantic Treaty Organization (NATO) military alliance too. As the Cold War heated up, Britain and the other Western countries could clearly see the benefit of bringing West Germans back into the fold, while at the same time ostracising East Germans living in the German Democratic Republic (GDR), who just happened to be stranded on the wrong side of the Iron Curtain.[3]

On quite another level, though, the treaty also represented a real diplomatic triumph for the Federal Republic. No longer would German war graves lie scattered throughout Britain, but instead were to be gathered together into one new military cemetery to be built somewhere on British territory. The VDK and its supporters had been pushing unsuccessfully for the establishment of a collective cemetery for decades. Politicians in the Weimar Republic had made some efforts in this direction but had always ended up bogged down in their own domestic troubles. As was their wont, the Nazis approached the whole issue with much greater fervour, but all they managed to achieve was another war and many more dead. When the 1959 treaty was finally agreed, therefore, West German officials had every right to congratulate themselves privately for making it possible to 'finally resolve' the war graves question.[4]

However, it was never the case that the German graves had simply been forgotten, before being miraculously rescued from decades of neglect by the new international treaty. The bereaved had generally gratefully acknowledged the work of local British communities in caring for the dead, while the IWGC itself had worked with the German authorities to ensure the graves were properly maintained. The issue instead was simply one of perceptions. In the early 1920s and again in the late 1940s, the IWGC had drawn up its own plans to move the British dead into new military cemeteries on German territory. As no such honour was bestowed on the German graves in Britain, it was very easy for the German Right, including more conservative organisations like the VDK, to claim that the German war graves were being unfairly treated in comparison to the British.[5] On paper at least, the 1959 treaty resolved forty years of dispute. Selling the virtues of this plan to the two publics, who by now were accustomed to the scattered graves, was a very different matter, which explains why a breakthrough treaty remained something of a secret.

Striding Out in Front

Forceville in northern France, with a population of only a few hundred souls, is a fairly unremarkable place. The odd house, some small farms and plenty of fields border the streets leading to the imposing spire of the village's eighteenth-century church. Forceville does have one other claim to fame, however, being home to the IWGC's very first war cemetery. When Beatrix Brice, wartime nurse and sometime poet, visited the newly completed cemetery in 1920, she could not help but marvel at the carefully laid out site. 'It is the most perfect, the noblest, the most classically beautiful memorial that any loving heart or any proud nation could desire,' she wrote with particular flourish.[6] Although slightly more reserved in their tone, the IWGC leaders were also satisfied with the results of their experimental cemetery and sought to roll out the basic design elsewhere too.[7] Imposing this same model onto defeated Germany, however, proved much more challenging. It was not so much that the German authorities resisted, but rather that the IWGC's leaders dithered. They had been very quick to seize control of the dead, barring relatives from repatriating the bodies, but they then proved much slower at deciding what should actually happen to the British dead still stranded on former enemy territory.

It was only in 1921, three years after the war's end, that the members of the IWGC finally seemed to be in agreement that the British dead were going to remain in post-war Germany. As had happened already in France, Belgium and elsewhere, the bodies would be moved from the hundreds of scattered burial sites to larger military cemeteries or, in IWGC parlance, to concentration cemeteries. The commission also planned to buy the land for its new war cemeteries outright, to ensure that it would have full control of the dead in perpetuity. Bringing the bodies together in this way meant that the Germans would no longer play a role in the maintenance of the graves, leaving the IWGC free 'to make beautiful British cemeteries' on German territory instead.[8]

The commission's vision for the British war dead was fine in principle, but it failed to provide an answer to one crucial question: where exactly were these large military cemeteries going to be? Even in its shrunken post-Versailles state, Germany covered a vast swathe of territory, which left plenty of potential sites for new military cemeteries. The dead could be moved to 'four or five cemeteries in the principal parts' of the country, suggested one leading voice in the IWGC. Rejecting this approach, another IWGC member preferred the idea of 'one large cemetery' in Cologne that the British occupation troops could easily protect.[9] Agreeing to leave the dead on former enemy territory was one thing, but deciding where exactly they were going to lie was quite another.

The British faced the same challenge after the Second World War, just with the added challenge of finding a suitable home in the ruins of Nazi Germany. As had been the case twenty-five years earlier, after thumbing through maps of Germany, everyone came to different conclusions as to where the cemeteries should be built. The RAF and Royal Navy asked that their dead be moved to new cemeteries west of the river Rhine, where they would be reassuringly close to friendly neighbours and of course the occupying British forces too. Taking a very different approach, the British army's adjutant-general, Ronald Forbes Adam, preferred the idea of having some cemeteries further into the heart of Germany, where they would 'serve as a salutary reminder' to Germans of the 'events of this war'.[10] One slight sticking point with Adam's plan was the Soviet occupation zone on the eastern side of Germany, out of which the GDR was later formed. With relations between the Western Allies and the Soviet Union increasingly tense, no one wanted to place the British dead in new danger. The Canadians, meanwhile, who seemed increasingly tired with the whole affair, threatened to go it alone and to send the bodies of their soldiers to cemeteries in the Netherlands.[11]

The competing aspirations of the IWGC, the War Office and service branches could not survive a confrontation with the realities on the ground. In the 1920s, the IWGC, for example, had been all set to develop a cemetery in the historic university town of Heidelberg, where they had identified some 'really beautiful sites' and 'very good stone' for construction. However, after visiting the town, the plans were quickly dropped. Darmstadt went the same way, when the local authorities demanded a hefty fee of £10 for each British body reinterred in the city, which would have quickly exhausted the IWGC's working budget.[12] This left the British with four main sites for their First World War dead, in Cologne, Berlin, Hamburg and Kassel. The first three were to be developed within the 'nucleus' of large German communal cemeteries, while the fourth – at Kassel – made use of the existing Niederzwehren POW cemetery, which was deemed suitable, just as soon as any 'Russian burials', which had been placed inconveniently in the way, were 'remove[d] and redistribute[d]'.[13] Finally, the development of two smaller sites was also agreed. Zehrensdorf, where the Germans had originally buried the Indian and colonial dead, was to become a permanent cemetery, as was Worms, where it proved too difficult to extract the British bodies from mass graves (see Map 1).

The British authorities went through the same long-winded process of selecting and then discarding sites in the 1940s too. Hagen, Cloppenburg and Xanten were all to host new military cemeteries, but then the plans changed. On this occasion, it was the army – assigned the task of finding suitable sites – that proved most indecisive. Eventually, though, its teams agreed on thirteen main locations in Berlin and in the Western occupation zones. The existing First World War cemetery in Hamburg Ohlsdorf was to gain a new section for the more recent conflict. Large cemeteries in Rheinberg and Reichswald, designed for those soldiers killed during the Western advance into Nazi Germany in 1945, were to be built in tandem with a series of smaller cemeteries sprinkled throughout the British occupation zone. One final cemetery, far away, in the Bavarian village of Dürnbach, was chosen mainly for RAF crews shot down on missions over southern Germany (see Map 1). Although the IWGC had not chosen the thirteen locations, its members seemed happy enough with the sites, acknowledging that 'good taste [had] been displayed' in making the selection.[14]

The IWGC's leadership may have been content with the plans to concentrate the dead, but the same cannot be said for the bereaved themselves, who were left largely in the dark. In the wake of the Second World War, neither the War Office nor the IWGC were in any rush to inform relatives about their planned military cemeteries, mainly out of a fear of complaints. This approach again left families scrambling around for scraps of information about the future of their loved ones' graves in Germany. The volume of enquiries 'on the subject of graves concentration' landing in the Air Ministry's in-tray was so large that the ministry struggled to hide its irritation with the whole process. 'Some of the questions that reach us', the Air Ministry moaned, are: ' "will isolated graves in Germany be concentrated into local churchyards or war cemeteries?" – "will graves in enemy countries be concentrated into an allied or neutral country?" ', and the list went on.[15]

The Air Ministry had answers to these questions of course, but an insistence on secrecy meant that it was in no position to make the cemetery plans public. There was good reason for this surreptitious approach, at least in the minds of the authorities. Back in the 1920s, the IWGC had learnt the perils of troublesome relatives the hard way. Generally, the commission had no qualms in brushing away enquiries that came its way, but in the case of Norman Robertson, who was buried in Hanover, it ended up revealing far more than it had perhaps intended. Determined to stop Robertson's brother from erecting a private headstone, the IWGC needed to convince him of the fallacy behind his plans. Even though they feared he 'may strongly object to the removal', the IWGC finally admitted outright that his brother's body was going to be moved to another cemetery. Robertson was enraged at the news. 'The proposal is prima facie repugnant to me,' he fumed.[16]

Robertson was not alone in bemoaning the official concentration plans. It was the lack of firm information that proved most unsettling. In summer 1946, an Oxfordshire mother discovered that her son's remains were to be exhumed and moved to a new military cemetery somewhere in Germany. One year later, there was still no firm news and no longer any certainty that his body would be moved. 'Is it beyond the power of whoever is the responsible authority to spare time to make some decision about the graves of English service men in Germany?' she asked.[17] Although this mother, like most of the bereaved, had no sight of it, there was actually a plan in place. By the early 1920s, and by 1946 at the latest, the British had decided not only that the dead were to be concentrated into military cemeteries in Germany, but also where these were to be located. Moving the bodies to the new sites and, perhaps more importantly, informing relatives of their plans, however, took much longer.

Perceiving Difference

The British approach to their war graves had been one of pragmatism. They took full control of their dead, even though, under the terms of the Treaty of Versailles, they were entitled to leave the bodies where they lay in German hands. But even the IWGC baulked at the thought of trying to sell this policy to the newly bereaved. The Germans, meanwhile, made their own very different choices. For once, the government became a firm enthusiast for the Treaty of Versailles, not of course because of the restrictions it placed on them, but rather because of the financial demands it made on the Allies, who, according to the agreement, had to pay for the upkeep of the German graves on their territory. 'We must abide by the Peace Treaty,' the German government repeated ad nauseam whenever the Allies tried to wriggle out of their obligations.[18] There might have been a financial logic to the Germans' approach, but it did have the effect of opening a visual divide. While the IWGC began to plan new military cemeteries, the German bodies remained scattered. With such a difference in approach, the charge of neglect quickly surfaced.

The impression that the German war graves had somehow been left behind proved very hard to shake, even though local communities across Britain often played a role in their maintenance. In Kent, for example, one family took on the care of the graves of two German airmen whose Gotha bomber had crashed on their land in 1918. Having had a son in the British air force, the family had particular 'sympathy with the German mothers whose boys' died in their midst.[19] Even when there were no willing custodians nearby, the IWGC took its responsibilities seriously, agreeing maintenance payments with local communities and then, in 1923, commencing a programme to erect a permanent marker over each grave. These were not conventional headstones as such, but rather German-designed concrete blocks that lay low to the ground; a raised face contained space for basic biographical details (see image 19).

19. During the 1920s, the IWGC gradually installed concrete grave markers, known as ZAK stones, over the German war graves in the United Kingdom. Sitting face up against the elements, however, meant that the inscriptions weathered very quickly.

Replacing the old wooden grave markers with these new concrete slabs, known as ZAK stones, got off to a bad start when some local communities complained about the move. The objection of a Catholic priest from the Cumbrian village of Frizington probably came as the greatest surprise. He pointed out that the German graves in the Catholic cemetery already had crosses that were 'really quite nice' and therefore he saw no need for new stones of what he called a 'pagan design'. No sooner had the IWGC resolved the Frizington issue by agreeing to erect one-off standing stone crosses than new problems emerged with the ZAK stones, which were being manufactured in Germany at IWGC expense.[20] While this arrangement ensured there was a material connection between the dead and the living back in Germany, it did increase the margin for error, with stones often arriving cracked, broken or wrongly inscribed. One consignment was delivered to Staffordshire, for example, with sixteen of the new stones already smashed. Much to the German manufacturer's annoyance, the IWGC informed them that this was due to 'insufficient packaging', and suggested they simply remake the order.[21]

Manufacturing faults and delivery problems prolonged the procurement programme by years, leaving the actual graves in a very unfinished state. This was something that relatives immediately noticed when they travelled across from Germany to visit the graves. Rather than finding neat new headstones in place, what often greeted them were the original wooden crosses, which by the mid-1920s were often in rather a sorry state. The churchyard of the twelfth-century church of St Mary Magdalene in Great Burstead, Essex, which contained the graves of a Zeppelin crew downed in 1916, became something of a *cause célèbre* for the Germans. In spring 1927, the father of the Zeppelin's commander, retired General Major Peterson, made his way to Essex to view his son's grave and was upset at the scene that greeted him. The paint was flaking off the original wooden grave markers, the ground over the graves was bare and an overgrown hedge, badly in need of a good prune, provided the backdrop (see image 20). Incensed at what he saw, Peterson stormed off to the German Foreign Office when he arrived home and demanded immediate improvements, threatening to go public with his complaints if the situation was not resolved.[22]

Later that year, the German press picked up on the story, but whether this was Peterson's doing or not is unclear. One extreme conservative newspaper drew a rather depressing picture of the final resting place of 'our German heroes' in Great Burstead for its readers.[23] They are 'right up against the hedge of an isolated and rundown part of the churchyard', the writer explained. 'Two rotten wooden crosses with barely legible inscriptions scarcely protrude above the high grass and weeds.' Fortunately for the German Foreign Office, the article chose to place most of the blame for the state of the Zeppelin graves on British, rather than German, failings. 'Soon the English will have achieved what they seem to want,' it proffered, 'which is for the Zeppelin graves to disappear.' The article did have one rather pointed suggestion for the German government, however. Given that the British government was obliged

20. The original wooden crosses marking the Zeppelin graves in Great Burstead, Suffolk. A decade after the Zeppelin's downing, the paint was peeling and the markers were already showing signs of decay.

to care for the German graves under the terms of Versailles, 'should it not be forced to do so?'[24]

The staff of the German embassy in London had every sympathy with this view, but getting the IWGC to complete the promised renovations proved something of a struggle. Joint visits to the graves in Great Burstead had little effect, while talk of improvements came and went. It got to the point where the embassy even considered escalating the matter by issuing a formal diplomatic note, but in the end it was forced to accept that the IWGC was probably working as fast as it could. 'Any further pressure from our side will only accelerate the British pace of work by a tiny degree,' it concluded.[25] Finally, in spring 1928, almost twelve years after the Zeppelin crew had first ended up in Great Burstead, the finished cemetery was rededicated as British and German officials looked on. Both sides expressed their satisfaction with the result. The British took comfort from the fact that the new grave markers listed the individual names of each crew member, replacing the original and much vaguer inscription of '21 Unknown German Airmen'. The Germans, meanwhile, emphasised that the new stone was 'from Germany', although conveniently omitting to mention that the IWGC had actually paid for the memorial.[26]

The problem of Great Burstead was eventually resolved, with even Peterson giving his begrudging approval, but this was only one of more than 235 cemeteries with German graves that the IWGC had to bring up to standard.[27] Just keeping an eye on the state of these separate sites was an enormous task for Germany's diplomatic staff in Britain. The German consul in Liverpool calculated that it would take him eighty-two days just to visit all of the different German gravesites in the north-west of the country, a task that would involve a drive of more than a thousand miles.[28] The German vice-consul in Lowestoft set himself a slightly less ambitious brief, limiting his visit to five of the largest cemeteries in his region, but this still involved 110 miles of motoring in a single day. 'We started at 10.30.am and completed at 6.30.pm,' he reported. The picture he discovered from his tour through rural England was rather mixed. While the graves were generally 'tidy and neat', there was still some maintenance work to be done to renew loose posts, rotten grave markers and faded inscriptions.[29]

For the German consular officials, the greatest frustration was that the concrete headstones, which had only started to be installed in the mid-1920s, were already failing. In Great Burstead, the new Zeppelin grave markers had been in place for less than four years when the vicar reported that most of the inscriptions were 'scarcely decipherable'. This was not an isolated problem. Throughout the country, local custodians experienced something similar. The low-standing ZAK stones proved entirely unsuitable for a damp climate, as the local council in Sutton, Surrey, explained. 'The 88 memorials and five wooden crosses are in a bad condition,' the council wrote. 'The inscriptions are almost illegible owing to [. . .] a raised moulding on the memorials which holds the wet and causes a green stain.' This was the last thing that the German authorities wanted to hear. After cajoling the IWGC into installing its ZAK stones across the country to ensure the war dead were not forgotten, the opposite had occurred. They were left with thousands of slimy, waterlogged concrete slabs, from which even the names of the deceased had started to fade.[30]

The ongoing problems with the German war graves in Britain during the years of the Weimar Republic were never just about maintenance. For the most part, the German graves were well cared for. Even the consular staff who visited the various graves were quick to admit this. Local custodians cut grass, pulled out weeds and kept the sites in a respectable condition, despite the ZAK stones themselves deteriorating rapidly.[31] But on its own, this always seemed somewhat inadequate. When the isolated and scattered German graves were compared to the IWGC's grand military cemeteries in Germany, then the treatment of the German war dead suddenly appeared to fall far short. This was a point that Germans were only too quick to note. 'I only hope that the British people have done the same for the German dead,' exclaimed one local resident visiting the British war graves in Hamburg.[32] Without concentrating the German graves in Britain into larger military cemeteries, bridging this perceived gap in the standard of care was always going to be a difficult task.

Fascists to the Fore

There was no group in Germany more convinced of the injustice of interwar remembrance than the National Socialists. Born out of the turmoil of war, defeat and revolution, the Nazis portrayed themselves as the 'political embodiment of the "front spirit"'.[33] When Adolf Hitler was appointed to the German chancellorship in January 1933, he and his acolytes placed the memory of the war at the very centre of their new dictatorship. For the Nazis, reversing the humiliating defeat of 1918, which had cast such a shadow over the Weimar Republic, was merely a springboard for conquest and the creation of a new racial empire. While the German war dead lying in British soil were of little real significance for the regime, their presence nonetheless provided the Nazis with some leverage in its dealings with the British. The small Nazi movement in Britain, never numbering much more than 550, for example, always took a keen interest in the German graves from the First World War, rushing in to protest at any hint of neglect.[34]

The people of Potters Bar were the first to experience the Nazis' obsession with the war dead and the spectacle of remembrance. Easily accessible from London, while also containing the graves of the crew of two airships shot down in 1916, the town had for many years attracted German visitors. A very different type of visitor, though, arrived in 1932. During the annual remembrance service, a Nazi supporter stood up and proceeded to make an unsolicited speech.[35] But this was just a light appetiser for what was to come. In subsequent years, the annual service at the small cemetery of St Mary's was invariably packed with crowds of mainly German guests who had travelled up from the capital to honour the Zeppelin dead. The German ambassador, Leopold von Hoesch, and later his successor, Joachim von Ribbentrop, joined the service, along with uniformed members of the German military. At the end of proceedings, all in attendance raised their hands to give the Nazi salute, turning this little part of Hertfordshire into a stage for something akin to a fascist rally (see image 21).

Back in Germany, the press was quick to capitalise on events in Potters Bar, regaling their readers with photographs of enthusiastic crowds standing amidst the Zeppelin graves in Middlesex. Their point was a simple one. The Nazi regime was reversing years of apparent neglect and finally giving the German war graves in Britain the respect they deserved.[36] This narrative of honouring Germany's supposedly forgotten war dead reared its head repeatedly through the 1930s. In March 1934, at around the same time as the ceremonies were taking place in Potters Bar, a fresh-faced young German lecturer arrived in Manchester, hoping to build his academic career. Hans Galinsky was not only a dedicated literary scholar but also a committed member of the Nazi party, having already apprised English audiences of the need to 'expel all the Jews' from Germany 'as undesirable aliens'.[37] In Manchester, he found a different outlet for his Nazi ideology, latching on to the state of the 155 POW graves in the city's Southern Cemetery. Raising a – by

21. The crews of two German airships, who had been killed in raids over southern England, were buried in Potters Bar. After Adolf Hitler's rise to power, the small cemetery became the focal point for Nazi supporters in Britain, who gathered in the front of the graves to hold their annual remembrance service.

now – familiar litany of complaints, he bemoaned the 'miserable' state of the graves that left him 'embarrassed to be a German'.[38]

In righting this perceived wrong, Galinsky also saw an opportunity to rally support for the Nazi cause. If the war graves were tidied up, he explained confidently, the city's 'older German community' would come to realise that 'we younger ones will care for our [German] war dead'. The only problem with Galinsky's plan was that the German embassy saw the situation very differently and proved reluctant to spend money on the graves, pointing out that under the Treaty of Versailles, this was in fact the IWGC's responsibility. Undeterred, Galinsky reined in his ambition somewhat and decided to restore just one of the cemetery's 155 German graves, so that there was 'at least [. . .] one reasonably decent grave'.[39] The lucky person chosen was Otto Frinke, who in October

1914 had been the first enemy soldier to be buried in Manchester. Galinsky and his acolytes symbolically cleaned Frinke's gravestone in time for the Nazis' annual Heroes' Memorial Day (*Heldengedenktag*) in March 1935.[40] On a dull spring day, forty-five people, including a small contingent from the British Toc-H Christian movement, gathered around Frinke's grave. Ever the optimist, Galinsky declared the service to be a complete success, as the city's German 'community was starting to come together'.[41]

Galinsky had arrived in Manchester with a burst of energy, but he soon departed for greater things in Berlin, a more senior lectureship and a new role in the party. His legacy in Manchester – beautifying a single grave and holding a small service – may have been extremely modest, but these actions represented just one tiny part of a renewed focus on the German war dead in Britain. Regional Nazi groups in the Midlands and Yorkshire followed the lead of Manchester and Potters Bar and staged their own ceremonies.[42]

While these small services tended to get picked up in the local press, it was larger set-piece events that really helped to bring the German war dead to the attention of the British public. The most spectacular act of remembrance occurred over the Yorkshire Dales in 1936. The giant airship *Hindenburg*, a symbol of the apparent dynamism of the new Nazi Germany, had been on a transatlantic run when it suddenly slowed down over the Yorkshire town of Keighley and lost altitude. Hearing the quiet whirr of the engines, people 'rushed into the streets and gazed heavenwards' to catch a glimpse of the 'silver hull and [. . .] the scarlet swastikas of her tail'. A small parcel was then thrown out to the crowd below; the neat package contained carnations, a silver cross and a hand-written note. The scrawled message asked the finder to place the objects 'on the grave of my dear brother, Lieutenant Franz Schulte', who had died in March 1919 as a POW in Skipton.[43] The British press lapped up the sentimental story of wartime death, explaining how the two boys who had found the parcel immediately travelled to Morton Cemetery, where they placed the flowers on Schulte's grave as a small 'tribute from brother to brother'.[44]

Schulte's elaborate stunt over Yorkshire, and local Nazi groups' new remembrance ceremonies, all helped to shine a spotlight on the German war dead. Unfortunately, what this illuminated was a rather gloomy picture. Local custodians and the IWGC were struggling to keep on top of the maintenance. Even the graves in Manchester's Southern Cemetery were reportedly 'wild and uncared for' once Galinksy's interest had waned. The increasingly weathered ZAK stones, not just in Manchester but in use throughout the country, only added to this picture of decay. 'In a few years' time,' the German embassy feared, 'it will scarcely be possible to make out any of the existing gravestones.'[45] None of this passed the public by either. 'Dear Herr Hitler,' wrote one young British girl. 'Last Sunday my Mother and Father and I went to Great Burstead and saw the graves where twentytowtwo Germans lie.' She helpfully wrote to the embassy to tell them that the graves were 'covered with weeds and looked very dull'. She thought they 'might like to know this'.[46]

This was really the last thing that the embassy staff wanted to hear. They had already been ground down by constant complaints from Nazi party members in Britain who were threatening to lodge formal complaints about the graves with the Nazi hierarchy back in Germany.[47] But it was the IWGC that had the most to lose. The decision to concentrate the British dead in Germany had been fine within the framework of the democratic Weimar Republic, but after Hitler's ascent to the Chancellorship, the stark disparities between the British and German dead became something of a problem. The Nazis had only been in power a few months when Ware reported that 'proper respect was not being paid to the Commission's cemeteries in Germany'. Graves were being vandalised and daubed with graffiti, while in its Stahnsdorf burial ground by Berlin, the wrong type of visitor scrawled swastikas in the margins of the IWGC's cemetery book. Much of this vandalism likely stemmed from the SA (Sturmabteilung – Brownshirts), who had started their own wave of violence after Hitler's rise to power. Ware's concern, though, was not to track down the perpetrators, but rather to ensure the long-term future of the British graves, which, because of his earlier choices, were now stranded in the heart of Nazi Germany.[48]

The solution that Ware hit upon was to establish a committee with 'Germans of the right type', meaning more conservative figures, to discuss the care of the war graves. By late 1935, the basis of his plan had evolved into an Anglo-German-French Mixed Committee that would meet annually in one of the three capitals. The membership included diplomatic staff as well as representatives from the IWGC and the VDK, whose leaders Ware must have viewed as 'the right type' of Germans. A lot of the committee's time was spent performing diplomatic niceties, visiting each other's graves, attending formal dinners and even enjoying a reception at Buckingham Palace.[49] The committee's most public set-piece was supposed to be a coordinated wreath-laying at the Cenotaph in Whitehall. However, when the delegates arrived in London, the French expressed their unease at publicly standing alongside the Germans. Given the ostentatious nature of the German wreath, a mixture of swastikas, lilies and laurels, this was perhaps understandable (see image 22). To get around the problem, the Germans laid their wreath first, then the French laid theirs fifteen minutes later, once the German delegation had left the scene. Ware still

22. General Hans von Seeckt in the centre and Fabian Ware to his right heading up a German delegation to the Cenotaph in June 1936. The unlikely group were together in London for the first meeting of the Anglo-German-French Mixed Committee.

managed to deem this a success, celebrating the French and German 'national colours [. . .] appearing side by side for the first time', even if the people themselves refused to appear together in public.[50]

The real significance of the wreaths adorning the Cenotaph was not so much French obstinacy, but rather that Ware and the IWGC seemed willing to negotiate with their opposite numbers in Germany on an equal footing. If they were now partners in the care of the war dead, then the IWGC had little option but to acknowledge German complaints about the apparent neglect of its war dead in Britain. After the first meeting of the committee, Ware sent off the IWGC's director of records, Henry Chettle, on a ten-day road trip around Britain with three of the German delegates as passengers. The four men criss-crossed the country, stopping off at different cemeteries to view the German graves; by all accounts, they must have hit it off. Once home, Chettle, who was known to be 'quite simply, a "character"', even sent his travelling companions a 'marked road map' as a 'small memento' of their many hours in the car together.[51] Both sides, though, drew very different conclusions from their trip. The IWGC thought that the VDK was only going to submit recommendations for the 'improvement of the general appearance of the graves', while the German delegates left the tour more convinced than ever that their dead needed to be concentrated into larger military cemeteries, akin to the IWGC's.[52]

Once their representatives had returned to Germany, the VDK wasted no time in drawing up concrete plans for a series of new military cemeteries across Britain. Based on the knowledge gleaned from their road trip with Chettle, they eventually settled on three potential sites. The first of these, earmarked for Potters Bar where the crews of two downed airships were already buried, was to become the final resting place for all those killed in aerial combat. For the naval dead, a second site on the cliffs near Saltburn-by-the-Sea, which had panoramic views over the North Sea, was to be purchased. Finally, some of the scattered German POWs were to be brought together into a much-extended version of the existing Park Hall Cemetery, near Oswestry in Shropshire (Map 2). Besides these new or expanded cemeteries, the VDK envisaged leaving some graves in situ, where circumstances allowed. The VDK could see little reason to abandon the Stobs camp burial ground, for example, which, as they pointed out, enjoyed a 'magnificent situation' in the Scottish borders.[53]

If the IWGC had any concerns at the thought of Nazi Germany establishing four military cemeteries in the heart of the British countryside, it kept these to itself. Instead, it approved the VDK's plans, so long as the 'whole costs of [. . .] acquisition' were met by the VDK. With the finance settled, Chettle then revisited the sites and started negotiations with local farmers for the land.[54] The IWGC's willingness to go along with the German plans was partly borne out of fear. As the British war graves remained in a precarious position in Nazi Germany, providing concessions to the VDK appeared to offer the best form of defence. But personal relationships also shaped the IWGC's response. After cosy drives around Britain, shared visits to war cemeteries and annual meetings of the Anglo-German-French Committee, members of the IWGC and VDK had actually struck up firm friendships. 'A band of friends' is how Frank Sillar, the IWGC's chief of finance, labelled relations. Leaning heavily on these personal contacts, Sillar somewhat cheekily arranged for his wife, a professional violinist, to play on German radio during a visit to Berlin in late 1938, shortly after the Nazis' November pogrom. 'We have returned to London with the happiest memories of German hospitality,' Sillar wrote, seemingly oblivious to the ongoing horrors being perpetrated against Germany's Jewish communities.[55]

However, while the IWGC seemed content with the VDK's concentration plans, not everyone was quite so pleased. In Potters Bar, there was some concern about the possibility of increased road traffic. During the 1937 remembrance ceremony, led by the then German ambassador, Joachim von Ribbentrop, there had already been problems with cars 'parked either off the highway or in quiet side streets'. Giving a foretaste of Britain's obsession with cars and motoring, the obvious concern was that a larger cemetery would result in more visitors and more parking problems.[56] What finally ended the German cemetery plans was not the problem of the automobile, but rather the Home Office's very real fear that the proposed sites could be used for spying. The Metropolitan Police objected to the expansion of Potters Bar 'from a point of view of national security', while their colleagues in Yorkshire reached a similar conclusion regarding the site near Saltburn, which should 'not be sold or handed over to any foreign power', they declared.[57] Before either the VDK or IWGC had had a chance to revise their plans, the outbreak of a second world war ended them for good.

Normalising Death

In 1947, by which time another generation of German military and civilians had been interred in British soil, the question of the enemy dead returned to the table, albeit in a rather limited fashion. Two policemen were called to the site of a former POW camp near Saunton in Devon, where the British army had come across a strange headstone hidden away in the wasteland dedicated to someone called 'Astrid von Eckernförde'. The two policemen had tentatively started digging, no doubt worried about what lay beneath, when their shovels hit upon the remains of a dog 'of the lurcher type' that had been wrapped in a blanket and 'enclosed in a wicker basket'. After discovering to their relief that this had probably been a POW's pet, they then had to dispose of the body elsewhere.[58] For the next two decades, this was about the extent of efforts to concentrate the German war dead. Yet, throughout this period, the VDK's desire to move its graves into a larger cemetery remained undiminished; it was just that the task they faced had grown considerably since they had devised their original concentration scheme in the late 1930s.

As an organisation, the VDK was initially in no position to reactivate its plans for the German war dead scattered throughout Britain. Siegfried Emmo Eulen, the driving force behind the interwar VDK, had been killed fighting near the Dutch border in 1945, while bombing raids had largely laid its Berlin headquarters to waste. Above all, though, any moral authority that the VDK may have once enjoyed had been tarnished through its close association to the Nazi regime. Although it retained some independence and never became a formal Nazi organisation during the Third Reich, its leadership threw themselves behind the regime, willingly cleansing the organisation of 'racially' or politically 'unwanted' members and promoting the Nazis' policies at every opportunity.[59] Yet, the VDK never let these awkward facts stand in its way. After the defeat of Hitler's Germany, it quickly brushed itself down, restarted its activities initially in the British occupation zone, before spreading out across the western side of Germany. By 1948, the VDK was ready to announce publicly that, after the 'most difficult time', it was back and ready to resume its important work of caring for the war dead.[60]

The reformed VDK pushed on with its activities with gusto. With the support of Konrad Adenauer's government, it took an increasingly formal role in the West, although never in the GDR, where its activities were banned.[61] Through the 1950s, the VDK landscaped existing cemeteries and also started to move scattered graves from the most recent conflict into larger sites in North Africa and Southern Europe.[62] While this work was all very familiar, it did come with the added benefit of institutional and national rehabilitation. By concentrating the dead and therefore replicating what other 'West European states [had] generally already done with their dead', the VDK hoped to reveal a different side of Germany.[63] The West has become 'used to judging the German people solely by the atrocity reports about the concentration camps', the VDK complained internally. It hoped that the sight of lovingly tended German cemeteries would make people realise that their criticism was 'wrong and unfair'. In short, then, the VDK believed that the new military cemeteries would help to cleanse the German war dead, turning them into ordinary soldiers who had done nothing more than to lose their lives fighting in a very ordinary conflict.[64]

If the VDK was going to demonstrate how honourably the Germans, in the western half of the country at least, dealt with their dead, then it also needed to create 'showcase cemeteries' in Britain.[65] Thousands of scattered graves from the two world wars hardly made the right impression on visitors. And with the number of German graves more than doubling after the most recent conflict, it was no longer possible to dust off the old interwar plans for four concentration cemeteries. What was required instead was a brand-new plan to match the VDK's post-war ambitions. The VDK's new General Secretary, Otto Margraf, a tall, wiry figure with slicked-back hair, was up for the challenge. Although Margraf had been a key figure in the VDK for years, it was only during the Second World War that he cut his teeth on the diplomatic stage, when he represented Nazi Germany in international negotiations. In trying to convince the IWGC of the need for a German military cemetery in

Britain, Margraf had to manoeuvre around a very different set of issues. What he quickly discovered was that the British had considerable 'unease' at the thought of placing a war cemetery designed 'according to German principles' on their territory.[66]

In an attempt to force the issue, Margraf went back to the VDK's earlier playbook and tried to make the case that the German graves had been unfairly neglected. The grave markers are 'now decaying, making a very bad impression', which he traced back to the 'IWGC's earlier approach' to the German dead.[67] Margraf drew what he considered to be the winning argument from these cases. 'The English', he sweepingly observed, 'do not understand how to care for graves in the way that this is generally performed in Germany.'[68] Given that he was trying to get the British to support his cause, criticising the IWGC's approach to maintenance might not have been the most sensible negotiating technique. Even though it acknowledged that there were occasionally German graves that needed more upkeep, the IWGC had always baulked at any criticism. When one West Berlin newspaper had previously had the temerity to criticise its work, the IWGC had replied with photographs and a list of evidence to prove categorically that it gave 'equal treatment' to the German graves 'in this country'.[69]

Deep down, Margraf must have known that claiming British neglect as a pretext for concentrating the German war dead did not entirely stack up. Stories from state officials, families and the casual visitor all confirmed that the German graves were generally in good order. 'Model Care' was the diagnosis of the West German daily, *Die Welt*. 'Surely not one of the other wartime opponents has [. . .] given the German military graves such attention as the British.'[70] Even the VDK was happy to repeat such stories when they suited its new post-war mantra of international harmony and cooperation. Its monthly newsletter was sprinkled with anecdotes about carefully tended German graves in Sheepstor on Dartmoor or Wick in Caithness.[71]

One of the most remarkable reports, however, came from Maldon in Essex. In 1956, Paul Ultsch, a businessman from Franconia, arrived in Maldon to visit the grave of his brother, Gottfried. Not only did he discover a well-tended plot but also an extremely generous local population. One family put Ultsch up in their house, providing him with home-cooked meals and a warm room for the duration of his stay. 'A hotel was out of the question,' the family told him. 'Besides he could stay as long as he liked.' Ultsch's visits to his brother's grave in Maldon Cemetery also brought him into repeated conversation with the locals. The parish priest explained how the congregation prayed for all the war dead, friend and enemy alike; another person insisted he come along to the next British Legion meeting, while a veteran of the Great War stopped to tell him that 'we are all brothers [now]'.[72]

The VDK basked in the warm glow of Ultsch's visit to Maldon, celebrating it as a 'bridge of friendship'. But this did very little for Margraf's claims of neglect. It was clear, therefore, that if the VDK was going to make a convincing case for concentration, then it needed to employ a different line of argument. Finance in the end proved something of an easier sell. The British had long bemoaned the arrangements, stemming from the Treaty of Versailles but continuing into the 1950s, that saw the IWGC paying £20,000 each year on the maintenance of German graves and another £40,000 on its own cemeteries in Germany. 'There was some inequality in the existing system,' the IWGC's then director general pointed out somewhat acerbically to Margraf.[73] The obvious solution to this problem, and one that Margraf was only too keen to push, was for the Germans to create a new military cemetery in Britain at their own expense.

Having previously congratulated themselves on having an 'extraordinarily favourable' arrangement with the IWGC, the West German authorities were certainly not thrilled at the thought of picking up the costs of the German war graves.[74] Nonetheless, the VDK grudgingly acknowledged that, to reach an agreement, it would have to compromise on the thorny issue of finance. This concession cleared the path to the 1959 war graves treaty that Profumo and Ritter signed off in Whitehall. Both sides could find something to applaud in the final deal. For the Germans, there was the fact that, after four decades, they finally had permission to concentrate their dead from across the United Kingdom, the Isle of Man and the Channel Islands. The IWGC, meanwhile, was equally pleased with the promise of an annual payment of £20,000 from the West Germans and agreement that any enemy graves within existing IWGC plots 'shall not be removed'.[75]

The one major omission in the agreement was where exactly the German dead were going to be moved to. All that appeared in the text was that the bodies could be transferred to a 'German war cemetery which has yet to be created'. Although the agreement was silent on the precise location, both parties already had a site in mind. In 1953, Margraf had visited the IWGC's Cannock Chase Cemetery, which contained the graves of British, New Zealand and German soldiers. He seemed pleasantly surprised by what he discovered. 'In its setting and in its design, this cemetery is so beautiful,' he gushed. From that point on, Margraf was convinced that Cannock Chase was the best location to move more, if not all, of the German dead.[76]

Yet, to fulfil this ambition, there was still the small issue of acquiring land either for a new cemetery or for extending the existing IWGC one. Fortune, though, was on Margraf's side. A few years after his initial visit, the Earl of Lichfield, whose family controlled great swathes of Cannock Chase, decided to donate 2,000 acres to Staffordshire County Council. This was not purely an act of altruism, it was also a way for the ageing earl to dispose of land that was subject to increasing complaints about 'unauthorised trading, litter and debris, motor-cycle trials, indiscriminate car parking, fairs and gypsy encampments'.[77] Regardless of motive, once the land was in the council's hands, it could then decide its future fate. Thus, when the IWGC made an approach about land for a German military cemetery, the council was able to set aside 5 acres for this purpose, although it did seek the Earl of Lichfield's approval before signing it away.[78]

Almost forty years after the British had first drawn up plans to concentrate its dead of the Great War into four new military cemeteries in Germany, the Germans, led by the VDK, finally followed suit in Britain. It was never the case that the German war dead had been wilfully ignored in the intervening period. On a basic level, the IWGC had a remit to maintain the graves. But beyond this, local communities often cared for them personally, as the VDK itself acknowledged, and were said to be 'even proud of the[ir] German graves'.[79] The issue instead was simply one of difference. Because the German war dead remained scattered, it was easy, as the Nazis demonstrated so effectively, to claim neglect. After the Second World War, when the British again moved swiftly to plan new war cemeteries in Germany, the VDK was even more desperate to follow in their footsteps. By creating its own military burial ground in Britain, it hoped to return Germany to the international fold. Once the dead had been concentrated, they would then no longer be participants in a racist and genocidal war, but would instead become just another group of military casualties common to all 'cultural nations', to which – by implication – the West Germans belonged.[80]

7

EXHUMING

One British gravedigger, who spent time exhuming the German war graves in the early 1960s, later spoke about the difficulties and dangers of the job. When excavating communal graves that could be 'twenty feet, if not more' deep, he remembered, there was always 'the awful business of water creeping in'. With muddy water dripping all the way down to the bottom of the open grave, he and his fellow gravediggers were forever 'worried about the sides falling in', which would have left them entombed together with the war dead.[1] This was clearly grim, gruelling and dangerous work. Yet, despite the risks, the same procedure was repeated time and again. Between April 1962 and May 1963, the VDK exhumed almost 5,000 bodies from across Britain. The British proved even more productive in this task. During the early 1920s, they moved some 6,500 dead within Germany and in the wake of the Second World War a further 26,500 bodies. In all three cases, these were immense operations, costing considerable time, labour and money.

Neither the British nor the Germans were strangers to such large-scale exhumation operations. On the former Western Front, the IWGC had reburied over 200,000 bodies by September 1921, while the VDK had already moved large numbers of the German dead within Southern and Central Europe during the 1950s.[2] These previous operations had been akin to a tidying exercise. Where human remains lay festering in muddy trenches or hastily dug graves, as was the case in France and Belgium, it was essential to move corpses not only for hygiene reasons, but also out of respect to the dead and to the bereaved. There was a similar urgency to operations in the late 1940s, with the British and other Allies desperately hunting out the strewn remains of their dead. However, the situation for the British in interwar Germany and for the VDK working in 1960s Britain was very different. For the most part, the dead already had a well-tended grave. The massive reburial exercises that the two countries pursued, therefore, amounted to moving a body from one marked grave to a new marked grave somewhere else in the same country.

As far as the two war graves commissions were concerned, the remains of their dead scattered on enemy territory were part of a massive jigsaw puzzle just waiting to be put back together in new national cemeteries. In the IWGC's view, expending vast amounts of energy on completing this puzzle was a matter of honour, ensuring that the graves would be 'maintained in perpetuity in British hands'.[3] The West Germans approached this exercise from a very similar starting point, albeit with the aim of returning themselves to the international stage. They too maintained that the war dead needed to be exhumed and reburied into large military cemeteries, such as Cannock Chase, for protection and out of respect. It is only 'in the military cemeteries', the VDK argued, 'where our war dead have an "eternal burial right"', which was only partly true, as a 1922 law had already guaranteed the permanence of all war graves.[4]

Regardless, exhuming a body is always a disruptive process. The corpse has to be disentangled legally from its existing owners and physically from its current location. While compliance with the legal procedures can be completed in advance from the comfort of an office, which was also what happened in these cases, the physical disinterment of the body of course has to happen on site.[5] As became quickly clear from the British and German exhumations, no matter how carefully they worked, the gravediggers always disturbed the quiet of the cemetery and left traces of their presence long after they had departed. Workers piled in, sometimes with machines, holes were dug, mounds of soil stacked up and previously manicured ground often ended up scattered with mud. Unsurprisingly, the sight of scars gouged into the landscape never went down particularly well with local communities. Exhuming the dead, therefore, was never just a case of reopening graves, it also reopened old wounds between the former foes that had slowly started to heal in the post-war world.

Dirty Work

In a letter to *The Times* in July 1947, Major-General Edgeworth-Johnstone from the War Office stressed the care and dedication of the British exhumation teams operating in Germany. 'Units carrying out these sad tasks have set themselves a high standard,' he confirmed, before praising the 'devotion and respect' that the British workers had for the dead.[6] The British and German war graves commissions made very similar points in their own public pronouncements. The VDK pointed out that the task of removing the bodies is always carefully carried out by 'a team of experts', while the IWGC explained that its workers 'have received a thorough training'.[7] This general line of argument helped to cloak the general grimness of the task in sterile, scientific terms. It also gave the impression to anxious relatives that if the exhumations were to be carried out properly and with due reverence to the dead, then only properly trained experts should be employed.

The RAF personnel working for the MRES, on a mission to hunt out missing airmen in post-war Europe, certainly appeared to possess all the requisite qualities that the role demanded. Before commencing their task, the MRES members received full training in search techniques from military personnel. Once on the ground, they worked in a meticulous fashion to locate and identify the bodies of aircrew that had been lost over wartime Europe, before handing over the remains to the Army Graves Service that completed the final interments. Many of the MRES members were veterans of the recent war, often they had even been involved in bombing raids over the very towns in which they were now working. Flight Lieutenant C.A. Mitchell, who served with the MRES in post-war Germany, noted that this had been a deliberate recruitment choice. 'By virtue of their training and operational experience', he later reflected, veterans of the air war 'could identify with their fallen comrades'.[8]

This same principle had guided the recruitment of the other exhumation teams too. When the IWGC started its mass exhumations in interwar Germany, it consciously sought out members of the British Legion already living in the country to perform the work. 'All whom we employ [in the exhumations] will be members of the Legion,' the IWGC's supervisor on the ground assured his superiors back in London.[9] There was also a more practical reason for this approach. By employing British citizens resident in Germany, the IWGC had a bilingual workforce at its disposal, which immediately resolved any potential communication problems. This same thought had occurred to the VDK in the 1960s, which is why they initially planned to recruit former German POWs who had stayed in Britain after the war to do the digging.[10]

However, these dreams of employing only workers from the same country as the dead evaporated fairly quickly. The VDK had to face this reality long before it had even put a spade in the ground. It turned out that German war veterans who had built a new life in Britain had little desire to put on their boots and start digging up bodies, even if they were those of former comrades who had died several decades earlier. For the British digging away in the ruins of recently defeated Nazi Germany, labour difficulties came from the continual pressure to complete operations as quickly as possible. Lieutenant Colonel Stott, who headed up the army's exhumation work in north-west Europe, spent much of his time repeatedly begging for more men, pointing out that progress 'depends upon the extend [sic] to which Units of the Graves Service' are used.[11] Although his demands eventually bore fruit and more units were put at his disposal, there was a trade-off. The War Office decided having more workers meant that Stott could complete his operations a full year earlier, by summer 1947.[12]

The need to expedite the exhumation operations, combined with the difficulties in recruiting workers, left both the British and Germans scrambling around for alternatives. The most obvious solution was to ask the former enemy to exhume the dead, but this of course raised the awkward question of whether the gravediggers might have killed the person they were exhuming in the first place. To circumnavigate this problem, both sides insisted that foreign workers would do nothing more than dig, although even then, as the British admitted, 'it is not considered policy to publicise this'.[13] Even in their internal reporting on their work in 1920s Cologne, the IWGC was keen to stress that the 'Germans were not allowed to handle the remains'.[14] Some twenty years later, the British followed a very similar approach when exhuming their dead from the ruins of Nazi Germany. Upon arriving to extricate war casualties, they instructed local workers to do the digging. Following earlier precedent, the British stated clearly that German labourers were only permitted to dig 'to within 1 inch of the bodies'.[15] Soldiers, it seems, remained the property of the nation even in death.

To the chagrin of the Germans, however, the British often departed not only with their corpses, but also without paying their bills. In Braunschweig, the British had accrued a debt of 822.75 Reichsmark for local labour, while in Wiesbaden the city authorities demanded 1,855 Reichsmark from the British military after providing them with local gravediggers.[16] Despite repeated requests, the bills went unpaid, which put the German authorities in a rather awkward position. On the one hand, labour had been provided, a service rendered and thus a debt was owed. Yet, on the other hand, the authorities were in effect chasing payment for exhuming bodies whose deaths the German side had originally caused.[17] Such quandaries had already led to diplomatic unpleasantry in the south-west German city of Pforzheim. When the city authorities had tried to charge the French for the exhumation of their dead, the Parisian daily, Le Figaro, was outraged, calling this an example of the 'Teutonic mentality'.[18] Faced with the prospect of similar criticism coming their way, the authorities in Wiesbaden and Braunschweig reluctantly waived the charges.

While the British almost paid the price for relying on ad hoc local labour, the VDK was forced to adopt even more ambitious plans. After failing to attract German war veterans, it decided instead to recruit its own personal team of British gravediggers, who would tour around the country digging one site after the next. However, the prospect of exhuming thousands of decaying corpses proved no more appealing to British workers than it had to former German POWs. After placing advertisements in labour exchanges across Britain for gravediggers, who also just happened to have a good knowledge of German, the VDK received a paltry eight enquiries. Of these, five turned up to interview, and in the end only two had the requisite language skills.[19] One person to make the cut was M.A. Rawley, whose well-to-do family had distant ties to the aristocracy.

Recently returned from skiing in Banff and with no immediate plans, Rawley had taken the job primarily for the pay. Everyone thought he was 'stark raving mad', he later admitted. However, for a young student, the work had some financial benefits. After a week's digging and with money in his pocket, Rawley jumped into his Jaguar XK150 convertible every Friday evening. He then sped down to London for the weekend before returning the following Monday for another round of exhumations.[20]

Neither the German nor the British exhumation teams ended up with the labour force they had originally envisaged or even desired. Instead of the carefully trained workers proficient in the latest exhumation techniques, they ended up employing a disparate group of diggers with no actual experience and often with little interest in the task at hand. Unsurprisingly, many of these workers often moved on fairly quickly, leaving the VDK forced to start recruiting once again. Its supervisors struggled to hide their frustrations, reserving much of their anger for the 'coloured workers', who they claimed were 'scared of the exhumations' and then simply 'ran away'. Yet, besides deeply embedded racism, there was a whole host of reasons for the constant rotation of gravediggers. The job itself was obviously unpleasant, but conditions outside the cemetery were not much better either. There was constant travel, poor food and only basic accommodation in British guest houses. During the winter, the workers 'froze in their rooms', the Germans complained, sometimes 'even while in bed'. British windows were 'draughty', they moaned, probably with some justification, and the gas heating was generally inefficient.[21]

Alcohol seemed to play a key role in helping the workers to navigate through the discomforts of the job. In Münster, the local cemetery authorities paid its gravediggers 20 Reichsmark and a bottle of spirits for exhuming the war dead, although if the bodies were 'already fairly decomposed', they only received half a bottle, as presumably the task was then only half as grim.[22] Back in Britain, Rawley recalled that at the end of a hard day's exhumations, the diggers often retired to a local pub.

The 'very strait-laced' German supervisors, who apparently liked to douse themselves liberally in some 'dreadful aftershave', normally had just the one drink before leaving, while some of the British workers interested in 'football and the pub' managed to consume much more. Almost inevitably perhaps, the mixture of alcohol and an unsavoury working environment led to punch-ups, although these were strictly between the British workers themselves or with local people, rather than with the German supervisors.[23]

The VDK did its best to distance itself from heavy drinking and fighting. In their final report, the supervisors complained of the British workers' 'dishonesty, lax punctuality, drunkenness and laziness'.[24] Clearly, the difficult conditions on the ground had done very little to improve relations between the two countries. However, what these complaints also highlighted was the disconnect between the gravediggers and the actual dead. The only real exemption to this came with the MRES units operating in post-war Germany, who had the task of disinterring the bodies of fellow airmen. For the most part, exhuming the dead was a purely transactional arrangement, a means for those involved to earn a wage. But of course there was an expectation that they would have to work for their money. Rawley remembered that the VDK supervisors 'were always a bit twitchy' about meeting their daily exhumation targets, constantly shouting to the diggers 'hurry up, hurry up'.[25] When the speed of the operation was combined with the diggers' detachment to the dead, then it becomes clear how disruptive the process must have been. These were not forensic, carefully considered removals, but something more akin to a snatch and grab affair.

Visible Intruders

For the most part, exhumations, whether in Britain or Germany, took place in long-established burial grounds. Even when these were situated in an urban environment, they had been designed as places of calm and for peaceful reflection. The nineteenth-century garden cemetery movement, in particular, had created parkland burial grounds that became destinations in their own right. When digging in carefully tended sites, such as Hamburg's massive Ohlsdorf cemetery, it proved very difficult for the exhumation teams to blend into their wider surroundings. In a vain attempt to keep the peace, but also in the hope of avoiding any confrontation, the exhumation teams did their best to keep their plans out of the public eye. 'The work should be carried out with as little publicity as possible,' Ware stressed to his exhumation teams in Germany. 'The less it is talked about the better.'[26] The only people to be given advance warning of a disinterment were local health authorities and the landowners where the bodies lay. Before commencing its operations in Britain, the VDK agreed to conduct exhumations early in the morning, and always with 'due care and attention to decency'. Their plan was for the gravediggers to creep into the cemeteries, remove the dead and then creep out again without disturbing the quiet of their surroundings.[27]

In practice, it proved very tricky to enter a community, remove the corpses and then depart unobserved. After all, the gravediggers rarely operated alone, but tended to be an all-male affair of five or more young men in one team. Women were given a strictly-behind-the-scenes role, providing administrative support or completing translation work.[28] As socialising and drinking played a big role in their daily routines, it is easy to imagine that the gravediggers may well have turned up for an early start loudly chatting and joking, not necessarily attuned to their wider environment. The men also had to drag a great deal of cumbersome equipment with them onto site. The large-scale disinterment of bodies required everything from picks, shovels and spades through to screens for shielding the work and then finally coffins or containers in which to deposit the remains.[29]

It would have been very difficult to have fitted the paraphernalia required for the exhumations into a standard vehicle. There was a lot to carry: a team of gravediggers, all their luggage, digging equipment and finally the exhumed bodies had to find a space in the vehicles too. What was needed, therefore, were trucks or large vans, which due to their size also had the unintended consequence of making the operations even more visible. The Army Graves Service operating in post-war Germany, for example, had wanted specialist trailers for carrying the corpses for reburial. A large canopy over the top for privacy was to be provided, along with steel grooves in the floor panel to allow for 'washing out with disinfectant after transport of the bodies'. Somewhat reassuringly, it was noted that the trailers would not 'be used for any other purpose'.[30] In the end, though, the Army Graves Service received very few of the trailers and tended to use large 15 hundredweight Bedford trucks instead.[31]

However, it was not just the size of the vehicles that made them conspicuous, but also their visible foreignness. The Bedford trucks had military markings, while in the 1920s the IWGC had imported its own Ford trucks into Germany. These were then adapted to give space for workers up front and enough room for nine coffins to be stacked in the rear. In an attempt to 'conceal the nature of the load from the public', some form of 'canvas screen or curtains' was supposed to provide cover.[32] The VDK followed a similar approach, shipping their own fleet of specially adapted Volkswagen vans into Britain through Harwich port. As imports, the vans were all left-hand drive and also retained their original German registration plates.[33] The visual cues of a foreign vehicle, whether the VDK's Volkswagens or the IWGC's Fords, also helped to identify the occupants as outsiders.

Once the trucks had been unloaded and the digging could finally commence, it still proved extremely difficult to disinter the bodies and then to retreat discreetly. Extracting the remains generally ended up taking far longer than had initially been planned. Regulations in both Britain and Germany often dictated the presence of a local official or public health officer to oversee proceedings, but all too often the grave-diggers would be left waiting for the official to arrive.[34] Even just digging down to the corpse could take a remarkable amount of time. This was the case with the German graves in Darenth Park Asylum in Kent, the site of a military hospital for POWs during the First World War. The VDK's team arrived in the hospital grounds where the cemetery was located, and started to dig down to the first of 280 bodies. Only after several hours hard labour did they discover that the remains lay 5–6 metres below the surface, with four to six corpses to a grave.[35] Trying to disentangle the bodies from mass graves, such as the ones in Darenth, also proved a considerable drag on operations. In Fürstenfeldbruck in Bavaria, the site of a former POW camp, the IWGC not only had to pick their way through mass graves, but also had do so without a plan. The German cemetery authorities apologetically explained that 'unskilled personnel' had originally buried the dead during the 1918 influenza pandemic and had failed to note their locations.[36]

In all operations, the supervisors in charge on the ground made great efforts to check the identity of the remains. Everyone wanted to avoid the embarrassment of exhuming the wrong body and dispatching it to some distant cemetery, although this did nonetheless happen on occasion. In the wake of the First World War, the French even managed to exhume one British soldier, as their own, and to deposit his remains in Giessen, before he was found and moved instead to Kassel.[37] To mitigate such mistakes, the Germans and British followed the same basic procedure. The supervisors donned their thick rubber gloves and prodded around the body for anything to confirm the identity. Duncan Torrance, a fresh-faced young British army officer, had his own technique for this; he kept his left hand gloved and his right hand bare 'so that [his] fingertips would never miss a useful clue'. He then recorded details of the corpse, including the position of teeth and bones, in a one-page report.[38] Fifteen years later, when the VDK carried out its exhumations in Britain, they filled in very similar forms, purely designed to ensure the body and name matched.[39]

By the time the identities of the corpses had been confirmed, even more time on site had been expended. The final stages of each exhumation operation, though, generally proceeded far more quickly. The exhumation teams proved to be very adept at quickly packing the remains onto their waiting trucks ready for a swift departure. The Army Graves Service followed the most basic method, albeit the least hygienic one, and simply wrapped the corpses in old blankets tied together at the top with wire.[40] With a nod to earlier mortuary traditions, the IWGC in 1920s Germany had used something that was at least akin to a coffin. It deployed special, reduced height wooden coffins, for holding the corpses, that crucially were 'not too demanding on transport space'.[41] The VDK, meanwhile, designed its own plastic 'sarcophagus' for the German bodies (see image 23). At a mere 68 cm in length, the corpse could only fit into the 'sarcophagus' if the body was reduced to its composite parts. Although this method had little aesthetic appeal, it did nonetheless offer a simple solution. The VDK's workers dropped the remains into the 'sarcophagus', which was apparently similar to placing

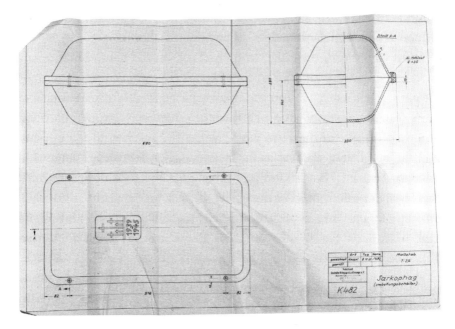

23. Before commencing its work to exhume the German war dead, the VDK commissioned a new plastic 'sarcophagus'. The compact design allowed its workers to efficiently pack the remains of the war dead ready for transportation.

items into 'a supermarket trolley'. They then put the lid on and simply sealed the top with four rivets. The whole process may not have been the most pleasing on the eye, but it was at least practical.[42]

At the end of a day's digging, the VDK's Volkswagen vans, as Rawley recalled, were 'very well loaded down', with two men sitting in the front, three behind, then their luggage and finally ten to twelve caskets of remains stacked in the back. The team drove their load to a central repository, where the caskets were collected by a larger lorry and then taken to Cannock Chase for eventual reburial.[43] In Germany, the IWGC and later the Army Graves Service took the exhumed remains of their soldiers to the new collective cemeteries direct. Whatever method was adopted, the entire process required considerable travel. The job, as Torrance remembered it, involved as much driving as digging. 'Our lives seemed to revolve round [sic] transport,' he joked.[44] At the end of the operation in Britain, the VDK calculated that its teams had covered around 400,000 kilometres in less than a year.[45] With so much time on the road, accidents and breakdowns were a frequent occurrence. War-damaged roads took their toll on the Army Graves Service's heavy lorries to the extent that it was 'impossible for the repair units to keep up with the work'.[46] The VDK, meanwhile, not only suffered from breakdowns, but also from crashes and theft. On one occasion, returning refreshed from a stop at a roadside café, the exhumation team found their van – fortunately not loaded with bodies at the time – gone.[47]

However, the hazards of a British lay-by paled in comparison to the British operations in post-war Eastern Europe. Soldiers and airmen had died in all parts of Nazi Germany, but with defeat some of these bodies were no more accessible than they had been during the conflict itself. The Soviets, who occupied the eastern part of Germany and also annexed territory further east, proved reluctant to let British investigators in, unless they were given greater access to the British zone of occupation in turn. But as a Foreign Office official in Whitehall put it, there were 'very strong objections to more Russians swanning about the British Zone than is necessary', which rather left the war dead as pawns in the early Cold War.[48]

It was only in autumn 1946 that British investigators finally gained some limited rights to enter the Soviet zone. However, this was access with strings attached, which meant the exhumation teams had to demonstrate considerable persistence if they were going to recover any remains at all. This certainly proved to be the case in the Baltic port town of Warnemünde. MRES investigators had a strong suspicion that two RAF personnel lay buried as unknown airmen in the town's main cemetery. Getting to the graves, however, turned out to be a challenge in itself. First, they were banned from the Warnemünde region, then they were not allowed near the crash site and, finally, attempts to meet the local mayor were also vetoed. The investigators did eventually reach the cemetery, by which point it turned out that the Americans had already exhumed the remains of the two airmen and returned them to France. In the eastern part of Germany, therefore, the mission was not so much to creep into a cemetery and escape quietly without notice, but rather to cross the Iron Curtain and come back with any remains at all.[49]

Clashes

When everything went to plan, the local population should have had very little to do with the exhumation teams. The MRES, which conducted interviews with Germans who had witnessed aircraft crashes, was the only group to actively seek out local people, but even this was done at a preparatory stage, rather than as part of the actual disinterment process. For the most part, locals only learnt that bodies had been removed long after the event. Yet, the carefully laid plans of the exhumation teams did not always run as smoothly as intended, and they sometimes found themselves caught in the act. This was the case in Swindon, where seventy-one German bodies lay buried. A journalist must have got word of the VDK's plans, for just as they were about to start digging, the team started to be asked a swathe of questions. Clearly annoyed at this intrusion, the VDK supervisors 'refused to give their names' and did their best to ignore the journalist.[50] With the exhumation teams having to set foot on the territory of their former enemy to rescue the bodies, clashes between local people and the newly arrived gravediggers could easily occur.

The fiercest clashes undoubtedly occurred in interwar Germany where the new Weimar Republic struggled to establish itself under the weight of defeat and revolution. Protests on the streets, paramilitary violence and soaring inflation affected the lives of all Germans in the immediate post-war years. The IWGC, therefore, had not chosen the most conducive time to start digging up its dead and, in doing so, stirring recent memories of the conflict. Even before exhumations were added to the mix, there appeared to be a marked antipathy towards the victorious Allies. In Berlin, there was an 'increasing distrust of foreigners', observed one British journalist, and 'a peculiar increase of distrust towards the English'. There was greater antipathy further west, where several battalions of the British army were stationed in the Rhineland around Cologne, ostensibly to secure the peace settlement. In attempting to recover its dead, therefore, the IWGC waded into an already extremely tense atmosphere.[51]

Thomas Greig, one of the IWGC's registration officers deployed to Weimar Germany, experienced the full force of this anger. In early

1924, Greig, who had served in the First World War as a captain in the Argyll and Sutherland Highlanders, led a group of six gravediggers to the Franconian town of Bayreuth, in northern Bavaria. The town is surely better known for being the home of the annual Bayreuth Festival than for housing a First World War POW camp. Nonetheless, it was in this camp, located south of the town centre, that French, Russian, Italian and British prisoners had died, mainly during the final months of the war.[52] Greig's task was to exhume the twenty-four British bodies buried in Bayreuth. However, as the British lay in shared graves, they had to be first disentangled from the other dead, before their remains could be exhumed and brought to Kassel for reburial.[53]

When Greig arrived at Bayreuth's cemetery to commence the exhumation operation, he found that a 'large crowd of civilian sight-seers had [already] assembled' around the graves. They may have descended on the cemetery curious to watch the exhumations, but the 'sight-seers' never confined themselves to a mere passive role. They 'trampled over the plots [and] over graves', Greig complained, and even over the piles of earth that his team had excavated from the graves. The German crowd also had plenty to say, hurling abuse at the IWGC's workers, calling them 'Swinehund Englander [sic]' among other pleasantries. Desperate to calm the situation and to get on with the job, Greig left to call the police, who did at least try to move the crowds on. Having failed to disrupt the exhumations in person, local people then placed other hurdles in the way. Greig was given a pile of new forms to fill in, was told that the bodies would have to be embalmed after disinterment and that his team could only dig before 8 a.m. and after 5 p.m., which given that it was only March left only a small window of daylight hours for digging.

Greig was of the opinion that the people of Bayreuth cared little for the graves themselves and were being difficult simply for the sake of it. 'This sort of thing happened almost everywhere in Germany,' he complained. His report of events in Bayreuth, however, also hints at a deeper set of reasons for these clashes. At one stage in the stand-off between the locals and the gravediggers, a German shouted out demanding to know why he and the other locals in the crowd should be 'put out of our <u>own</u> cemetery'.[54] It was this palpable sense of inequality that seemed to rile local people the most. As citizens of the vanquished wartime power, they could only watch on as foreigners charged into their cemeteries and exhumed bodies, while their own dead remained scattered overseas. The process of exhuming the war dead effectively came to embody the most despised aspects of the Versailles settlement. Back in London, the IWGC's legal advisers clearly had some sympathy with the German complaints and sought to ease tensions by paying Bayreuth town council 70 Reichsmark in compensation for any inconvenience caused.[55]

However difficult the working arrangements in Bavaria, they paled in comparison to those in the industrial Ruhr. In January 1923, after ongoing debates over reparations, the French decided to march into the Ruhr to help themselves to what they believed the Germans owed. Relations between Germany and France deteriorated rapidly the longer events in the Ruhr went on. With strikes, protests and violence becoming an all-too-common occurrence, the British were perilously stuck between the two sides. They attempted to pursue a policy of 'benevolent neutrality', hoping to maintain a positive relationship with both the Germans and the French.[56] This put the IWGC in something of a predicament, as it still needed to exhume hundreds of bodies from the Ruhr. The French, who were also in the process of reburying their own dead, suggested partnering up. For the British, there was a certain logic to working with their wartime ally who could provide protection should clashes occur with the local German population.

Yet, at the same time, the IWGC had very real concerns. Ware had sent Major-General Edward Perceval, a long-serving Royal Artillery officer, to oversee the concentration process in Germany. With thinning white hair and a clipped military-style moustache, Perceval brought an aura of authority to the spreading tensions. He was very concerned about being dragged into what he saw as France's dispute. 'I would rather work independently of them,' he told Ware, 'as there is now such very strong feelings against them [the French].'[57] Ware, whose instincts were always to avoid any scandals and unwelcome attention, advised Perceval to work with the French but to make 'every endeavour' to keep any incidents out of the press.[58]

The atmosphere was far less charged when the VDK began its exhumation work in Britain in the 1960s. Nonetheless, problems did emerge and relations between the German-led teams and the local British communities were never entirely smooth. Considering their own openly racist stance towards the employment of black British gravediggers, it was perhaps somewhat ironic for the VDK's German leaders to complain repeatedly of the 'Englishman's prejudices against foreigners'.[59] Yet, as far as they were concerned, a British reluctance to deal with the Germans made their work much more difficult. Presumably reflecting its position at the geographical centre of the wartime air war, the VDK experienced the strongest anti-German sentiments in southern England, where local officials apparently placed hefty bureaucratic barriers in their way. To navigate around these, the leaders of the VDK's operation explained that they had to deploy 'considerable organisation and improvisation', while at the same time relying on their own 'personal diplomacy and quick thinking'.[60]

Despite drawing on their apparently deep reserves of tact, the VDK's workers still experienced the odd clash with local people. The most significant of these occurred not amidst the apparent Germanophobia of the south, but further north, in Dishforth, Yorkshire, where the VDK attempted to exhume the bodies of Hartwig Hupe and Ernst Weiderer. The two men, both of whom had been in their late twenties at the time of their deaths, had been killed on a cold winter's night in 1942. Their Dornier Do217 bomber was travelling at speed towards a target in York, when it suddenly lost height and hit the lumbering presence of Easterside Hill on the North Yorkshire Moors. The bomber disintegrated on impact, spreading metal parts over the hillside. Of the four-man crew, only the bodies of Hupe and Weiderer were recovered; the remains of their colleagues, Syrius Erd and Rolf Häusner were never found.[61]

Almost twenty years later, the VDK's attempts to extract Hupe and Weiderer from Dishforth started smoothly enough. They managed to dig halfway down to the bodies and were in the process of excavating further when the chairperson of Dishforth Parish Council suddenly appeared. Catching them in the act of exhuming the two bodies, he demanded they lay down their shovels and leave the graves intact. 'The man in charge was arrogant,' the councillor complained. 'I had to get very cross with them before they would stop.' Indeed, the councillor became so incensed that he called the police to the cemetery.[62] Finally grasping the seriousness of the situation, the VDK's representatives fished out their Home Office exhumation licences. Unable to contest these official documents, the chairperson beat a hasty retreat and the exhumations continued.[63] While this clash never descended into angry abuse, as had been the case years earlier in Bayreuth, the general contours of the debate were very similar. This was ultimately a squabble over the ownership of the war dead and over the rights of the former enemy to trample through local communities to reclaim the bodies.

Both the VDK's team in the 1960s and the IWGC's in the 1920s had been operating at a time when the immediacy of war had started to pass. Despite this relative distance, they still found themselves clashing with communities and local bureaucracy over the exhumation process. When the members of the MRES and the Army Graves Service carried out their own work in the 1940s, they did not even have this temporal buffer for protection. Instead, they were operating amidst the ruins of recent conflict and with a population still suffering the effects of a war of destruction. In this atmosphere, the British frequently experienced local hostility wherever they exhumed. As an MRES officer, C.A. Mitchell could still remember working in this hostile environment when he penned his memoirs some fifty years later. 'The mere sight of an officer bearing the insignia of aircrew on his left breast', Mitchell remembered, 'was like red rag to a bull to some [Germans].' Mitchell went on to explain rather matter-of-factly that many people remained angry at the sight of Allied airmen after their experience of wartime bombing. It was still the presence of the former enemy in local communities that remained the catalyst for clashes over the war dead, but in 1940s Germany the exhumation teams went about their business already prepared for confrontation.[64]

Destruction

In a 1920s report, the IWGC laid out very carefully its working methods in German cemeteries. With reassuring words, it explained that at the end of an exhumation operation, 'the grave is filled in, paths cleaned and the Cemetery left in a tidy condition'.[65] However, the reality, both in the interwar period and later, was often very different. As the digging operations started, carefully tended cemeteries turned into something more akin to a muddy building site. Local people generally only discovered the destruction of their mortuary landscapes when the gravediggers had already packed up their tools, taken the bodies and moved onto the next site. By then there would have been little chance of confronting the culprits directly. Understandably, such episodes left a bitter aftertaste for the communities that had originally tended the graves.

On a warm summer's day, it might have been possible to excavate a grave without causing too much damage to the surrounding environment. Performing the same feat in the depths of winter, however, was far harder. This was particularly the case in Germany, which suffered unusually low temperatures during 1947. For the British busy trying to exhume their dead, it first proved impossible to break into the ground, but then when the thaw came, everything just turned into a cold mush.[66] Conditions also proved challenging for the VDK's teams digging in 1960s Britain. The problem for them was not the snow, but the rain. In 'the worst weather for 100 years', as they saw it, graves flooded and cemeteries turned into quagmires.[67] Sutton Cemetery, south of London, suffered the worst. After the gravediggers had failed to find all ninety-six bodies by hand, they had to bring in a mechanical digger. However, in the damp clay soil, the digger failed to gain traction and kept sliding on the ground. The result was a muddy, churned-up cemetery, and still no trace of the two missing bodies.[68]

When they did manage to find a body, the exhumation teams generally retained any personal items that might help with identification, but any other non-human remains were supposed to be carefully disposed of for sanitary reasons.[69] Often, this just involved properly clearing away old rotten coffins so that the sites could be returned to their original condition. There were different methods of going about this. The IWGC's workers in interwar Germany chose to spray the coffins with creosote and then set them alight, while the VDK tended to pour over a liberal amount of petrol before throwing in a match. As far as the Home Office in London was concerned, it was less important how the coffins were destroyed, so long as 'fragments of old coffins are not left about'.[70] Due to the constant rain, even burning the coffins proved more difficult than expected. 'The wood is often wet and cold,' the German supervisors complained, which made it difficult to burn and 'cost even more time'.[71]

Refilling the empty graves was also a time-consuming, albeit necessary, part of the exhumation process. Sometimes more soil had to be brought in to fill the hole, after which the earth always needed stamping down and the grass reseeding. The task of refilling the graves was also the one that local communities were most insistent upon. The vicar of St Eval in Cornwall, for example, only consented to the exhumation of seven German airmen from the Second World War if the graves 'shall be filled in up to turf level'.[72] Almost forty years earlier, the director of Saarbrücken cemetery in the Saarland had made a similar demand of the IWGC before granting permission for them to carry out exhumations in the city. The graves would need to be refilled twice to allow for the settling of soil, he explained, and only then seeded. He argued that 'the town is not ready to accept [. . .] costs' for this work on its own, and that he would bar entry to the cemetery until the money had been paid 'in full'.[73]

The VDK discovered that one easy way to save time in backfilling the empty graves was simply to throw in the headstones that had once stood proudly over the bodies. They clearly saw little problem with this approach and never sought to keep it a secret. Indeed, in its communications with local cemetery administrators, the VDK always asked the direct question: 'Is it possible for these graves [sic] markers to be buried in the vacated grave?'[74] This seemed to make perfect sense as once the corpse had been exhumed, there was no longer a grave that needed marking. At the same time, the VDK had been left with a large hole to fill and also headstones awaiting disposal. The vicar of St Eval agreed to the VDK's demand; the vicar of Potters Bar, where some of the Zeppelin dead lay, went a stage further and even suggested that the grave markers be 'broken up into small pieces to be used on the paths'.[75] Although the vicars of St Eval and Potters Bar were very accommodating, to the annoyance of the VDK, not all parishes were so enamoured of the idea. 'Destroying and removing the headstones and memorials over the graves takes a lot of time,' the War Graves Association later complained.

'Only in a few cases are we actually allowed to use the smashed-up stones as rubble for filling the graves.'[76]

The IWGC had faced a similar problem of disposal at the end of the First World War. Rather than immediately reaching for the sledgehammer, the commission had instead shown greater reverence for the abandoned grave markers. Recognising that some families might have formed an emotional attachment to the wooden crosses, the IWGC invited relatives to request their return. By December 1920, the IWGC had already received some 11,000 enquiries, predominantly concerning the former Western Front.[77] The IWGC later made provision for the return of old grave markers from Germany, but in the end very few families took up the offer. The parents of 21-year-old Basil Garrod, who had their son's old wooden cross returned from Cologne, were one of only about twelve families to make such a request.[78] By 1926, with crosses, stakes and rotting wooden markers piling up in a corner of Cologne's Southern Cemetery, a decision was taken to have them destroyed. Back in Britain, many of the regional newspapers blamed the Germans for 'these tragic mementos' being 'thrown into the flames'.[79] The *Daily Mirror* was probably closer to the mark, however, when it implied that the old markers were simply unwanted. It printed an image of the bedraggled crosses piled high in Cologne with a comment underneath from the IWGC confirming that families had had every opportunity to claim them, and nothing more could be done, 'but to destroy them'.[80]

As was the case in Cologne, the destruction of grave markers, even when they stood forlornly over an empty grave, proved to be particularly contentious.[81] In the vast commemorative infrastructure that the war graves commissions developed after 1918, the headstone had a prominent place; it not only marked the grave, but also helped to connect the living to the recently deceased. During and immediately after the two world wars, the Red Cross worked hard to fulfil families' demands for photographs of their loved one's grave and wooden marker. Later, a headstone gave relatives something tangible to touch if they managed to make a pilgrimage to the gravesite, while they also provided the focal point for wreaths or flowers during annual remembrance services. Becontree Cemetery, where fifty Second World War German airmen lay buried, served this very purpose for the London staff of the West German embassy, who travelled out to Essex on the Day of National Mourning (*Volkstrauertag*) each year to lay a wreath. In 1962, the VDK even delayed its exhumations in Becontree to allow the annual commemorative service to take place first. Once it was over, however, the VDK's team arrived with their spades, shovels and sledgehammers to clear the site.[82]

Many of the other sites that stood on the VDK's exhumation lists had been maintained to a similar standard as Becontree. On arriving at the Stobs POW camp cemetery in Scotland, the VDK supervisors noted that the graves were 'well kept', while in Dormansland, Surrey, they praised the 'extraordinary beauty and care' of both the graves and the cemetery.[83] Yet, these fine words were not enough to spare the grave markers in Stobs, Becontree or Dormansland, from the gravediggers' wrecking ball; in all three sites, the bodies were removed to Cannock Chase and all markers destroyed. The remains of the headstones in Stobs and the large stone memorial that had once watched over the site were discovered in the undergrowth many years later.[84] Further south, in Sutton, one local resident was so incensed to discover the 'destruction of war grave memorials' that they penned an angry letter to the local newspaper. 'Was it necessary to smash the stones?' they lamented. 'What if such a thing was to happen to memorial plaques of "Our Glorious Dead" in some foreign field "forever England"?'[85]

Invoking the words of Rupert Brooke was a means to stress the seriousness of the apparent destruction of Sutton Cemetery. The bodies of the dead, even those from the enemy side, were supposed to rest peacefully 'in some foreign field', but had suddenly been disturbed. Such complaints should never have marked the end point of the exhumation operations. The German and British gravediggers were supposed to enter former enemy territory, recover their deceased, then quietly depart, restoring the site to the condition in which they had found it. All too often, though, these basic requirements were not met. Instead, once the exhumation teams had left the scene of their digging, often what remained were muddy cemeteries, smashed headstones and sometimes angry local residents too.

Removing bodies was always going to cause some disturbance, but the situation was not helped by a lack of properly trained workers. The two war graves commissions may have publicly claimed that they were only using their own highly skilled teams but, in reality, they both had little choice but to employ anyone who could dig a hole. A lack of time and money meant that these ad hoc exhumation teams had to rush from one gravesite to the next, doing their best to rescue what they could from each cemetery before moving on. The speed of the operations added to the frustrations of local communities, who often viewed the intrusion of the gravediggers with a mixture of suspicion and contempt. A process that was apparently supposed to improve British–German relations generally did the reverse. It is 'pure and simple desecration', complained one Scottish Highlands councillor, expressing a sentiment that would no doubt have been shared by many other communities in both Britain and Germany.[86]

8

BREAKING

Plymouth's Ford Park Cemetery, with its commanding views down towards the city, lies a good mile north of the English Channel and the more renowned landmark of the Hoe. With woodlands down one side, mature trees and bushes throughout, the cemetery makes for a beautiful place for an early morning stroll. Christel Eulen, the wife of the VDK's founder, Siegfried Emmo Eulen, visited Ford Park for slightly different reasons in 1956. Eulen, short in stature and fairly stern in appearance, was by this time a 55-year-old widow, her husband having been killed in the final months of the last global conflict. She was in Plymouth looking for the graves of German airmen shot down over the city in the Second World War. Hidden alongside the imposing headstones of various nineteenth-century Devonians, Eulen eventually discovered six white wooden crosses set neatly in the grassy hillside that marked the final resting place of the German dead (see image 24). Seven years after Eulen's visit, the VDK's gravediggers pulled up at the same spot in their Volkswagen van, pulled down the crosses and started to recover their remains.[1]

With more than fifty corpses to exhume from three different cemeteries, the gravediggers ended up spending a lot longer in Plymouth than they had originally intended; heavy rain and sodden ground also hampered their progress.[2] Their prolonged stay gave local journalists an opportunity to write more fully about the VDK's plans and, at the same time, to ask questions as to how the German airmen had ended up in

24. In June 1956, six white wooden crosses still marked the graves of German Second World War airmen buried in Plymouth's Field Park Cemetery.

Plymouth in the first place. Focusing on four of the bodies in Ford Park Cemetery, the *Western Independent* relived the moment when the German crew lost their lives. It was a 'rainy, gale-swept evening in August, 1941', when one 'lone German bomber' set out to attack Plymouth. The German aeroplane, a Junkers Ju 88, dropped its load but never made it back home; 'it crashed into Gawton Woods and exploded', the newspaper reported. The article then named the four men – Ernst-Otto Wentzler, Alexander Reimann, Roderic von Heimann and Hans Otto Pusch – who had been 'blown to pieces' over Devon some twenty years earlier.[3]

In other towns where the VDK worked, there had been a similar response. Local newspapers often ran stories about the enemy dead and how they had first come to rest in their communities.[4] In Plymouth, as was the case elsewhere, it was of course the act of exhumation that provided the prompt for this renewed focus on the lives of those killed in conflict. The dead had always played an active role in connecting the former foes; their very presence in local communities forced the British and Germans into discussions.[5] However, once the dead had been extracted from their existing site of rest, the reverse happened. In place of these sites of memory that could prompt reflection, even reconciliation, there was nothing left but empty voids in the ground and slowly fading memories of past conflict.[6]

Seizing Control

The German and British war graves commissions had both decided that their dead should be cared for in national cemeteries. While this was extremely convenient for them, it did rather overlook the small matter of other groups who had a similar claim to the dead: the bereaved and the current custodians of the bodies on whose land they were buried. The war graves commissions were certainly aware that both of these groups might have their own plans for the dead, which could potentially be diametrically opposed to the large reburial operations. If they were to move the dead to new national military cemeteries, the war graves commissions realised very early on that relatives and the current custodians of the graves were potential obstacles that could, as the IWGC none too subtly put it, 'hamper [. . .] our work'.[7] Seizing control of the bodies, therefore, and silencing any other claimants was the only sure way of guaranteeing the success of the various exhumation operations.

Seemingly the most straightforward way of avoiding complaints from the bereaved was to leave them out of the exhumation process entirely. George Perley, the Canadian High Commissioner to the United Kingdom and also an adviser to the IWGC, expressed this point most succinctly. With years of experience as a Conservative politician back home, Perley was well aware of how best to shape a potentially thorny situation to one's advantage. On the matter of moving the British dead in interwar Germany, he suggested that it was 'inadvisable to make any public statement in the matter, as it would at once arouse opposition'.[8] Maintaining silence and, where possible, avoiding any discussion of the exhumations, even with relatives, became the IWGC's preferred approach. Only those people 'who had given any trouble' were given advance warning that their loved one's body was to be moved; everyone else only discovered the good news after the event.[9]

When the VDK commenced the exhumation of the German dead in Britain some forty years later, it did at least try to give the impression that relatives had agreed to the plan. Indeed, the CWGC, which represented the VDK in some of the local negotiations in Britain, confidently stressed that all ethical issues had been fully considered. 'The German authorities have taken into full account the wishes of the next-of-kin of the deceased,' the CWGC maintained.[10] Yet, this statement never stood up to any real scrutiny. There was a marked difference between following the exact requests of a relative and just taking them into 'account'. In practice, the VDK's operation was much closer to the earlier British approach and avoided discussing the reburials with the bereaved unless absolutely necessary.[11] The CWGC was fully aware of this sleight of hand but chose to remain ignorant as long as the VDK took 'full responsibility for any complaints from German relatives'.[12]

However, as the exhumations were apparently being undertaken for the benefit of the bereaved, it proved impossible to leave them out of the process entirely. This was particularly the case when a private memorial had already been placed over the grave. It was one thing to come into a cemetery, remove a temporary marker and exhume a body; it was quite another to knock down a private headstone that belonged to a bereaved relative. Even the VDK had to concede that in these circumstances it would have to consult with the families before commencing work. It managed to write to these relatives outlining its plan, making clear that, should the grave remain in situ, then relatives would have to take responsibility for any future upkeep.[13]

While the VDK's approach was never a direct threat as such, it certainly gave those wavering pause for thought. A Frau T. Paul faced this dilemma with her husband Otto's remains. He had died in November 1940, when his Heinkel bomber had ditched in the sea off the Dorset coast; the other crew members waded ashore, but Paul died in the impact. Once they had recovered his body, the British then buried Paul in the parish churchyard of St Peter's in the tiny village of Eype, just inland from the crash site. The local vicar was reluctant to see the grave go, particularly as Paul's family had 'paid a visit to this parish last summer'. His wife was also unsure what to do for the best. She dithered for many months until eventually agreeing to the move, after the VDK had promised that doing so would ensure she had 'no expenditure for the future'.[14]

The IWGC had deployed a similar line of argument after 1945 to 'dissuade', as it put it, families from leaving graves in situ.[15] In careful terms, the IWGC explained to relatives that its 'first duty in Germany' was to create military cemeteries. The maintenance of any graves left outside these sites, it stressed, will 'rest with yourself'.[16] Such persuasive arguments did not always convince, however. In Oberschleißheim, a small community just north of Munich, workers from the Army Graves Service had readied themselves to remove the bodies of six RAF crew members killed in a raid over the Bavarian capital in December 1942. Before they could dig, however, the relatives of Edward Fenwicke-Clennell, who had piloted the doomed Lancaster bomber, requested that the bodies of the crew be left where they lay. The family even offered to form a trust fund to pay for any future upkeep of the graves. Wrong-footed by this request, and seemingly unable to agree a way forward with the IWGC, the army ended up leaving the bodies resting in Oberschleißheim's historic Hochmutting cemetery, amidst the graves of local German civilians.[17]

While the relatives of Edward Fenwicke-Clennell and Otto Paul managed to have some say in what happened to their loved ones' remains, the majority of people were not quite so lucky. In 1923, the parents of William Legge made the gruelling journey from their home in Edinburgh via Luxembourg to Trier. The object of their trip was the grave of their 23-year-old son, who had died in air combat during the final year of the Great War. Legge's parents eventually made it to the ancient city of Trier and found the main municipal cemetery. However, what should have been the culmination of a long physical and emotional journey turned out to be nothing of the sort. Unbeknown to them, the IWGC had helpfully moved their son's remains to Cologne's Southern Cemetery, some 150 kilometres further north. Unsurprisingly, Legge's parents were 'rather aggrieved' to discover the news, although according to the IWGC, they apparently 'took the matter very well'.[18]

The geographical confusion stemmed from the fact that the IWGC, and later the VDK too, chose to move the bodies first, before giving the relatives news of what they now termed the 'final resting place'.[19] The belated news of a reburial, though, was not always enough to satisfy the bereaved, particularly if they had already formed a strong emotional bond to the grave. One of the most distressing responses involved E.H.R. Stephens. He was at home one summer's morning in 1924, when a note dropped through his letterbox informing him that his son's grave had been moved from Landshut in Bavaria to the central German city of Kassel. Stephens was 'distraught', but presumed it a 'mistake', as he had already placed a private headstone over the grave of his son, Donald, in Landshut.[20] Unfortunately, there had been no mistake. It was again the lack of information that riled him the most. The IWGC are like 'a thief in the night', he complained. 'The truth is that the relatives are not considered in the matter.'[21] Placing the IWGC's loyalties in question, he called the commission's action 'inhumane [. . .], not only unfair but [also] un-English'.[22]

The mass exhumation of the dead not only sparked complaints from families, but also led the existing custodians of the bodies to express concern. As was the case with the next-of-kin, the war graves commissions had to placate these voices if they were to realise their concentration plans. In Britain, one of the biggest hurdles facing the VDK came from the requirement to apply for a faculty, effectively the Church of England's permission to conduct work on consecrated ground. Although most clergy simply signed off this paperwork, there was nonetheless some disquiet within the Church over the VDK's plans. What proved most contentious was the temporal distance between death and the date of exhumation. Reverend Slocombe, vicar of Shelsley Walsh, a quiet hamlet some 20 kilometres north-east of Worcester, had only a single German grave in his care, that of Ernst Altmann, a 26-year-old infantryman who had died of 'double pneumonia' on Christmas Day 1918.[23] Asked by the VDK to consent to Altmann's disinterment, Slocombe replied simply: 'This grave has been here since 25th December 1918.'[24] He then made the same point to the Diocese of Worcester, indicating that Altmann 'has been resting undisturbed' for forty-three years. 'There can be little but bones left now,' he added. As far as Slocombe was concerned, the remains should be left 'quietly and individually at rest' and not moved to some 'vast regimental war cemetery'.[25]

After much pressure, Slocombe eventually signed the faculty. It was the response of the Diocese that led Slocombe to fall into line. The decision to support the exhumation of the German dead had been taken at a 'high level', he was told, with the Dean of Arches offering direction. Therefore, while others shared his 'sentiments', there was little that could be done to halt the process.[26] Very similar concerns surfaced in the Salisbury Diocese, but again pressure was brought to bear and the faculties passed. The Chancellor of the Diocese noted 'some disquiet' with the VDK's plans, particularly given the length of interment.[27] 'The large-scale mass exhumation of virtual communities which have laid at rest for some 45 years and are now gone to dust', the chancellor complained, 'raises a difficult question.'[28] Invoking the Christian burial refrain of 'ashes to ashes and dust to dust', the Chancellor highlighted the theological dilemma of wrenching the dead from the soil. However, before he could ponder the matter much further, the CWGC waded in to point out that the procedure had the 'blessing of the Dean of Arches'.[29] Faced with this evidence, the Bishop of Salisbury conceded the point. 'My feeling is that we ought to go ahead,' he wrote, none too enthusiastically.[30]

The objections raised in the dioceses of Worcestershire and Salisbury were not enough to halt the exhumations and the German war dead in these areas were also gradually moved to Cannock Chase. However, the VDK did suffer the occasional setback which forced it to make the reluctant decision to leave the dead exactly where they were. In Tangmere, Sussex, it was a case of not neglect, but rather too much remembrance that forced the VDK's hand. The village churchyard contained the graves of thirteen German airmen killed in the Second World War, shot down by aircraft from an RAF base that neighboured the village. The VDK had these war dead firmly in its exhumation sights and had planned for its teams to collect the bodies when they worked their way along the south coast.

What threw things off course was the intervention of Group Captain W.D. David, the incumbent RAF station commander. In 1959, David proposed a series of joint British–German commemorative events to foster reconciliation between the former foes. The catalyst for David's intervention had actually been something far more mundane: the realisation that the organ in the parish church was beyond repair. 'It has been decided to purchase a Minster Mark II (electric organ) as a replacement,' David explained, which should at the same time act as a 'memorial to British, Commonwealth and German airmen who are buried in the churchyard'.[31] To meet the £700 cost, he ran a well-publicised fundraising appeal, even managing to get Konrad Adenauer, the West German Chancellor, to donate £100. The two war graves commissions, however, dismissed the entire enterprise. There are 'no funds available' was the IWGC's curt response, when asked to contribute. They advised the VDK to respond in the same way, particularly as the graves would soon be 'reinterred at Cannock Chase'.[32]

Unfortunately for the two war graves commissions, the organ was just the start of David's joint British–German commemorations. With the funds in place, he planned for a large dedication ceremony in Tangmere to unveil the memorial organ to which he also invited German relatives. As a further sign of reconciliation between the former adversaries, David arranged for the printing of a special memorial calendar that listed the names of all the war dead, regardless of which side they had fought on. During the dedication ceremony, the German relatives were presented with the calendar but also with small walnut urns containing soil from the graves (see image 25).[33] As was the case with other sites of memory, such as the Tomb of the Unknown Warrior in Westminster Abbey, soil added authenticity and allowed survivors almost to touch a distant grave.[34]

This was all rather awkward for the war graves commissions. The events in Tangmere were a spectacular example of genuine reconciliation made possible because of the presence of British and German graves together in a local parish churchyard. As the Bishop of Chichester rightly stated during the dedication, in Tangmere, there are 'two countries at least, united here around one memorial'.[35] However, while the British and German war graves commissions were not averse to reconciliation, this all happened in the wrong place and at the worst possible time for them. But after such a wealth of attention, even they had to acknowledge that it was no longer possible to exhume the dead.[36] Elsewhere, the war graves commissions had managed to push such barriers to one side, but in Tangmere the publicity was too great, and the dead were allowed to remain at peace.

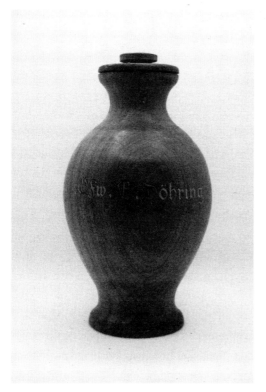

25. In 1959, the RAF station commander in Tangmere, Sussex, presented wooden urns to the relatives of the German war dead buried in the village. Each urn was filled with soil from the graves.

Welcome Departures

The small village of Sutton Veny, nestled in the Wylye Valley, situated just to the south of Salisbury Plain, has always been an important area for military training. During the First World War, its location made Sutton Veny an ideal site for army bases and also for a POW internment camp. After the conflict, the parish church of St John's bore witness to this history. The graves of 143 Australian and twenty-six British servicemen lay alongside those of thirty-eight German POWs, many of whom had died from their wounds in the village's military hospital. Their presence, however, had always sat uncomfortably with the IWGC. Frederic Kenyon, the director of the British Museum and IWGC's chief artistic adviser, was quite clear that he regretted the German graves' position in front of the 'Cross of Sacrifice', which, as he pointed out, 'is the monument to <u>our</u> fallen', and by implication not for the German dead.[37] Over thirty years on from Kenyon's original complaint, the IWGC was still unhappy with the German graves, bemoaning their 'conspicuous position' and their apparent attractiveness to ants, which caused 'periodic disturbance of the soil'.[38] Clearly, few tears were shed when the former enemy was exhumed and moved to Cannock Chase; the cemetery finally gained a more pleasing appearance, although whether the ant problem was resolved at the same time is unclear.

For the communities on the Channel Islands, seeing the German war dead gone was always about more than just aesthetics. After five years of Nazi occupation, there was far less of a warm attachment to the 475 enemy graves there than was generally the case on mainland Britain. The islands' authorities were very insistent that the Germans would have to remove their dead, but ruled out any form of concentration cemetery on Jersey, Guernsey or Alderney from the start. The authorities presented their call as being driven by a need to provide their own citizens with adequate burial plots, while also ensuring that German headstones did not 'spoil the beauty of [. . .] particularly attractive corner[s] of the island', as the Bailiff of Jersey put it.[39] Yet, there were clearly deeper issues running through these demands. As collaboration had been as much a part of the Channel Islanders' occupation experience as resistance, many people were keen to move on. Removing the enemy bodies, therefore, had the benefit of cleansing soiled ground, helping to erase signs of the German occupation at the same time.[40]

It was not just the current custodians who were sometimes pleased to see the German graves cleared, some of the bereaved also welcomed the large-scale exhumation operations, primarily because it seemed to provide an opportunity to bring their loved ones back home. The 1959 British–German war graves agreement certainly leant in this direction: 'Any application for exhumation and transfer of a body shall be made by the duly entitled relatives to the competent German authority.'[41] The VDK never went out of its way to advertise this clause; nonetheless, nineteen families seized the opportunity and negotiated the repatriation of remains. Once exhumed, these bodies were temporarily stored in Cannock, before being packed into oak coffins and transported to continental Europe, either by boat or aeroplane.[42]

One such case involved the body of Graf Gustav Friedrich zu Castell-Castell, a member of the aristocratic Castell family, whose Heinkel bomber had been shot down over Steyning, Sussex, in 1941. On learning of the VDK's plans for Cannock Chase, the mother of Castell-Castell requested her son's remains be repatriated to the family tomb in Hochburg, Austria.[43] The only slight difficulty with the request was that the body of the bomber's radio operator, Xaver Kroiss lay on top of Castell-Castell's coffin. The obvious solution to the problem, and one that had been applied elsewhere, was to complete the repatriation at the same time as the reburials to Cannock Chase. However, on this occasion, the VDK took a different approach. Perhaps swayed by Castell-Castell's aristocratic lineage, the VDK decided to expedite the process by exhuming both bodies at once, then reburying what was left of Kroiss until he could be dug up again and then moved a few months later to Cannock Chase.[44]

Once Castell-Castell and the rest of his flight crew had been removed from Steyning, there was then immediately more space for new burials. For some local councils in Britain, this was reason enough to welcome the removal of the enemy war dead. With very little sentiment at all, one council worker in Swindon explained that the empty German plots would be 'left a while' before being reused 'for burying local people'. 'We are very busy at the moment, and could do with more space,' he added.[45] In Park Hall, near Oswestry, where 109 First World War POWs had been buried, the CWGC was again keen to offload the empty land to interested parties. Given its isolated location surrounded by fields and alongside a railway line, it had no future use as a burial ground. Instead, a local farmer took on the site, which still contained a 'granite cross and shrine', a reminder of the now absent dead. Once these had been flattened and the ground seeded with wheat, however, the former German cemetery flowed seamlessly into the surrounding fields; nobody would ever know simply by looking that there had once been a cemetery there.[46]

In the Rhineland city of Duisburg, which had been heavily bombed in October 1944, some residents had not even waited for the dead to be exhumed before they started to plant crops. Less than two years after the heaviest raids, MRES officers were hard at work trying to track down the graves of the Allied war dead. A tip-off led one of the investigators, C.A. Mitchell, to a garden behind a large block of flats to the south of the city centre. There he found some well-tended vegetables; the green leaves of pea and cabbage plants protruded through the soil, alongside 'a metal cross roughly stuck in the ground' that bore the inscription: 'Two Unknown British Flyers'. Mitchell made arrangements for the two bodies, which had not even been placed in coffins, to be exhumed from the garden and moved to one of the new concentration cemeteries. Although the identities of the corpses could not be ascertained, they did at least receive a more dignified resting place than the back-garden allotments of Duisburg.[47]

Mitchell had feared being at the receiving end of local anger when the bodies were exhumed, not because locals were reluctant to see the corpses depart, as the VDK later experienced in Britain, but rather because they feared their cabbages and peas might be killed off at the same time. The general ambivalence towards the disinterment of the British dead reflected the exigencies of post-war German life, where housing, fuel and food were all in short supply. Such was the desperation for basic supplies that people clearly had no qualms about planting their vegetable seedlings in the same ground as rotting corpses.[48] However, German ambivalence towards the exhumations was also a sign of the ubiquity of death. By 1945, as the Allies closed in on Nazi Germany, the country had become 'a land of the dead'. In areas with the fiercest fighting, 'corpses lay scattered across the spaces once inhabited by the living', with both soldiers and civilians hastily buried in gardens and fields or left uncovered under the rubble of bombed-out buildings.[49]

For local communities, there was good reason to expedite the disinterment of the British dead. Not only did exhumations play a role in moving society towards a new post-war era, but the act of removing corpses also had the added benefit of distancing people from the scene of war crimes.[50] In many cases, there was only one reason why British bodies lay in a particular German cemetery: a crime had been committed. This was the case for the small town of Bösel, south-west of Oldenburg, where the remains of one British airmen, Harry Horsey, lay alone in the graveyard of the Catholic church of St Cäcilia. Horsey's Hawker

Tempest fighter had been forced down near Bösel in April 1945, just a few days before the war's end. Two German soldiers were instructed to escort Horsey, who had survived the emergency landing unscathed, to a POW camp. The group had not walked far, when one of the guards turned his weapon on Horsey, shooting him in the back.

Horsey's body in effect became a silent witness to a crime. When the MRES investigators turned up in Bösel and in other communities, they not only hunted for the dead, but they also sought to ascertain how and why the person had been killed. The corpse, which they recovered from the town's Catholic cemetery, provided the first piece of evidence for investigators. A medical officer performed a full autopsy on the exhumed remains, examining clothing and the body itself, which revealed 'two separate sets of injuries': a shot through the neck and another bullet hole in the chest.[51] As was the case with Horsey, the presence of the body often helped to confirm that a crime had been committed. Under these circumstances, of course, it was easier for local communities to see the war dead moved than to have the remains there drawing attention to a wartime atrocity. Nazism then became someone else's problem, leaving the original community cleansed.

Back in Bösel, after concluding their investigations, the British were able to arrest the two guards who had escorted Horsey to his death, putting them on trial for murder in 1946. Rolf Brinkmann, who was only a couple of years older than the man he killed, tried to defend his actions by claiming that the unarmed Horsey had tried to seize his weapon. 'I believed myself to be in very serious danger,' Brinkmann pleaded trying to save himself. '[I] only intended to use the weapon to defend myself.' His co-defendant, Werner Assmussen, had a more plausible defence; he had briefly left the scene, returning only to find Horsey dead and Brinkmann drinking in a nearby pub.[52] After listening to the evidence, the British court found Assmussen not guilty, but sentenced Brinkmann to life imprisonment for 'shooting an unarmed prisoner'. As with many of those committed for war crimes, Brinkmann was released early, returning home in 1952, having served a mere six years behind bars.[53] By this point, the British had already exhumed Horsey's body from Bösel and moved him to the IWGC's large military cemetery at Sage. With the body gone and the perpetrators released, the local community could concentrate instead on their own wartime victim-hood at the hands of Allied air raids.[54]

Cutting Ties

Before the VDK embarked on the exhumation of the German dead in Britain, it conducted a very similar, albeit much smaller, operation in the Republic of Ireland, moving 134 bodies to a new collective cemetery in Glencree, County Wicklow. Prior to the work starting, a German journalist visited the town of Bantry on the Atlantic coast, where the bodies of two German aircraft crew, killed in 1942 and 1943 respectively, lay buried. After a long conversation with a grave-digger in the cemetery, who could still recall the original wartime funerals, the journalist left Bantry with a real sense of melancholy:

> [Removing the dead] will leave a void for the people of Bantry [...] as the foreign soldiers in the quiet graves belong to them. There will be something missing when the wooden crosses, which are so neatly lined up, are not there anymore. The graves will also no longer encourage Germans to take the road to Bantry. It will only be his [the gravedigger's] grandchildren who get to hear now and again about the graves for the airmen that he once dug and then filled in.[55]

The journalist's reflections about the dead in Bantry applied equally to communities throughout Britain. Having been custodians of the bodies for years, even decades, local people found themselves suddenly redundant when the VDK entered their communities and reclaimed the dead. On a basic transactional level, this meant the immediate cancellation of any contracts that the CWGC may have made for the maintenance of the German graves. As soon as the VDK had recovered the remains of sixteen Zeppelin crew members from Theberton in Suffolk, for example, the commission contacted the Rector of St Peter's Church, informing him that, from now on, they would only pay him for the upkeep of the two remaining British graves.[56] At the same time, any informal labour that communities had once offered also came to an abrupt end. In the Norfolk community of Starston, the local rector had taken personal responsibility for the care of the grave of a single German pilot killed in 1940, requesting no fee for his work. With the removal of these remains, his interest in the German airman of course also stopped.[57]

The act of tending the enemy graves may have started from a contractual basis, but over time, the dead often became embedded within local remembrance calendars, featuring in annual remembrance services or commemorative anniversaries. Notions of friend and foe gradually blurred as personal relations developed around the graves. Visitors to Lennoxtown's Campsie Cemetery, located some 15 kilometres north of Glasgow, need first to pass through a stone arch dedicated to the local men who 'Fell in the Great War'. Yet, for many years, alongside the local dead were the graves of two German airmen killed in 1941. Following conversations with the wife of one of the airmen, the community planted two saplings behind the graves. Throughout the year, local people volunteered to tend the graves, then at Christmas they laid wreaths in memory of the two Germans who had been killed many years earlier. The exhumation of the enemy dead and their removal to Cannock Chase ended these and other horticultural interventions, but at the same time also severed personal relations between the old adversaries too.[58]

If the grave was no longer in its original location, then there was also clearly no reason for relatives to make pilgrimages to the many small, local cemeteries across Britain and Germany. In the Weimar Republic, British families who had once sought out their loved ones' graves in Trier or Landshut travelled instead to the large collective cemeteries. After the VDK's exhumation operation, the same applied to German families visiting Britain, who could go directly to Cannock Chase rather than having to trek to Lennoxtown, Oswestry or elsewhere. Indeed, the VDK was always very keen to stress that one of the reasons for moving the war dead in the first place was to help German families visit the graves. 'Arranging trips to scattered graves is extremely difficult,' the VDK explained, whereas moving them to Cannock Chase makes 'it easier for bereaved relatives to make these visits, and to help administration generally'.[59]

Whether relatives prioritised the apparent ease of travel to remote Cannock Chase over leaving the remains undisturbed is a moot point. Nonetheless, it is clear that the removal of graves from small, far-flung graveyards also destroyed relationships that had gradually developed between the British and Germans. Nowhere was this loss more painfully experienced than in the south coast town of Poole. What had brought the former foes together in Dorset was the grave of 30-year-old Horst Gündel. In May 1941, Gündel had been a crew member aboard a Heinkel He 111 bomber heading to targets over England. Reaching Poole Harbour, the aircraft swept down to drop its bomb load, but took a direct hit and crashed onto mud flats, killing Gündel and two other members of the crew.

After the war, Gündel's widow made frequent visits to the grave in the town's Parkstone Cemetery. It was on one of these pilgrimages that she had a 'chance meeting' with R. Dourass, a local man who lived opposite the cemetery. An unlikely friendship then developed. Dourass kept the grave tidy, laid flowers and placed candles on it for her each Christmas. Gündel's widow visited him whenever she travelled to Dorset and Dourass even stayed at the family's home in Giessen. 'Her former husband's photographs and mementos are everywhere about the house, he has certainly not been forgotten by his family,' Dourass later remarked.[60]

This friendship, however, was irreparably broken when the VDK exhumed Gündel's remains in spring 1963 and moved them some 250 kilometres further north to Cannock Chase. Discovering that the grave had suddenly disappeared, Dourass thought it best to inform Gündel's widow of the news. 'It came as a great shock to her,' he remarked, 'and has caused her much misery.' What seemed to upset her the most was that no one had taken the time to give advance warning of the move, even though she still lived in the same house in Giessen that she had once shared with her husband Horst. As the VDK should have had her address on file, she decided that the disinterment could only have been arranged by the British. Very quickly, a friendship that had developed around the care of one wartime casualty faded through suspicion, sadness and distance. After the reburial, Gündel's widow stopped making her frequent journeys to Poole and Dourass, in turn, no longer needed to write with regular updates on the grave. The dead airman who had once worked to bring the pair together now seemed to push them apart.[61]

This was a scene repeated across Britain. Relations between former foes that had tentatively developed were once again lost when the exhumations started. In Weldon, Northamptonshire, the relationship was never as close as in Poole; nonetheless, the presence of the bodies of five German Second World War airmen in the village's historic St Mary's churchyard had helped to foster close interactions. After some of the initial wartime 'bitterness' had tailed off, the graves were regularly tended, 'on occasion flowers were placed' and a wreath was 'sent regularly by the relatives of one of the airmen'. Given the strength of these relations, the Rector of St Mary's thought it a 'pity that they [the airmen] cannot remain', but, as in Poole, there was never any opportunity to stop the exhumations. Somewhat ironically, as the families were rarely consulted, the VDK justified the move on the basis that they had to 'consider the feelings of the German next-of-kin'.[62] Once removed from Weldon, Poole or Lennoxtown, then relations between the British and Germans that had gradually developed were swiftly lost.

Unwelcome Arrivals

Once the dead had been exhumed from their original burial spot, the majority were moved to concentration cemeteries, many of which were in rural locations. After some forty-five years buried in the bustling West End of London, the remains of Erich Wutke, a German civilian of the First World War, were dug up and moved to the much quieter setting of Cannock Chase. Set in isolated moorlands with only deer for company, Wutke's new home had a very different ambience. In this regard, Cannock Chase seemed to provide the perfect setting for a concentration cemetery, with space for thousands of graves and few neighbours to disturb the peace. For the same reason, the British also decided to place most of their military cemeteries in rural locations. Niederzwehren cemetery, constructed for the dead of the First World War, for example, sits on the hills surrounding Kassel, while the large Rheinberg and Reichswald cemeteries occupy isolated locations in Nordrhein-Westfalen. The few exceptions to this pattern occurred where existing municipal cemeteries were expanded to accommodate a British war cemetery, such as in Hamburg, Cologne and Kiel.

Regardless of the precise location, one thing seemed to unite the local communities surrounding these various sites: a hostility towards their new skeletal arrivals. The British army's approach to establishing the military cemeteries in the wake of the Second World War was based more on requisition than negotiation. In 1946, the British seized a small 'piece of land used as a military cemetery' on the northern fringes of Celle. The town council had little say in the matter other than to sign away the land, but it clearly saw the British dead as something of an inconvenience.[63] As the West German economy boomed during the 1950s, the local authorities designated both the cemetery and the area surrounding it as an industrial zone, and not a peaceful resting place for their former enemy. The solution, as far as they saw it, was for the burial ground to be moved to a more appropriate location. Rather than keeping the cemetery in an industrial area, 'our suggestion is to consider moving the few graves to a dignified military cemetery', they argued in vain.[64]

The new British cemeteries established in Sage and Dürnbach at least benefited from more peaceful surroundings, but this certainly did not mean that the local communities were any more amenable to the arrival of the war dead. Sage war cemetery lies around 25 kilometres south of Oldenburg in the plateaux of the Wildeshausen Geest nature park. The IWGC's inspectors commended its 'pleasant roadside site with a wood of small trees on North and West sides'.[65] On the other side of Germany, Dürnbach, in deepest Bavaria, occupied a much hillier location. 'It can best be likened to the English Lake District, only on a grander scale,' noted the IWGC inspector.[66] As with Sage, though, the site was very isolated, surrounded by fields and woodland. When the Army Graves Service first started to move bodies into the new sites, locals could do little more than look on, as once familiar pockets of land were turned into what one British officer called a 'civil engineering project'.[67]

Unsurprisingly, it was the actual landowners who were most aggrieved at the arrival of the dead. Where they had once sown their crops, the

British now started the process of planting bodies. The cemetery land in Sage belonged to an H. Barabas, whose family had long farmed in the area. She bemoaned the fact that the field, which had been taken 'against our will', was the 'most valuable land in our possession'.[68] The landowner in Dürnbach, P. Haltmair, also stressed the positives of the field that had been seized, stressing that it was in 'perfect condition' and 'very close to my farm'. What annoyed Haltmair even further was the randomness of the confiscation that included not only his pastureland but also neighbouring woodland that he used for mulching the fields.[69] There might have been some basis to this complaint, as one of the British army officers also found himself confused at the parcel of land, which looked to have been 'drawn up in an office from maps' rather than from an actual field visit.[70]

Both Barabas and Haltmair struggled to connect the arrival of several thousand Allied bodies to their own circumstances, or indeed to Nazi Germany's genocidal war. Instead, their main concern was the interruption to their own livelihoods that had occurred once the dead had been deposited on their land. Haltmair described himself as an 'upstanding taxpayer, with a completely clean record'. The implication, therefore, was that he should never have inherited the dead in the first place. For this apparent injustice, he demanded 'appropriate compensation' that would put him on an equal footing with all the 'old Nazis', who had apparently got away with their crimes.[71] Haltmair had equivalent land in mind, whereas in Sage Barabas sought financial recompense for her losses. Unfortunately for them, they both went empty-handed; there was no land of similar quality available, and the state authorities of Lower Saxony offered far less compensation than Barabas believed the field was worth.[72]

For both Barabas and Haltmair, the British dead came to embody all their resentments. Barabas stubbornly refused to relinquish full control of the plot to the IWGC, while Haltmair ended up lashing out against the British. In a moment of rage, he threatened to 'get hold of some dynamite' and use it to blow up the cemetery. Once the headstones had been smashed from their foundations, he was then going to let his cows chew over what remained. After his anger had subsided somewhat, Haltmair claimed that his remarks were 'of course not to be taken seriously' and were merely borne out of frustration at the loss of prime farm-land.[73] Regardless of the specific lines of dispute in Sage and Dürnbach, what is clear is that the arrival of the dead in new national cemeteries, often did very little to improve the British–German relationship.

On Cannock Chase, where the VDK wanted to site its new ceme-tery in an Area of Outstanding Natural Beauty, there was remarkably little opposition to the prospect of building in a protected environment. When it came to the reason for this development, however, there was more disquiet. Upon hearing of the plans to bring thousands of German bodies to Staffordshire, one local councillor pondered whether it might not be better to build a new hospital on the site instead. 'The Chase could then help [British] people in life, rather than in death,' he mused.[74] There were also rumblings of discontent from the members of the Friends of Cannock Chase, a volunteer body that sought to protect the region's unique environment. 'I fought against the Germans and I [do] not particularly want to see them on the Chase,' was one of the most pointed reflections to surface. In the end, the chair of the group managed to silence such views by reminding members that the Germans had given 'great assistance' in caring for the British war dead. Constructing a German cemetery, therefore, was really just a matter of reciprocity, he added, before calling on members to start 'falling in with the idea'.[75]

Whether they were being moved to Cannock Chase, Sage or Dürnbach, the enemy dead arrived in their new homes as disruptors. None of them had originally died at these sites nor, for the most part, anywhere even near them. Instead, their place of death was in faraway POW camps or in aircraft that had crashed down in some distant regions. Being buried near where they had breathed their last had given the enemy a particular connection to the surrounding communities, particularly as local people may have witnessed their original deaths or wartime burials. It was these shared experiences that had encouraged the later deep relations that often blossomed between the bereaved and local custodians.

Once exhumed and moved to the large military cemeteries, however, the enemy dead became interlopers. They had no connection to the new sites or to the local communities surrounding them. What, for example, connected a Zeppelin crew killed over Suffolk in 1917 to

Cannock Chase or an RAF airman shot down and then murdered near Heidelberg but later moved to Dürnbach? The lack of any close bonds to their wartime fate left the new arrivals not only entirely disconnected from their new surroundings, but often unwanted too. It proved much easier for local communities to rally against these mass concentrations than had been the case with the original wartime burial of far smaller numbers of war dead. In the new cemeteries, not only was the original relationship between the enemy and local custodians broken, but any new bonds that emerged were incapable of reconnecting the two sides.

9

NATIONALISING

One of the reasons for moving the German war dead, as the VDK repeatedly explained, was to help 'bereaved relatives to make [. . .] visits' to their loved ones' graves, something that was apparently 'extremely difficult' with the scattered graves.[1] It was something of a surprise, therefore, to discover that four soldiers who had died in Imperial German army uniforms remained in one of the most inaccessible cemeteries, located inside Feltham Borstal Institution, a prison for young people to the west of London. The VDK's brochure, produced for visitors to the new Cannock Chase Cemetery, added more confusion than clarity. It explained that the only 'German dead excluded from the exhumations' were those 'already buried in British military cemeteries' cared for by the CWGC.[2] But the four men in Feltham Borstal were neither in a CWGC cemetery, nor were their graves adorned with the commission's standard headstone. Instead, the graves lay in front of a huge granite boulder, wedged up tight against the Borstal's boundary fence, designed to keep prisoners inside, not to allow visitors in.[3]

On closer inspection, the boulder, inscribed with three lines in Danish, seems to give a strong indication as to why this group of war dead never made it to Cannock. The four men, originally from the German-annexed province of North Schleswig, had died in Feltham during the First World War, when the British had established a POW camp on the site for supposedly friendly prisoners.[4] The VDK was all set to remove the four men to Cannock Chase but, before they could start digging, the Danish embassy halted proceedings. The plans were causing 'great distress' for relatives and war veterans, who did not want to see the four soldiers 'considered as Germans', it explained.[5] After the Danes had recovered their territory in 1920, there had been years of difficult negotiations with Germany over the identity of the Danish soldiers who had fought in German uniforms.[6] Such sensitivities over national identity passed completely over the head of one junior minister in Harold Macmillan's Conservative government who asked simply: 'Why should Germans decide not to remove Danish bodies from English earth to other English earth!'[7] Had the minister taken time to ponder Germany's repeatedly shifting borders in the decades since the First World War, then he might have understood why the idea of Germans removing Danish bodies had the potential to cause upset.

It was not just in Germany's north that the territorial lines had moved; in the east, an independent Polish state had been re-formed after 1918, and this was reconstituted once again after the defeat of Nazi Germany in 1945. There had been signs of these national shifts in Feltham too. Originally, buried alongside the four Danish POWs, there had been eight men from Polish areas who had also died in First World War captivity as members of the German army. However, when the VDK came to exhume the dead in the 1960s, at the height of the Cold War, nobody came out to advocate for the Poles, so their bodies were simply shifted to Cannock Chase to become part of the German Military Cemetery. At least the Danes and Poles managed to retain a marked grave. There had once been another enemy burial at Feltham: a civilian internee, named J. Chudzick, had also originally lain alongside the Poles and Danes. However, there is no longer any sign of Chudzick either in Feltham or in Cannock; his life and wartime death have simply been erased.[8]

On paper, the British and German plans for their war dead appeared to be quite straightforward. Both commissions set out to reclaim their dead by 'renationalizing [the] corpses'.[9] Once in possession of their bodies, they could then reinter the remains in vast national cemeteries, whether on Cannock Chase or in one of the IWGC's military cemeteries in Germany. Yet, as the case of the eight Polish-German soldiers demonstrated, not everyone who actually arrived at these sites had necessarily wanted to be labelled as German or as British. And, as the unfortunate fate of Chudzick also showed, many more bodies were left outside the cemetery gates. Both the British and the Germans had made decisions about which of the war dead were to be given a space in the national cemeteries and which were to be denied a spot. What transpired, therefore, was a rather narrow interpretation of wartime sacrifice and national identity, with ideas of gender, race and military status playing a massive role in decisions as to who was to be allowed entry into these new national pantheons.

National Landscapes

Winston Churchill had set a very high bar for the design of Britain's new military cemeteries when he spoke in the House of Commons in 1920. 'As long as we remain a great nation and Empire,' he pronounced, these sites will 'remain an abiding and supreme memorial to the efforts and the glory of the British Army and the sacrifices made in that great cause'.[10] His words may have been intended to calm public disquiet over the IWGC's concentration policy, but they also helped to demarcate what Churchill called 'ordinary cemeteries' from these new national places of remembrance. The task of the IWGC, and later of the VDK too, was to create resplendent military cemeteries that lived up to such lofty aspirations. In short, this meant designing cemeteries that embodied the national values for which the individuals had apparently given their lives.

Once land had been secured for military burial grounds, either by requisition or negotiation, both the British and the Germans worked quickly to separate their new space from the territory of their former enemy. The IWGC tended to favour the natural aesthetics of a hedge over wire fences for its German cemeteries. However, as the authorities in Hamburg pointed out – no doubt with some disdain at British efforts – a hedge was always going to need considerable time to become properly established. 'The plants used are so small and spread so far apart', they complained, 'that a complete hedge will take decades to grow, if it grows at all.'[11] Avoiding any horticultural niceties entirely, the VDK went for a much more dramatic approach on Cannock Chase, digging a deep trench around the entire perimeter of the site that had an uncanny resemblance to fortifications on the Western Front (see image 26). Fortunately for the VDK's leadership, building the earthworks did not fall to them, but rather to a group of 250 'German boys' from Bremen, who spent their summer digging in Staffordshire. Whether with fences, hedges or ditches, the result was the same: everything within the boundaries was British or German; everything outside was effectively foreign.[12]

26. After the exhumation of the German war dead from across the United Kingdom, there was still much work to be done on Cannock Chase before the new cemetery could be dedicated. To help with preparations, this youth group from Bremen spent their summer in 1962 digging the boundary ditches.

After sealing the sites from their surroundings, the two war graves commissions had to find a way to embed particular national characteristics into the space that remained. While the IWGC had a design model that it had honed to perfection over the years, the VDK found it more of a struggle to draw out the Germanness of Cannock Chase. It faced the twin challenge of needing a cost-effective design for the dead of the two world wars that also avoided the Nazis' adulation of its 'fallen heroes'.[13] Robert Tischler, the VDK's long-standing architect, thought he had found the perfect solution with his plans for a memorial in the Libyan desert outside Tobruk. His imposing fortress-like structure avoided the need for individual graves by bringing the remains of some 6,000 German soldiers together into a central sarcophagus.[14] Tischler might have been pleased with his design, but not everyone else was. A Berlin bishop helpfully reminded the VDK that neither the bereaved nor the Allies had ever shown much enthusiasm for Tobruk. 'The Germans lost the war but are building victory monuments of huge proportions,' was apparently the British view. With Tischler's approach firmly off the table, the VDK instead looked for a more subtle design that would better turn Cannock Chase into a 'slice of German Heimat'.[15]

The VDK's final design for the cemetery envisaged rows of dark granite headstones lined up in regimental fashion, centred on an 11-metre-high metal cross. Completely ignoring the stark differences between the world wars, the VDK viewed its plans as being about universal suffering and 'the shared fate of all of the dead'.[16] In a further attempt to distance the new Federal Republic from the recent German past, the VDK planned a representative sculpture, which would be the first thing visitors saw as they walked through the modest, flat-roofed entrance hall. It was somewhat unfortunate, therefore, that the man charged with the task, the Munich sculptor Hans Wimmer, had honed his skills in the late 1930s and early 1940s, when he enjoyed considerable success creating sculptures of heroic figures in the classical style.[17] Elements of this earlier style lived on in Wimmer's design for Cannock Chase of a semi-nude soldier, lying peacefully on the ground having done his duty. The VDK was evidently pleased with Wimmer's efforts, praising its 'high artistic value', which in their view made it 'surely one of [their] best sculptures'.[18]

Cannock Chase's German Military Cemetery sits just down the road from a smaller British equivalent, although far enough removed to avoid upsetting what the VDK called at the time, a particular 'English mentality'[19] (Map 2). The two cemeteries' close proximity, however, did have the advantage of amplifying the Germanness of the VDK's site when contrasted with the IWGC's earlier approach. The British utilised much lighter materials for their headstones, walls and paving than the dark German granite, which the VDK had imported from Belgium to Staffordshire. In place of figurative sculptures, like Wimmer's fallen warrior, the IWGC also preferred more symbolic pieces. Each large military cemetery received a Stone of Remembrance, an altar-like structure bearing the simple inscription 'Known unto God', a phrase chosen by Rudyard Kipling, the imperialist writer and long-time supporter of the IWGC. Finally, the commission's towering Cross of Sacrifice, embedded with a bronze sword, added religious and militaristic symbolism to the British cemeteries.[20]

However, none of the new military cemeteries, whether in Germany or Britain, were complete until landscaped with plants carefully chosen to represent each country. Heather, with its deep green foliage and bright autumnal flowers, was planted between the graves on Cannock Chase, apparently to resemble the typical landscapes of the North German Lüneburg Heath. In designing their own cemeteries, the IWGC favoured plants typical of a 'feminine English garden', such as roses, bulbs, lavender and irises, softening a space otherwise associated with war and death. These flowers were set off perfectly by neatly clipped green turf, which the IWGC also viewed as a uniquely English approach to gardening. There was no point other people even dabbling with such horticultural styles, one IWGC officer suggested, as they simply were 'not accustomed to the maintenance of lawns'.[21] The IWGC and the VDK, therefore, set out to 'delimit a piece of land' on the other's territory as German or British, providing the architecture and horticulture to match.[22]

Sometimes the surrounding environment had the potential to undermine these attempts to create national spaces. This was always a particular concern of the British, who even sought to alter the surroundings when they appeared to upset the look they were hoping to achieve.

After visiting Berlin in the 1930s, for example, Ware decided that the aesthetics of the IWGC's Stahnsdorf cemetery were being undermined by the presence of a row of large pine trees. He therefore petitioned his opposite numbers in Nazi Germany to have the trees felled, so as to 'transform this cemetery into an English Garden' more fitting for Germany's capital.[23] After the Second World War, it was 'ugly concrete walls' in Celle and 'unsightly barracks' in Kiel that caused the most offence. The judicious planting of English favourites – 'Climbing Roses, Clematis Jackmanii, Wistaria multijuga [sic]' – again came to the rescue, helping to blot out any surrounding urban blight.[24]

The IWGC's desire not only to build new war cemeteries but also to turn these into shining symbols of Britishness always seemed destined to put it on a collision course with local German communities. The city of Münster's Lauheide cemetery sits in a beautiful, forested setting containing 'a wide variety of trees, including beech, oak and pine'.[25] Presumably drawn to the peace and tranquillity of Lauheide, in 1947 the British decided it offered the perfect surroundings for a further concentration cemetery. However, there were two difficulties with this choice. First, the British requisitioned more land than they actually required and, second, the Germans were building their own war cemetery in Lauheide, which just happened to run into the requisitioned area. With the two cemeteries rubbing up against – and even over – one another, Lauheide proved to be a constant source of British–German bickering over the apparently 'out of place' British design. Yet, neither side was going to let their desire to create national cemeteries be derailed by such local distractions and eventually the trees grew sufficiently to provide some screening between the two.[26]

Welcoming Home

Berlin's 1939–1945 British war cemetery, with lavish planting of English roses and lavender, has become the final resting place for soldiers from across the world. William Caldwell, a 19-year-old New Zealander originally from Lyall Bay, a little residential suburb backing onto a glorious sandy cove, lies in Berlin not far from another downed airman, Wilfred Rattigan, who came from Sleeman, a one-horse community in rural Ontario. Aside from having died in the fight against Nazi Germany, the only thing that really united them both was that they had once been part of Britain's global empire. But, for Fabian Ware, a man who fully embraced the idea of a world governed by the 'white Dominions', this in itself was crucial. Ware firmly believed that the IWGC's cemeteries in Germany and elsewhere should symbolise a British empire that, in his words, was united as 'one and [was] indivisible when assailed'.[27]

The empire may have flowed through Ware's veins, but not everyone was quite so enthused by the idea. As Britain's colonial system started to crumble and countries finally started to gain independence, deciding who owned the dead became much trickier. The IWGC faced an early test of its principles when it came to exhuming the Irish war dead from across Germany in the mid-1920s. Although the new Irish Free State, which had emerged out of the Irish War of Independence against the British, made no particular claim to these bodies, the IWGC still found itself in a delicate position.[28] In the historic town of Limburg an der Lahn, where the German military had established its own equivalent of Feltham, only for supposedly friendly Irish POWs, the aesthetics could not have been any worse. During the war, the Irish prisoners had erected a striking Celtic Cross memorial, reportedly the largest in continental Europe, for their forty-five comrades who had perished in Limburg (see image 27). The sight of the British not only removing the Irish bodies but also flattening the memorial would surely not have done much for the fabled image of imperial unity.[29] Fortunately, the IWGC's Principal Assistant Secretary stepped in to avoid any diplomatic embarrassment and declared that the memorial 'should not be removed'.[30]

After the Second World War, the IWGC faced a similar dilemma, only this time with the Indian war dead, as British control in South Asia dissolved. There was never any thought of leaving the hundred or more Indian soldiers and airmen who had died in Germany outside the IWGC's plans; after all, they had lost their lives as a formal part of the empire's war effort. Yet, Ware's original dream of the military cemeteries becoming symbols of imperial strength increasingly looked like an archaic relic from a bygone age. When it came to concentrating the

27. During the First World War, Irish prisoners of war interned in the Limburg an der Lahn internment camp erected a tall Celtic Cross in memory of their forty-five comrades who had died in captivity.

bodies of the Indian dead in defeated Germany, however, the British did give due consideration to religious sensibilities. The plan was to cremate Hindus and Sikhs 'on the spot' wherever bodies happened to be found, while Gurkhas and Muslims were to be exhumed and moved to one of the new military cemeteries.[31] The actual implementation of this policy was at times a bit more haphazard; some Hindu soldiers, for example, ended up being moved from a POW cemetery in Hoyerswerda and reburied in Berlin, when really they should have been cremated.

If the shrinking British empire threw up difficulties for the IWGC's planning, then the issues of shifting national allegiances were even more complicated for the Germans. By the time the VDK came to start exhumations to Cannock Chase in the 1960s, Germany's expansionist visions had shrunk significantly. After wartime defeat, its borders in both the east and west repeatedly shifted, meaning some soldiers might have departed in German uniforms but returned to their homes in what was now France or Poland. Even the VDK, which once boasted of local groups from Saarbrücken to Königsberg, was much curtailed. The German Lutheran Church took a sporadic interest in the war graves in the German

Democratic Republic but anything further east behind the Iron Curtain was firmly off limits. Yet, none of this stopped the VDK from laying claim to large groups of people, who may have had only a very tentative link to the regions within the borders of the post-war Federal Republic.[32]

The Austrian war dead of both world wars lying on British soil caused the most difficulties for the VDK. In theory, their bodies appeared to fall outside the Federal Republic's responsibility. This was certainly how the British had interpreted the matter so far. There had been one test case in 1954, where it was decided that nationality trumped military uniform. The grave in question belonged to Hans-Georg Pramesberger, an Austrian Luftwaffe pilot, who had been buried in Aylesham, Kent, during the Battle of Britain. With the help of a British family, Pramesberger's parents managed to make a request for the body to be cremated and then returned to their hometown of Bad Goisern in Upper Austria.[33] It was at this point that the British hit a problem. Pramesberger had undoubtedly died 'while serving in the German forces', but his relatives were 'apparently resident in Austria'. The conundrum, therefore, was whether the Germans or the Austrians needed to give permission for the exhumation. After much deliberation, the Home Office labelled Pramesberger an 'Austrian national' and never informed the Germans that the body had gone.[34]

At first glance, dealing with the Austrian dead from the First World War appeared to be much more straightforward than was the case with those Austrians, like Pramesberger, killed fighting for Nazi Germany. Having died as civilians or as members of the Austro-Hungarian army, it was much harder to mislabel these 108 men as Germans. Yet, scratch below the surface and certain administrative problems existed here too. Vazal Marzsinean, who died as a POW in Surrey in February 1919, was a typical example of Central Europe's fluid populations. Marzsinean had been captured the previous year at a point in the conflict when some Austrian divisions were seeing service in the west. Shipped across the English Channel into captivity, Marzsinean soon fell ill and was taken to the Belmont POW Hospital in Surrey, where he rapidly succumbed to tuberculosis. At the time of his death, the Red Cross recorded Marzsinean as an Austro-Hungarian from the village of Magyarherepe. But even this was open for interpretation as, at the end of the war, Magyarherepe was formally ceded to Romania and renamed Herepea, leaving Marzsinean himself presumably as a Romanian.[35]

Whether or not Marzsinean was Austrian, Hungarian, Romanian or even German did not really concern the VDK. Its overriding aim was simply to scoop up all the dead who vaguely came within its remit and move them to Cannock Chase. This was neither an act of altruism nor an act of mortuary aggrandisement; it rather came down to what was most practical. The British had often buried the enemy as one, some-times even mixing together different nationalities in the same common grave. To get to their dead in Sutton Cemetery, where Marzsinean was buried, the VDK needed first to move him and the remains of another seven Austrians. It was far easier, therefore, simply to move them all at the same time, rather than having to disentangle any non-Germans from the grave.[36]

The Austrian government, though, failed to share the Germans' enthusiasm for concentrating the dead. It insisted that any Austro-Hungarians from the Great War should remain where they were currently buried, as should Austrian refugees from the Second World War, leaving only Austrians who had fought for the Nazi regime destined for Cannock Chase. Try to remember that we were 'brothers in arms during the war', insisted the VDK, but the Austrians refused to budge. They rightly pointed out that under German plans, Austrian Jews who had died in the First World War and refugees from the later conflict could feasibly end up buried in the new German cemetery next to 'members of the SS'.[37]

The Austrians were certainly not exaggerating when they raised these concerns, for some particularly unsavoury characters did end up in Cannock Chase. One of these was Aril Knoppert, a Dutchman, who had originally been buried in Knutsford, Cheshire. After the Second World War, the Dutch government had denied any claim to Knoppert, labelling him a traitor. The VDK later proved less discerning and rein-terred him as a German.[38] In Cannock Chase, he could enjoy the company of an unknown number of Ukrainian Waffen-SS members, who had died in British captivity. Their former comrades even added their own vaguely worded plaque for 'Ukrainian Soldiers' in the 1980s.

However, the most notorious reinterment was surely that of Maximilian von Herff, head of the SS personnel office, a Waffen-SS general, who had also played a role in crushing Jewish resistance during the 1943 Warsaw Ghetto uprising. Von Herff died as a POW in the much more genteel surroundings of a Lake District POW camp in September 1945.[39] When it came to exhuming his remains in the 1960s, neither the British nor the Germans raised any issues, and he too made the journey to the new German Military Cemetery.

Just as the Austrians had predicted, von Herff and other war criminals ended up in Cannock Chase lying near the victims of Nazi Germany. The British government's decision to 'collar the lot' in June 1940, following the fall of France, led to the arrest and internment of all 'enemy aliens', including thousands of refugees who had fled Nazi Germany.[40] Some of these people were ill, infirm or already in a poor way having fled persecution in Central Europe. Being thrown into camps behind barbed wire in a supposedly friendly country hardly helped matters. Many people's physical and mental health deteriorated further, and suicides were common. In the Huyton internment camp, which occupied a newly built council estate to the east of Liverpool, men took their own lives on six separate occasions.[41]

The situation was little better on the Isle of Man, where men and women were stranded far from friends and family in the middle of the Irish Sea. One of those to suffer loss on the island was 28-year-old Anna Ortner. Originally a domestic servant in Vienna, she left Austria in late 1937, arriving first in Dover, before eventually finding work in Surrey. With the outbreak of hostilities, and in the early stages of pregnancy, she was sent to the Rushen Camp on the Isle of Man, which the British established primarily for women and children who had been branded as 'enemy aliens'.[42] Ortner's son John, baptised Joannes, was born in early 1941, but sadly died some twelve months later from diphtheria and was buried on the island. Twenty years later the VDK arrived to take his remains to the new German Military Cemetery, even though the young Ortner had never even set foot on German soil and was hardly of fighting age when he died. Fortunately, for the VDK, the dead cannot speak, so they kindly imposed a German identity on the bodies, whether Ortner and others liked it or not.[43]

However, the living also raised their voices and were sometimes even heard. Originally, the VDK had planned to concentrate the German and Austrian Jewish dead in its new military cemetery. Some of these men had died as members of the First World War armies, while others were refugees from Nazi Germany. Bernard Seidel, a Frankfurt bookseller, fell into this second category. After the First World War, Seidel and his wife, Johanna, had both severed their ties with the city's Jewish community, but of course this was of little concern to the Nazis once they came to power. The pair managed to reach England in the late 1930s, together with their two children, but for some reason Johanna returned to Germany. All that is then known is that she was 'deported in the direction of Lublin in May/June 1942 and has not returned', which was ominous as the Nazis' Lublin District was at the centre of the Operation Reinhard extermination camps.[44] Bernard Seidel, meanwhile, was interned in the Central Camp on the Isle of Man, as part of the British policy of screening 'enemy aliens'. The precise details are sketchy, but what is clear is that he died there in August 1940.[45]

Seidel's body was brought back to the mainland and laid to rest in Liverpool's Long Lane Cemetery. The private headstone makes visible the family's suffering: 'In Loving Memory of our Dear Father, Bernard Seidel [. . .] Also in Loving Memory of our Dear Mother, Johanna Seidel (née Neu). Died in a Polish Concentration Camp. Deeply Mourned by their Daughters.'[46] On a human level, the VDK should never have even contemplated removing the remains of Seidel and other Jewish dead to Cannock Chase. At a time of rising antisemitic incidents in West Germany, including the vandalism of hundreds of Jewish sites, it would have been politically illiterate too. Indeed, when vandals scrawled swastikas on Cologne's synagogue in December 1959, there was international outrage. *The Times* feared the attacks were a sign of 'a new birth of an old evil' that threatened to undermine a supposedly democratic Federal Republic.[47] It was paramount for West German institutions, therefore, to demonstrate greater sensitivity to the recent Nazi past, which, in the case of the VDK, clearly meant not disturbing Jewish bodies.[48]

In the end, it fell on the British-Jewish communities to point out the incongruity of the VDK's plans. The United Synagogue in London demanded that the Home Office stop the exhumations, which went against Jewish law, while the Isle of Man Hebrew Congregation lodged a 'strong protest' against 'the disturbance in any way' of the Jewish graves on the island.[49] Bringing the Jewish dead, whether First World War soldiers or later refugees to Cannock Chase, would have been beneficial for the VDK, further helping to blur the lines between perpetrators and victims. After all, if Jews had died alongside other Germans in the world wars, then it became much easier to ignore the particularities of death and instead to speak more generally of shared losses.[50] However, given the protests, even the VDK had to concede that the Jewish bodies should remain where they lay.

Closing the Cemetery Gates

The two war graves commissions may have been very keen to bring a random assortment of people into their new cemeteries, some of whom only had a tentative connection to either Britain or Germany, but at the same time they also expended considerable energy on trying to bar others from making the same journey. One of those never to make it was Thomas French, Master of the SS Rubens, a slender single-funnelled cargo vessel which had been impounded in Hamburg in 1914 and the crew interned. When French died in October 1915 in the Ruhleben internment camp, his wife, Clementine, had sought just 'one comfort' which was to have his body repatriated home from the Spandau cemetery, west of Berlin, where he lay. But it was a familiar story; the Foreign Office rejected her request, as 'quite impractical', adding that the 'expenses would be prohibitive'.[51] Resigned to leaving her husband in Germany, Clementine erected her own memorial plaque in the parish church of Old Lakenham, outside Norwich. French himself is still in Spandau. A small concrete plinth, covered in moss and whitish-green lichen, unceremoniously marks his final resting place.

It was never the case that the IWGC had simply forgotten French; it was rather that they were simply not interested in him. As far as the IWGC was concerned, French was a civilian and therefore fell outside its strict military sphere of operation. The apparent inequity from an organisation whose mantra was 'equality of treatment', struck Victoria de Voss, an Englishwoman living in Berlin, as particularly unfair.[52] 'May I put in a plea for those who have died in a civilian camp?' she asked Rudyard Kipling, who was an early supporter of the IWGC. Without waiting for his reply, Voss explained that many of the internees would have fought for their country and, given half a chance, would have probably 'met a glorious death on the field of battle'. Therefore, she wanted to know why they should be denied their own 'Cross of Sacrifice and Stone of Remembrance [just] because there is no regimental badge, only a prison number'.[53] Such arguments made little impression on Kipling and his colleagues in the IWGC. When the commission came to move the dead to its new site in Stahnsdorf, French and the other British civilians buried in another eight Berlin cemeteries were left behind. These are 'not War Graves and should not be concentrated', was the blunt instruction.[54]

Just as the IWGC barred civilians from its cemeteries, so it also objected to the presence of any post-war dead. It imposed two somewhat arbitrary cut-off points of 31 August 1921 and 31 December 1947; anyone unfortunate enough to die after these dates was denied entry to the hallowed ground of its military cemeteries. This was already a highly contentious policy, but the inequities of it were really laid bare in Germany in the two post-war eras.[55] On the Rhineland, partly occupied during the 1920s, British troops continued to die in uniform. Most of these deaths were either accidents – drowning while bathing in the Rhine was common – or caused by sickness or disease.[56] William Thomas Ellerker, for example, a decorated war veteran, arrived in Cologne to work with the Intelligence Corps. He had not been in the historic city long when he fell ill with an infection, dying only four days later in December 1921. A large crowd gathered in Cologne's Southern Cemetery to pay their respects to a 'tremendously popular' officer. However, as he 'happened to die after the date when the war had "officially"' ended, as one newspaper later put it, Ellerker was laid to rest in a civilian section of the burial ground.[57]

Although Ellerker just missed out on a place in one of the IWGC's military cemeteries in Germany, surely the thirty-nine members of the British military killed during the Berlin airlift in 1948 and 1949 had more of a claim. In June, the Soviets sealed off all land routes into the divided city of Berlin, which sat like an island in the middle of the Soviet zone of occupation. Determined not to give physical and metaphorical ground in a deepening Cold War, the Americans and British started a series of dangerous airdrops to keep Berliners fed, watered and warm. Flying at night from tight landing strips on land and water required commensurate skill and considerable luck too. Illustrating the lethal nature of these flights, one British transporter, a Handley Page Hastings, took off from Berlin Tegel in July 1949. It rose steadily into air before suddenly dropping and hitting the ground almost vertically. It took the fire brigade more than thirty minutes to dampen the flames which had engulfed the wreckage, by which point the five-man crew were long dead.[58]

As had been the case with Ellerker a quarter of a century earlier, the dead men received a lavish military funeral. British forces stationed in the then former German capital marched the coffins, draped in Union Jack flags, into the cemetery. With groups of uniformed men looking on, a military padre then conducted the funeral service, before the bodies were lowered into a grave (see image 28). However, this turned out not to be their final resting place. After the commission decided to close the site, the five men were exhumed and moved to the IWGC's larger 1939–1945 Berlin military cemetery. Even then, their graves remained something of an awkward presence, consigned to a separate post-war plot, where they lay with a mixture of civilian personnel and later military casualties. Trying to get these different elements to mesh gave the IWGC's horticultural experts a big headache. Plantings needed to be rethought, the 'narrow' borders widened and the 'poor'-quality grass re-sown with 'one of our own best mixtures' was the advice.[59]

Other British servicemen did not even enjoy the luxury of close proximity to a national cemetery. In Wiesbaden, 132 civilian and military bodies, mainly from the 1920s occupation era, remain in the city's main cemetery, quietly resting under what the IWGC considered to be 'unsightly headstones'.[60] By far the most neglected post-war graves, though, were surely those in the Polish city of Opole, formerly German Oppeln. The graves all belonged to British soldiers who had died in the early 1920s as members of an Allied peacekeeping force overseeing a

28. Thirty-nine members of the British forces lost their lives in the post-war Berlin airlift. In July 1949, five of these airmen were laid to rest in the city's Olympische Strasse Cemetery. A decade later, the IWGC exhumed their remains to the larger Berlin military cemetery.

plebiscite for determining whether Upper Silesia was to come under German or Polish control.[61] Some of those killed had suffered extremely violent deaths; Sergeant Selvester was shot in the abdomen, while Sergeant Waknell took a bullet to the face.[62] But the IWGC's concern was solely with their self-imposed 31 August 1921 cut-off point, not how the soldiers had lost their lives. Therefore, when their exhumation teams arrived in Opole to concentrate the dead, they took eleven of the correct type of dead to Berlin Stahnsdorf, leaving behind the bodies of thirty British soldiers who 'did not conform with the regulations'. The unwanted graves lay neglected for many years in an ever-worsening state until vanishing into obscurity behind the Iron Curtain after the Second World War.[63]

The VDK generally seemed less picky as to who entered its new cemetery on Cannock Chase. Germans, Austrians, Poles, Dutch and even Czechoslovaks found a spot, as did military and civilians, which is how one-year-old John Ortner ended up being moved from the Isle of Man.[64] The VDK was also less concerned with a strict cut-off point. At one point, it even tried to make the case for the inclusion of a former member of the Waffen-SS who had died in an accident while working in Dundee in the 1950s. 'The grave does not have a headstone and the parents, both pensioners who were bombed out in the war, are in no position to pay for one,' the VDK pleaded. The West German Foreign Ministry, though, was less convinced, pointing out that the deceased had not even been a POW at the time of his death and had 'made the choice to stay in England [sic]'.[65]

However, even the VDK drew the line somewhere. The one group it was fairly determined to keep out of Cannock Chase were the slave labourers who had perished as part of the Nazis' Organisation Todt. Like so much of the Nazi regime's power structures, the organisation had developed haphazardly. Initially responsible for the task of accelerating the building of new roads and *Autobahnen*, it grew haphazardly to become the major player in all matters of infrastructure construction, from canals and docks, through to major military fortifications. Building on this scale clearly required a large labour force; up to 2 million workers, according to some estimates. The vast majority laboured against their will, having been recruited from occupied territory, POW camps and concentration camps. With brutal conditions and high death rates, the organisation acquired a reputation among its workers for 'murderous brutality'.[66]

On the British mainland, there were only three foreign worker graves recorded, which should not come as a surprise, as the Organisation Todt's purpose was engineering and construction.[67] Cross over the sea to the Channel Islands, however, and the picture was very different.

Under German occupation from June 1940 until the war's end, the islands became a key cog in the Nazis' Atlantic Wall, a line of defensive fortifications stretching around the coast of continental Europe. Organisation Todt, which oversaw much of the planning, started to bring large numbers of workers to the islands in summer 1942, to start building the giant fortifications. The workforce, which numbered 16,000 at its height, consisted of conscripts and forced labourers from as far east as Ukraine and as far south as Algeria. Conditions were abysmal, particularly on Alderney, with workers dying from malnutrition, sickness, deliberate killings and accidents. The brutal end to Antoni Onuchowski's life was sadly typical. Rounded up in occupied Poland, Onuchowski eventually ended up on Alderney, where he became severely ill in September 1942. With swelling to his feet, he was unable to keep up with the other workers; the guards' response was to beat him with their truncheons, leaving him for dead.[68]

When the German occupation of the Channel Islands officially ended in May 1945, 389 workers had died, although the precise number is still unknown and likely to have been far higher. The dead were buried unceremoniously in a mixture of unmarked and often incorrectly marked graves. The name of Onuchowski, for example, appeared on two separate grave markers. Of course, even if the Germans had buried Onuchowski properly, which is uncertain, his remains can only ever have been in one of the grave plots, but which one remained unclear.[69]

In stark contrast, the occupiers also left behind several 'beautifully maintained' military cemeteries containing the remains of some 475 Germans who died during the occupation.[70] Under the terms of the 1959 British–German War Graves Agreement, the VDK had permission to exhume German war dead, but the bodies of Organisation Todt workers were a grey area. The Foreign Ministry in Bonn was of the view that 'non-uniformed foreign workers', which included the Todt members, fell outside the agreement, but the British proved less particular. Fearing it was going to be left with these graves, the CWGC thought it better for Germans to take all the dead in one go, thinking it 'unlikely that we shall be able to persuade them to return'.[71] While everyone was distracted with the issue of the forced workers, the VDK suddenly declared that it was also going to remove both groups of bodies – the

German military dead and the forced workers – to Normandy, rather than to Cannock Chase. Even though it had been mooted previously, the choice of destination seemed to be news to the British, who meekly noted that moving the dead overseas broke the terms of the 1959 Agreement, but otherwise had no interest in intervening.[72]

The VDK had no intention of hanging around on the Channel Islands. In December 1961, only two months after its first workers had stepped off the ferry, the local press announced that the 'German War Cemeteries [had] Disappear[ed]'.[73] Allowing the graves to vanish from sight suited all concerned. The CWGC was pleased that it was not going to be burdened with the 'considerable extra expense' of dealing with the Organisation Todt dead, while the Channel Islanders were happy to close a 'further chapter' from the 'dark days of 1940–1945', helping them quietly to forget less palatable moments of collaboration and even denunciation.[74] Sending the dead to Mont-de-Huisnes in Normandy had distinct advantages for the VDK too. As a mausoleum rather than a cemetery of individual marked graves, it made it much easier to lose the Operation Todt workers among the 11,000 or so other bodies. Had the foreign workers, taken from all corners of Europe and North Africa, instead ended up on Cannock Chase, it would have made the Nazis' crimes visible to a much wider British audience. What was supposed to be the shining face of a new Germany would have been sullied from the start. Once the dead were in France, this was no longer the case and these past crimes appeared to conveniently 'disappear'.

Absent-Minded Gravediggers

On the Channel Islands, the Nazi occupiers' record keeping had been so poor and so derisory when it came to the forced labourers that the VDK may well have missed bodies during their exhumation operations.[75] After all, if the dead had already vanished from the administrative record, then it was very difficult to come along and attempt to find them later. This was not just an issue for the VDK on the Channel Islands. Across both Britain and Germany, remains were sometimes abandoned or lost, and therefore these individuals, who had lost their lives as the wartime enemy, never made it to one of the new national cemeteries.

Civilian internees were the most likely group to end up excluded in this way. Unlike the military prisoners, who had the support of their respective war ministries and later the war graves organisations, the civilians had fewer formal institutions advocating on their behalf. The ease with which some internees were forgotten was evident from the medieval city of Winchester. When the VDK arrived to exhume the German war dead, their lists contained the names of eight men from the First World War and three from the Second. One name not on their records was that of Oskar Steinwarz, a 34-year-old writer, originally from Offenburg, who before the war had lived near Winchester with his English-born wife. With the outbreak of hostilities in 1914, Steinwarz eventually ended up behind wire as an 'enemy alien', at which point his health deteriorated rapidly. In February 1917, he was admitted to Camberwell House Lunatic Asylum with 'self inflicted' wounds to his 'neck & side' and died just a few weeks later.[76] As was the case with many of the civilian dead, a family member took care of the funeral arrangements, but this meant the name never appeared on official records as a war casualty. Steinwarz, along with many other civilians, has therefore entirely vanished from the history of the war.[77]

A narrow concept of what constituted a wartime death made it all the easier for civilians like Steinwarz to vanish from public memory. Along with those dying in asylums, female deaths also tended to be long forgotten before the war graves commissions had even started to plan their exhumation schedules. This is clear from the completed British war cemeteries in Germany. Of the 32,000 graves from the two world wars, fewer than fifty are of women. The CWGC's war cemeteries may give the impression that wartime death was an entirely male affair, but women also died on German soil during and immediately after the two world wars. There are the well-known cases of female operatives executed in Nazi concentration camps, of women dying as part of the British occupation forces and of civilian internees losing their lives while held behind wire.[78] In the southern German town of Bad Wurzach, for example, five women, who had been deported from the Channel Islands in 1942 as part of the Nazis' round-up of British-born islanders, died in its elegant baroque castle that doubled as a temporary internment camp. The IWGC took only a cursory interest in these graves, stressing that they were entirely 'outside our powers', even if this did seem a little 'unreasonable', they admitted.[79]

In Britain, women also died under the stigma of being the wartime enemy. Even when their deaths were high profile, taking place in a glare of publicity, many of these women were still overlooked when it later came to filling the national cemeteries. The dramatic death of Emma Ahlers, the wife of the German consul in Sunderland, is a case in point. Despite taking British citizenship in 1905, the Ahlers had come under immediate suspicion when Britain declared war against Germany in August 1914 and were arrested on charges of treason. 'Sunderland Sensation', declared the press, revelling in their misery.[80] Although the charges were dropped and the family escaped the limelight for a while, the former consul was rearrested in 1915, with Emma Ahlers following him into captivity the year after. Described as a 'delicate, nervous woman', Ahlers' health suffered, and she died in Holloway Prison from an overdose of Veronal barbital in March 1917. German reports blamed her death on the 'jingoistic English', who continued to attack 'everything German'. Yet, decades later, when the VDK arrived to exhume its dead, nobody came looking for Ahlers, leaving her as yet another person excluded from the new German cemetery and destined to be forgotten.[81]

One of the reasons that Ahlers, Steinwarz and others never made it back into the national fold was that their graves were already long lost, which clearly made concentration tricky. There were, however, plenty of other cases where, although the whereabouts of the enemy graves were known, the remains were also never exhumed. It should have been very difficult for the VDK to fail to find the grave of the Bavarian officer, Georg Eid, in Altrincham, just to the south of Manchester. The headstone from the First World War, which towered almost up to shoulder height, was not only inscribed with a German inscription, but also contained an Iron Cross relief in the centre (see image 29). Despite the monumentality of the headstone, the VDK's exhumation team somehow missed Eid's grave. They arrived in Altrincham in 1962, but left empty-handed, apparently because the grave 'could not be recovered'.[82]

Labelling graves as irretrievable or unrecoverable was really just a more palatable way of describing the VDK's policy of abandonment. It was not that the VDK failed to find Eid's grave in Altrincham; it was

29. The grave of Georg Eid, a Bavarian officer who died in May 1917 while
being held as a prisoner in Altrincham. Standing to the left of the headstone
is Mr Heyworth, the British translator for the town's POW camp; to the
right is the vicar of Altrincham with his wife.

rather the case that they consciously chose to leave his remains behind.
The VDK had already floated the idea of disposing of First World War
graves, like Eid's, as 'most of the relatives were now dead'.[83] But what
really condemned Eid to obscurity was the fact that he shared the burial
plot with a further twelve bodies. It would have been impossible to
disinter Eid without disturbing them, which meant the VDK would
have required the permission of the relatives of the other people buried
in the same grave. In these circumstances, the British 'induced the
Germans to desist from pressing for the right to exhume' from common
graves. The VDK proved only too willing to oblige, leaving Eid and
many other Germans stranded outside its new military cemetery purely
for the sake of convenience.[84]

The policy of leaving behind bodies in shared graves could easily
have been justified on the basis that these dead already rested under
well-maintained headstones. But even this appeared to be too much for
the two war graves commissions, who decided that if the bodies were
not going to move, then they were not going to stay either. Acting as

one, the VDK and CWGC confirmed that any German graves that 'could not be regrouped' to Cannock Chase 'will be abandoned and markers will be removed'.[85] Eid fell into this category, as did many more graves in Greenwich, Newton-le-Willows, Chester, Carmarthen and numerous places in between. The irony was that the Germans had pushed for a national war cemetery to secure the future care of their war dead, but in achieving their dream, they also willingly allowed hundreds of other marked war graves to be flattened.

The British occasionally took a similarly pragmatic approach to their graves in Germany, always prioritising the aesthetics of the national cemeteries over any individual bodies that fell foul of their plans. When concentrating the First World War dead in the 1920s, the IWGC's exhumation teams recovered three bodies from a cemetery in Hillesheim, but then hit a problem with the fourth. The remains of Henry Wilkes, who had died in the final months of the conflict, had unhelpfully been discarded in a grave 'with those of other nationalities', making it 'impossible to distinguish the British [body] from the others'. The gravediggers, therefore, reluctantly left Wilkes behind. However, rather than marking the grave, they decided to abandon it instead, placing a new headstone at the entrance with the vague inscription of 'Known to be Buried'. The incongruity of this solution was not lost on a later generation of IWGC personnel, who decided there was little point in having a headstone, if it 'did not mark the actual grave', which rather ignored how this issue had ever come about in the first place. With that, Wilkes's non-grave marker was removed from Hillesheim to be replaced with a new headstone in the British cemetery in Cologne with the generous, albeit slightly duplicitous, inscription: 'Buried at the Time in Hillesheim Cemetery but whose Grave is now Lost'.[86]

Simply abandoning graves in Hillesheim and elsewhere seemed a step too far, even if the IWGC's determination to ensure it retrieved the correct remains was entirely understandable. The commission placed great store on the accuracy of its record keeping; it certainly wanted to avoid a scenario where it allowed the wrong person into its national space. There was, therefore, considerable consternation when it emerged that the Air Ministry had been arranging for the remains of aircrews who had been killed on bombing raids over Nazi Germany to be exhumed to concentration cemeteries, when there were never any bodies to start with. The Air Ministry's 'view of the matter', the IWGC explained, was that if little of the body remained after a high impact crash, then 'removing a certain quantity of earth [. . .] to form a "grave"' was a sensible compromise. The IWGC was less convinced, fearing the 'unfortunate consequences if such a thing leaks out'.[87]

The IWGC may have tried to brush such issues away, but the Air Ministry's seemingly unorthodox approach to exhumations does raise questions about the extent of the remains actually brought to the new war cemeteries. One man who knew about this better than most was M.A. Rawley, who joined the VDK's exhumation operations in Britain during the early 1960s. When Rawley's team reached the Zeppelin graves in Theberton in Suffolk, he remembered that they had found some of the bodies in 'flying suits' still wearing 'leather boots with all the fur inside'. But then under other headstones they found nothing at all, presumably because the bodies had been destroyed during the Zeppelin's original crash. Determined not to leave empty-handed, however, they filled the coffins with 'whatever it was' lying around and simply made up the coffins in this way.[88]

It was only when these slightly unorthodox practices came to the attention of more assiduous officials that difficulties arose. The local medical officer for health for Westmorland, whose official responsibilities covered the southern half of the Lake District, certainly fitted this category. He had observed the VDK's gravediggers at work in Kendal and was fairly shocked at their practices. After opening a grave, he complained, the gravediggers then proceeded to 'scrape' the bones, leaving behind 'soft parts, clothing or shroud' in the now empty plot. In his view, these were nothing more than 'partial exhumations' as some of the remains had simply been 'discarded'. All parties concerned just wanted the matter 'treated [. . .] confidentially' and kept away from the court of 'public opinion'. The key issue was ensuring that the new national cemeteries gave the impression of totality; whether this was ever really achieved was less of a concern, so long as the public did not stop to ask difficult questions.[89]

Had there been an opportunity to examine the details of these new military cemeteries more closely, people would probably have been surprised to discover how incomplete the sites actually were. The war graves commissions had set out to translate the messiness of the two world wars into something that could be more easily consumed by the bereaved, the public at large and, crucially, by their former enemy on whose territory the cemeteries sat.[90] With their manicured lawns, neat rows of regimental headstones and clever architectural flourishes, it is safe to say that in this regard both the British and German war graves commissions achieved their aims.

Yet, not everyone who died in conflict gained entry to these new national spaces; the communities of the dead had been carefully curated to ensure the finished cemeteries projected acceptable narratives of the world wars. Some bodies, therefore, had to fall by the wayside, whether these were civilians, the post-war dead or, in the case of the Germans, members of Organisation Todt. If the West Germans were to present themselves as a new Germany, unburdened by the legacies of a genocidal war, then there could be no place for forced labourers in the heart of Staffordshire. But at the same time, neither the British nor the Germans had any qualms about welcoming in other groups of the dead, who, by the time of the cemeteries' creation, had only a tentative link to West Germany or to Britain's crumbling empire. It did not matter if Austrians, Irish, Indians or even Dutch people entered these spaces, so long as both the VDK and the IWGC were left with something that they could label a national cemetery. The illusion of national homogeneity mattered far more than the realities on the ground.

10

RITUALISING

By the late 1950s, the much-troubled British cemetery in Dürnbach, which had been plagued by problems over unsuitable materials and poor workmanship, finally played host to the first of what were to become annual remembrance ceremonies. After all, this was not just about the creation of a new cemetery, it was also about the invention of tradition.[1] From the start, these services were very formal affairs. Military uniforms, highly polished boots and lines of upright servicemen filled the cemetery space, with its commanding views out towards the Alps. An RAF band, bussed in from the British sector, provided the musical accompaniment, while a military clergyman then led the religious part of the ceremony, before the obligatory wreath-laying brought proceedings to a close. Many of the early services had a guest list to match the grandeur of the setting. The British consul general from Munich, the British ambassador, an air commodore and local American commanders all showed their faces in Dürnbach during these first years. Given local arguments that surrounded the cemetery's initial construction, it was perhaps a surprise to see the German mayor from the neighbouring community, decked out in a smart jacket and tie, also putting in an appearance.[2]

Both the British and Germans, who by this time were Cold War allies rather than wartime enemies, were quick to frame the remembrance services in terms of post-war reconciliation. The RAF's official photographs, printed to accompany its operation reports, included a close-up of the German mayor seemingly in deep conversation with the air commodore, as the pair made their way into the cemetery. Even more explicitly, the regional Bavarian press commented on the two nations' 'shared suffering', almost as if no perpetrators had ever been involved, and praised the mayor's attendance as a sign that 'a lot has changed in Germany'.[3] Whether they liked it or not, the dead, who had been brought together into a single site, had now been given the job of working for peace and reconciliation. No doubt with one eye on improving its own reputation overseas, the VDK was particularly attached to the idea that the war cemeteries could function as a vehicle for international understanding. It plastered its activities with the phrase 'Versöhnung über den Gräbern', which it very loosely translated as 'Reconciliation at the Graves', before later adding the less than subtle suffix 'Working for Peace' to the motto.[4]

However, trying to turn the national cemeteries into arenas of British–German understanding was really just a post-factum attempt to rationalise the reason for their original creation. There was very little left of the more spontaneous gestures of reconciliation that had once actually brought local communities and the bereaved together. These earlier custodians had been replaced by official dignitaries, such as the ambassadors, military commanders or regional mayors who lined up for set-piece services, but then quickly dispersed. Other than as bystanders to formal remembrance services or ceremonies, the British and German people had very little to do with these new sites. If they paid any attention to them at all, it tended to be with curiosity, even ambivalence, towards their former enemy's new national sites of memory. The war graves commissions were happy to claim their new military cemeteries helped to bring the erstwhile foes together but, beyond the cemetery gates, the effects were far more limited.

The Label of Reconciliation

There had been a long history of British remembrance services in Germany. In November 1920, three German firemen, Friedrich Braun, Jacob Vogt and Wilhem Fromme, became unsuspecting witnesses to one of the first British Armistice Day ceremonies to be held in the Weimar Republic. The three, who had been busy working at the dockside in Cologne, laid down their tools to watch, as the British military parade marched in. Only, instead of standing in solemn silence as the buglers sounded the Last Post, they apparently 'saw fit to laugh and sneer'. A British sergeant present at the ceremony later testified that he saw 'these blokes', meaning Braun, Vogt and Fromme, 'jeering and gesticulating and generally [being] insulting towards us.' The three German firemen protested their innocence, claiming they had been laughing at a joke; it had presumably just been bad timing that the punchline came in the middle of the two minutes' silence. After inevitably rejecting their plea, the British presiding officer sentenced the three men to a one-month jail term. 'To make fun of a parade [...] is not only an insult to the living but also to the dead,' he reprimanded them.[5]

This was rather an inauspicious start to any notion that the presence of the war dead could bring about reconciliation. Admittedly, Germany after defeat and revolution was hardly the ideal test case, particularly as the British entered the Rhineland as an occupying army.[6] But as the immediacy of the war's end passed, there were occasional signs that the war cemeteries could help with British–German peace-making, however optimistic this might have seemed. In November 1929, the city authorities in Cologne got in on the act for the first time, laying a wreath in the British section of the Southern Cemetery, which they had decorated suitably in the Rhineland city's red and white.[7] This act was a far cry from the jeering firemen who had initially sullied such remembrance events. The following year, Hamburg's city parliament followed suit by laying a wreath in the IWGC's section of the sprawling Ohlsdorf cemetery. Their actions, which had happened without any advance warning, caught the British consul by surprise. 'When I was visiting the British war cemetery on Sunday,' he wrote, 'to my pleasure, I suddenly noticed the friendly gesture [...] of the wreath.'[8]

However, damage to these wreaths the following November, when someone hacked off the ribbons, only served to highlight the fragility of such gestures for any meaningful sense of reconciliation.[9] There was more success, at least on paper, from a series of international visits which used the new British war cemeteries as a backdrop for their own diplomatic efforts. An amateur football team from Ilford, for example, found time to break their continental tour to lay their own wreaths in Cologne's British war cemetery. This was not just about honouring the dead; the visit also provided the group with an opportunity to make profound gestures about war, peace and reconciliation. Herbert Dunnico, Labour MP and peace campaigner, who had joined the tour, helped to push forward the message of peace. After laying their wreaths, the players stood and listened as Dunnico explained how the British and German soldiers buried in the Southern Cemetery were all united in a 'brotherhood' of death.[10] The problem with such gestures was they only spoke to the converted. All that the local press was interested in was the fact that the players of Ilford FC had thrashed local favourites, Kölner SV 1899, by five goals to two.[11]

Some six years later, it was suddenly very difficult to avoid reading about wreaths being laid in the same cemetery. The German and British newspapers were filled with stories and pictures of floral tributes on the war graves in Cologne. However, despite their prominence, the wreaths were something of a sideshow. The real focus of attention was on a delegation of war veterans, all leading figures in the British Legion ex-servicemen's organisation, who had stopped off in Cologne in July 1935. The leader of the little party was Francis Fetherston-Godley, a moustachioed army major and chair of the legion, who could be guaranteed to appear at any occasion with a row of highly polished medals pinned to his chest. Once the delegation had reached the Cross of Sacrifice in the IWGC's cemetery, Fetherston-Godley took a few steps forward before carefully laying down his wreath. At first glance, this ritual appeared comfortably familiar, but further back a row of brown-shirted SA men, Hitler Youth and girls in the Nazis' Bund Deutscher Mädel, lined the path of the cemetery. After a series of speeches, the legion members and their hosts retreated to the salubrious setting of Cologne's town hall for an official luncheon, which concluded with a round of 'Sieg Heils' in honour of the legion and the British king.[12]

This sustenance break in Cologne actually marked the culmination of what had been a ten-day nationwide tour. As was befitting for an ex-servicemen's group, the Great War and its fraught legacies was a constant theme for the delegates. German war veterans accompanied them for parts of their journey, and the IWGC's cemeteries in Germany featured prominently in their schedule. In Berlin, which had been the delegation's first destination, there was time for an afternoon trip down to the British war graves in Stahnsdorf. A similar ritual played out to that in Cologne, with Nazi uniforms lined up as far as the eye could see, supposedly there in honour of both their British visitors and the war dead. After another series of speeches, members of the Nazi youth organisations placed a single rose on each of the British war graves. 'Visibly touched' by the gesture, Fetherston-Godley then personally thanked the young Germans.[13] When the British Legion delegation arrived at their next destination, Hamburg, the whole scene repeated itself once again. In the British cemetery in Ohlsdorf, the same mixture of uniforms, flowers and wreaths was again on display, as the legion members paid respects to their dead.[14]

The British Legion had a long-held aim of fostering better relations with Britain's erstwhile enemy, but even so, its tour of Nazi Germany still marked a major policy departure, taking it from the national to the international arena. The fact that the trip included a meeting with Adolf Hitler and his entourage did not overtly concern Fetherston-Godley, who later found time to tick off another fascist dictator when he visited Benito Mussolini in Rome; his main concern was simply to ensure that the British Legion increased its public and political profile.[15] If the legion's ordinary members were at all concerned by their leaders' dalliance with international fascists, then some supportive words from the Prince of Wales, the future Edward VIII, surely helped to calm nerves. 'I feel that there could be no more suitable body or organization to stretch forth the hand of friendship to the Germans than we ex-Service men,' the prince reassured the membership.[16] Once home after their whirlwind tour of Nazi Germany, Fetherston-Godley was quick to reiterate this same sentiment. 'The Germans and we ourselves', he proudly told the press, 'hope that ex-Service men [. . .] will work together in the cause of peace.'[17]

However, any trip endorsed by a royal with a penchant for Nazi Germany surely raises questions over the whole endeavour. And this certainly proved to be the case here. If the British Legion's activities were truly a form of British–German reconciliation, then they can only ever have been partial. A whole section of Germany's ex-servicemen community had already been excluded, as more moderate veterans' groups were either banned or subsumed into the Nazis' own war veterans' organisations. Worse still was the fate of some 100,000 German-Jewish war veterans, who were already facing increasingly violent persecution in Nazi Germany.[18] But as the British Legion's trip to Germany included a meeting with Hitler and a visit to Dachau concentration camp, initially a well-publicised camp for political opponents, reaching out the hand of friendship to the German-Jewish war veterans was never one of their main priorities. For the British Legion, as for the Nazi regime, the relationship was all about improving their own image on the international stage.[19] The IWGC's war cemeteries just happened to provide the perfect setting for photographers to capture the former foes appearing to come together to honour the war dead.

Further opportunities for good publicity shots occurred through the remainder of the decade, as different British Legion branches made the journey over to Germany, with some German veterans making the return journey to Britain. Almost without fail, each delegation conducted a short remembrance service at one of the IWGC's British cemeteries. As the ex-servicemen laid their customary wreaths with local German dignitaries looking on, the same message of reconciliation was repeated time and again. 'It made me feel really comfortable', declared one Yorkshire veteran, 'that there can be friendship between us even though we have fought in the past.'[20] But even the legion's obdurate leadership was forced to acknowledge the emptiness of such gestures during the 1938 Munich crisis. Surprisingly, it was not the Nazi regime's threat to invade Czechoslovakia that led to this conclusion, but rather that international events moved on without them. Revelling in the moment, Fetherston-Godley and colleagues had initially tried to act as an international mediator, offering up 10,000 of their members as a peacekeeping force. Neville Chamberlain's decision to throw the Czechs to the Nazis for a short-lived 'peace for our time' put paid to such dangerous schemes, and a chastened legion withdrew from the international stage.[21]

Yet, the British cemeteries continued to be the focus of attention. Two days before the Nazi regime broke the Munich agreement and invaded the Czech provinces of Bohemia and Moravia, the war dead were apparently still working for peace. To mark Nazi Germany's annual Heroes' Memorial Day (*Heldengedenktag*), functionaries from the SA and the Nazis' war veterans' organisation, gathered in Stahnsdorf to lay wreaths on the British war graves. Their not-too-subtle presence was marked by a sea of swastika flags, draped over the IWGC's Stone of Remembrance (see image 30). The Nazis framed their ceremony as a sign that 'Germany needs and wants peace'.[22] But with representatives from the British Legion and the IWGC conspicuously absent, it was more of a German takeover of a British space than an act of genuine reconciliation. What this curious incident in Stahnsdorf had really confirmed was the potential of military cemeteries, with their heady mix of war graves and national symbols, to act as a magnet for international power politics. Far from acting as vehicles of reconciliation, they instead became dangerous arenas of contestation.

30. The Nazi regime ensured that its Heroes' Memorial Day in March 1939 was a spectacular occasion. During a ceremony held in the British military cemetery in Stahnsdorf, swastika flags and German military uniforms drowned out the IWGC's own symbols of remembrance.

Off Limits

If the British Legion had been bruised by its missteps with the Nazi regime, it was determined not to show it. When fighting in Europe came to an end for a second time in 1945, it gradually ratcheted up its continental operations. With many of the war graves initially inaccessible to relatives and to veterans too, the legion pitched itself as a service provider that could connect the living with the dead. It announced proudly that the bereaved could place orders for 'wreaths to be laid on any graves' in Germany, including on the First World War graves in 'Berlin South-Western (Stahnsdorf)' cemetery.[23] The promise to lay wreaths at Stahnsdorf, however, was possibly a stretch too far. The cemetery nudged up against the border to the American sector of Berlin but, frustratingly for all concerned, landed just in the Soviet zone of occupation. Consequently, even getting to Stahnsdorf proved rather a challenge. A representative of the IWGC, accompanied by a British officer, a translator and a 'scruffy Russian Officer', did manage a brief visit in spring 1948, but only after months of diplomatic pressure. The cemetery itself turned out to be generally in 'good condition', but the grass and 'all shrubs [were] overgrown'.[24]

After this visit, the IWGC's main concern was if and when it could return to Stahnsdorf to make repairs. Using the cemetery as a means to improve international relations, therefore, was clearly not the priority at this stage. Although it received far less attention, the IWGC's First World War Indian cemetery at Zehrensdorf, which lay deep in the Soviet zone, was also off limits. The cemetery had the unfortunate distinction of sitting within a military training area, which had already made access tricky during the Nazi era. After witnessing the troops liberally shooting off their machine guns during one visit in the 1930s, Charles Batty, the IWGC's representative on the ground, concluded that it was too dangerous for workers and the public to visit, as anyone 'could be accidentally shot'.[25] The situation was even worse a decade later. A local resident, who had lived near Zehrensdorf for years, filled Batty in on the cemetery's current state. Making sure to paint the Soviet forces in the worst possible light, she explained that Zehrensdorf had been well cared for and had even survived the end of the war 'undamaged'. In more recent times, however, 'rows of graves have been driven over by tanks and stamped into the ground'.[26]

Without proper access, such reports were hard to verify. Unfortunately, the transformation of the former Soviet occupation zone into a new German Democratic Republic in 1949 made it even harder to traverse the border. After the formation of this other Germany, the British found themselves in a rather awkward position. Following the lead of the Federal Republic, which was by now their Cold War partner in the west, the British government refused to recognise the GDR as a legitimate state. Relations that did exist had to operate below the level of the state, whether through trade missions, fact-finding visits by friendly politicians or even through the GDR's unofficial travel agency, Berolina, which promised a holiday 'where more pleasure can be extracted for less money'. With a choice between East Germany and destinations in Greece, Italy or Austria, however, few British holidaymakers took Berolina up on their appealing offer.[27] But all this left the IWGC in a quandary. If there were no formal relations between the GDR and Britain, then there was little chance of ever discussing the future of the British war graves in the East.

All the IWGC could really do was to rely on small snippets of information garnered from other sources, such as newspapers or occasional reports from across the Iron Curtain. A few lines in one East Berlin newspaper outlining the chance discovery of a Halifax bomber with skeletal remains still inside provided one such prompt to action. 'After 15 years, finally back in daylight: pipe, compass, morphine and munition, munition, munition,' reported the newspaper.[28] However, as the wreckage remained out of their reach, the best the British could do was to try to negotiate for the return of the airmen's remains. To everyone's surprise, the Soviets proved to be 'unusually friendly' and agreed to an exchange. On a damp, overcast day in late October, a 'small R.A.F. party' made their way to the Brandenburg Gate, which at that time was right on the border between East and West. A Soviet officer met them, took the delegation to an East German police post, where they were then handed a box of unidentified human remains, and with that the party returned.[29]

While it was just about possible for the remains of these two airmen to cross the border, the chances of anyone from the IWGC going in the opposite direction were slim, particularly after the construction of the Berlin Wall in 1961. However, one small branch of the British military, the British Commanders'-in-Chief Mission to the Soviet Forces in Germany – fortunately shortened to BRIXMIS – did have some freedom to step foot on East German territory. Effectively a hangover from the early post-war years when there was some hope of better relations between the different occupying forces, BRIXMIS members had the right to roam into the East, while Soviet forces could do the same in return. Kitted out with a range of specially equipped four-wheel-drive vehicles, cameras and filming equipment, BRIXMIS's regular tours into East Germany were primarily about observing the Soviets' military manoeuvres. As Brigadier David Wilson, who headed up BRIXMIS in the 1960s, later put it, 'the amount of intelligence we produced over the years was out of this world'.[30]

Alongside these more pressing Cold War matters, BRIXMIS members also managed to make the occasional detour to the Stahnsdorf military cemetery. The first British person to set foot there for many years arrived on a 'gloomy' day in October 1968. It had been so long since there had been any British visitors that a cemetery worker 'initially thought [he] was a Swede'. Even though the cemetery workers were clearly not expecting too many British visitors to check up on their work, it was clear that some basic maintenance had been done. The grass had 'recently been cut with a scythe' and while the site was 'somewhat overgrown', there was at least 'no evidence of dilapidation' to the stone structures.[31] The following November, a 'handful' of BRIXMIS members and their driver, 'who just happened to play the bugle', returned to Stahnsdorf. The men, no more than four in number, then conducted their own remembrance ceremony amidst the weathered headstones with only the sound of the Last Post to accompany their thoughts.[32]

This was quite possibly the first service to be held in the cemetery since the Nazis had gathered there for their Heroes' Memorial Day commemorations in 1939. On this occasion, nobody even pretended that the BRIXMIS service was somehow an act of peace and reconciliation between former foes. Indeed, the very opposite was the case. The ruling Socialist Unity Party (Sozialistische Einheitspartei Deutschlands,

SED) in East Germany would dearly have liked to put a halt to such gatherings. But as the BRIXMIS agreement was with the Soviets, and not with them, it was powerless to intervene. What the East Germans could do, however, was to erect as many hurdles as they possibly could to discourage the British from staging their ceremonies in Stahnsdorf. Over the years, they added new requirements, restricted transit permits and even turned back a padre and buglers who apparently lacked the 'necessary clearance'.

BRIXMIS persevered in the face of such opposition, primarily because it regarded the ceremonies in Stahnsdorf to be in the British 'national interest'. If it conceded ground on the annual remembrance ceremonies, the fear was that it would be 'a foot in the door' for the East Germans, who would then try to restrict BRIXMIS's activities in other areas too.[33] With both sides refusing to give way, the services in Stahnsdorf turned into a game of cat and mouse between the East Germans and the British. Each year, when the small delegation of mainly BRIXMIS members arrived at Stahnsdorf for their ceremony, the East German police (Volkspolizei) and state security operatives in the Stasi were there waiting to welcome them. Only on one occasion did this tinderbox of competing interests threaten to go up in flames. Drawn by the sound of a Scottish piper playing a lament, some local civilians tried to follow the British into the cemetery. The crowd ignored the shouts of an East German policeman and continued to push forwards. He was just about to 'draw his pistol' when a BRIXMIS member intervened and managed to restore some semblance of order.[34]

Threats to shoot Remembrance Day visitors were hardly conducive for promoting a message of peace or for improving British–German relations in the East for that matter. Yet, these issues were never the CWGC's main concern. As had always been the case, aesthetics played a dominant role in CWGC thinking. Without proper access to Stahnsdorf itself, the commission's big fear was that visitors might mistake the slightly overgrown cemetery as being representative of the way it managed its other overseas sites.[35] Desperate to protect its own reputation, the CWGC continued to push the Foreign Office in Whitehall for a solution. Although the East Germans saw the situation very differently, the obvious way forward, as far as the commission was concerned, was for it to retake responsibility for the cemetery and to employ its own gardeners again.

Given the GDR's obstinacy in such matters, conducting maintenance work in Stahnsdorf was easier said than done. There was, though, one small glimmer of light that provided a way forward. When it came to international agreements, the GDR was like a moth to a flame. Desperate for international legitimacy, it had already signed a string of diplomatic agreements with Western states.[36] Although it was harder to 'make a big political fuss' about a war graves agreement, the Foreign Office still thought that the promise of a treaty might bring the East Germans to the negotiating table.[37] As it turned out, they were right. Through the first half of the 1980s, the two parties engaged in fairly tedious negotiations that went on for years about the cost of 'Crocus bulbs', 'Hand tools' and a 'Large Watering can (plastic)'. It was not just the cost of materials that had to be agreed, but also maintenance schedules. If the CWGC decided to 'create a small bed of roses around each headstone', a British official explained in one meeting, then they would pay for the roses. However, who would 'care for them once they were planted', he asked. This question seemed to take the East German official by surprise. 'They would have to be watered and pruned,' he stuttered in reply, clearly shocked at the thought of the extra expense.[38]

British and East German state officials finally put their signatures to a new war graves treaty in April 1987, bringing a particularly long-winded set of negotiations to a close. The GDR celebrated its 'Intergovernmental Agreement with Great Britain' in the press, while the CWGC was simply relieved. It finally had permission to 'access the Südwestfriedhof of Stahnsdorf' according to a binding international treaty, although the Indian cemetery in Zehrensdorf was still conspicuous by its absence.[39] The new treaty did nothing to bring local communities and relatives together, nor did it do much for British–German post-war reconciliation. Nonetheless, the atmosphere of the annual remembrance services in Stahnsdorf was much improved. The 1988 ceremony 'went off smoothly', reported British officials, with a 'less restrictive attitude of the GDR police'. These were all 'welcome developments' that they hoped would be 'repeated next year'. As it turned out, they need not have worried too much. On the 9 November 1989, the Berlin Wall came down, so Stahnsdorf came back under CWGC control and thereafter gradually drifted back into obscurity.[40]

National Vandals

The Staffordshire moorlands offered a far more serene setting for cultivating a narrative of peace and reconciliation than Cold War Berlin. In June 1967, the flags of the Federal Republic, the United Kingdom and the VDK fluttered in the early summer breeze, as people gathered for the dedication of Germany's first and only war cemetery in Britain. The ceremony itself started with religious blessings from Catholic and Protestant clergymen, before formal speeches and a choreographed wreath laying brought proceedings to a close. The only element missing was the VDK's planned torchlit parade, which was vetoed, not because of the unwelcome images of the Nazis' own processions, but because of the obvious fire risk. As the VDK pitched the whole event as one of British–German reconciliation, it conceded that setting fire to the surrounding landscape would likely lead to 'severe criticism'.[41] There were, however, plenty of other opportunities to demonstrate what was apparently a new British–German era. An RAF band beat out some Germany military favourites, including 'Ich hatt' einen Kameraden', while the VDK's then president, Walter Trepte, spoke of 'both nations unit[ing] in friendship'.[42]

The formal opening of the Cannock Chase cemetery did indeed mark a new chapter in British–German relations. Despite the VDK's public rhetoric, what emerged, though, was a very different relationship, not necessarily a stronger one. A warm friendship certainly developed between state officials, in particular between members of Staffordshire County Council and the city of Bremen, whose local VDK branch helped with the organisation.[43] Long rounds of planning in the run-up to the dedication had already helped to breed familiarity among officials. Once the formal ceremonies were over, there were then plenty of opportunities for more relaxed socialising. The Mayor of Bremen hosted his own reception in Stafford 'to show [. . .] appreciation' for the County Council's help, inviting officials along to sample a 'glass of wine from the cellars of the Bremen Ratskeller'.[44] Some of those attending might have enjoyed more than one glass, as several hours later, a small British–German group descended on the house of the County Council's public relations officer to continue with drinks and snacks. 'I shall never forget having the Mayor of Bremen washing up [in my house],' he later joked.[45]

While relations between the state officials flourished in new ways, the same was less true for the bereaved and local communities, all of whom played a much more minimal role in the proceedings. The dedication had been planned largely around the needs of the visiting West German state officials and VDK dignitaries. They flew into Birmingham Airport, were picked up on landing and then enjoyed the opulent surroundings of a former manor house-turned-hotel just outside Stafford. The relatives, meanwhile, could pay a very reasonable DM 699 to take the ferry from Hook of Holland to Harwich, followed by the train to Stafford. There had been some suggestion that Staffordshire Rotary Club members might like to host relatives during the dedication. The VDK was quick to nip this idea in the bud, pointing out that the Rotary Club attracted 'highly educated individuals', which made it 'very difficult' to find 'suitable [German] relatives for such accommodation'. Instead, a large motel-style hotel further from the centre was deemed far more fitting.[46]

The relatives may have been shunted off to enjoy the delights of their more functional accommodation, but the VDK was keen to stress that they would nonetheless 'form the centre of the ceremony'.[47] What this meant, it turned out, was that relatives could look on at everything that had been achieved on their behalf, but they were certainly not going to play a role in the main proceedings. Instead, it was officials from the VDK and CWGC who took centre stage. Flanking them, in closely demarcated sections to avoid too much interaction, were the British Legion, a delegation from Staffordshire County Council and then other German dignitaries. Finally, the German relatives were able to look on from a safe distance, almost as spectators at the consecration of their loved ones' graves.[48]

Once the formal ceremony was complete, relatives were then free to spend some time in the cemetery, while the British and German officials retreated to the elegance of the County Buildings in Stafford for a luncheon. Over a sit-down meal washed down with 'German table

wines', as a cultural nod to the international guests, they could congratulate themselves on a job well done. To the VDK's regret, however, four
relatives did receive invites to the meal, but such compromises had to
be made. The County Council had originally wanted to allow all 150
relatives to attend, so a small representative group, was certainly prefer-
able. Inviting German widows to partake in lunch in what had been
planned as a mainly male gathering, though, did add a further layer of
complexity. Fortunately, the Staffordshire councillors resolved this by
bringing along their wives 'so that the ladies will have some company'.[49]

At least the four relatives allowed in for lunch managed to get some
food and wine. There was certainly no place at the table, or at the dedication ceremony for that matter, for the local custodians who had once
cared for the scattered graves. The only person to sneak into the ceremony was the vicar of Alresford who had booked a spot four years
earlier when the VDK had first exhumed the German bodies from his
parish churchyard. 'I visit the military cemeteries in Arnhem and
Reichswald every year as a military chaplain,' he explained to the VDK.
'It would be a great honour to be present at the official dedication of
your own cemetery.' The vicar's military connections may well have
cleared the path for him, but for other former custodians the road was
blocked. As far as the British and German officials were concerned,
there seemed little point in inviting other people along who once may
have cared for the German war dead. That was now all in the past; the
future was Cannock Chase.[50]

Yet, even the war graves commissions' carefully crafted efforts at
constructing a new British–German relationship did not entirely go to
plan. When the cemetery caretaker arrived early on the day of the dedication to make the last preparations, he was greeted not by an ordered
site, but by a scene of devastation. Someone must have broken into the
cemetery during the night, armed with red paint and a thick brush.
Offensive messages had been daubed across the seats laid out for guests,
over headstones, the memorial cross and through the entrance hall. The
graffiti was hardly in the spirit of reconciliation and renewed British–
German relations. 'Go Home' was scrawled across one row of graves;
the misspelt word 'Belson' was left in several locations; and on the
reverse of one stone, the far from welcoming message 'Our Lads?' had

been daubed in thick paint (see image 31). The name of Bergen-Belsen, the Nazis' infamous concentration camp, liberated by the British in April 1945, may have been misspelt, but the question mark was grammatically correct. The implication was clearly that the Germans, the enemy, had usurped the country's own dead: 'Our Lads'.

31. The dedication of the German Military Cemetery on Cannock Chase had been planned well in advance for 10 June 1967. On the eve of the ceremony, someone broke into the grounds and vandalised many of the headstones with red paint.

With guests due in a matter of hours, there was understandable panic at the discovery of the graffiti. Not only did the whole site make a terrible impression, but if any of the bereaved were to stumble across the vandalism, it would no doubt have been emotionally distressing too. Finding the culprits, therefore, could wait; the most immediate issue was trying to find a way to remove the paint. The local police rushed into action and managed to secure 'a quantity of cotton waste, petrol, acetate and other cleaning materials' from the English Electric Company, which had a plant nearby. A German youth group staying in Staffordshire for the dedication then spent several hours scrubbing away at the graffiti trying to make good the damage.[51]

Fortunately for all concerned, the paint came off relatively easily. 'With the weathering and passing of time', the cemetery's architect was even hopeful that 'any slight stain' would soon 'disappear'. But the incident did leave rather a bitter aftertaste.[52] Local officials were not just embarrassed at what had occurred but also completely confused as to the point. The Germans buried 'on the Chase', explained one exasperated councillor, 'were not the cause of war, but its victims.' They were 'just ordinary folk', nothing but 'rank and file' soldiers, he added. The implication was that there had been good and bad Germans in the recent conflict; Staffordshire had just happened to inherit the former. Spelling this dichotomy out more bluntly, one local journalist asked of the vandals: 'Who are they hitting at? There are no Gestapo chiefs buried here, just ordinary servicemen.' As the VDK knew all too well, this was not strictly true. For this reason, the VDK was keen 'to forget this incident as soon as possible', before more awkward questions emerged. Burying Germany's recent past on Cannock Chase may have allowed the cemetery to be built in the first place, but it was surely not a secure foundation for a new British–German relationship.[53]

Fading Out

An article appeared in the *Daily Telegraph* in 1990 about an enduring love story between an elderly German woman, Lore Scheuplein, and her long-dead husband, Alfons Scheuplein. He had been shot down during the air war over Sussex in August 1940, leaving her at home in Uelzen, a town some way south of Hamburg, alone with a 10-month-old baby. Ever since, it had been 'her dream' to be reunited with her husband. As this was no longer going to happen in life, she formulated a plan for the pair to be brought together in death instead. Scheuplein arranged that at the time of her own death, her ashes would be brought from Germany to Britain and then scattered over her husband's grave. The CWGC, which only learnt of Scheuplein's elaborate plan from the *Daily Telegraph*, was unsure how to respond for the best. After the press had celebrated this story of the reunited lovers, it would have been tricky to veto the idea, which left the CWGC with little option but to approve the plan. 'This case in no way sets a precedent,' it begrudgingly conceded.[54]

The CWGC's annoyance stemmed from a major difference between civilian and military cemeteries. Churchyards and municipal burial grounds, particularly those in continental Europe, almost have their own life cycle. They are never static; new burials are added, while older graves gradually fade, as ownership rights end and the living themselves pass on.[55] By contrast, the British and German war graves commissions viewed their cemeteries as complete. Once the dead had been concentrated, whether this was in the 1920s, 1940s or 1960s, then no further movement of bodies was supposed to take place. Without any changes to the sites, they effectively became repositories of the dead, sealed in perpetuity at the moment of their original creation. Instead of being living, vibrant spaces, the military cemeteries became merely a backdrop for a calendar of annual rituals, from remembrance services through to diplomatic visits. Such occasions were often dressed in the language of reconciliation, but their reach was increasingly limited.

In civilian life, the bereaved tend to give life to individual graves. Relatives might visit annually on particular religious or personal days, to say a prayer, speak a few words to the dead or simply to maintain the grave.[56] Once they have departed, flowers, mementos and other grave gifts often remain as a sign of their recent presence. In the military cemeteries, such moments were much rarer. The biggest difficulty for relatives, whether in Britain or Germany, was finding a way to make the long and expensive journeys to the large cemeteries overseas. Elsie

Cook, from Taunton in Somerset, was certainly not going to be dissuaded from visiting her husband's grave in Stahnsdorf, even if she did choose the most inauspicious moment to travel. Having never been to Germany before and 'unable to speak the language', she arrived in Berlin, in the heart of Nazi Germany, in April 1937, ready to hunt out the grave of her husband, Percy Cook, who had died as a POW almost twenty years earlier. She was fortunate that a member of the IWGC happened to be Berlin at the same time and was able to take her to Stahnsdorf which otherwise was 'not easy to find'.[57]

However, not everyone had as much fortitude as Cook, which is why, in the 1920s, the British Legion and some Christian organisations started to put on their own 'pilgrimages' to cemeteries on the former frontlines, and occasionally Germany too. After the Second World War, the British Legion gradually restarted its German trips, taking 175 'pilgrims' to the IWGC's cemeteries in 1957. This was a moment for families to see their loved ones' final graves for the first time.[58] One widow on a later tour to Becklingen expressed the view of many 'pilgrims': 'I shall have the memory of seeing it [the grave] for ever.' However, despite how 'beautifully kept' everything was, she was rather disappointed that the headstone gave his age as 23, when he was in fact '25 years old when he was killed'. After the birth certificate was studied, it turned out that everyone was wrong; he had actually been 24 years old at the time of his death. 'She unfortunately misled us,' complained the IWGC before reluctantly altering the stone.[59] This was one of the dangers of organised tours. But for a brief period at least, relatives did at least manage to breathe some life into the large cemeteries, before they departed and the graves again fell silent.

The VDK was keen to keep a firm hold on 'pilgrimages' and established what was effectively its own in-house travel bureau, with organised tours across North Africa and Western Europe.[60] The VDK's members keen to visit cemeteries abroad would no doubt have been delighted when the brochure listing the trips planned for 1980 landed in their letterboxes. The main draw was probably the tours of France and Italy, but there was also one trip to Britain hidden away in the programme. For those with a spare DM 905, plus an extra DM 55 for a room with a shower, people could join a seven-day coach tour in June, leaving from Mönchengladbach to Cannock Chase.[61] Twenty-one people leapt at the chance and signed up for the adventure. The vast majority of this number were West Germans wanting to visit a relative's grave in Staffordshire. They were also joined by two siblings from Poland, whom the VDK helpfully marked as 'from the East (*Osten*)' on its lists. They had come along hoping to visit the grave of their father, Josef Drabik, whose body had been fished from the sea off Sussex in May 1944.[62]

By the time the little group of travellers arrived in Staffordshire on day two of their journey, not everyone was in the best of spirits. Even though the coach driver, Herr Wolf, had mastered 'driving on the left without a problem', it had still been a long and tiring journey from Mönchengladbach. Frau Mai and her sister, who had signed up for the tour to visit the grave of their father, a Second World War airman, were already tired of travelling, when Herr Wolf got lost trying to navigate the coach through the 'slums of London'. Nonetheless, the sisters tried to look on the bright side; they were 'anthropologically inquisitive people', so it was good to be confronted with sights that 'they would not normally get to see'. Either side of their visit to Cannock Chase, there was a series of 'bad hotels', which were a further source of complaint. Three hours lost in Southampton on the way back to the ferry was the final straw for Frau Mai and her sister. While Herr Wolf and the tour guide went off to get directions, the passengers were left on the bus with Dr Geßner, a senior member of the group, who gave an impromptu lecture on the 'different currents in port basins and their impact on marine life'. Whether this lightened the mood for those stuck on board is hard to say.[63]

Frau Mai, in her late fifties at the time, was actually one of the younger members of the group. An ageing demographic led to a more general decline in the numbers signing up for the VDK's cemetery tours during the 1980s.[64] Indeed, further tours to Cannock Chase in 1981 and 1982 had to be cancelled due to a lack of interest. Two years later, when the VDK next managed to muster the numbers to justify hiring a coach to drive all the way from Mönchengladbach, nine of the eighteen people signed up had no direct connection to the dead buried in Staffordshire and were just travelling out of interest. As a result, the tour became less of a pilgrimage to the gravesites and more of a package holiday. After a 'final short cemetery trip with a wreath laying', it was off to Lichfield to see the cathedral, followed by further trips to Llangollen – 'with an opportunity to travel on the mountain railway' – followed the next day by a drive down to Stratford-upon-Avon to take in the 'birthplace of William Shakespeare'.[65]

The difficulties of finding enough people to join organised cemetery tours did highlight a broader problem facing both war graves commissions. As the actual generation most touched by the violence of war themselves died out, it raised uncomfortable questions about the future and purpose of the large military cemeteries. The CWGC came to this realisation somewhat belatedly. It was only in the 2010s that it launched a series of new initiatives designed to 'inspire, inform, educate, involve and engage people', by which it meant young people, 'with stories of sacrifice that must never be forgotten'.[66] The VDK, however, was already way ahead of the curve. Building on some of its work with German youth in the interwar years, it had developed a comprehensive plan to attract the next generation to its activities as early as the 1950s. For the VDK, bringing young people on board had the double attraction of cheap labour and sustainability. With some cynicism, Christel Eulen was sure that 'the experience of going to war cemeteries stayed with young people', which she added, had 'long-term benefits for the VDK'.[67]

Boosted by such sentiments, the VDK sent its first contingent of young people to Belgium in 1953, followed in 1962 by the very first of what was to become an annual youth trip to Cannock Chase. These early German pioneers enjoyed fresh air, a campsite near the cemetery and hearty meals provided by a Bundeswehr cook who joined the party. After six hours each day spent shifting rocks and stones at the new cemetery, the group probably needed the army rations to keep them going. This was no bad thing, as far as the VDK was concerned, as these were supposed to be character-building trips. '[The girls] are all nice; all natural, with no make-up and definitely not like models,' the VDK reported proudly. 'Just like the boys, their knees and bones are aching.'[68] However, there was a reward for the hard labour. Each year, the VDK put on a series of local outings to keep the German youth enthused.

One year a visit to see the police training dogs was on the menu; another year there was an evening of English country dancing; but the highlight was surely a tour of the General Electric Company (GEC) factory in Stafford, during which a slightly bewildered group of young Germans got to witness the actual assembly of industrial turbines.[69]

Engaging young people with the sights and sounds of post-war Britain, even if it only involved an industrial site in the Midlands, allowed the VDK to pitch its youth visits as a form of British–German understanding under its motto of 'Versöhnung über den Gräbern'.[70] The star turn in this programme was unleashed in August 1965. Stanley Matthews, the great England footballer who had recently taken over as manager of the far less successful Port Vale FC, agreed to host something akin to an international friendly. On the rugged pitch of Chell Heath, an outer suburb of Stoke-on-Trent, the visiting German youth squared up against Port Vale's youth team under Stanley Matthews's experienced guidance. This should have been a complete mismatch, but then in the first half, the Germans took the lead with an 'excellent shot'. To the relief of the small crowd, which watched on from the housing estate surrounding the pitch, Port Vale equalised, with what the Germans called a 'doubtful goal'. But then in the final stages of the match, the German youth 'dug into their last reserves of energy' and scored the winner. The contest ended with the all-too-familiar headline: 'Vale Youth Beaten by Germans'.[71]

Whether a footballing defeat amounted to successful reconciliation is debatable, particularly as even the German match report admitted to some 'differences of opinion' over the rules.[72] What does come through from such events, however, is how the war dead themselves were increasingly a sideshow. The youth were dragged along to Cannock Chase to help with the cemetery's construction, but the real attraction always seemed to be elsewhere. A decade or so after the Germans' famous victory over Port Vale, another little group of German youth gathered in Cannock Chase. By then, the cemetery was complete and their task was to help with general maintenance. However, before setting to work, they first had to be inducted into the site. Standing passively in a half-circle, the young people half listened as a much older official regaled them with the cemetery's history. But while he looked back, their thoughts were somewhere else. Wearing flares, their hair freshly styled, they seemed all set to sample the nightlife of Stafford (see image 32). Whether it was the youth or the families on the VDK's coach trips, these ritualised tours ended up being as much about the other activities on offer as the war graves themselves.

In 1987, a quarter of a century since the first German youth visits to Cannock Chase, and twenty years on from its dedication, the cemetery was the setting for another formal ceremony. Senior members of the VDK and the CWGC again donned their best suits and gathered in the German Military Cemetery. They were joined by Prince Edward, the Duke of Kent, who had been invited to unveil a large memorial stone commemorating '25 years of friendship Staffordshire – Bremen' in caring for the war cemetery. Before the duke could whip off the white sheet that shrouded the memorial, the then president of the

32. Youth exchanges between Bremen and Staffordshire have taken place regularly since the 1960s. However, this group of young Germans, visiting the Cannock Chase German Military Cemetery in 1978, appear to be less than enthused with the tour.

VDK, Eduard Hasskamp, gave a short speech to the assembled guests. He looked back fondly to the first youth visit to Cannock Chase in 1962, praising the young people of that time for daring to 'build a bridge across to a people, who only 20 years earlier had been their [wartime] enemy'. What Hasskamp failed to point out was that in building this bridge, the VDK had had to smash down hundreds of other smaller bridges that had originally existed linking together local communities and the bereaved. But in 1987, nobody wanted to hear this; they were there instead to honour the official narrative of reconciliation and of jointly 'working for peace' together.[73]

The war dead had never asked to perform this role of international diplomacy. This was a task that the two war graves commissions had kindly bestowed upon them. But ultimately, it required 'real living people' to perform the work of reconciliation.[74] The difficulty was that in the new military cemeteries, the living had often gone AWOL. State officials and senior members of the war graves commissions, like those watching the Duke of Kent's memorial dedication, appeared of course for occasional remembrance rituals. But for the majority of the year, the dead could rest quietly alone. While the number of visiting relatives dwindled as the passing of time caught up with them, a younger generation, who came to tend the graves, were themselves already fairly disconnected from the dead. All that remained, therefore, was a series of well-tended cemeteries, isolated as small British or German overseas islands, that had been largely left alone to perform the tricky task of peace-making.

11

MYTHOLOGISING

In May 1938, the city of Breslau, Germany's Silesian capital, played host to the VDK's annual general meeting or *Führertag*. Siegfried Emmo Eulen, the group's leader, had dutifully renamed it as such after the Nazis' rise to power. With its medieval marketplace, gothic town hall and twin-towered cathedral, the city undoubtedly made a lovely setting in which to bask in the warm glow of Germany's recent *Anschluss* of Austria. 'The historic German Ostmark has come home,' Eulen excitedly proclaimed to his newly arrived delegates.[1] Breslau's main concert hall, a modernist jumble of straight-edged balconies and sweeping ceilings, had been dressed in the same spirit. The VDK's emblem and several judiciously placed giant swastika pendants hid much of the building's expressionist architecture that the Nazis so loathed. The rows of uniformed men who had taken their seats in the hall were something of a rogues' gallery. Erich von dem Bach-Zelewski, the SS leader in Silesia, Fritz Bracht, the province's deputy Gauleiter, and the Wehrmacht general, Ernst Busch, had all managed to elbow their way to the front row. Tucked in between these friendly faces were the dark-suited figures of Fabian Ware, Henry Chettle and Oliver Holt, three of the IWGC's leading lights. They had made the long journey east after accepting an earlier invitation to attend (see image 33).

Ware and his colleagues did not have much time to get to know their German neighbours in the hall, as Eulen had filled his *Führertag* with a packed calendar of events. The most important trip, as far as the VDK

33. In May 1938, the VDK's annual general meeting took place
in Breslau. Seated in the front row in dark suits from left to right are
Oliver Holt, Henry Chettle and Fabian Ware, who had been invited to
the main events to represent the IWGC.

was concerned, was to the Annaberg, a good 130 kilometres further
south. Other than a steep hill, a Franciscan monastery and the barren
workings of a former quarry, the Annaberg appeared not to have much
appeal for the casual visitor. However, this seemingly inconsequential
place also happened to be the location of the 1921 'Battle of Annaberg',
where Freikorps fighters had forced back Polish insurgents in the
disputed German-Polish borderlands. The Nazis were only too happy
to mythologise this moment as an example of spirited resistance – not
only against Poland but also in defiance of an impotent Weimar government. For their visit, the VDK's delegates, including the small IWGC
contingent, were bussed down to the same site to witness the dedication of a new memorial, not for the dead of the Great War but for
paramilitary fighters killed in skirmishes over the post-war settlement.[2]

Designed by Robert Tischler, the VDK's favoured architect for all
monumental constructions, the memorial was a ten-sided building

with a domed roof. Sitting imposingly on the clifftop above the disused quarry, Tischler's fortress-like structure was a show of strength, deploying the Freikorps fighters as defenders of the German East even in death.[3] To add further weight to this message, the VDK also needed some actual bodies. Therefore, in advance of the dedication, it exhumed fifty dead Freikorps fighters and reinterred their remains within its new memorial on the Annaberg. The lucky fighters were supposed to represent all other Freikorps soldiers and to act as 'messengers of faith in [Hitler's] Germany'.[4]

Some fifteen years earlier, IWGC exhumation teams had also trudged around Silesia hunting for British bodies. After recovering them from municipal cemeteries and POW camp burial grounds, they moved most of the remains to their new Stahnsdorf cemetery near Berlin. The British efforts had had the effect of clearing the landscape of more complex signs of recent conflict. With the enemy graves removed, it proved far easier for Germans on the Right to fill the voids with newer narratives of ongoing battles for the nation's survival. The revanchism of the Annaberg memorial may have been specific to the Nazi regime's toxic war memory, but the actual act of mythmaking certainly was not. The VDK's reinterment of the German dead in Cannock Chase in the 1960s also gave the British space to create new inward-looking myths of conflict, focused on their own soldiers' apparent heroism and stoicism. In very different ways, therefore, the removal of the enemy from both countries had the effect of turning transnational histories of the world wars, in which both sides had suffered losses, into purely national stories.

Revanchism

Long before the crowds had gathered at the Annaberg in 1938, Germans had been obsessed by the legacies of war, defeat and revolution. Politicians expended considerable energy debating the 1918 military collapse; the war wounded bemoaned their fate, while war films became something of a staple in the modern cinema palaces.[5] Yet, the vitriol of this later discourse took a while to appear. Indeed, when the Reich Association of Former Prisoners of War

(Reichsvereinigung ehemaliger Kriegsgefangener, ReK), which went on to become one of the Weimar Republic's major veterans' groups, had first formed in 1919, it was not mythologising but reminiscing that most occupied its time. Some of the ReK's members wrote the first histories of the French and British POW camps, while one former captive even raised funds by selling his genteel sketches of the English countryside.[6] Local ReK groups were also often the first to take on the care of enemy POW graves that had been left throughout Germany. In Oldenburg, the local ReK branch went a stage further. It organised a joint remembrance service for the German and enemy dead in 1922; a scene repeated elsewhere by other ReK groups.[7]

However, such sympathies wilted as quickly as a bouquet of freshly cut flowers in the sun. Faced with the political and economic instability of the new Weimar Republic, many Germans became too engrossed in their own daily lives in the present to worry too much about their former enemy's war graves. At the same time, the ReK's leading voice and later chairman, Wilhelm von Lersner, a stern-faced former army officer with cropped dark hair, set the association on a less than concil-iatory path. Like members of other veterans' organisations of this era, Lersner was happy to wade into politics, campaigning against the Treaty of Versailles and demanding more 'living space' (*Lebensraum*) for the German people. For him, the members of the ReK had made unique sacrifices for the German military cause, facing untold suffering and cruelty while stranded for years in enemy hands.[8]

The exhumation of the enemy dead from cemeteries across Germany made it much easier for the ReK to ignore the Allied POWs who had died in German captivity from mistreatment and neglect. It was a case of out of sight, out of mind. In their place, Lersner and his comrades in the ReK were free to create their own myths of the recent past. In the northern industrial city of Bielefeld, for example, at least six British POWs had originally been buried in the Sennefriedhof, a landscaped forest cemetery to the south of the centre. Twenty-two-year-old Arthur Bugg, who made up one of this number, had been captured at the Battle of Mons and transported to Bielefeld, which is where, in November 1914, he eventually succumbed to his wounds, far from his family back home in Ipswich.[9] Once the British had exhumed the remains of Bugg and his comrades to Kassel in the mid-1920s, the German war veterans had the space to themselves. Without the enemy there to complicate matters, the ReK erected its own memorial to 'The Fallen Prisoners of War'. The group could have legitimately added the word 'German' between 'Fallen' and 'Prisoner', for this was a memorial purely about German suffering. Clearly, none of the three anguished figures depicted on the memorial were Arthur Bugg; instead, these were German POWs, whose robust torsos suggested an inner willingness to survive (see image 34).

34. The Reich Association of Former Prisoners of War spent a lot of time in the interwar years erecting new memorials for its own war dead. This memorial, dedicated in Bielefeld in March 1931, was for the 'Fallen Prisoners of War'.

The POW memorial in Bielefeld was no fleeting aberration. During a period of intense navel-gazing, the ReK repopulated spaces across Germany with memorials dedicated to its own members' captivity.[10] A hundred kilometres to the west of Bielefeld, Friedrich Heyenga, a former POW himself and leader of the Brambauer branch of the ReK, was determined to see his own hometown in the industrial Ruhr get in on the act. The ever-energetic Heyenga and his fellow members spent weeks shifting a huge 100-kilogram boulder to the entrance of the town's old cemetery. 'Pleasant hours of comradely teamwork' were needed, 'and many drops of sweat flowed too', joked Heyenga to his comrades. Their hard labour eventually paid off. On a late summer's day in 1929, they could watch on – no doubt still with aching backs – as the memorial to 'comrades who had died in captivity' was officially unveiled. Yet, it was never clear as to why Brambauer even needed its own giant POW memorial. Only two POWs had failed to return home, both of whom had died in French captivity a few months after the armistice.[11] However, commemorating one's own suffering was never really about a specific need; it was rather a means to stamp the experience of German POWs into the public's imagination.

Brambauer's two POWs may not have died in the town, but they did at least have some connection to the community. Five years later in Lübeck, Nazi officials were determined to find their own wartime hero or heroes to commemorate in the Hanseatic city. Clearly, Charles Slocombe, a 23-year-old British sergeant who had died in 1917 as an internee in a Lübeck hospital, was not exactly who they had in mind. In any case, by 1934, Slocombe's remains had already been taken from the city to the IWGC's cemetery in Hamburg. The Nazi enthusiasts in Lübeck eventually found someone to fill the voids left by the removal of Slocombe and the other enemy bodies: Carl Hans Lody, the German spy executed by the British in 1914. Lody had been born in Berlin, died in London and had spent most of his life at sea. How he fitted in Lübeck was not immediately clear, but nobody appeared to mind too much. The city finally had a proper war hero to celebrate. A local artist designed a relief of a medieval knight, representing Lody, while a slithering snake curling around his legs, none too subtly symbolised British treachery.[12]

The Lody memorial, which was given a prominent position in Lübeck's city walls, was far more aggressive than the ReK's earlier efforts in Bielefeld or Brambauer. The accompanying plaque, for example, reminded Germans that Lody had 'Died For Us', while the dedication, a spectacle of Nazi uniforms and swastikas, turned into a public celebration of heroism.[13] Despite a clear difference in tone, these new sites of memory shared much in common. They all prioritised the experience of German wartime captivity, constructing comforting stories around the themes of valiant heroism or unjust suffering behind the barbed wire of internment camps. The memorials that sprang up across Germany during the final years of the Weimar Republic also appeared in artificial sites – city walls, cemeteries or town squares – that had no connection to the German POWs' original place of death or burial. All the time, the soldiers and civilians who had actually breathed their last in German communities were absent, both physically and mnemonically, as the focus of local memories had long moved elsewhere.

Instead of turning a blind eye to these new memorials, the British occasionally engaged with them directly, which only had the effect of giving them even greater credence. Albert Foster, a 'hawk-faced' Special Branch officer from Scotland Yard, had no particular intention of hunting out the Lody memorial when he took a short holiday to Lübeck. After all, he was the policeman, who had originally arrested Lody twenty-four years earlier, starting a trail that eventually led to the firing squad in the Tower of London. However, an 'enthusiastic Nazi guide', blissfully unaware of Foster's role in the whole affair, took him down to the memorial to pay his respects. Foster simply stood there 'grim-faced' and said nothing.[14]

The veterans in the British Legion proved far less circumspect about being associated with Germany's new wave of POW memorials. In September 1935, just as the Nazi regime was implementing the racial Nuremberg Laws, members of the British Legion's Brighton branch travelled over to Germany, bound for Grundschöttel, a small community not far south of Dortmund. The German war veterans in the ReK who had invited them over pulled out all the stops, decorating the streets with swastikas and even arranging for the Union Jack to fly from Grundschöttel's historic water tower, a local landmark. Not wanting to appear ungrateful, the British visitors laid their own wreath at the foot of the ReK's new memorial in Grundschöttel. No German POWs had died at this spot, of course, and no bodies were involved. It was, therefore, more of a memorial to German suffering than to the actual dead, which perhaps made it more palatable to the British visitors. The British Legion group then travelled north to Münster, where they crowned their trip with a reception in the city's gothic town hall. After signing the city's 'golden book', which was an honour reserved for only the most prominent of guests, they politely thanked their German guests with a loud refrain of ' "Heil" for Hitler'.[15]

Suffering Again

Ten years after the British Legion's cosy visit to Münster, aerial bombing and street fighting during the final months of the Second World War had left many of Germany's urban areas in ruins. Münster's Prinzipalmarkt, a gable-roofed ensemble of medieval buildings leading to the town hall – the site of the legion's earlier meeting – was nothing more than a pile of dusty rubble and charred timbers. The very visible signs of human destruction were also hard to escape. Surveying the fresh graves around the eastern fringes of the city, a German official totted up the damage. Six German soldiers lay in a wood, not far from the main road to Dülmen; an Austrian had been buried behind a hedge and an unknown solider lay near a farmhouse; single graves near a road contained the bodies of two British soldiers and a bit further along a member of the Scots Guards, killed in the final weeks of the war, had also been buried. The survey made no effort to record the graves of the Nazis' victims, even though slave labourers and foreign workers had been killed in and around Münster.[16]

By 1958, Münster's town hall and Prinzipalmarkt were standing again, having regained much of their old shine. Judging by the thousands of people who gathered in the streets for the final unveiling, the local population was also pleased to be able to draw what they hoped was going to be a line under this dark chapter in the city's history. Similar scenes were repeated across the Federal Republic, and at a slower pace in East Germany, which, unlike the West, had no economic miracle (*Wirtschaftswunder*) to help fuel reconstruction. The bodies of the war dead that had once littered Münster had also been tided away. The British Army Graves Service had moved the Scots Guardsman and the remains of their two other soldiers to the IWGC's Reichswald Forest cemetery, near the Dutch border, while the French and Americans had repatriated most of their dead directly home. This left the German war dead buried in local cemeteries, plus a smaller number of Soviet soldiers and civilians trapped the wrong side of the Iron Curtain, as the most visible mortuary reminders of the recent conflict.

The process of tidying away the bodies, sending the remains to different national cemeteries mainly outside Germany, may have been a necessary step towards moving on from war, but – once again – it created huge voids in local memory. Where communities had once had to face a patchwork of victims, this changed very quickly, leaving only the German dead with a strong visible presence in cemeteries and memorials. In the West, these gaps proved an open invitation for Germans to emphasise their own seemingly unique victimhood. German expellees who had fled the Soviet Army's westwards advance told their own stories of loss, as did the many thousands of Germans who had directly experienced the Allied air war.[17]

Returning POWs were also keen to get in on the act. The interwar ReK may have been dead, but like a phoenix from the ashes, it re-emerged in a new form as the snappily named Association of Returnees, Prisoners of War and Relatives of the Missing (Verband der Heimkehrer, Kriegsgefangenen und Vermisstenangehörigen, VdH). In Brambauer, Friedrich Heyenga, noticeably greyer and more wrinkled in complexion, made a remarkable reappearance as the head of the town's newly formed VdH group. It was just like '30 years ago', he announced, clearly relishing the chance to get back in the saddle and start campaigning for the rights of a new generation of former POWs.[18]

With little chance of being confronted with the graves of the Allied war dead, many of whom had died in German internment, Heyenga and his comrades could easily return to the ReK's old playbook. They were quick to emphasise the misery of internment and their members' acute anguish behind wire, although, as the VdH was careful to point out, 'they were no German nationalists from 1918'.[19] Instead, the message they tried to put across was rather that West Germany's former prisoners were genuine war victims, whose suffering was still ongoing. Not only had the Allies apparently mistreated them during the conflict, but thousands of German soldiers were still living in intolerable conditions, stranded in Soviet camps. To keep these POWs in the public eye, the VdH again started to fill the public realm with new memorials to German suffering. By the mid-1960s, they had erected almost 1,800 of these throughout the Federal Republic.[20] Heyenga ensured that his VdH group was not going to miss out, commissioning a small memorial plaque for the foyer of Lünen's newly built fourteen-storey town hall. The imagery was none too subtle. An oversized prisoner, hands held out in a Christ-like pose, maintained his moral worth, despite the unchristian barbed wire camp depicted below (see image 35).[21]

From a distance and while squinting, Heyenga's memorial could easily have been confused for a plaque in memory of the Nazi concentration camp victims.[22] But then appearances can be deceptive. The VdH never showed any particular interest in the actual victims of Nazi persecution nor, for that matter, in the fact that many of its own members in the supposedly 'clean Wehrmacht' may well have perpetrated war crimes themselves. Victimhood, according to the pages of the VdH's newsletter and its public pronouncements, was entirely about the German soldiers who had been locked away in Britain, France and, above all, in the Soviet Union. The organisation even sponsored an exhibition that toured through 1950s West Germany highlighting the horrors of the POW camp system in the East. 'A display of human suffering and deepest misery,' proclaimed one Bavarian branch of the VdH, optimistically trying to entice the casual visitor.[23]

Taking such a narrow line may have been possible in the 1950s, when the Soviets still held thousands of Wehrmacht soldiers in the East and many Germans were focused only on their own woe, but it was not sustainable. A series of high-profile war crimes trials, the probing of literary figures coupled with a wave of antisemitic desecrations all helped to shed light on the fate of Germany's Jewish communities and the unspoken continuities from the Nazi era.[24] In a slowly liberalising society, the VdH found itself left behind – something of an 'anachronism' in a rapidly changing world.[25] It continued to repeat the same

35. In post-war West Germany, a new organisation for former prisoners of war followed in the footsteps of its interwar predecessor and also constructed memorials across the new Federal Republic. In Lünen, this simple plaque urged visitors to the town hall to 'Remember the Prisoners'.

stories of wartime suffering, but fewer and fewer people were actually listening. POWs drifted away from the association as they rebuilt their lives and membership numbers dwindled. When Heyenga passed away in 1967 aged 70, the Brambauer branch of the VdH died with him. First emerging in 1919 as the ReK, before relaunching under the guise of the VdH in 1945, its time was finally up.

After the group's dissolution, the ReK's memorial boulder from 1929 continued to sit in Brambauer cemetery, even if some large rhododendrons did their best to disguise its very existence. The newer memorial plaque in Lünen remained for a while after Heyenga's death, but at some point, the frame cracked and the whole thing fell to the ground. The council cleared away the mess, leaving behind a slightly faded wall and four empty screw holes.[26] There was something fitting in the memorial's demise, for it had always been something of an interloper. Not only did its overblown depiction of the German POWs' wartime victimhood sit uneasily in an increasingly liberal and self-aware society, but the setting was also questionable.[27] After all, the POWs' war experiences had played out not in Lünen, but in camps far removed from the town's 1950s concrete town hall, home to Heyenga's memorial plaque.

Narratives of German victimhood did not entirely dissipate with the fading of the wartime generation. Wehrmacht cemeteries, war memorials and family tales of loss all ensured that stories of German suffering continued to maintain a presence. Yet, the focus of local memory started to shift. A younger generation, determined to know more about their communities' dark past, asked awkward questions. It was about trying to 'discover the truth', explained Anna Rosmus, who, as a young woman in the late 1970s, had worked hard to highlight the persecution of the Jewish community in her hometown of Passau.[28] Lünen might have lacked its own Rosmus, but there were still gradual attempts to think more deeply about the Nazi past. At around the time Rosmus was probing away in Passau, the town council erected a memorial on the site of the former synagogue that acknowledged its destruction in the 1938 pogrom.[29]

This connection between persecution and place, something badly missing from the VdH's memorials, became increasingly central to the Federal Republic's memory culture. From the 1980s onwards, community after community commissioned their own Holocaust memorials, often placing them on sites directly associated with Jewish persecution and suffering. In the university city of Erlangen near Nuremberg, the first new memorials were dedicated to prominent German-Jewish academics whose lives and legacies were destroyed under the Nazi regime. These early, fairly uncontroversial efforts paved the way for more substantial memorials, including a plaque to mark the site of the Nazis' book burning in 1933, a memorial to Erlangen's Jewish victims of Nazism, followed by the publication of an official remembrance book in 2001.[30] The face behind most of these initiatives was Ilse Sponsel, an energetic local politician and historian who dedicated her later years towards reconciliation with Erlangen's former Jewish citizens. It is about 'keep[ing] the memory of the [town's] small Jewish community alive' and ensuring 'its members are not forgotten', she later reflected.[31]

In Germany's new memorial landscape, there was never any mention of the British dead of the two world wars, who had died in Erlangen and elsewhere. But then this was quite understandable. By the time Germans started to think more broadly about the range of people who had perished in their wartime communities, the enemy dead had already been exhumed and removed. The absence of the enemy surely had the benefit of ensuring there was a clear local focus on the victims of Nazi persecution, without any threat of dilution. But, at the same time, it reduced Germany's memory culture to two seemingly opposing groups: the victims of Nazism and the German dead. The thousands of enemy soldiers and civilians killed in the two conflicts, who might have added greater depth and colour to this history, were missing.

War and Heritage

Anyone taking a stroll through London's Gladstone Park in the late 1960s might have left with the distinct impression, albeit a mistaken one, that the British were making far greater efforts to commemorate both friend and foe alike. The source of such confusion lay in a set of five sculptures that stand in one corner of the park. Collectively, the sculpted figures reimagine the stages of wartime internment, from capture and dreams of escape through to resignation and despair as the months of confinement add up, before finally the prisoner rises out of captivity and strides forward with hopes for a better future. While this was clearly a memorial dedicated to the internment experience, it is far less clear who these prisoners actually were. The dating and phrasing of the inscription only confuses matters further. It was dedicated to both 'Prisoners of War and Victims of Concentration Camps' for the years '1914–1945'.[32]

The mixture of different victim groups, conflicts and even nationalities that the memorial encompasses reflected the complexities of the sculptor's own life. Fred (Fritz) Kormis, a talented artist known for his portrait medallions, had himself experienced internment during the

First World War, having been captured on the Eastern Front while serving in the Austro-Hungarian army. 'I think it has shaped my life,' he later reflected.[33] Fifteen years after the war's end, he then suffered persecution at the hands of the Nazis; the memorial's other message. Born into a Frankfurt Jewish family, Kormis had managed to flee over the border into the Netherlands after the Nazis' rise to power, before eventually arriving in London in 1934. Some thirty-five years later, Kormis, by now grey-haired and sporting a pair of thick-rimmed spectacles, proudly watched as the two sides of his life between Britain and Germany were dedicated in stone. 'It has been a long time waiting for this day,' he remarked, 'but I am very happy now that it has arrived.'[34]

The fact that Kormis's idiosyncratic sculpture set spanned Britain and Germany, friend and foe, was quickly forgotten. Over the years, the five statues provided a backdrop for the occasional remembrance event. Throughout the 1970s, for example, Jewish war veterans gathered there each autumn to remember their comrades who had served in the British army, but the broader British-German context had vanished. Gradually, even these events petered out and the memorial became ever more dilapidated. In one incident, the figures were daubed with antisemitic graffiti, leading the Board of Deputies of British Jews to make an official protest to David Waddington, the then Home Secretary. Although Waddington expressed 'serious concern' at the incident, his words failed to make much of a difference: some years later someone took a hammer to the statues, pockmarking them with holes.[35] But by then, Kormis, who had so embodied the British–German relationship, had passed on, dying in his nineties 'still at work in his studio'.[36]

It was not until the new millennium that the next POW memorial appeared on British soil. The driving force behind the memorial was the National Ex-Prisoner of War Association, an ad hoc group of former POWs led by the jovial figure of Les Allan, who had been a private in the First Buckinghamshire Battalion during the Second World War.[37] Unlike Kormis, who had straddled the twin worlds of wartime Britain and Germany, the members of the association were more squarely focused on representing a British experience of internment. Allan himself had been captured, aged just 19, at Dunkirk. He then spent a truly horrific five years in various POW camps. It started with a 'Nazi rifle between my eyes', as he put it, and ended 'with a 1,000-mile "death" march across Poland'.[38] Allan's later attempt to memorialise the POW experience was made somewhat easier as the enemy war dead, who for so long had provided a salutary reminder of transnational loss, had already been cleared away to Cannock Chase. With the enemy no longer casting a shadow over proceedings, the association had the space to rethink the past in new ways.

Using these freedoms to full advantage, Allan took inspiration from a recently built memorial in northern Germany that recreated the entrance to the Stalag XIB POW camp near Fallingbostel. Eschewing the trend for modernist or abstract memorial sculptures, the design was in fact an exact replica of the camp's original entrance, replete with brick wall and barbed wire gates resting slightly ajar. But at least this memorial marked an actual site. The association's version, which was finally dedicated in July 2007, simply took the same design and placed it in a British setting. Nonetheless, Allan and his fellow members were delighted with the result. In the words of Allan, the memorial represented the 'soul destroying yearning for freedom' that his members had experienced in captivity, only relieved when the British army liberated the camps in April 1945. During the dedication, a swathe of bright umbrellas brought out to ward off the early summer rain almost drowned out the military uniforms and regimental colours that were also on display. Vera Lynn, the iconic British wartime singer, who had wisely decided to stay home given the inclement weather, later sent a note of praise. 'A fitting memorial that makes us all very proud,' she wrote.[39]

As the POW memorial had been created by the self-titled 'National' ex-servicemen's organisation, it was perhaps fitting that Allan located it in the National Memorial Arboretum (NMA). Occupying a flood-prone patch of land in Staffordshire at the confluence of the rivers Tame and Trent, the Arboretum officially opened in 2001. However, its origins lay a decade or so further back, when David Childs, a retired Royal Navy commander, conceived of creating a British version of America's Arlington Military Cemetery, a place where, as he put it, 'graves lie between wonderful lines of trees'. It may have been impossible for Childs to place actual war graves in his new memorial site, but trees were easier to come by. With the backing of a coalition of conservative groups and figures, ranging from the then prime minister, John Major, through to the British Legion and Rotary Club, he managed to start planting both trees – mainly poplars, willows and alders – as well as memorials on the newly acquired land. For Childs, the whole venture was a 'living tribute to all who served their country [meaning Britain] in an age of violence'.[40]

As a 'National' site of military commemoration, the Arboretum was designed as a predominantly British space for British war memories, or at the very most for those from 'across the Commonwealth who have served and sacrificed for the United Kingdom', as the Arboretum's guidance states.[41] It therefore reflects a fairly narrow conception of twentieth-century war and conflict. Although some civilians are represented at the site, mainly through charity or service memorials, the main focus is on male military sacrifice, figuratively represented in numerous statues of uniformed soldiers. Women also make an appearance, however. Members of the Women's Land Army, for example, are rewarded with their own separate memorial depicting two uniformed women, one holding a hoe and the other an axe. But, understandably, given the Arboretum's focus and priorities, there has been little interest in finding a space for the enemy dead, whose lives and wartime deaths are completely absent.

Named Visit England's 'Large Visitor Attraction of the Year' in 2018, the Arboretum is one of many recent sites and experiences focused on public remembrance. This memory boom started in earnest in the 1980s with the launch of attractions such as the Imperial War Museum's interactive 'Blitz Experience'. A decade later, the memory boom expanded even further into a series of extravagant public events to mark the fiftieth anniversaries of D-Day and VE-Day in 1994 and 1995 respectively, along with the First World War centenary twenty years later. These commemorations further embedded the idea of wartime stoicism, heroism and national unity into British culture.[42] Such heritage sites and events may not have been consciously designed as a cynical political 'distraction', as the cultural critic Robert Hewison once suggested, but nonetheless they did provide people with a means of accessing fortifying and consoling images of the past.[43]

The International Bomber Command Centre (IBCC), the latest in a long line of visitor attractions dedicated to the world wars, opened outside the city of Lincoln in 2018. Like the Arboretum, it was built on a blank site unrelated to either conflict. However, as Lincolnshire had been home to almost fifty RAF airfields during the Second World War, it had a direct connection. At the heart of the IBCC is a large visitor centre and a 31-metre-high memorial spire, based on the dimensions of a Lancaster bomber's wingspan. The IBCC has inscribed the names of almost 58,000 members of Bomber Command killed in the war on a metal wall that surrounds the memorial spire. The dead are listed equally, regardless of nationality and without 'ranks or awards'. Friends and relatives also have the option to purchase a more personal remembrance stone for their loved one set into the ground. The IBCC designates its purpose as a 'work to preserve history' and to honour the aircrews; the story it tells is largely one of bravery, sacrifice and fighting for freedom.[44]

Britain's wartime enemy does make an appearance, albeit fleeting, in these new heritage sites, being briefly mentioned in an exhibition accompanying the IBCC's memorial, for instance. But for the most part the dead enemy is largely absent. The irony with both locations, however, is that there had once been actual German war graves nearby, part of a much more complex, but long forgotten, remembrance culture. Less than 4 kilometres from the IBCC, fifteen German soldiers from the First World War and twenty-eight from the Second World War had been buried in Lincoln's main municipal cemetery. For the Arboretum, the numbers are smaller, but the German war dead had also lain undisturbed for decades within the communities nearby. By the time the two heritage sites were established, the enemy graves were long gone, removed to the German Military Cemetery on Cannock Chase. With those individual lives and stories transplanted elsewhere, the Arboretum and the IBCC have focused instead on British sacrifice against a more generic German enemy.

Ruptured Relations

If the presence of the enemy dead helped to nurture British–German relations in the wake of the two wars, their very absence has also shaped both countries' cultures of remembrance. Some of Britain's newer heritage sites certainly allude to the importance of fostering international understanding. The Arboretum, for example, is home to a tiny 'British–German Friendship Garden', admittedly somewhat lost in its military surroundings, and there is also a memorial to the 1914 Christmas 'truce' within the grounds.[45] Consisting of a British and a German hand clasped together within the frame of a football, the memorial commemorates the legendary moment when soldiers on the Western Front briefly stopped fighting. According to the story, the British and Germans climbed out of their trenches on Christmas Eve to chat, share cigarettes and to kick a ball around, although the precise course of events and level of participation has been debated ever since.[46]

A hundred years after the 'truce', Prince William, in his role as president of the English Football Association, arrived in Staffordshire on a cold December day to dedicate the new memorial. Wrapped in a dark jacket to protect against the elements, William took to the lectern and addressed the assembled audience, which included Roy Hodgson, the then England football manager. He stressed the importance of football as a unifier, then spoke of the 'truce' and the memorial as a sign of 'hope and humanity' between former foes.[47] William's warm words certainly seemed to be genuine and heartfelt. Yet, once the royal entourage and other guests had departed, it was unclear how exactly this memorial was going to improve British–German relations. It commemorates neither individual soldiers' lives, nor the complexities of the world wars. Instead, as has become a common trait in recent sites of memory, it is effectively a memorial to itself, merely commemorating popular narratives of the past.[48]

In reunified Germany, by contrast, memory of the Nazi past is neither comforting nor popular. Indeed, right-wing politicians in the AfD spend more time belittling Holocaust remembrance than participating in it, wilfully stoking antisemitism and downplaying Jewish victimhood.[49] Nonetheless, the memory of the Nazis' genocidal crimes, which Rosmus, Sponsel and other grassroots activists fought so hard to reveal in the 1970s and 1980s, has come to occupy a place at the very centre of Germany's remembrance culture, with almost every town having at least one Holocaust memorial. The *Stolpersteine* or stumbling block initiative, for example, has covered the pavements of town and cities with thousands of small shiny brass blocks. Each one marks the former homes or workplaces of the Nazis' victims.[50] If the country were to be judged solely on the number of public memorials, then the Germans could rightly praise themselves for dealing with a dark past. Yet, a continual 'inflation of memorials', as one historian has remarked, does not necessarily equate to a deeper sense of the Nazi era.[51] Familiarity can also breed complacency, particularly as the generations most connected to the victims and perpetrators of the Holocaust pass on.[52]

Holocaust remembrance may be firmly established in reunified Germany, but as soon as these familiar boundaries are stretched, there is much greater hesitancy.[53] Breaking out of the country's established memory framework to draw in other victims of Nazism, or even other genocides, has been extremely difficult. Mention colonial atrocities, such as the genocide of the Herero and Nama people in early-twentieth-century German South West Africa, for example, and there is far less appetite for 'coming to terms with the past'. Attempts to remove colonial-era street names, to decolonise exhibitions or to repatriate pilfered objects to their countries of origin have all faced considerable opposition. These atrocities just happen to represent the wrong past.[54]

The British dead of the two world wars have obviously not been absent in the same way; after all, their remains reside in self-contained, and beautifully maintained, CWGC war cemeteries. Nonetheless, with the original graves gone, there is generally very little awareness that British soldiers and civilians once died in the midst of local communities. It is only through the doggedness of campaigners that some trace of the enemy has very occasionally re-emerged. In the west of Germany, Traugott Vitz, a retired Protestant priest, has spent his golden years researching the murder of Second World War Allied airmen. His efforts have certainly paid off. On a road bridge to the south of Essen, where three RAF members were murdered in 1944, Vitz campaigned for an information board to be erected to mark these crimes. It was essential to stop these events from 'sinking into oblivion', he explained during the memorial's dedication.[55] Despite Vitz's diligence, this was something of an exception. The vast majority of British dead from the two conflicts have simply vanished from local memory, removing a foundation which might have fostered a much closer British–German relationship.

The circumstances are very different, but it is clear that in Germany there have been genuine efforts to engage with the country's wartime crimes, as manifested in its public memorials. Ironically, in Britain it has proved much harder to move beyond the era of the world wars, which is perhaps a reflection of the country's victorious fight against European fascism.[56] This popular memory of the world wars has never been confined solely to the Arboretum or the IBCC, but has taken root in heritage sites up and down the country, from Portsmouth's D-Day Story in the south through to Liverpool's Western Approaches exhibit in a Second World War bunker in the north. One of the most popular heritage experiences, however, remains the long-running Battle Proms. Held in the grounds of Britain's finest stately homes, including Winston Churchill's own Blenheim Palace, it is a mixture of classical music and military re-enactments. Each evening guests tuck into their picnics, as a Spitfire flies overhead and the orchestra start their performance of 'The Dam Busters March' and 'Rule Britannia'.[57]

Even where visitor attractions have little to do with the two conflicts, few have been able to resist the allure of staging their own wartime festivals or weekends. The annual Great Dorset Steam Fair, which, in the words of the organisers, showcases Britain's 'rich industrial, agricultural and leisure history', has also broadened its remit to include the world wars. When the gates to the 2014 Fair opened in the otherwise tranquil Tarrant Valley, visitors could enjoy the sights and acrid smell of hundreds of traction engines, and also take in a series of new military recreations, designed in 'honour and memory' of all those British soldiers who made the 'ultimate sacrifice'.[58] To represent the Great War, a line of freshly dug trenches and underground tunnels recreated the Western Front in the chalky soil of southern Dorset. Directly alongside the trenches, what the organisers called, an 'authentic re-creation of a blitzed small English town' stood in for the second global conflict.[59]

The Great Dorset Steam Fair did touch on the history of wartime death. Indeed, the site even contained its own replica war memorial, replete with poppy wreaths at its base (see image 36). Yet, unlike the actual war graves that were once dotted throughout British and German

36. The Great Dorset Steam Fair has for many years displayed its own First World War recreation trenches. In August 2022, the scene also contained a replica memorial for the 'Fallen Men of Kent'.

local communities, this recreated site of memory offered little scope for reconciliation. There was no sign of other war stories; the only narratives to feature were those of the victorious British. The Steam Fair was certainly not alone in offering an extremely narrow vision of the world wars. Whether the D-Day Story museum or the Battle Proms, the focus of these heritage attractions has been largely on a singular British war experience. Perhaps unsurprisingly, the enemy lives lost in conflict very rarely feature, which, if nothing else, removes an opportunity to foster British–German reconciliation.

Ironically, at one time, more complex narratives of the world wars could be found near most of these contemporary heritage sites. In Dorset, for example, had visitors chosen to leave the Steam Fair, then a brisk fifteen-minute walk would have taken them to the village of Tarrant Monkton, which contains both British and German war graves. In the churchyard of All Saints, opposite the popular village pub, a black metal marker, lying low in the long grass, still records the final resting place of '4 Unknown German Soldiers' (see image 37). This is an accurate description as the four graves have always had something of a mysterious presence. They are most likely for First World War POWs from the nearby Blandford camp, but their names, and indeed even whether the bodies are still there, is unclear.[60] The British and German soldiers may have died in the peace and quiet of rural Dorset, but they lost their lives in an actual conflict, not in an imagined one. The memorial in Tarrant Monkton, along with thousands of others that once stood in communities across Britain and Germany, was the site of a genuine British–German relationship, but today the odd faded relic is all that remains.

The flurry of new memorials and heritage sites, which have usurped both the original war graves and the war graves commissions' large military cemeteries, shows no sign of abating. In March 2016, residents from Handforth, which lies on the train line running south of Manchester, finally had a chance to join in with this remembrance wave. The Lord Lieutenant of Cheshire, sporting a dark blue ceremonial uniform, arrived in the town to dedicate a new war memorial that had been constructed on a grass verge just to the edge of the main centre. Why Handforth required another memorial, when there were

37. The churchyard in Tarrant Monkton, close to the site of the Great Dorset Steam Fair, still has metal markers for four German First World War soldiers.

already similar plaques in the town, is unclear. Nonetheless, after a series of short speeches, the Lord Lieutenant was invited to pull away the giant Union Jack that had been wrapped around the light-stone memorial for the dedication. This revealed the names of twenty-six soldiers from the First World War, ten from the Second and one from the more recent conflict in Afghanistan.[61] The Handforth memorial is very similar to the earlier German POW memorials. Just as in Germany, none of the dead listed in Handforth had actually died in the town and there was nothing particular about the chosen site that connected it to the dead or even to conflict.

The artificiality of the Handforth memorial, like its forerunners in Lünen, Brambauer or indeed the NMA in Staffordshire, would not be so problematic if they were not so selective. However, in each case, a distinct group of British or German dead has been chosen for commemoration, leaving all the others excluded, even though the enemy had also died in or near these places. The particular irony in

Handforth was that more German than British soldiers actually lost their lives in this part of rural Cheshire, breathing their last in the town's First World War POW camp. By the time the new memorial was built, more than fifty years had passed since the German bodies had been exhumed from the town and reinterred in the new Cannock Chase German Military Cemetery. As had been the case earlier in Germany, the absence of the enemy dead left the road clear for local communities to create their own purely national sites of memory, overlooking the potential for a shared culture of remembrance.

CONCLUSION

The Ghosts of War

The dead are never far from the surface. In June 2023, a violent explosion ripped through the concrete walls of the Kakhovka Dam in southern Ukraine that, at the time, was held by occupying Russian forces. After the breach, millions of litres of water from the Dnipro River cascaded down the streets and through the houses of communities stretching over an area in excess of 600 square kilometres. At least, fifty people, thousands of livestock and other animals were dragged to their deaths in the flood waters.[1] While the attack on the dam caused new deaths, it also revealed the remnants of earlier destruction. Entombed in the muddy marshes of the once colossal reservoir, some locals spotted a human skull, then more skeletal remains surfaced; one body still even sported a rusting Wehrmacht helmet. These appeared to be the remains of German soldiers killed in bitter fighting with Soviet forces during the Battle of Dnieper in late 1943.

Such was the brutality of the conflict in the East that many of the dead had not received proper burials at the time, particularly during the frozen winter months. Around the Dnipro River, bodies were simply left to fester where they fell until the construction of the Kakhovka Dam in the 1950s looked certain to consign them forever to a watery grave.[2] It is, however, very rare for human remains to disappear completely, even in an aquatic environment; bones remain intact long after flesh and any clothing have decomposed.[3] And, as was the case in both Britain and Germany after the two world wars, the bereaved continued to demand information about their missing loved ones, hoping they might still be alive, but as a bare minimum wanting a grave. Looking at these skeletal discoveries in Ukraine against the backdrop of another deadly conflict is a salutary reminder that not only do military conflicts cost the lives of friend and foe alike, they also always leave mortuary traces behind.

The soil of Britain and Germany has already given up the remains of most of the enemy dead, although bodies still occasionally resurface. One of the bodies discovered most recently, in 2014, belonged to Wilfred Lawson, an RAF airman who had been shot down near Dresden in 1944. At the time of the Lancaster bomber's crash, the Germans had managed to capture some of the crew and to recover the remains of the others, but the 25-year-old's body remained missing. The belated discovery of his remains seventy years later, and his subsequent burial in Berlin, was something of a rare case.[4] For the most part, the enemy dead already lay in the large CWGC and VDK war cemeteries in Britain and Germany. Although these sites give the impression of unending permanence, they are merely the enemy's latest resting place. With the move from parish churchyards and municipal burial grounds to the new national cemeteries, local communities lost many of their connections to the dead, and to broader histories of the world wars. Once the enemy bodies were hidden away in remote, secluded national cemeteries, space opened for other, often less inclusive, narratives of the wars to flourish instead.

Local Enemies

In the late 1930s, a diplomatic storm erupted over a war memorial that had been erected a decade earlier in the Yorkshire village of Sledmere. What was so unusual about the memorial in question was that it eschewed the typical platitudes and depicted the enemy at their worst. Dedicated to the men of the Wagoners' Special Reserve, a local Territorial Army unit, the panels adorning the cylindrical structure depict the story of one volunteer's wartime journey from the farms of Yorkshire to the battlefields of the Western Front. The little figures, carved in a jocular style, suddenly meet their enemy midway through the frieze, when they come face to face with the German soldiers, all grimacing teeth, Pickelhaube helmets and serrated bayonets. Nothing is left to the imagination, as the Germans then set fire to a church, before grabbing a Belgian woman by the hair and finally decapitating her with a sword (see image 38). The German embassy discovered the depictions of their fellow countrymen somewhat belatedly in 1938. An exchange of letters then followed, including the demand that the scene be deleted. The whole memorial is 'symptomatic of the British mentality', crowed commentators from within Nazi Germany, somewhat ironically as they were just about to invade the Sudetenland and set fire to hundreds of synagogues.[5]

Mark Sykes, the aristocratic landowner who had originally designed the Wagoners' memorial, had the freedom to meditate on the Great

38. After the First World War, a local landowner in Sledmere erected a memorial for the men who had served in the Wagoners' Special Reserve. Scenes from the conflict inscribed around the sides of the memorial were the source of some controversy, particularly as one section depicted German war crimes in Belgium.

War and to depict its history as he saw fit. Sykes had neither bodies nor an actual site of conflict to constrict him in this endeavour. Elsewhere, though, such constraints did exist, which, if nothing else, ensured that Sykes's peak of jingoism remained an isolated incident. In communities across both Britain and Germany, the enemy was never some abstract figure made up of fears, prejudices and national cliches, but rather an increasingly familiar presence. With the graves of the enemy in their midst, local people got to know their new mortuary neighbours as individuals, whose lives had ended in a global conflict. Letters from loved ones abroad, the first family visits and annual remembrance ceremonies all helped to rehumanise the enemy dead. Over time, therefore, the thick lines that had divided the British and German people, separating out the 'grievable' and 'ungrievable' dead, also started to fade.[6] What had initially been a war against a faceless, dangerous enemy became a transnational history of shared loss.

The relations that developed between the former foes in the wake of the two conflicts were very different from the more familiar diplomatic, political and commercial exchanges that adorn many a history book.[7] Indeed, in the case of the British and German war graves, the dead often continued to provoke diplomatic incidents long after the fighting was over, with heated complaints over maintenance, care and respect all too common. But on the local level, in rural villages and small towns where the enemy just happened to be buried, relations flourished more easily. Members of these communities often saw it as their responsibility to take on the care of the freshly dug enemy graves. This was not unique to Britain or Germany, with a similar role performed, albeit less willingly, by French communities in the 1940s and 1950s.[8] Reconciliation was rarely the main driver of these local activities, at least at first. Far more important was a sense that those killed, regardless of their actions in life, deserved proper care in death.[9] Families, mothers in particular, who had lost sons themselves, found it easy to imagine grief beyond borders. They ended up tending the enemy graves out of a shared experience of wartime loss, but also in the hope of reciprocity.

The dead may have been able to draw the former foes together, but these rather ad hoc relations fell outside the scope of more official plans. The two war graves commissions, while keen on the idea of reconciliation, would have rather this happened as a result of their own actions, and not because of local interventions. In Bishop's Stortford, for example, where mother and daughter team, Muriel Wright and Ivy Coppen, earned international praise for their care of local German war graves, the IWGC proved to be less keen. The commission's inspectors disliked the pair's informal approach to commemoration, particularly after they placed 'a painted metal flower container on each grave'.[10] The final straw, though, came in the late 1950s, when there was some suggestion that the West Germans were planning to honour Wright for her work maintaining the German war graves. The thought of rewarding Wright for her 'rusty vases and jam jars' filled the IWGC with such dread that it demanded an 'opportunity to express a view'.[11] Both the IWGC and the VDK had long-established modes of operating which they did not want to see disrupted by other people, whether this was the bereaved or members of local communities.

Concentration of the scattered graves into central cemeteries provided the war graves commissions with the simplest way of retaining complete control.[12] Once the dead had been interred in neatly laid out military cemeteries, enclosed safely behind high walls and fences, then they no longer needed to fear the influence of any other custodians. However, the bodies were not going to travel to these new cemeteries on their own. The result was three massive exhumation schemes conducted by the British in 1920s and 1940s Germany, followed by the West Germans recovering their dead in Britain in the early 1960s. In all three cases, lorries and vans filled to the brim with makeshift coffins and sarcophaguses criss-crossed the two countries moving thousands of corpses and body parts from one location to another. Despite the scale of these operations, they passed largely under the radar; even most of the bereaved only discovered what had happened to their loved ones' remains after the event. Yet, these were huge examples of mortuary realignments. The VDK's twelve months of gravedigging in Britain constituted one of the largest examples of mass exhumation in the modern era, surely only rivalled by the much larger project of disinterment for London's Elizabeth Line and the neighbouring High Speed 2 railway line.[13]

Present-day exhumations, whether of individual or mass graves, are strictly regulated and conducted according to standard operating procedures. Today's agencies also benefit from scientific advances, such as the use of DNA, that make identification much easier.[14] Nothing of the sort, of course, was available to the exhumation teams working in the years after the two world wars. Reliant on more primitive techniques, with limited time and often reluctant workers, all three exhumation schemes suffered from errors in recovery and identification. One particularly unfortunate episode occurred in north Germany. In 1951, a Dutch exhumation team arrived at a small cemetery in Salzgitter to recover the remains of Louis Engelander, a Jewish coffeeshop owner from Amsterdam. Engelander had died in unexplained circumstances in 1944 while held in a nearby slave labour camp. When the Dutch team arrived at the marked grave, they dug down, only to find it completely empty. After much investigation, it turned out that the British had taken the body to the IWGC cemetery in Hanover four years earlier. They had read Engelander's name on the grave marker as 'Engländer', taking it to be the grave of an unknown Englishman.[15]

The mix-up with Engelander was clearly unfortunate, no doubt exacerbated by the fact that the exhumation teams were working through the chaos of post-war Germany. The same, however, cannot be said for the VDK's large-scale disinterments in the 1960s. Often the German war graves commission knew the precise location of an individual grave. Yet, as soon as problems occurred with the exhumation operation, it chose to declare the grave as missing rather than leave it in situ. The case of Grenadier Paul Löhofer, who had died from wounds in a London hospital in December 1914 and been buried in Greenwich Cemetery, is a typical example. The VDK's casualty database simply lists Löhofer as having no known grave; he could not be recovered 'during our exhumation work', the record innocently states.[16] Reports from the 1920s and 1930s, however, noted his grave was 'permanently and adequately commemorat[ed]'.[17] And when Christel Eulen visited Greenwich in 1956, she left with a photograph showing a very solid-looking headstone (see image 39). The reason for the loss of Löhofer's grave was actually that he shared a burial plot with seven other bodies. Rather than disturb these other corpses to find the one they wanted, the VDK simply abandoned the grave and smashed up the headstone, almost as if Löhofer had never existed.

39. Slightly hidden in the high grass of Greenwich cemetery, the headstone
for Paul Löhofer, a German soldier of the Great War, is still visible in 1956.
Only six years later, the VDK's exhumation teams were unable to locate the
grave when they visited the cemetery.

Whether bodies made the journey to the new military cemeteries or
not, the disappearance of the enemy still had a dramatic effect on the
original custodians. Communities that had spent years, even decades in
the case of the British, caring for these war dead suddenly found themselves redundant. Left with little option but to watch on as the gravediggers set to work, it seemed that their own efforts to tend the graves
had been ignored or, worse still, that the war graves commissions
no longer trusted them to care for the dead. This was often a cause of

local resentment, as one British newspaper expressed it, the Germans from the VDK were the 'Unwelcome Gravediggers'.[18] Where the enemy graves had once provided a foundation for rebuilding the fragile British–German relationship, there was only bitterness and sadness. In Theberton, the Zeppelin graves and the steady stream of German visitors had been a feature of village life since the airship's downing in 1917. When the VDK disinterred the remains, there was little cheer; it was like 'another bit of Suffolk history [was] gone', lamented one local.[19]

Once the enemy had been removed from places like Theberton, local interest and local care vanished at the same time. A similar relationship to the enemy could never be replicated in the new, artificially created, large military cemeteries. But then this was never the primary aim of the two war graves commissions. After all, one of the reasons for concentrating the dead was to centralise maintenance and to ensure uniformity of treatment, thereby avoiding future Wrights or Coppens from putting their 'jam jars' of flowers on the graves. The almost inevitable consequence of these mortuary moves, though, was the cessation of contacts between the bereaved and local communities; with this, the tentative – sometimes awkward – but always vital, local British–German relations were also lost. Had international relations been a priority for the war graves commissions, then the lesson to take from this wave of exhumations was that local burials were far more productive for breaking down barriers than was the case with the large national cemeteries. But sadly, national homogeneity always trumped reconciliation and indeed the wishes of relatives too.

If there was one lesson that seemed to percolate down through the war graves commissions, it was that leaving bodies on former enemy territory could be more difficult than returning them. The IWGC discovered this to its cost in the 1930s, after their four large military cemeteries were left isolated in Nazi Germany and open to abuse. Fifty years later and this same lesson still rang true. In 1996, German intelligence suggested that the CWGC cemeteries, these very British symbols, were potential targets of the Irish Republican Army (IRA), which resulted in them being effectively locked down. Indeed, anyone wanting to attend the annual Remembrance Day in Münster that year had to pass through a ring of mounted police and sniffer dogs just to enter the British cemetery, while the drone of a helicopter circling overhead accompanied the two minutes' silence.[20]

Partly to avoid a repeat of such scenes, it has largely become the norm to repatriate the British dead. The bereaved successfully pushed for this during the 1982 Falklands War; an approach that has been repeated in all subsequent conflicts too. John Keegan, the renowned military historian, lamented the loss of 'islands of something distinctly British' overseas, but therein lay the problem.[21] Imposing large national sites onto another country, particularly when it was the former enemy, often ended up doing little more than stirring old animosities. The Federal Republic also learnt this same lesson. When the German government dared to dip its toes into international conflicts again from the 1990s onwards, casualties were repatriated home rather than left in graves overseas. Completing this circle, in 2009, the German Defence Ministry constructed a new memorial for its post-war dead in central Berlin. The grey concrete and steel cube-like structure was not only an acknowledgement that soldiers were still dying in conflict, but also that they were to be remembered within Germany and not overseas.[22]

Beyond the Grave

Cemeteries are very good at telling stories.[23] The type of headstone or wording of the inscription reveal something about the deceased, but often far more about the living who made these choices. However, the very presence of different graves also raises questions for the visitor: how and why did a particular individual die and how come the body ended up being laid to rest in one particular spot? When looking at the grave of a 90-year-old local man buried in a parish churchyard, the answers are obvious, but this is not always the case. Few cemeteries raise as many questions as the British or White Cemetery in Afghanistan's capital, Kabul. Tucked away behind a high perimeter wall and sturdy wooden gate lie the remains of foreigners who lost their lives in the region from the British colonial wars of the nineteenth century through to the West's more recent Afghan conflicts. Seeing the graves of Danish explorers alongside those of colonial-era troops and, much later, aid workers reveals something of the region's tumultuous past and present.[24] Although the British returned their dead from the 2001–2021 war to RAF Lyneham, near Wootton Bassett, and the Germans to Cologne/Bonn airport, plaques to the dead remained in the cemetery in Kabul as a lasting reminder that British, Germans and others had once served and died in Afghanistan.[25]

Very few British or German cemeteries are still able to tell such diverse stories. Visitors to the nineteenth-century cemetery in Fürth, on the northern edge of Nuremberg, might be able to marvel at the graves of the city's long-deceased great and good, but they would never know that at least ten RAF airmen had once been buried there during the Second World War. Similarly, in the Devizes Road Cemetery in the cathedral city of Salisbury, there is no longer any sign of the twenty German airmen killed in the Second World War and buried in the city, while further across Wiltshire at the village of Sutton Veny, anyone walking around the parish churchyard would have little inkling that this was once the resting place of thirty-eight German POWs from the Great War. With the removal of the enemy dead, the burial grounds in Fürth, Salisbury, Sutton Veny and elsewhere have all reverted back to being local cemeteries, almost solely for local people.

Although the enemy dead have taken their stories of conflict with them to the large concentration cemeteries, there is no reason why other, more diverse narratives of wartime death, should not continue to feature locally. Yet, the CWGC's efforts to promote its work have so far only ended up in further cementing these absences. At the entrance to St John's Parish Church in Sutton Veny, for example, a CWGC information board explains how the different groups of war dead ended up coming to rest in this part of Wiltshire. The British war graves, the panel explains, mainly had some familial connection to the region, while many of the Australian dead had been stationed locally and died in the influenza pandemic. But what of the German POWs? Their graves are gone, so no longer even earn a mention. These other stories are also absent from 'War Graves Week', an 'annual celebration of the work of the Commonwealth War Graves Commission'. For the very first of these new annual weeks in May 2021, the public were asked to 'discover the World War heritage on their doorstep'. But, just as in

Sutton Veny, this was about current graves, not anyone else, particularly the enemy, who may also have died 'on their doorstep'.[26]

The absence of the other casualties of war only leads to introspection. In the interwar years, the German people were the masters at wallowing in their own war stories. The Treaty of Versailles was unjust, the reparations bill financially crippling and Germany's almost 2 million war dead had been unfairly forgotten went the complaints. The British and other Allied war dead who might have provided some wider context had been removed from local burial grounds by the mid-1920s. The IWGC's four large military cemeteries in Hamburg, Berlin Stahnsdorf, Cologne and Kassel, which replaced local burial grounds, clearly demonstrated that the British had also died in the recent conflict, but they did nothing to soften the mood. Indeed, the new cemeteries only served to deepen German self-pity. While Britain's dead were honoured in grand manicured gardens on German soil, their own dead still lay scattered, apparently forgotten, in hundreds of separate cemeteries throughout Britain. For the Nazis, such visible differences only made them all the more determined to reassert German wartime heroism through new memorials, ceremonies and military parades.[27]

Since the 1990s, it has been the British that have led the field when it comes to having an obsessive focus on the world wars, particularly the 1939–1945 conflict. However, British navel-gazing has been very different from that of interwar Germany. It is not revanchism or remilitarisation that has driven the British fascination with war and conflict, but rather heritage. A heady mixture of wartime nostalgia and a good day out – tanks and a cup of tea – is at its heart. Staffordshire's NMA and the IBCC in Lincoln – two of the largest wartime heritage sites – have demonstrated the endless possibilities of this ever-growing genre. They enjoy high visitor numbers, royal patronage and an annual income reaching into the millions.[28]

However, the NMA and the IBCC are just the tip of the iceberg. As anyone visiting the Great Dorset Steam Fair would know, the world wars have managed to permeate heritage attractions up and down the country. The fifteenth-century Tudor House in Southampton, a beautiful timber-framed building in the centre of the city, provides a glimpse into the lives of the people who once ate and drank in its exquisite oak-framed banqueting hall. During school holidays, however, attention moves from the 1490s to the 1940s, when children can take part in Second World War 'Civil Defence training', learning the 'correct way to put out an incendiary bomb and bandaging the wounded'. With a slight nod towards good taste, this was only suitable for children aged over 6 years old.[29] Steam railways, whose numbers are legion in Britain, have few qualms about the age of their audience, when they stage their ubiquitous 1940s weekends. The Kent and East Sussex Railway invites everyone to 'join in the fun' as the 'railway turns back the clock to wartime Britain', with the promise of a 'whole weekend of pure nostalgia'. The Grand Central Railway in Loughborough goes a stage further, with flypasts from Spitfires and Lancaster bombers, as well as a 'mock battle', while still offering 'something for all the family'.[30]

In an attempt to tone down the militarism, the Grand Central Railway is keen to stress that 'remembrance is at the heart' of its 1940s weekend, as visitors can attend a church service and view a 'poppy shower tribute'. Yet, as much as they may try, it is hard to avoid the triumphalism in this and other events, which take Britain's earlier 'culture of victory' to a new level. The booming wartime heritage sector has done very little to foster a reflective and sustainable relationship between Britain and Germany. Instead, it is very much a case of a return to more simplistic narratives of us and them. At the East Lancashire Railway, which runs restored steam trains into the countryside north of Manchester, military re-enactors have helpfully emphasised this distinction by appearing in SS uniforms during the railway's own wartime weekends. While this uniform choice provided the re-enactors in Allied uniforms with an obvious target, it hardly suggested a deep reflection on the past or on a post-war future. It was left to Manchester's Jewish community to point this out, as one member rightly stressed: 'What's this got to do with wartime England?'[31]

The complainant could have also legitimately questioned why 77 per cent of Britain's swathe of heritage railways have felt the need to hold wartime re-enactment weekends or, indeed, why so many of Britain's heritage venues are saturated with world war-themed events, even when there is no obvious connection to twentieth-century conflict.[32] While this repeated telling of the same stories of the British people's wartime exploits might help to draw the crowds into cash-strapped heritage sites, it has done little to improve the British–German relationship. Regaling later generations with comfortable stories of military fortitude in the trenches of the Great War or of 'standing alone' in the second global conflict encourages nothing but separation and insularity.

Breaking this spiral into ever greater introspection requires a deeper focus on the complexities of twentieth-century conflict, on the breadth of actors involved and, above all, on the immense scale of wartime death that ensnared friend and foe, as well as soldier and civilian. Ironically, the very circumstances for pursuing such conversations did once exist. For years, even decades after the two world wars, enemy bodies lay intermingled with their former foe in cemeteries across Britain and Germany. It is now too late to return the physical remains of these other dead to local landscapes, but it is still possible to tell broader narratives of war and conflict, if the will exists. France's 'Ring of Remembrance' memorial, inaugurated in 2014 on a windswept hill north of Arras, hints at what is possible. The circular memorial records the lives of some 580,000 soldiers who died in the region of Nord-Pas-de-Calais in the First World War, ordering them not by rank or nationality but by name. Tens of Lefèvres, Müllers or Smiths silently line up on the memorial's metal plaques.[33] There is perhaps little appetite for another 'Ring of Remembrance' in Bristol, Berlin, London or Lübeck. Nonetheless, recovering earlier, more expansive histories of shared wartime death, should be at the heart of a strong and sustainable British–German relationship.

NOTES

Introduction

1. 'Nazi Down in N.E. Scotland', *Dundee Courier*, 15 July 1941, p. 3.
2. 'Hans Steggemann', *Westfälische Tageszeitung*, 20 August 1941, p. 6.
3. Wendy Ugolini, '"When Are You Going Back?" Memory, Ethnicity and the British Home Front', in Lucy Noakes and Juliette Pattinson (eds), *British Cultural Memory and the Second World War* (London: Bloomsbury, 2014), pp. 89–110. On differences in commemorations within the British Empire, see: Commonwealth War Graves Commission, *Report of the Special Committee to Review Historical Inequalities in Commemoration*, 2021: https://www.cwgc.org/media/noantj4i/report-of-the-special-committee-to-review-historical-inequalities-in-commemoration.pdf (accessed 10 May 2022).
4. For the classic study, see: Angus Calder, *The Myth of the Blitz* (London: Jonathan Cape, 1991). In addition: Malcolm Smith, *Britain 1940: History, Myth and Popular Memory* (London: Routledge, 2000).
5. Judith Butler, *Frames of War: When is Life Grievable?* (London: Verso, 2010), p. xxii.
6. Kevin Hall, *Terror Flyers: The Lynching of American Airmen in Nazi Germany* (Bloomington: Indiana University Press, 2021); Georg Hoffmann, *Fliegerlynchjustiz: Gewalt gegen abgeschossene alliierte Flugzeugbesatzungen 1943–1945* (Paderborn: Ferdinand Schöningh, 2015).
7. Norbert Frei, *Vergangenheitspolitik: Die Anfänge der Bundesrepublik und die NS-Vergangenheit* (Munich: Beck, 1996).
8. Robert Moeller, *War Stories: The Search for a Useable Past in the Federal Republic of Germany* (Berkeley: University of California Press, 2003).
9. Jay Winter and Antoine Prost, *The Great War in History: Debates and Controversies, 1914 to the Present* (Cambridge: Cambridge University Press, 2020), p. 238.
10. For general overviews of the war at home, see: Adrian Gregory, *The Last Great War: British Society and the First World War* (Cambridge: Cambridge University Press, 2008); Benjamin Ziemann, *War Experiences in Rural Germany 1914–1923* (Oxford: Berg, 2007). In Alexander Watson's magnificent study of the Central Powers by contrast, there is a brief discussion of wartime slave labour: Alexander

Watson, *Ring of Steel: Germany and Austria-Hungary at War, 1914–1918* (London: Allen Lane, 2014), pp. 384–92.

11. Panikos Panayi, *Prisoners of Britain: German Civilian and Combat Internees during the First World War* (Manchester: Manchester University Press, 2012), pp. 123–65; Oliver Wilkinson, *British Prisoners of War in First World War Germany* (Cambridge: Cambridge University Press, 2017), pp. 89, 110, 119; Uta Hinz, *Gefangen im Großen Krieg: Kriegsgefangenschaft in Deutschland 1914–1921* (Essen: Klartext, 2006), pp. 235–49.

12. For the term, see: Jay Winter, *Sites of Memory, Sites of Mourning: The Great War in European Cultural History* (Cambridge: Cambridge University Press, 1995).

13. This has been an ongoing objective of historians of twentieth-century conflict, for example: Jörn Leonhard, *Die Büchse der Pandora: Geschichte des Ersten Weltkrieges* (Munich: Beck, 2014).

14. Tim Grady, 'Dying with the Enemy: Prisoners of War Deaths in First World War Britain', in Holly Furneaux and Matilda Greig (eds), *Enemy Encounters in Modern Warfare* (Basingstoke: Palgrave, 2024), pp. 173–93. More generally: Alison Fell, 'Nursing the Enemy in the First World War', *European Journal for Nursing History and Ethics* (2022), pp. 1–23.

15. George Mosse, *Fallen Soldiers: Reshaping the Memory of the World Wars* (Oxford: Oxford University Press, 1990), pp. 163–4.

16. *Montrose Standard*, 25 July 1941.

17. Volksbund Deutsche Kriegsgräberfürsorge (hereafter, VDK), 'Aufstellung', VDK, A100/975; L. Worthington Evans to C.K. Howard-Bury, 24 May 1928, Commonwealth Graves Commission (hereafter, CWGC), CWGC/1/1/7/C/11.

18. This is an example of what is termed 'multidirectional memory', see: Michael Rothberg, *Multidirectional Memory: Remembering the Holocaust in the Age of Decolonization* (Stanford: Stanford University Press, 2009), p. 3.

19. 'Frau Becker Achieves an Ambition', *Dundee Courier*, 23 September 1954, p. 2.

20. Agathe Becker to Auswärtiges Amt, 27 October 1954, Politisches Archiv des Auswärtigen Amts (hereafter, PA-AA), B 10-ABT.2/2248.

21. On tensions during and after the Great War, see: Matthew Stibbe, *German Anglophobia and the Great War, 1914–1918* (Cambridge: Cambridge University Press, 2001), pp. 194–209. For the importance of local relations: Jan Rüger, *Heligoland: Britain, Germany, and the Struggle for the North Sea* (Oxford: Oxford University Press, 2017), pp. 4–5.

22. David Blackbourn, '"As dependent on each other as man and wife": Cultural Contacts and Transfers', in Dominik Geppert and Robert Gerwarth (eds), *Wilhelmine Germany and Edwardian Britain: Essays on Cultural Affinity* (Oxford: Oxford University Press, 2008), pp. 15–37, p. 26.

23. On gender and the history of emotions, see: Ute Frevert, *Emotions in History – Lost and Found* (Budapest: Central European University Press, 2011), pp. 87–147. And in the context of war: Claire Langhamer, Lucy Noakes and Claudia Siebrecht (eds), *Total War: An Emotional History* (Oxford: Oxford University Press, 2020).

24. For an account of a much trickier relationship in post-war France, see: Zoe Rose Buonaiuto, 'A Grave Reconciliation: The Establishment of German War Cemeteries in Normandy, 1944–1964', *International Journal of Military History and Historiography*, 38 (2018), pp. 170–95.

25. Writing on pilgrimages to the gravesites generally focuses on the battlefields, rather than the home front. See: David Lloyd, *Battlefield Tourism: Pilgrimage and*

Commemoration of the Great War in Britain, Australia and Canada, 1919–1939 (Oxford: Berg, 1998).

26. 'Touching Scene', *Stapleford & Sandiacre News*, 27 July 1928, p. 1.
27. Thomas Laqueur, *The Work of the Dead: A Cultural History of Human Remains* (Princeton: Princeton University Press, 2015).
28. Existing cemeteries in Cologne and Hamburg received bodies from the 1939–1945 war, while new sites were added in Kiel, Becklingen, Celle, Hanover, Sage, Münster-Heath, Rheinberg, Reichswald, Dürnbach, Berlin Heerstrasse and Berlin Olympische Strasse.
29. On the VDK, see: Jakob Böttcher, *Zwischen staatlichem Auftrag und gesellschaftlicher Trägerschaft. Eine Geschichte der Kriegsgräberfürsorge in Deutschland im 20. Jahrhundert* (Göttingen: Vandenhoeck & Ruprecht, 2018); Bernd Ulrich et al., *Volksbund Deutsche Kriegsgräberfürsorge: Entwicklungslinien und Probleme* (Berlin: be.bra Verlag, 2019). For more on these resentments, see: Tim Grady, 'A Dance with Death: The Imperial War Graves Commission and Nazi Germany', *The English Historical Review* 138 (2023), pp. 1307–36.
30. Most of the dead were moved to the new Cannock Chase German Military Cemetery, although a smaller number, including Becker, ended up in the neighbouring Cannock Chase War Cemetery.
31. For one exception, albeit for more recent exhumations, see: Layla Renshaw, 'Anzac Anxieties: Rupture, Continuity, and Authenticity in the Commemoration of Australian War Dead at Fromelles', *Journal of War and Culture Studies*, 10 (2017), pp. 324–39.
32. There is a wealth of literature on established military cemeteries: Simon Rietz, 'Deutsche Soldatenfriedhöfe des Ersten Weltkrieges und der Weimarer Republik. Ein Beitrag zur Professionsgeschichte der Landschaftsarchitektur' (PhD, Leibniz Universität Hannover, 2015); Mandy Morris, 'Gardens "For Ever England": Landscape, Identity and the First World War British Cemeteries on the Western Front', *Ecumene*, 4 (1997), pp. 410–34.
33. The book, therefore, follows the 'forensic turn', see: Zuzanna Dziuban (ed.), *Mapping the 'Forensic Turn': Engagements with Materialities of Mass Death in Holocaust Studies and Beyond* (Vienna: New Academic Press, 2017). For an important case study, see: Lucy Noakes, *Dying for the Nation: Death, Grief and Bereavement in Second World War Britain* (Manchester: Manchester University Press, 2020).
34. Anthony Nicholls, 'Always Good Neighbours – Never Good Friends? Anglo-German Relations 1949–2001', German Historical Institute London, Annual Lecture (2004).
35. Wiebke Kolbe, 'Trauer und Tourismus: Reisen des Volksbundes Deutsche Kriegsgräberfürsorge 1950–2010', *Zeithistorische Forschungen*, 14 (2017), pp. 68–92.
36. Morris, 'Gardens "For Ever England"', p. 424. See also: Stéphane Audoin-Rouzeau and Annette Becker, *Understanding the Great War, 14–18* (New York: Hill & Wang, 2002), pp. 191–2.
37. Sam Edwards, 'An Empire of Memory: Overseas British War Cemeteries, 1917–1983', *International Journal of Military History and Historiography*, 38 (2018), pp. 255–86, p. 263.
38. 'Royal Visit in Memory of the Dead', *Uttoxeter Newsletter*, 24 April 1987, p. 4.
39. Mosse, *Fallen Soldiers*, p. 7.
40. Manfred Hettling and Jörg Echternkamp, 'Deutschland: Heroisierung und Opferstilisierung Grundelemente des Gefallenengedenkens von 1813 bis heute',

in Manfred Hettling and Jörg Echternkamp (eds), *Gefallenengedenken im globalen Vergleich: Nationale Tradition, politische Legitimation und Individualisierung der Erinnerung* (Munich: Oldenbourg, 2013), pp. 123–58, p. 140.

41. Geoff Eley, 'Finding the People's War: Film, British Collective Memory, and World War II', *American Historical Review*, 106 (3) (2001), pp. 818–38; Nick Hewitt, 'A Sceptical Generation? War Memorials and the Collective Memory of the Second World War in Britain, 1945–2000', in Dominik Geppert (ed.), *The Postwar Challenge: Cultural, Social, and Political Change in Western Europe, 1945–1958* (Oxford: Oxford University Press, 2003), pp. 81–97, p. 91; David Reynolds, 'Britain, the Two World Wars, and the Problem of Narrative', *The Historical Journal*, 60 (2017), pp. 197–231.

42. Patrick Wright, *On Living in an Old Country: The National Past in Contemporary Britain* (London: Verso, 1985), p. 46; Paul Gilroy, *Postcolonial Melancholia* (New York: Columbia University Press, 2005), p. 87.

43. On gift shops and the commodification of the past, see: Tony Kushner, 'One of Us? Contesting Disraeli's Jewishness and Englishness in the Twentieth Century', in Tony Kushner and Todd Endelman (eds), *Disraeli's Jewishness* (London: Vallentine Mitchell, 2002), pp. 201–62.

44. 'Frau Becker Achieves an Ambition', *Dundee Courier*, 23 September 1954, p. 2. The IWGC was rebranded as the CWGC to reflect the end of empire in 1960.

45. Eduard Becker: https://www.volksbund.de/erinnern-gedenken/graebersuche-online/detail/36113a38d9423776dc3718ed3a09cc0e (accessed 15 May 2022).

46. These are the words of Corinne Fowler, who in very different circumstances, stresses the importance of a site or object's prehistory: Corinne Fowler, *Green Unpleasant Land: Creative Responses to Rural England's Colonial Connections* (Leeds: Peepal, 2020), p. 133.

1 Locating

1. 'Vermischtes', *Norddeutsche Allgemeine Zeitung*, 3 July 1909, p. 7; 'Mit der deutschen Gartenstadtgesellschaft durch England', *General-Anzeiger der Stadt Mannheim und Umgebung*, 2 August 1909, p. 1. Deutsche Gartenstadt-Gesellschaft (ed.), *Aus englischen Gartenstädten* (Berlin: Renaissance, 1910), pp. 6–7, 118–28.

2. 'Garden City Association Visit to Port Sunlight 9th July 1909. Speech of Mr. Lever in the Auditorium', Unilever Archives, Port Sunlight, GB1752.UNI/BD/2/1/1/21.

3. Ulrike Lindner, 'Imperialism and Globalization: Entanglements and Interactions between the British and German Colonial Empires in Africa before the First World War', *German Historical Institute London Bulletin*, 32 (2010), pp. 4–28. For a wider discussion, see: Jan Rüger, 'Revisiting the Anglo-German Antagonism', *Journal of Modern History*, 83 (2011), pp. 579–617.

4. 'Garden City Association'. For the classic work on these tensions: Paul Kennedy, *The Rise of the Anglo-German Antagonism, 1860–1914* (London: Allen & Unwin, 1980).

5. Heinrich August Winkler, *Der lange Weg nach Westen – Deutsche Geschichte I: Vom Ende des Alten Reiches bis zum Untergang der Weimarer Republik* (Munich: Beck, 2020 [orig. 2000]), p. 274.

6. Stephanie Coontz, *Marriage, a History: How Love Conquered Marriage* (London: Penguin, 2005), p. 293.

7. 'Day Respondent Survey', 11 November 1937, Mass Observation Archive, Brighton, DS080.
8. Christopher Clark, *The Sleepwalkers: How Europe Went to War in 1914* (London: Penguin, 2013), pp. 204–14.
9. 'Wettlauf um den Marokkopreis', *Simplicissimus*, 7 August 1911, p. 333. Peter Hugill, 'German Great Power Relations in the Pages of "Simplicissimus", 1816–1914', *Geographical Review*, 98 (1) (2008), pp. 1–23.
10. Esmé Wingfield-Stratford, 'Before the Lights Went Out', in I.F. Clarke (ed.), *The Great War with Germany, 1890–1914* (Liverpool: Liverpool University Press, 1997), pp. 256–8.
11. George Tomkyns Chesney, *The Battle of Dorking* (London: Blackwood's, 1871).
12. One of the most well-known was: Erskine Childers, *Riddle of the Sands* (London: Smith, Elder & Co., 1903).
13. William Le Queux, *The Invasion of 1910* (London: Macmillan, 1906), pp. 255–6.
14. Ailise Bulfin, 'The International Circulation and Impact of Invasion Literature', *Critical Survey*, 32 (2020), pp. 159–92, pp. 164–6.
15. 'Book-Makers', *Weekly Dispatch*, 10 June 1934, p. 6.
16. Their book even opens with Baldwin's words: Frank McIlraith and Roy Connolly, *Invasion from the Air: A Prophetic Novel* (London: Grayson & Grayson, 1934), pp. 5, 120, 244, 266.
17. Julian Freeman, 'Boswell, James Edward Buchanan', *Oxford Dictionary of National Biography*, September 2004: https://doi.org/10.1093/ref:odnb/57139 (accessed 10 December 2023).
18. Brett Holman, *The Next War in the Air: Britain's Fear of the Bomber, 1908–1941* (Farnham: Ashgate, 2014), pp. 62–3.
19. 'Postcards for Parliament', *Gloucester Citizen*, 4 June 1934, p. 4.
20. Norbert Frei, *1945 und wir: Das Dritte Reich im Bewußtsein der Deutschen* (Munich: Beck, 2005), pp. 113–16.
21. Karina Urbach, '"England is pro-Hitler": German Popular Opinion during the Czechoslovakian Crisis, 1938', in Julie Gottlieb, Daniel Hucker and Richard Toye (eds), *The Munich Crisis, Politics and the People: International, Transnational and Comparative Perspectives* (Manchester: Manchester University Press, 2021), pp. 171–91, p. 181.
22. 'The Adonis of the Boxing World', *The Sketch*, 15 July 1914, p. 1; 'A Battle of Titans', *The Tatler*, 15 July 1914, p. 1. For a more general discussion of pre-war attitudes, see: Catriona Pennell, *A Kingdom United: Popular Responses to the Outbreak of the First World War in Britain and Ireland* (Oxford: Oxford University Press, 2014), pp. 23–35.
23. There was a shift in British press reporting too: Martin Schramm, *Das Deutschlandbild in der britischen Presse 1912–1919* (Berlin: Akademie, 2007), pp. 286–300.
24. Wolfgang Krapp, 'Germersheim im Ersten Weltkrieg. Tagebucheinträge der Elisabeth Kreiter – Feldpostbriefe des Kurt Kreiter', in Regionalgeschichte.net: https://regionalgeschichte.net/link/urn/urn:nbn:de:0291-rpf-015677-20221214-0 (accessed 12 December 2023).
25. 'The Prime Minister's Answer', *The Times*, 18 March 1939, p. 12. 'Auch Herr Chamberlain ist verständnislos', *Stuttgarter Neues Tageblatt*, 18 March 1939, p. 10; 'Chamberlain sieht die Dinge falsch', *Der neue Tag*, 19 March 1939, p. 2. On popular responses: Nicholas Stargardt, *The German War: A Nation under Arms, 1939–45* (London: Bodley Head, 2015), pp. 25–6.

26. Albert Deibele, 3 September 1939, in David Schnur (ed.), *Tagebücher eines Stadtarchivars. Die Schwäbisch Gmünder. Kriegschronik von Albert Diebele (1939–1945)* (Schwäbisch Gmünd: Stadtarchiv Schwäbisch Gmünd, 2020), pp. 78–9. Diarist, 30 August 1939, Mass Observation Archive, D5205.

27. Neville Chamberlain, House of Commons, 11 March 1935, Volume 351, Column 292.

28. 'Aufruf des Führers an das deutsche Volk', *Der Erft-Bote*, 4 September 1939, p. 1.

29. Panikos Panayi, *The Enemy in Our Midst: Germans in Britain during the First World War* (Oxford: Berg, 1991).

30. Panikos Panayi, *German Immigrants in Britain during the 19th Century, 1815–1914* (Oxford: Berg, 1995), p. 35.

31. J.M. Cohen, *The Life of Ludwig Mond* (London: Methuen, 1956), pp. 69–83, 155–64.

32. 'Obituaries', *Journal of the Chemical Society*, 113 (1918), p. 331. Thomas Adam, *Transnational Philanthropy: The Mond Family's Support for Public Institutions in Western Europe from 1890 to 1938* (Basingstoke: Palgrave, 2016), p. 43.

33. Interview with Marie Trapp, 14 January 1999, Kendal Oral History Group, Nr. 0070. Rob David, ' "Once a German always a German": Attitudes to People of German and Austrian Extraction in Cumbria During the First World War', *Transactions of the Cumberland & Westmorland Antiquarian & Archaeological Society*, 16 (2016), pp. 73–93.

34. Daniela Caglioti, *War and Citizenship: Enemy Aliens and National Belonging from the French Revolution to the First World War* (Cambridge: Cambridge University Press, 2020), p. 152; Thomas Weber, ' "Cosmopolitan Nationalists": German Students in Britain – British Students in Germany', in Dominik Geppert and Robert Gerwarth (eds), *Wilhelmine Germany and Edwardian Britain: Essays on Cultural Affinity* (Oxford: Oxford University Press, 2008), pp. 249–70, p. 263.

35. J.C. Masterman, *On the Chariot Wheel: An Autobiography* (Oxford: Oxford University Press, 1975), pp. 88–95.

36. 'Memory Corner: Marie's Story', *Grange Now*, April 1999, p. 13.

37. Aliens Restriction (Amendment) Act 1919: https://www.legislation.gov.uk/ukpga/1919/92/pdfs/ukpga_19190092_en.pdf (accessed 15 December 2023).

38. 'Suicide Rather than Return to Germany', *The Cologne Post*, 28 July 1920, p. 1.

39. Rolf Gardiner and Georg Götsch, 'Englandreisen sind schwierig!', Archiv der deutschen Jugendbewegung, Witzenhausen, A228, Nr. 8058.

40. 'A Tramp in Germany', *Derbyshire Times*, 24 March 1928, p. 5. On tourism to the Weimar Republic more generally, see: Colin Storer, *Britain and the Weimar Republic: A History of a Cultural Relationship* (London: I.B. Tauris, 2010), pp. 11–33.

41. 'Day Respondent Survey', 22 May 1937, Mass Observation Archive, DS409.

42. Christabel Bielenberg, 'Desert Island Discs', BBC Radio 4, 8 November 1992: https://www.bbc.co.uk/sounds/play/p0093xgf (accessed 16 December 2023). Christabel Bielenberg, *The Past is Myself* (London: Chatto & Windus, 1968), p. 16.

43. Peter Heinrich Bielenberg, in Jamie Bulloch (ed.), 'Peter Heinrich Bielenberg: 13 December 1911–12 March 2001' (Marlborough, 2002), p. 36.

44. Gerwin Strobl, *The Germanic Isle: Nazi Perceptions of Britain* (Cambridge: Cambridge University Press, 2000), p. 93.

45. Dan Stone, *Responses to Nazism in Britain 1933–1939: Before War and Holocaust* (Basingstoke: Palgrave, 2012), pp. 168–88.

46. Helen Roche, *The Third Reich's Elite Schools: A History of the Napolas* (Oxford: Oxford University Press, 2021), pp. 157–65.

47. Ian Kershaw, *Hitler, 1936–45: Nemesis* (London: Allen Lane, 2000), pp. 192–3.

48. Norman Hillson, *I Speak of Germany: A Plea for Anglo-German Friendship* (London: Routledge, 1937), p. 2.

49. Diarist, 30 August 1939, Mass Observation Archive, D5205.

50. Friedrich Stampfer, *Erfahrungen und Erkenntnisse* (Cologne: Verlag für Politik und Wissenschaft, 1958), p. 168.

51. 'A Taffy not a German', *Chester Chronicle*, 22 August 1914, p. 5.

52. Masterman, *Chariot Wheel*, p. 98.

53. Interview with Marie Trapp.

54. Ringo Müller, *'Feindliche Ausländer' im deutschen Reich während des Ersten Weltkrieges* (Göttingen: Vandenhoeck & Ruprecht, 2021), p. 351.

55. 'Stadt-Chronik', *Dresdner Volkszeitung*, 5 August 1914, p. 3.

56. 'Shops Wrecked', *Northern Daily Telegraph*, 26 October 1914, p. 7. See more fully: Panayi, *Prisoners*, pp. 48–52.

57. Arnd Bauerkämper, *Sicherheit und Humanität im Ersten und Zweiten Weltkrieg. Band 1: Erster Weltkrieg* (Oldenbourg: De Gruyter, 2021), p. 298.

58. Peter Gillman and Leni Gillman, *'Collar the Lot!' How Britain Interned and Expelled its Wartime Refugees* (London: Quartet, 1980), pp. 39–46.

59. 'Unsere lieben Engländer', *Kölnische Zeitung*, 23 October 1914, p. 1.

60. 'Those "Influential Friends" of Dangerous Aliens', *Sunday Express*, 21 January 1940, p. 1.

61. Matthew Stibbe, 'A Question of Retaliation? The Internment of British Civilians in Germany in November 1914', *Immigrants & Minorities*, 23 (2005), pp. 1–29; Tony Kushner, 'Clubland, Cricket Tests and Alien Internment, 1939–40', in David Cesarani and Tony Kushner (eds), *The Internment of Aliens in Twentieth Century Britain* (New York: Routledge, 1993), pp. 79–101.

62. Mass Observation, 'Supplementary Report on Public Opinion about Aliens', 16 July 1940, FR276.

63. Interview with Marie Trapp.

64. Stefan Manz and Panikos Panayi, *Enemies in the Empire: Civilian Internment in the British Empire during the First World War* (Oxford: Oxford University Press, 2020), p. 227.

65. Minister des Innern to Regierung Cassel, 5 November 1914, Hessisches Staatsarchiv Marburg, Bestand 165, Nr. 737.

66. Masterman, *Chariot Wheel*, p. 101. On Ruhleben, see: Matthew Stibbe, *British Civilian Internees in Germany: The Ruhleben Camp, 1914–18* (Manchester: Manchester University Press, 2008).

67. 'Dr Ludwig Mond', *Westminster Gazette*, 14 December 1909, p. 7.

68. 'Ludwig Mond, ein deutscher Chemiker', *Berliner Tageblatt*, 27 December 1909, p. 10; 'Ludwig Mond', *Kölnische Zeitung*, 15 December 1909, p. 15.

69. *Daily Mirror*, 21 May 1934, p. 5; 'The Late Colonel Thelwall', *The Times*, 18 May 1934, p. 13.

70. 'Baron Von Hoesch Germany', *John Bull*, 20 May 1933, p. 10. For reflections on Hoesch, see: Karl-Günther von Hase, 'Aus der Geschichte der Deutschen Botschaft in London', in Wilhelm Reissmueller, *Der Diplomat: Eine Festschrift zum 70. Geburtstag Hans von Herwarth* (Ingolstadt: Donau Courier, 1974), pp. 103–14.

71. Caroline Sharples, 'A Legend of the London Landscape: Giro the "Nazi" Dog' (unpublished paper, 2014).

72. 'Der Tod im Schlafzimmer', *Pester Lloyd*, 26 April 1936, p. 350.

73. Anthony Eden, *The Eden Memoirs: Facing the Dictators* (London: Cassell, 1962), p. 354.

74. 'German Ambassador's Last Journey', *Western Mail*, 16 April 1936, p. 6; 'The Late German Ambassador', *The Times*, 16 April 1936, p. 12.

75. Eric Phipps, 19 April 1936 in Gaynor Johnson (ed.), *Our Man in Berlin: The Diary of Sir Eric Phipps, 1933–1937* (Basingstoke: Palgrave, 2008), p. 169.

76. Kate Connolly, 'The Fatal Hike that Became a Nazi Propaganda Coup', *Guardian*, 6 July 2016: https://www.theguardian.com/world/2016/jul/06/fatal-hike-became-nazi-propaganda-coup (accessed 18 December 2023).

77. Phipps, 19 April 1936.

78. 'Nach dem Unglück am Schauinsland', *Neue Mannheimer Zeitung*, 20 April 1936, p. 4; 'Die Opfer des Schneesturms', *Der Patriot*, 21 April 1936, p. 9.

79. 'Das Denkmal für die verunglückten Engländer', *Hakenkreuzbanner*, 7 October 1938, p. 6.

80. Bernd Hainmüller, *Tod am Schauinsland. Das 'Engländerunglück' am 17. April 1936 und seine Folgen* (Freiburg: Rombach, 2021), pp. 165–70.

81. For the hostility narrative, see: Heather Jones, *Violence against Prisoners of War in the First World War: Britain, France and Germany, 1914–1920* (Cambridge: Cambridge University Press, 2011), pp. 67–9.

2 Dying

1. Mick Holness, 'Oral History', November 2003, Imperial War Museum (hereafter, IWM), 26527.

2. Marjolijn van Daalen, 'An Aquatic Decomposition Scoring Method to Potentially Predict the Postmortem Submersion Interval of Bodies Recovered from the North Sea', *Journal of Forensic Sciences*, 62 (2) (2017), pp. 369–73.

3. Such was the frequency of bodies washing up on Jersey that the German occupation forces had to remind locals to report them: Feldkommandant to Bailiff Jersey, 18.10.1940, Jersey Archive, B/A/W56/1.

4. Noakes, *Dying for the Nation*, pp. 2–5; Lucy Noakes, 'Valuing the Dead: Death, Burial, and the Body in Second World War Britain', *Critical Military Studies*, 6 (2020), pp. 224–42.

5. On notions of a 'good death', see: Allan Kellehear, *A Social History of Dying* (Cambridge: Cambridge University Press, 2007), p. 90.

6. 'Deaths of Interned Germans', *Isle of Man Examiner*, 4 December 1915, p. 3. Geislinger's death certificate records his name as Gisslinger, but all other records list Geislinger.

7. 'The Public and the Zeppelin Raids', *Lancashire Evening Post*, 26 September 1916, p. 2.

8. Notes on Destruction of L48, Suffolk Archives, Ipswich, HD1295/2/33.

9. Ian Beckett, *The Making of the First World War* (New Haven and London: Yale University Press, 2012), pp. 162–80.

10. 'German Witness to Crash of John Valentine's Aircraft', International Bomber Command Centre Archive, Lincoln (hereafter, IBCC), SValentineJRM125 1404v20026; 'Deposition of Gustav Otto', 15 September 1947, The National Archives, Kew (hereafter, TNA), WO 309/1060.

11. 'Story of the Last Few Minutes of JB529, DX-F', IBCC, MTansleyEH149542-160929-02.

12. 'German Plane Hits North-East Farm House', *Yorkshire Evening Press*, March 1945.

13. 'It Was a Night of Drama', *Evening Star*, 14 June 1983, p. 6.

14. Peter Lyons, 'Oral History', March 2001, IWM, 21101.

15. Untitled Newspaper, June 1961, Suffolk Archives, HD1295/2/33.

16. Reserve Lazarett Köln-Nippes, 'Nachweis über Sterbefall eines Wehrmachtangehörigen', 19 September 1942, Historisches Archiv der Stadt Köln, Best. 756, A20.

17. East Sussex Constabulary, 'Air Raid Incident', 10 April 1941, East Sussex Record Office, SPA/1/1/1/69; East Sussex Constabulary, 'Crashed Aircraft Report', 11 May 1941, East Sussex Record Office, SPA/1/1/1/498.

18. Naval Officer Sylt, 'Number of War Graves in Sylt Area', 17 October 1945, TNA, FO 1006/489.

19. H.F. Chettle to Baron W. zu Putlitz, 30 July 1935, VDK Archive, Kassel, R13.

20. Hinz, *Gefangen im Großen Krieg*, pp. 49–58. Civilian internees were more reliant on the protection of neutral states: Caglioti, *War and Citizenship*, p. 115.

21. Five died at the scene, with a sixth internee – Rudolf Dorflinger – dying in hospital some days later: 'The Alien Camp Riot', *Peel City Guardian*, 5 December 1914, p. 5.

22. 'The Camp Mutiny', *Isle of Man Examiner*, 5 December 1914, p. 8.

23. 'Disturbance at the Aliens Detention Camp at Douglas on Thursday, November 19th 1914. Official Report of the Proceedings' (Douglas, 1914), Manx National Heritage, M 06104/71.

24. 'End of Spy Trial', *The Times*, 3 November 1914, p. 4; Leonard Sellers, *Shot in the Tower: The Story of the Spies Executed in the Tower of London during the First World War* (Barnsley: Pen & Sword, 1997), pp. 17–42.

25. All were shot in the Tower of London, bar Robert Rosenthal who was hanged in Wandsworth prison.

26. The following camps reported the killing of enemy prisoners: Leigh in 1915, Oldcastle in 1916, Reading in 1917, Handforth in 1918, Brocton in 1919, Park Hall in 1919 and Dorchester in 1919.

27. 'German Prisoner Shot', *Manchester Evening News*, 7 August 1918, p. 2.

28. Innes McCartney, *Scapa 1919: The Archaeology of a Scuttled Fleet* (Oxford: Osprey, 2019), p. 49.

29. 'Die Opfer von Scapa Flow', *Berliner Börsen-Zeitung*, 23 July 1919, p. 1.

30. 'German Shot at Scapa', *Daily News*, 10 February 1920, p. 1.

31. Josef Jakobs was the last German spy to be executed in the Tower of London in 1941. For examples of camp deaths, see: 'Two Germans Prisoners Shot', *Coventry Evening Telegraph*, 5 March 1945, p. 3.

32. IWGC to Volksbund Deutsche Kriegsgräberfürsorge, 7 June 1956, CWGC/1/2/E/5; Rachel Pistol, *Internment during the Second World War: A Comparative Study of Great Britain and the USA* (London: Bloomsbury, 2017), p. 102. On British policy: Renate Held, *Deutsche Kriegsgefangenschaft in Großbritannien: Deutsche Soldaten des Zweiten Weltkriegs in britischem Gewahrsam* (Munich: Oldenbourg, 2008), pp. 45–52.

33. 'Fatality at Knockaloe', *Isle of Man Examiner*, 30 September 1916, p. 6.

34. Eduard Levi, 'Einiges über Knockaloe', Bundesarchiv Berlin (hereafter, BArch Berlin), R67/1437.

35. Helen Fry, *The London Cage: The Secret History of Britain's World War II Interrogation Centre* (New Haven and London: Yale University Press, 2017), pp. 15–16.

36. A.P. Scotland, *The London Cage* (London: Evans Brothers, 1957), pp. 61–3; Fry, *London Cage*, pp. 107–12.

37. Gerhart Rettig was murdered in similar circumstances the following year: 'German Prisoners on Murder Charge', *Dundee Evening Telegraph*, 7 August 1945, p. 8.

38. Arieh Kochavi, *Confronting Captivity: Britain and the United States and their POWs in Nazi Germany* (Chapel Hill: University of North Carolina Press, 2005), p. 282; Helmuth Forwick, 'Zur Behandlung alliierter Kriegsgefangener im Zweiten Weltkrieg', *Militärgeschichtliche Mitteilungen*, 2 (1967), pp. 119–34, p. 126.

39. Hinz, *Gefangen im Großen Krieg*, p. 215; Neville Wylie, *Barbed Wire Diplomacy: Britain, Germany and Politics of Prisoners of War, 1939–1945* (Oxford: Oxford University Press, 2010), p. 218.

40. 'Prison Camp Horrors', *Sheffield Independent*, 22 May 1917, p. 3; 'Savage Dogs in German Camp', *The Derbyshire Advertiser*, 27 November 1915, p. 10.

41. 'Portrait of John Player Genower', IWM, HU 114957.

42. 'Correspondence with the German Government Respecting the Death by Burning of J.P. Genower, Able Seaman, when Prisoner of War at Brandenburg Camp', Miscellaneous, No. 6. (London: His Majesty's Stationery Office, 1918); Admiralty to Prisoner of War Department, 28 August 1917, TNA, FO 383/292.

43. Alan Kramer, *Dynamic of Destruction: Culture and Mass Killing in the First World War* (Oxford: Oxford University Press, 2009), p. 337.

44. More generally, see: Susanna Schrafstetter, ' "Gentlemen, the Cheese is All Gone!" British POWs, the "Great Escape" and the Anglo-German Agreement for Compensation to Victims of Nazism', *Contemporary European History*, 17 (2008), pp. 23–43.

45. Clare Makepeace, *Captives of War: British Prisoners of War in Europe in the Second World War* (Cambridge: Cambridge University Press, 2017), p. 15; 'Proceedings of an Inquiry', 31 August 1944, TNA, WO 309/24. More generally, see: S.P. MacKenzie, *The Colditz Myth: British and Commonwealth Prisoners in Nazi Germany* (Oxford: Oxford University Press, 2006), pp. 235–6.

46. Hall, *Terror Flyers*, p. 62.

47. 'Ein Wort zum feindlichen Luftterror', *Völkischer Beobachter*, 27 May 1944, p. 1; Barbara Grimm, 'Lynchmorde an alliierten Fliegern im Zweiten Weltkrieg', in Dietmar Süß (ed.), *Deutschland im Luftkrieg: Geschichte und Erinnerung* (Munich: Oldenbourg, 2007), pp. 71–84, pp. 79–80.

48. Hall, *Terror Flyers*, p. 5.

49. 'Deposition of Adolph Wolfert', 10 April 1946, TNA, WO 309/176. See also: Marie-Christian Werner, 'Der englische Flieger', SWR2, 26 March 2014: https://www.swr.de/swr2/leben-und-gesellschaft/aexavarticle-swr-37802.html (accessed 5 March 2022).

50. 'Brief for Investigation', 11 September 1947, TNA, WO 309/176; Ortsgemeinde Dirmstein (ed.), ' "Dirmstein erinnert sich". Tage des Gedenkens an die Opfer des Nationalsozialismus' (Dirmstein, 2009).

51. For a wider discussion of these wartime relations, see: Raffael Scheck, *Love Between Enemies: Western Prisoners of War and German Women in World War II* (Cambridge: Cambridge University Press, 2021).

52. Hall Caine, *The Woman of Knockaloe: A Parable* (Toronto: Ryerson Press, 1923), pp. 89, 184–5. For the background, see Peter Skrine, 'Hall Caine's *The Woman of Knockaloe*: An Anglo-German War Novel from the Isle of Man', in Susanne Stark (ed.), *The Novel in Anglo-German Context* (Amsterdam: Rodopi, 2000), pp. 263–76; Panayi, *Prisoners*, pp. 8–10.

53. 'Inquiry into the Death of Ernest Knappenberger', 25 November 1947, National Records of Scotland, Edinburgh, SC1/16/1947/17.

54. 'Two Germans Killed', *Belfast News-Letter*, 28 May 1945, p. 4; '2 Dead Germans', *Nottingham Journal*, 27 July 1945; 'Five German P.O.W. Killed', *Bury Free Press*, 5 April 1946, p. 1. For a German POW's experience of such an accident, see: Kurt Glaser, 28 November 1946, in Wolfgang Benz and Angelika Schardt (eds), *Kriegsgefangenschaft: Berichte über das Leben in Gefangenenlagern der Alliierten* (Munich: Oldenbourg, 1991), pp. 212–17.

55. 'Eleven Die as Hull Train Hits Lorry at Crossing', *Hull Daily Mail*, 17 September 1947, p. 1. Ministry of Transport, 'Report on the Collision which occurred on the 17th September, 1947, at the Burton Agnes Level Crossing on the London and North Eastern Railway' (London: His Majesty's Stationery Office, 1947).

56. 'She Put Off Breakfast to Aid 10 Injured', *Daily Mirror*, 2 March 1948, pp. 4–5.

57. Kochavi, *Confronting Captivity*, pp. 62–3.

58. Auswärtiges Amt, 'Verbalnote', 22 October 1917, TNA, FO 383/292.

59. 'Fatality at Beachley Shipyard', *Gloucestershire Echo*, 1 April 1919, p. 4; International Committee of the Red Cross (hereafter, ICRC), 'List No. 154 of German Prisoners of War', A10420: https://grandeguerre.icrc.org/en/List/20253/898/10420/ (accessed 10 March 2022).

60. Reinhard Nachtigal, 'The Repatriation and Reception of Returning Prisoners of War, 1918–22', *Immigrants & Minorities*, 26 (2008), pp. 157–84, p. 175; Johann Custodis, 'Employing the Enemy: The Contribution of German and Italian Prisoners of War to British Agriculture during and after the Second World War', *Agricultural History Review*, 60 (2012), pp. 243–65.

61. Swiss Legation to Swiss Minister London, 19 March 1919, TNA, FO 383/506.

62. 'Lot of the German Prisoners', *Nottingham Evening Post*, 11 January 1947, p. 3.

63. Donald Elles to the Sheriff of Ayr and Bute, 18 May 1947, National Records of Scotland, SC7/19/1947/4.

64. 'Prisoner's Fatal Dive', *Staffordshire Advertiser*, 27 July 1946, p. 5.

65. 'P.O.W. Drowned', *Staffordshire Advertiser*, 7 June 1947, p. 6.

66. See for example: 'Fatal Accident at Stotzheim', *The Cologne Post*, 13 September 1919, p. 1.

67. 'Grip of Death', *The Cologne Post*, 19 August 1919, p. 1.

68. 'Neck Broken in Dive', *Staffordshire Newsletter*, 20 July 1946, p. 4.

69. American Consul General to American Ambassador, London, 9 February 1917, TNA, FO 383/294; Reserve-Lazarett III, 'Beerdigungs-Erlaubnis', 23 May 1918, Staatsarchiv Hamburg (hereafter, StAHH), 325-1, 219.

70. Vasilis Vourkoutiotis, *Prisoners of War and the German High Command: The British and American Experiences* (Basingstoke: Palgrave Macmillan, 2003), p. 126.

71. Swiss Legation, 'Brooker Hall', 15 March 1918, BArch Berlin, R901/83129.

72. Florence Emily Hardy, *The Later Years of Thomas Hardy 1892–1928* (London: Macmillan, 1930), p. 173.

73. James W. Gerard, *My Four Years in Germany* (New York: Hodder & Stoughton, 1917), p. 118.

74. Government Committee on the Treatment by the Enemy of British Prisoners (ed.), *The Horrors of Wittenberg: Official Report to the British Government* (London: Pearson, 1916), pp. 18–24. For British responses to the outbreak, see: John Palatini, ' "A German Horror" – Das Kriegsgefangenenlager Kleinwittenberg in der englischen Propaganda', in John Palatini (ed.), *'Gäste des Kaisers'. Die Kriegsgefangenenlager des Ersten Weltkrieges auf dem Gebiet Sachsen-Anhalts Teil I* (Halle: Landesheimatbund Sachsen-Anhalt, 2018), pp. 83–96.

75. American Embassy Berlin, 'Lower Southern Hospital for Prisoners of War at Dartford', 3 February 1917, BArch Berlin, R901/83051. See also: Panayi, *Prisoners*, pp. 107–9.

76. Joseph Powell and Francis Gribble, *The History of Ruhleben: A Record of British Organisation in a Prison Camp in Germany* (London: W. Collins, 1919), p. 106. Stibbe, *The Ruhleben Camp*, pp. 71–3.

77. Kochavi, *Confronting Captivity*, p. 15.

78. Adolf Lukas Vischer, *Die Stacheldraht-Krankheit: Beiträge zur Psychologie des Kriegsgefangenen* (Zürich: 1918); Matthew Stibbe, *Civilian Internment during the First World War: A European and Global History, 1914–1920* (Basingstoke: Palgrave, 2019), pp. 214–21.

79. Swiss Legation, 'Knockaloe', 21 May 1918, TNA, FO 383/432.

80. Albert Jones, 'Oral History', 26 October 1993, IWM, 13573.

81. See, for example, the movement of prisoners from Handforth camp to the Parkside Asylum in Macclesfield: 'Civil Register', 1912–1917, Cheshire Record Office, NHM/8/9/9.

82. Parkside Asylum, 'Notice of Death', 22 March 1917, Cheshire Record Office, NHM/8/3/2.

83. Estimates range from 30 million to 100 million influenza deaths: Susan Kingsley Kent, *The Influenza Pandemic of 1918–1919* (Boston: Bedford/St Martin's, 2013), p. 1.

84. Swiss Legation, 'Tendring', 24 May 1919, BArch Berlin, R901/83131.

85. Reserve-Lazarett III, 'Beerdigungs-Erlaubnis', 18 October 1918, 4 November 1918, 8 October 1918, StAHH, 325-1, 219.

86. Foreign Office, 'Memorandum for Communication to the Netherland Minister at Berlin', 14 July 1917, BArch Berlin, R901/84121.

87. Kriegsministerium Berlin, 16 February 1918, Bundesarchiv Militärarchiv, Freiburg, PH2/588.

88. Swiss Legation, 'Dartford War Hospital', 30 July 1917, BArch Berlin, R901/83051.

89. 'Nursing the Enemy', *Hull Daily Mail*, 19 December 1914, p. 3.

90. Interview with Jean Campbell, 2001, North Devon Record Office, B723/OHA/24/2.

91. Alison Fell, 'Far from Home? Perceptions and Experiences of the First World War Nurses and their Patients', in Alan Beyerchen and Emre Sencer (eds), *Expeditionary Forces in the First World War* (Basingstoke: Palgrave, 2019), pp. 57–78, p. 69.

92. Santanu Das, *Touch and Intimacy in First World War Literature* (Cambridge: Cambridge University Press, 2006), p. 26.

93. Shelia Bambridge, cited in Eric Taylor, *Combat Nurse* (London: Robert Hale, 1999), p. 55.

94. 'Kindly Treatment of a Wounded Scottish Officer', *Dundee Evening Telegraph*, 24 December 1915, p. 5.

95. 'German Prisoners' Deaths', *Bognor Regis Observer*, 27 November 1918, p. 2.

3 Burying

1. ICRC, 'Engländer III', PA221: https://grandeguerre.icrc.org/en/List/4140157/698/221/ (accessed 7 May 2022).

2. 'B. Murphy', *Dortmunder Zeitung*, 8 September 1914, p. 4.

3. ATLAS to Auswärtiges Amt Berlin, 9 September 1914, BArch Berlin, R901/84157.

4. John Horne and Alan Kramer, *German Atrocities, 1914: A History of Denial* (New Haven and London: Yale University Press, 2001).

5. Katherine Verdery, *The Political Lives of Dead Bodies: Reburial and Postsocialist Change* (New York: Columbia University Press, 1999), p. 28.

6. Convention (IV) respecting the Laws and Customs of War on Land and its annex: Regulations concerning the Laws and Customs of War on Land, The Hague, 18 October 1907, Article 19, in ICRC, 'International Humanitarian Law Databases': https://ihl-databases.icrc.org/en/ihl-treaties/hague-conv-iv-1907 (accessed 7 May 2022); 'Convention relative to the Treatment of Prisoners of War', Geneva, 27 July 1929, Article 76, in ICRC, 'International Humanitarian Law Databases': https://ihl-databases.icrc.org/en/ihl-treaties/gc-pow-1929 (accessed 7 May 2022).

7. 'The Fate of a German Prisoner', *The Scotsman*, 17 September 1918, p. 2; War Office to Imperial War Graves Commission, 2 January 1926, CWGC/1/1/8/35. ICRC, 'List No. 228 of German Prisoners of War', A32971: https://grandeguerre.icrc.org/en/List/165107/898/32971/ (accessed 7 May 2022).

8. Seumas Spark, 'The Treatment of the British Military War Dead of the Second World War' (unpublished PhD, University of Edinburgh, 2009), pp. 167–9.

9. RAF Mepal to Mrs I.D. Bain, 24 August 1943, IBCC, EAeroMepBainID430824; Casualty Branch to Mrs A. Bain, 9 September 1943, IBCC, ESmithJA BainID430909; Air Ministry to Mrs I.D. Bain, 9 November 1943, IBCC, ECasBraBainID431109; British Red Cross Society to Mrs I.D. Bain, 8 November 1943, IBCC, EAmpthillMBainID431108.

10. Stuart Hadaway, *Missing Believed Killed: Casualty Policy and the Missing Research and Enquiry Service 1939–1952* (Barnsley: Pen & Sword, 2008), p. 16.

11. No. 22 Section, No. 4 M.R. & E.U. RAF 'Investigation Report', 25 May 1946, IWM, 9046.

12. Martin Francis, *The Flyer: British Culture and the Royal Airforce, 1939–1945* (Oxford: Oxford University Press, 2008), pp. 124–5.

13. '12 German Dead', *The Scotsman*, 13 February 1940, p. 1.

14. Naval Officer Sylt to Naval Officer Husum, 17 October 1945, TNA, FO 1006/489.

15. Prisoner of War Information Bureau, 'Willy Max Hüller', 22 October 1918, BArch Berlin, R67/909; Prisoner of War Information Bureau, 'Albert Stettner', 9 September 1918, BArch Berlin, R67/1039.

16. 'Queensferry', *Flintshire Observer*, 26 November 1914, p. 5; 'German's Death at Chester', *Runcorn Guardian*, 20 November 1914, p. 3.

17. Herbert Sulzbach, *With the German Guns: Four Years on the Western Front* (Barnsley: Pen & Sword, 1998), p. 189; Joanna Bourke, *Dismembering the Male: Men's Bodies, Britain and the Great War* (London: Reaktion, 1996), pp. 214–15; Bart Ziino, *A Distant Grief: Australians, War Graves and the Great War* (Crawley: University of Western Australia Press, 2007), p. 25.

18. Rudyard Kipling, 'Mary Postgate', in Rudyard Kipling, *A Diversity of Creatures* (London: Macmillan, 1917), pp. 419–41. For reflections: Norman Page, 'What Happens in "Mary Postgate"?', *English Literature in Transition 1880–1920*, 29 (1986), pp. 41–7.

19. Andy Saunders, *Finding the Foe: Outstanding Luftwaffe Mysteries of the Battle of Britain and Beyond Investigated and Solved* (London: Grub Street, 2010), pp. 11–23.

20. IWGC, 'Investigation Report', 19 June 1952, CWGC/1/2/A/585.

21. IWGC, 'Minutes of Proceedings', 19 July 1945, CWGC/2/2/1/271.

22. VDK, Kreisverband Uelzen to Bezirksverband des VDK Lüneburg, 8 June 1948, Landesarchiv Hannover, Nds. 120 Lüneburg, Acc. 46/79 Nr. 205.

23. 'Camp of Death Brings Back a Grim Memory', *Aberdeen Evening Express*, 14 July 1962, p. 4.

24. 'Germans' Graves', *Derby Daily Telegraph*, 14 June 1945, p. 2.

25. Feldkommandant to Bailiff of Jersey, 27 November 1941; Feldkommandant to Bailiff of Jersey, 12 April 1943, Jersey Archive, B/A/W56/1.

26. Interview with Jean Ramon, 9 December 1945; BAOR, War Crimes Section, 'Brief for Investigation', 4 October 1946, TNA, WO 309/1060.

27. IWGC, Chief Maintenance Surveyor, 25 March 1921, CWGC/7/4/2/1137.

28. Lutz Miehe, 'Zu den Gräbern der Kriegsgefangenen des Ersten Weltkrieges auf dem Gebiet des heutigen Landes Sachsen-Anhalt', in John Palatini (ed.), *'Gäste des Kaisers'. Die Kriegsgefangenenlager des Ersten Weltkrieges auf dem Gebiet Sachsen-Anhalts Teil I* (Halle: Landesheimatbund Sachsen-Anhalt, 2018), pp. 119–43, p. 125.

29. Gerhard Höpp, *Muslime in der Mark: Als Kriegsgefangene und Internierte in Wünsdorf und Zossen* (Berlin: Das Arabische Buch, 1997), pp. 131–7.

30. Bericht des Stadtbauamtes, 29 May 1916, Stadtarchiv Worms, 005/1:03635. Wolfgang Hasch, 'Gräberfelder und Denkmäler für Opfer und Teilnehmer von Kriegen', in Ralf-Quirin Heinz and Gerold Bönnen (eds), *100 Jahre Hauptfriedhof Hochheimer Höhe Worms 1902–2002* (Worms: Stadt Worms, 2002), pp. 57–64.

31. Botschaftsarchitekt, 'Besuch der deutschen Kriegsgräber im Metropolitan Asylum Board Cemetery in Direnth [*sic*.] bei Dartford', 23 August 1927, VDK, R13.

32. Deutsches Konsulat Liverpool, 2 May 1930, VDK, R13.

33. Pat Jalland, *Death in War and Peace: Loss and Grief in England, 1914–1970* (Oxford: Oxford University Press, 2010), p. 98.

34. 'Familienanzeigen', *Bonner Nachrichten*, 8 July 1942, p. 5.

35. Wilhelm Hinkämper to Oberstadtdirektor, 19 January 1947, Stadtarchiv Münster, Amt 32, Nr. 26.

36. 'Beerdigung eines englischen Hauptmanns', *Niederrheinisches Tageblatt*, 29 April 1916, p. 1.

37. George Soane, 'Oral History', 9 June 1981, IWM, 4896.

38. Ludwig Bogenstätter and Heinrich Zimmermann, *Die Welt hinter Stacheldraht: Eine Kronik des englischen Kriegsgefangenlagers Handforth bei Manchester* (Munich: Piloty & Löhle, 1921), pp. 83–5.

39. Metropolitan Police, 'Funeral of the Crew of the Zeppelin Destroyed by Fire', 7 September 1916, TNA, MEPO 2/1652.
40. War Office to Prisoners of War Department, 19 August 1918, TNA, FO 383/405.
41. 'Funeral of Two Nazi Airmen', *Edinburgh Evening News*, 19 October 1939, p. 7; 'Seventh Week Ends', *Edinburgh Evening News*, 21 October 1939, p. 4.
42. 'Nazi Airmen's Funerals', *Newcastle Evening Chronicle*, 10 February 1940, p. 4; Deutsches Nachrichtenbüro, 4 February 1940, PA-AA, RZ 407/47875.
43. 'Air Ministry on Nazi Funerals', *Aberdeen Press and Journal*, 24 July 1941, p. 2.
44. 'Military Funeral of German Prisoner of War', *Dorset County Chronicle*, 2 September 1915, p. 5.
45. Matthias Range, *British Royal and State Funerals: Music and Ceremonial since Elizabeth I* (Woodbridge: Boydell, 2016), p. 201.
46. 'German Prisoner's Funeral at Inverness', *Aberdeen Press and Journal*, 11 November 1916, p. 4.
47. William Lister, 'Verzeichnis', 24 April 1916, TNA, FO 383/206; Alfred Lustgarten, 'Verzeichnis', 14 July 1918, TNA, FO 383/521.
48. In contrast, hostility towards actual enemy POWs was more common: Hinz, *Gefangen im Großen Krieg*, pp. 185–203; Jones, *Violence against Prisoners of War*, pp. 33–69.
49. War Office to Prisoners of War Department, 19 August 1918, TNA, FO 383/405.
50. War Office to Prisoners of War Department, 5 May 1917, TNA, FO 383/303; IWGC, 'German Graves in Kent', 29 December 1943, CWGC/1/2/A/60.
51. Der Reichsstatthalter in Hessen, 7 August 1941, Stadtarchiv Worms, 005/1:07736.
52. 'The British Cemetery at Cologne', *Dundee Courier*, 27 November 1926, p. 7.
53. British Red Cross Society to Captain V.G. Housden, 24 August 1943; Prisoner of War Department, 24 October 1941; Prisoner of War Department, 10 December 1941, CWGC/1/2/A/60.
54. IWGC South Eastern Division to IWGC, 16 August 1943, CWGC/1/2/A/60.
55. Captain A.J. Dix to IWGC, 15 July 1943, CWGC/1/2/A/60.
56. On the trials, see: Caroline Sharples, '"Where Exactly is Auschwitz?" British Confrontation with the Holocaust through the Medium of the 1945 "Belsen" Trial', in Tom Lawson and Andy Pearce (eds), *The Palgrave Handbook of Britain and the Holocaust* (Basingstoke: Palgrave, 2021), pp. 181–200.
57. 'Deposition of Max Markowicz', The Trial of Joseph Kramer and 44 Others, 17 September 1945: http://www.bergenbelsen.co.uk/pages/Trial/TrialAppendices/TrialAppendices_Affidavits_41_Markowicz.html (accessed 7 May 2022).
58. Christine Lattek, 'Bergen-Belsen: From "Privileged" Camp to Death Camp', in Jo Reilly et al. (eds), *Belsen in History and Memory* (London: Frank Cass, 1997), pp. 37–71.
59. IWGC to Prisoners of War Department, 29 May 1941, CWGC/1/2/A/58.
60. IWGC, 'East London Cemetery, Plaistow', 10 November 1924, CWGC/8/1/4/1/2/341.
61. Anne Buckley (ed.), *German Prisoners of War in Great Britain: Life in a Yorkshire Camp* (Barnsley: Pen & Sword, 2021), p. 221. Translation of: Fritz Sachsse and Willy Cossmann, *Kriegsgefangen in Skipton: Leben und Geschichte deutscher Kriegsgefangener in einem englischen Lager* (Munich: Reinhardt, 1920).
62. 'German Prisoners' Graves at Castle Donington', *Nottingham Evening Post*, 17 January 1919, p. 2.
63. Miehe, 'Zu den Gräbern', pp. 132–3.

64. 'Prisoner in Hunland', *Leicester Daily Mercury*, 29 January 1919, p. 4. Netherlands Legation, 'Parchim', 22 February 1918, BArch Berlin, R901/84409.
65. Mosse, *Fallen Soldiers*, pp. 220–2.
66. Kristen Alexander and Kate Ariotti, 'Mourning the Dead of the Great Escape: POWs, Grief, and the Memorial Vault of Stalag Luft III', *Journal of War & Culture Studies*, 16 (2022), pp. 1–22, p. 11. Anthony Eden, House of Commons, 23 June 1944, Volume 401, Column 481; Alan Bryett, 'Oral History', April 2004, IWM, 27051.
67. 'Tombstones in Six Languages', *Isle of Man Examiner*, 1 January 1921, p. 2.
68. Stefan Manz, Panikos Panayi and Matthew Stibbe, 'Internment during the First World War: A Mass Global Phenomenon', in Stefan Manz, Panikos Panayi and Matthew Stibbe (eds), *Internment during the First World War: A Mass Global Phenomenon* (Abingdon: Routledge, 2019), pp. 1–18, p. 5.
69. Miehe, 'Zu den Gräbern', pp. 135–6.

4 Tending

1. Joe Fitzpatrick, 'Oral History', July 1989, IWM, 10767. See: Panayi, *Prisoners*, p. 278.
2. 'Abschied', *Stobsiade*, January–February 1919, p. 2.
3. Buckley, *German Prisoners of War*, pp. 276–7.
4. 'German Prisoners Depart', *Leicester Journal*, 12 September 1919, p. 4.
5. In Oswestry, the POWs left £314: Zentralnachweiseamt für Kriegerverluste und Kriegergräber to Auswärtiges Amt, 30 July 1920, VDK, R13.
6. UK representation in The Hague to A.J. Balfour, 14 November 1918, TNA, FO 383/420.
7. Neil Gregor, ' "Is he still alive, or long since dead?": Loss, Absence and Remembrance in Nuremberg, 1945–1956', *German History*, 21 (2003), pp. 183–203, p. 184. On the German POWs in the Soviet Union, see: Andreas Hilger, *Deutsche Kriegsgefangene in der Sowjetunion, 1941–1956: Kriegsgefangenschaft, Lageralltag und Erinnerung* (Essen: Klartext, 2000), p. 389.
8. Zentralnachweiseamt für Kriegerverluste und Kriegergräber to Deutsche Botschaft London, 17 August 1923; Foreign Office to German Embassy, 27 October 1923, VDK, R13.
9. Richard van Emden, *The Quick and the Dead: Fallen Soldiers and the Families in the Great War* (London: Bloomsbury, 2011), p. 251.
10. Jane Potter, 'Livingstone [née Stickney], Dame Adelaide Lord', *Oxford Dictionary of National Biography*: https://doi.org/10.1093/ref:odnb/52029 (accessed 10 July 2022). 'To Trace the Missing in France', *Yorkshire Evening Post*, 24 July 1919, p. 3. Zentralnachweiseamt für Kriegerverluste und Kriegergräber to Auswärtiges Amt, 7 June 1920, PA-AA, RZ 407/47737.
11. Hadaway, *Missing Believed Killed*, pp. 56–9; Spark, 'British Military War Dead', pp. 186–8.
12. 'British Soldiers' Graves in Germany', *Army and Navy Gazette*, 22 July 1922. Spark, 'British Military War Dead', p. 200.
13. Adelaide Livingstone to War Office, 2 February 1922, CWGC/1/1/7/C/11.
14. C.A. Mitchell, 'The Missing Research and Enquiry Service', IWM, 9046.
15. G.R.J. Vick to Winston Churchill, 21 May 1945, TNA, AIR 20/9050.
16. G. Street & Co. Ltd to Foreign Office, 11 March 1919, TNA, FO 383/499.

17. Erna Pancke to Prisoner of War Information Bureau, 15 December 1957; Deutsche Dienststelle to British Embassy Bonn, 15 September 1960, TNA, FO 371/154249. 'Former German POW Believed Dead', *Yorkshire Post*, 9 March 1954, p. 7.

18. 'A German Mother's Search for her Son', *Cheshire Observer*, 28 July 1967, p. 1; '22 Year Search for Son Switches to Ireland', *Belfast Telegraph*, 11 February 1967, p. 1.

19. Wing Commander, 158 Squadron to Mr Barr, 7 January 1945; S. Clyde to Mr Barr, 11 October 1945, Tower Museum, Derry-Londonderry, DMS 2017/121.

20. Ernest Barr, translations, Tower Museum, Derry-Londonderry, DMS 2017/121. 'Missing Derry Airman', *London Sentinel*, 28 September 1946, p. 5.

21. For the main proponent of the brutalisation thesis, see: Mosse, *Fallen Soldiers*.

22. George Dutton to the Chief Clerk, A. Bodenheim, 14 January 1920, Stadtarchiv Worms, 005/1:03634.

23. Leo Grünfeld to George Dutton, 17 January 1920, Stadtarchiv Worms, 005/1:03634.

24. Mary Strasser to Town Clerk Oswestry, 11 January 1951; Oswestry Burial Committee to Frau Steffen, 16 January 1951; Albert Steffen to Oswestry Burial Committee, 21 January 1951, Oswestry Town Council Archives, OTC/10/12/2/7/1-4.

25. War Organisation of the Red Cross Society to IWGC, 15 March 1944; Comité International de la Croix-Rouge to IWGC, 22 October 1947, CWGC/1/2/A/67.

26. Tony Walter, *On Bereavement: The Culture of Grief* (Buckingham: Open University Press, 1999), pp. 48–9.

27. 'The Late Rifleman Aubrey Fraser', *Jewish Chronicle*, 28 July 1916, p. 19.

28. IWGC to E.M. Perceval, 17 March 1922, CWGC/8/1/4/1/4/58.

29. IWGC Germany to IWGC London, 22 September 1924, CWGC/8/1/4/1/2/69.

30. John Cox to Mrs Warren, 14 May 1945, IBCC, SWarrenGC1580687v30002; 'A Brief Introduction to George Warren's Life', IBCC, BWarrenBWarrenGCv10001; Mary Carter to Mrs Warren and Beryl, 13 May 1946, IBCC, SWarrenGC 1580687v30003.

31. 'Bericht über die besuchten deutschen Kriegsgräber in England in der Zeit vom 11. – 23.6.1956', VDK, A11/55.

32. Ludwig Wittmann to Mrs Warren, 16 July 1952, IBCC, E[Author] WarrenGH520716-0001; Photographs of Ernst Hohlheimer, IBCC, SWarrenGC 1580687v10002.

33. On the number of deaths, see: Antoine Prost, 'War Losses', International Encyclopedia of the First World War, October 2014: https://encyclopedia.1914-1918-online.net/article/war_losses (accessed 10 January 2024).

34. Erik Goldstein, 'Great Britain: The Home Front', in Manfred Boemeke, Gerald Feldman and Elisabeth Glaser (eds), *The Treaty of Versailles: A Reassessment after 75 Years* (Cambridge: Cambridge University Press, 1998), pp. 147–66.

35. 'Französische Gräberschändungen', *Salzburger Volksblatt*, 7 August 1919, p. 6.

36. 'Treue den Toten!', *Volkswille*, 31 October 1919, p. 1.

37. Nina Janz, 'Deutsche Soldatengräber des Zweiten Weltkrieges zwischen Heldenverherrlichung und Zeichen der Versöhnung' (unpublished PhD, Universität Hamburg, 2018), p. 206. See also discussion of continued responsibilities: IWGC to Foreign Office, 9 May 1955, TNA, FO 369/5162.

38. J.E. Talbot to Fabian Ware, 28 October 1919, CWGC/1/1/7/C/11.

39. Der Reichsminister des Innern to sämtliche Landesregierungen, 8 December 1921, Niedersächsisches Landesarchiv Oldenburg, Best. 136, Nr. 20482.

40. In Hamburg, for example, the cemetery authorities designed new markers for the British graves: Das Protokoll der Friedhofsdeputation, 2 May 1922, StAHH, 325-1, 205.

41. Der Oberbürgermeister to Garten- und Friedhofsverwaltung, 8 November 1945; Garten- und Friedhofsverwaltung to Stadtrat Greis, 28 November 1945, Stadtarchiv Wiesbaden, WI/3, 11082.

42. Land and Legal Adviser to Vice Chairman IWGC, 1919, CWGC/1/1/6/7.

43. IWGC, 'Agreement for Maintenance of War Graves', 10 July 1922, Wiltshire and Swindon Archives, PR132, 1858/9.

44. Fordington Burial Joint Committee to Office of Works, 8 April 1921; Office of Works to Fordington Burial Joint Committee, 15 April 1921, CWGC/7/4/2/11573-1.

45. 'Fallen in Germany', *Daily Telegraph*, 14 December 1946, TNA, WO 32/11593.

46. Office of Works to Vicar Kenninghall, 12 May 1921, Norfolk Record Office, PD 108-41.

47. Jon Lawrence, 'Forging a Peaceable Kingdom: War, Violence, and Fear of Brutalization in Post-First World War Britain', *Journal of Modern History*, 75 (2003), pp. 557–89. Rex Pope, 'British Demobilization after the Second World War', *Journal of Contemporary History*, 30 (1995), pp. 65–81, p. 75.

48. For more on this case, see: Saunders, *Finding the Foe*, pp. 87–95.

49. 'Memorial to Nazis Splits a Village' (undated newspaper cutting), VDK, A100/124.

50. In Germany, one memorial was later erected to mark an RAF crash site: Ministry of Defence, News Release, 'Germans Honour Lancaster Crew', 11 October 1974, IBCC, SJenkinsonPR1826262v10041.

51. 'German's Letter', *Dundee Evening Telegraph*, 13 January 1919, p. 2.

52. R.A. Jones to German Embassy London, 3 July 1928, VDK, R13. On the administrative hurdles, see: Ann-Marie Foster, 'The Bureaucratization of Death: The First World War, Families, and the State', *Twentieth Century British History*, 33 (2022), pp. 475–97.

53. 'German Father and the War Grave', *Walsall Observer*, 14 April 1928, p. 9.

54. Hedwig Sopkowiak to Deutsche Botschaft London, 23 March 1935, VDK, R13.

55. 'Auf der Heldengedenkstätte deutscher Soldaten bei Park-Hall, Oswestry, England', *Kriegsgräberfürsorge*, September 1934, p. 10.

56. 'Flowers are Appearing on German Graves', *Crawley and District Observer*, 5 September 1952, p. 5; 'Boldon PoW's Body to be Moved', *Newcastle Journal*, 18 May 1962, p. 9.

57. 'Town and District Topics', *Herts and Essex Observer*, 2 December 1955, p. 8.

58. 'An deutschen Gräbern in England', *Kriegsgräberfürsorge*, June 1951, p. 65.

59. 'She Tends Graves of 24 Germans', *Weekly Dispatch*, 27 July 1952, p. 3; 'Town and District Topics', *Herts and Essex Observer*, 2 December 1955, p. 8.

60. J.W. Nicholas to German Consul Liverpool, 6 July 1933, VDK, R13. German coverage in: 'Kameradengräber in England', *Der Heimkehrer*, 1 February 1934, p. 26.

61. H. Cohen to German Consul, 18 October 1926; Carlton White to Deutsche Botschaft, 4 November 1926, VDK, R13.

62. 'Für den Frieden unter den Völkern', *Tägliche Rundschau*, 16 December 1926; Meynen to Cohen, 9 December 1926, VDK, R13. 'British Tribute to German

Dead', British Pathé, 18 November 1926: https://www.britishpathe.com/asset/52625 (accessed 15 July 2022).

63. 'Silver Inkstand', *Liverpool Echo*, 27 June 1956, p. 13; 'Grammar School Pupils Should Use "Privilege"', *Runcorn Weekly News*, 7 December 1956, p. 5.

64. 'German War Graves are to be Transferred', *Runcorn Weekly News*, 29 December 1960, p. 5.

65. 'Sales by Auctions', *Dorset County Chronicle*, 24 June 1920, p. 4.

5 Controlling

1. Ron Robin, '"A Foothold in Europe": The Aesthetics and Politics of American War Cemeteries in Western Europe', *Journal of American Studies*, 29 (1995), pp. 55–72.

2. Bürgermeister Worms to Hohe Interallierte Rheinkommission, 7 January 1921; American Graves Registration Service to Commandant d'armes de la Place de Worms, 9 September 1921, Stadtarchiv Worms, 005/1:3629.

3. Stadt Worms, 'Notiz für die Akten', 12 August 1924, Stadtarchiv Worms, 005/1:2332.

4. 'Clemenceau über unsere Kriegsgefangenen', *Vorwärts*, 23 May 1919, p. 1.

5. Laqueur, *Work of the Dead*, pp. 453–9.

6. Winston Churchill, House of Commons, 8 July 1919, Volume 117, Column 1594.

7. Kriegsministerium to Auswärtiges Amt, 4 December 1916; Foreign Office, 9 February 1918, BArch Berlin, R901/85256.

8. Kriegsministerium to Auswärtiges Amt, 22 September 1919, BArch Berlin, R901/85256.

9. IWGC to Zentralnachweiseamt, 6 August 1924, VDK, R13; Birmingham Crematorium to IWGC, 10 May 1927; IWGC to Home Office, 31 December 1929, CWGC/1/1/8/35.

10. IWGC, 'Exhumation from Germany', CWGC/1/1/5/25.

11. Curzon to Smith, 17 February 1920, CWGC/1/1/5/25.

12. C. Stein to K. Markel, 21 February 1921, CWGC/1/1/8/25.

13. Valerie Beudel to Österreichische Botschaft, 28 February 1956; IWGC to VDK, 12 March 1956, CWGC/1/2/E/5.

14. Edward Sabarsky to IWGC, 2 June 1949; IWGC to Foreign Office, 23 June 1949, TNA, FO 369/4223.

15. Böttcher, *Geschichte der Kriegsgräberfürsorge*, pp. 69–74, 160–78.

16. Werner Böhme, 'Siegfried Emmo Eulen', *Niedersächsische Lebensbilder*, 6 (1969), pp. 143–59, p. 152; Ulrich et al., *Volksbund Deutsche Kriegsgräberfürsorge*, p. 493; Johann Zilien, 'Der "Volksbund Deutsche Kriegsgräberfürsorge e.V." in der Weimarer Republik', *Archiv für Kulturgeschichte*, 75 (1993), pp. 445–78, p. 460.

17. Auswärtiges Amt to Deutsche Botschaften in London, Paris, Rome, 13 January 1921, VDK, R13.

18. Kurt Deglerk, 'Anfrage 830', 21 June 1921, VDK, R13.

19. ZAK to Reichsminister des Innern, 26 September 1921, VDK, R13.

20. 'Überführungen in die Heimat', *Kriegsgräberfürsorge*, December 1921, p. 90. See also: Ulrich et al., *Volksbund Deutsche Kriegsgräberfürsorge*, p. 133.

21. IWGC to War Office, 9 March 1925, CWGC/1/1/8/25; Botschaftsarchitekt, 'Bericht ueber meinen Besuch der deutschen Kriegsgraeber in Cannock Chase Military Burial Ground', 4 July 1928, VDK, R13.

22. 'German Officer's Remains Exhumed', *Leicester Daily Mercury*, 2 May 1939, p. 11.

23. Town Clerk Leigh to IWGC, 17 May 1928; IWGC, 'Memorandum for W.G.843/4', 26 February 1926; German Embassy to Arthur Henderson, 29 May 1930, CWGC/1/1/8/35.

24. War Office to IWGC, 20 August 1948, CWGC/1/2/E/5.

25. Home Office, 'Application for Licence to Remove Remains of Lieut. Eugen Beudel to Austria', 30 April 1956, TNA, HO 282/20.

26. Home Office, 'Form of Application for the Removal of Human Remains', 19 July 1954, TNA, HO 282/20; VDK to IWGC, 28 July 1954, CWGC/1/2/E/5.

27. Town Clerk Thornaby to Home Office, 19 July 1954; Thomas Rea & Sons to Home Office, 19 July 1954, TNA, HO 282/20. Mrs Riley to IWGC, 4 August 1954, CWGC/1/2/E/5.

28. Oliver Holt, 'First Steps with the Commission', CWGC/1/2/D/17/10.

29. Michèle Barrett, 'Subalterns at War: First World War Colonial Forces and the Politics of the Imperial War Graves Commission', *Interventions*, 9 (2007), pp. 451–74. Commonwealth War Graves Commission, *Report of the Special Committee to Review Historical Inequalities in Commemoration* (Maidenhead, 2021).

30. P.N. Dolan to Otto Margraf, 16 August 1954, CWGC/1/2/E/5.

31. 'The Glorious Dead', *The Times*, 18 December 1919, p. 13. Michael Heffernan, 'For Ever England: The Western Front and the Politics of Remembrance in Britain', *Ecumene*, 2 (3) (1995), pp. 293–323, p. 297.

32. Rudyard Kipling, 'The Graves of the Fallen' (Imperial War Graves Commission, 1919).

33. IWGC to War Office, 25 June 1948, CWGC/1/2/E/5.

34. F. Hibberd to David Lloyd George, 21 June 1921, CWGC/1/1/5/25.

35. 'Graves in Germany', *The Times*, 5 December 1946, p. 5.

36. IWGC, 'Report of Discussion at War Office Lunch', 7 June 1945, CWGC/1/2/D/1/89.

37. IWGC, 'Minutes of Proceedings', 15 November 1921, CWGC/2/2/1/38; IWGC, 'Report of Discussion at War Office Lunch', 7 June 1945, CWGC/1/2/D/1/89.

38. Godfrey Nicholson, House of Commons, 23 October 1945, Volume 414, Column 1849.

39. 'Cabinet 29 (45)', 6 September 1945, TNA, CAB 128/1/12.

40. 'War Dead Not Being Brought Home', *The Times*, 4 October 1945, p. 6.

41. 'Graves in Germany', *The Times*, 28 December 1946, p. 2.

42. IWGC, 'Minutes of Proceedings', 29 November 1921, CWGC/2/2/1/39.

43. Margaret Staveley to 14 June 1920; IWGC, 'Memorandum', 18 June 1923; IWGC, Principal Assistant Secretary to M. Staveley, 22 June 1920, CWGC/8/1/4/1/1/87.

44. E.H.R. Stephens to IWGC, 1 November 1920, CWGC/8/1/4/1/2/69.

45. Hempsons Solicitors to IWGC, 4 August 1949; War Office to Hempsons Solicitors, 3 October 1949; Hempsons Solicitors to War Office, 15 November 1949; War Office, 'Minute Sheet', 28 September 1949, TNA, WO 32/13526.

46. Dominiek Dendooven, '"Bringing the Dead Home": Repatriation, Illegal Repatriation and Expatriation of British Bodies during and after the First World War', in Paul Cornish and Nicholas Saunders (eds) *Bodies in Conflict: Corporeality, Materiality and Transformation* (New York: Routledge, 2014), pp. 66–79.

47. On the family background, see: Ann Noyes, 'Memorials and Landscape', *Surrey History*, 7 (2005), pp. 3–13.
48. W.A. Robertson to IWGC, 18 October 1921; W.A. Robertson to IWGC, 19 May 1920, CWGC/8/1/4/1/3/59.
49. IWGC to W.A. Robertson, 4 June 1920; IWGC to W.A. Robertson, 14 October 1921; W.A. Robertson to IWGC, 18 October 1921, CWGC/8/1/4/1/3/59.
50. ZAK to X. Armeekorps Hannover, 22 January 1920, Niedersächsisches Landesarchiv Oldenburg, Best. 230-12, A, Nr. 125.
51. 'England', *Kriegsgräberfürsorge*, April 1922, p. 39; 'England', *Kriegsgräberfürsorge*, September 1922, p. 102.
52. W.A. Robertson to IWGC, 4 July 1922, CWGC/8/1/4/1/3/59.
53. 'Wills and Estates', *The Scotsman*, 5 July 1937, p. 13. Noyes, 'Memorials', pp. 3–13.
54. Petition to H.R.H. the Prince of Wales, June 1919, CWGC/1/1/5/21.
55. On the British War Graves Association, see: Alison Fell and Susan Grayzel, 'Women's Movements, War and the Body', in Ingrid Sharp and Matthew Stibbe (eds), *Women Activists between War and Peace: Europe 1918–1923* (London: Bloomsbury, 2017), pp. 221–49.
56. 'J. Clemenson' and 'Ivy Clemenson', June 1919, CWGC/1/1/5/21; ICRC, 'Engländer', 13 August 1918, PA34792: https://grandeguerre.icrc.org/en/List/1802940/698/34792/ (accessed 29 July 2022).
57. S.A. Smith to Sir Worthington-Evans, 10 January 1922; War Office to IWGC, 12 January 1922, CWGC/1/1/5/21.
58. British War Graves Association to Secretary of State for War, 10 December 1924, CWGC/1/1/5/21.
59. IWGC to British War Graves Association, 18 June 1936, CWGC/1/1/5/22.
60. 'German Cemetery for Welsh Fallen', *Western Mail*, 16 September 1946, p. 1.
61. George Thomas to Jack Lawson, 16 September 1946, WO 32/11593.
62. A.W. Holerook to IWGC, 11 December 1946, WO 32/11593.

6 Concentrating

1. 'Agreement between the Government of the United Kingdom of Great Britain and Northern Ireland and the Government of the Federal Republic of Germany regarding German War Graves in the United Kingdom', 16 October 1959. Foreign, Commonwealth and Development Office, UK Treaties Online: https://treaties.fcdo.gov.uk/data/Library2/pdf/1960-TS0004.pdf (accessed 20 September 2022).
2. 'Care of German War Graves', *Birmingham Post*, 17 October 1959, p. 14. Other than the VDK's newsletter, the treaty was similarly overlooked in the German press: 'Kriegsgräberabkommen mit Großbritannien in London unterzeichnet', *Kriegsgräberfürsorge*, December 1959, p. 130.
3. Josef Foschepoth, 'Westintegration statt Wiedervereinigung: Adenauers Deutschlandpolitik 1949–1955', in Josef Foschepoth (ed.), *Adenauer und die deutsche Frage* (Göttingen: Vandenhoeck & Ruprecht, 1988), pp. 29–60.
4. Dr Kunisch to the Staatssekretär, 16 March 1960, PA-AA, B 92-REF.602/IV3/299.
5. This was a widespread complaint that even included the graves of executed German war criminals in the 1950s: Caroline Sharples, 'Burying the Past? The

Post-Execution History of Nazi War Criminals', in Richard Ward (ed.), *A Global History of Execution and the Criminal Corpse* (Basingstoke: Palgrave, 2015), pp. 249–71, p. 259.

6. 'At Forceville', *The Times*, 2 September 1920, p. 13.

7. IWGC, 'Annual Report of the Imperial War Graves Commission, 1919–1920' (London: His Majesty's Stationery Office, 1920), p. 8.

8. IWGC, 'Minutes of Proceedings', 29 November 1921, CWGC/2/2/1/39.

9. IWGC, 'Minutes of Proceedings', 18 October 1921, CWGC/2/2/1/37; IWGC, 'Minutes of Proceedings', 29 November 1921, CWGC/2/2/1/39.

10. Principal Personnel Officers Committee, 14 May 1945, TNA, WO 32/11593.

11. British Army of the Rhine to Control Commission for Germany, 31 October 1945, TNA, WO 32/11593. 'Canadian War Graves', *The Times*, 30 October 1945, p. 3.

12. Edward Perceval to Fabian Ware, 24 April 1922, CWGC/1/1/7/C/18. IWGC, 'Minutes of Proceedings', 20 June 1923, CWGC/2/2/1/56.

13. 'Minutes of Proceedings', 18 July 1922, CWGC/2/2/1/47.

14. Robert Gordon-Finlayson to A.O. Stott, 25 May 1946, TNA, WO 171/8653.

15. Air Ministry to War Office, 1 November 1945, TNA, WO 32/11593. See: Spark, 'British Military War Dead', pp. 123–6.

16. IWGC, 14 November 1921; W.A. Robertson to IWGC, 23 November 1921, CWGC/8/1/4/1/3/59.

17. 'British Graves in Germany', *The Times*, 2 July 1947, p. 5.

18. 'Resumé of a Preliminary Conference of the Representatives of the Graves' Services of Belgium, England, France, Germany', 16 March 1922, PA-AA, RZ 407/47741.

19. Isobel Whitehead to Mrs Sthamer, 11 September 1923, VDK, R13.

20. J.A. Curran, St Joseph's Frizington, 12 January 1924, PA-AA, RZ 407/47920.

21. IWGC to German Foreign Office, 15 February 1926; Gebr. Friesecke to Auswärtiges Amt, 24 February 1926, PA-AA, RZ 407/47917. Auswärtiges Amt to Deutsche Botschaft London, 27 January 1927, VDK, R13.

22. Auswärtiges Amt to Deutsche Botschaft, 23 May 1927, VDK, R13.

23. The German Zeppelin crew came to be regarded as valiant heroes in the interwar years: Peter Fritzsche, *A Nation of Fliers: German Aviation and the Popular Imagination* (Cambridge, MA: Harvard University Press, 1992), pp. 58–9.

24. *Deutsche Zeitung*, 15 October 1927, reproduced in: VDK to Auswärtiges Amt, 19 November 1927, PA-AA, RZ 407/47918.

25. Deutsche Botschaft to Auswärtiges Amt, 7 October 1927, PA-AA, RZ 407/47918.

26. 'Zeppelin Crew's Grave', *Daily Mirror*, 27 June 1928, p. 3; 'Tageschronik', *Kölner Lokal-Anzeiger*, 28 June 1928, p. 2.

27. Generalmajor Peterson to Auswärtiges Amt, 7 September 1928, VDK, R13.

28. Deutsches Konsulat Liverpool to Deutsche Botschaft, 19 December 1924, VDK, R13.

29. Deutsches Vize-Konsulat to Deutsche Botschaft, 1 September 1931, VDK, R13.

30. Vicarage Great Burstead to German Embassy, 6 March 1932; Sutton and Cheam Urban District Council to German Embassy, 26 August 1931, VDK, R13.

31. Deutsches Konsulat Liverpool to Deutsche Botschaft, 2 May 1930, VDK, R13.

32. IWGC Visitors Book, 'Ohlsdorf Cemetery, Hamburg', 3 May 1931, CWGC/1/1/7/C/22.

33. Richard Bessel, *Germany after the First World War* (Oxford: Oxford University Press, 1993), p. 281.
34. James Barnes and Patience Barnes, *Nazis in Pre-War London 1930–1939: The Fate and Role of German Party Members and British Sympathizers* (Brighton: Sussex Academic Press, 2005), p. 166.
35. 'Honouring the German Dead', *Barnet Press, Finchley and Hendon News* (undated cutting), VDK, R13.
36. See for example: 'Deutscher Volkstrauertag in England', *Hamburger Nachrichten*, 12 March 1933, p. 6; 'Deutsche Heldenehrung in England', *Hakenkreuzbanner*, 27 February 1934, p. 3.
37. 'Jewish Danger in Germany', *West Middlesex Gazette*, 25 March 1933, p. 8. For a reverential review of Galinsky's academic career, see: Hans Helmcke, Klaus Lubbers and Renate Schmidt von Bardeleben (eds), *Literatur und Sprache der Vereinigten Staaten: Aufsätze zu Ehren von Hans Galinsky* (Heidelberg: Carl Winter, 1969).
38. Karl-Hans Galinsky to Generalkonsul, 1 March 1935, VDK, R13.
39. K.H. Galinsky to Generalkonsul, 13 March 1935; Generalkonsul to Dr Galinksy, 6 March 1935, VDK, R13.
40. 'German War Victim', *Manchester Evening News*, 13 October 1914, p. 2.
41. Deutsches Konsulat to Deutsche Botschaft, 23 March 1936, VDK, R13.
42. The Nazi movement in Britain had insisted on such services: Otto Bene to Deutsche Botschaft, 13 March 1935, VDK, R13.
43. '"Hindenburg" Drops Flowers', *Yorkshire Observer*, 23 May 1936, p. 1.
44. 'The Hindenburg Flies Over Yorkshire', *Leeds Mercury*, 23 May 1936, p. 1.
45. Deutsche Botschaft to Auswärtiges Amt, 27 June 1937, PA-AA, RZ 407/47874.
46. Marjorie Needham to Herr Hitler, 20 June 1937, PA-AA, RZ 407/47874.
47. See: Hans-Adolf Jacobsen and Arthur Smith, *The Nazi Party and the German Foreign Office* (London: Routledge, 2007), pp. 19–28.
48. IWGC, 'Minutes of Proceedings', 22 November 1933, CWGC/2/2/1/167. IWGC Visitors Book, 'Stahnsdorf (South-Western) British Military Cemetery', CWGC/1/1/7/C/25.1.
49. On the committee, see: Grady, 'A Dance with Death'.
50. Ware's private secretary, Oliver Holt, has a vivid account of the wreath laying: 'First Steps with the Commission'. IWGC, 'Anglo-German-French War Graves Agreement', 21 July 1936, TNA, WO 32/4377.
51. H.F. Chettle to Geheimrat Sethe, 23 May 1939, PA-AA, RZ 407/48153. This was Holt's description of Chettle: 'First Steps with the Commission'; 'Niederschrift über den 2. Führertag des Volksbundes Deutschen Kriegsgräberfürsorge', 30 October 1936, VDK, A11/19.
52. Fabian Ware, 'Anglo-German-French War Graves Agreement', 21 July 1936, TNA, WO 32/4377.
53. IWGC, 'Anglo-German-French Mixed Committee. Minutes of the Second Meeting held in Berlin', 29–30 April 1937, CWGC/1/2/D/12/5/10.
54. IWGC, 'Minutes of Proceedings', 13 July 1938, CWGC/2/2/1/217. IWGC to Geheimrat Sethe, 20 May 1939, PA-AA, RZ 407/48153.
55. J.C. Sillar to Auswärtiges Amt, 1 December 1938; J.C. Sillar to Dr Sethe, 12 January 1939, PA-AA, RZ 407/48152.
56. Metropolitan Police, 3 February 1938, TNA, MEPO 2/3059.

57. Metropolitan Police to Home Office, 3 February 1938; Chief Constable's Office, Yorkshire to Home Office, 25 January 1938, TNA, MEPO 2/3059.
58. 'Grave Discovery in Sandhills', *North Devon Journal*, 22 May 1947, p. 5.
59. Ulrich et al., *Volksbund Deutsche Kriegsgräberfürsorge*, pp. 287–8, 475–7; Böttcher, *Geschichte der Kriegsgräberfürsorge*, pp. 106–10.
60. 'Zum Geleit', *Kriegsgräberfürsorge*, 1948, p. 2.
61. The Lutheran Church tried to care for the war graves in place of the VDK: Laura Tradii, 'Conflicted Afterlives: Managing Wehrmacht Fallen Soldiers in the Soviet Occupation Zone and GDR', *Journal of Contemporary History*, 58 (2023), pp. 267–86.
62. Birgit Urmson, *German and United States Second World War Military Cemeteries in Italy* (Bern: Peter Lang, 2018), p. 86; Böttcher, *Geschichte der Kriegsgräberfürsorge*, pp. 224–31.
63. 'Die ersten Auslands-Verträge', *Kriegsgräberfürsorge*, October 1952, p. 115.
64. 'Kriegsgräberfürsorge im Auslande', 1 August 1950, VDK, A10/124.
65. VDK, 'Besprechungspunkte mit Außenminister', 17 February 1959, VDK, A10/66.
66. Otto Margraf, 'Bericht über Besprechungen in England', 9 October 1953, VDK, A10/81. On Margraf, see: 'Ein Lebenswerk für den Volksbund', *Kriegsgräberfürsorge*, December 1960, p. 131.
67. Otto Margraf, 'Bericht über Besprechungen in England', 9 October 1953, VDK, A100/124.
68. Otto Margraf, 'Bericht über eine Reise nach England', 9 November 1956, VDK, A10/81.
69. F.C. Sillar to Generalkonsulat der Bundesrepublik, 19 January 1953, VDK, A100/116.
70. 'Soldatengräber in England', *Die Welt*, 15 January 1951, p. 6.
71. 'England', *Kriegsgräberfürsorge*, July 1953, p. 111; 'Zwei Berichte aus Schottland', *Kriegsgräberfürsorge*, October 1955, p. 159.
72. 'Wir sind alle Brüder', *Kriegsgräberfürsorge*, September 1959, p. 74.
73. IWGC, 'Minutes of the First Meeting of the Commonwealth-German-French Joint Committee', 25 October 1956, CWGC/1/2/D/12/5/11.
74. Auswärtiges Amt to Bundeminister der Finanzen, 4 June 1954, PA-AA, B 92-REF.602/IV3 50.
75. IWGC, 'Minutes of the Second Meeting of the Commonwealth-German-French Joint Committee', 22 October 1959, CWGC/1/2/D/12/5/11.
76. Otto Margraf, 'Bericht über Besprechungen in England', 9 October 1953, VDK, A10/81.
77. 'Chase Acres Transferred to Council', *Rugeley Times*, 30 July 1955, p. 5; CWGC, 'Minutes of Proceedings', 16 February 1961, CWGC/2/2/1/445.
78. Minutes, Cannock Chase Sub-Committee, 23 November 1960, Staffordshire Record Office, CC/B/89/1.
79. Otto Margraf, 'Bericht über Besprechungen in England', 9 October 1953, VDK, A10/81.
80. 'Zum Beginn der Auslandsarbeit', *Kriegsgräberfürsorge*, August 1952, p. 86. Monica Black, *Death in Berlin: From Weimar to Divided Berlin* (Cambridge: Cambridge University Press, 2010), p. 242.

7 Exhuming

1. Interview between Tim Grady and M.A. Rawley, Norfolk, 31 August 2019.
2. Laura Tradii, '"Their Dear Remains Belong to Us Alone": Soldiers' Bodies, Commemoration, and Cultural Responses to Exhumations after the Great War', *First World War Studies*, 10 (2019), pp. 245–61, p. 247; Urmson, *Military Cemeteries in Italy*, pp. 260–87.
3. IWGC, *Fourth Annual Report of the Imperial War Graves Commission 1922–1923* (London: His Majesty's Stationery Office, 1923), p. 14.
4. 'Warum Umbettungen auf größere Soldatenfriedhöfe?', *Kriegsgräberfürsorge*, July 1952, p. 80. 'Gesetz über die Erhaltung der Kriegsgräber aus dem Weltkrieg, vom 29. Dezember 1922', *Reichsgesetzblatt*, 9 January 1923, p. 1.
5. Jennifer Green and Michael Green, *Dealing with Death: A Handbook of Practices, Procedures and Law* (London: Jessica Kingsley, 2006), pp. 132–6.
6. Major-General Edgeworth-Johnstone, 'War Graves in Germany', *The Times*, 10 July 1947, p. 5.
7. VDK to St Ervan and St Eval Rectory, 8 February 1961, Cornwall Record Office, P61/2/3/16; IWGC, 'Report', 1 July 1924, CWGC/1/1/7/C/20.
8. Mitchell, 'The Missing Research and Enquiry Service'; Hadaway, *Missing Believed Killed*, pp. 59–66.
9. Edward Perceval to Fabian Ware, 16 March 1923, CWGC/1/1/7/C/19.
10. 'Bericht über die Dienstreise von Herrn Seifert nach England von 8. – 25. August 1960', VDK, A10/81.
11. Stott to Brigadier Holbrook, 8 June 1946, TNA, WO 171/8653.
12. Spark, 'British Military War Dead', p. 121.
13. Army Graves Service, 30 September 1946, TNA, WO 32/12036.
14. IWGC, 'Report on the Progress of Work in Germany', CWGC, 12 June 1924, CWGC/1/1/7/C/19.
15. Captain Fowler to Oberbürgermeister Wiesbaden, 22 September 1947, Stadtarchiv Wiesbaden, WI/3, 11082.
16. Stadt Braunschweig to BAOR, 25 October 1947, Niedersächsisches Hauptstaatsarchiv Hannover, Nds. 120 Hannover, Acc. 67/68, Nr. 9.
17. To the Baudezernenten, 2 April 1949, Stadtarchiv Wiesbaden, WI/3, 11082.
18. 'Dummheit oder Schamlosigkeit', *Das Ziel*, 1948, Stadtarchiv Wiesbaden, WI/3, 11082.
19. VDK, 'Tätigkeitsbericht', 31 March 1962, VDK, A10/86.
20. Interview with M.A. Rawley, 31 August 2019.
21. VDK, 'Tätigkeitsbericht', 7 February 1963, VDK, A10/86.
22. Friedhofsamt Münster to Amtsdirektor Roxel, Stadtarchiv Münster, Roxel II, Nr. 1058.
23. Interview with M.A. Rawley, 31 August 2019.
24. VDK, 'Schlussbericht', 31 May 1963, VDK, A10/93.
25. Interview with M.A. Rawley, 31 August 2019.
26. Fabian Ware to Edward Perceval, 19 February 1923, CWGC/1/1/7/C/19.
27. CWGC, 'Exhumation of German War Dead buried in the United Kingdom', March 1961, Suffolk Archives, FC205/C/12/3.
28. Mitchell, 'The Missing Research and Enquiry Service'.
29. For a full list of equipment, see: VDK to Bailiff's Chambers Jersey, 14 August 1961, Jersey Archives, B/A/W56/1.

30. H. Sangster to BAOR, 3 May 1946, TNA, WO 171/8653.
31. Duncan Leitch Torrance, *Desert to Danube* (Berwick: Torrance, 2010), p. 127.
32. Transport Adviser, IWGC, 'Transport for Germany', November 1922, CWGC/1/1/7/C/16.
33. VDK, 'Tätigkeitsbericht', 31 March 1962, VDK, A10/86.
34. IWGC, 'Report', 1 July 1924, CWGC/1/1/7/C/20.
35. VDK, 'Tätigkeitsbericht', 7 November 1962, VDK, A10/86.
36. Zentral-Nachweiseamt to IWGC, 26 August 1922, CWGC/1/1/7/C/18.
37. IWGC, 'Burial Return', 27 March 1924: https://www.cwgc.org/find-records/find-war-dead/casualty-details/903147/f-s-cook/#&gid=2&pid=1 (accessed 11 January 2023).
38. Torrance, *Danube*, p. 120.
39. Examples of these are still held in the VDK archive in Kassel.
40. Torrance, *Danube*, p. 122.
41. P.H. Brown, 'Concentration of Graves in Germany', 30 December 1921, CWGC/1/1/7/C/1.
42. Interview with M.A. Rawley, 31 August 2019.
43. Ibid.
44. Torrance, *Danube*, p. 127.
45. VDK, 'Schlussbericht', 31 May 1963, VDK, A10/93.
46. 'Report on Graves Registration Service', 3 May 1947, TNA, WO 32/12036.
47. Torrance, *Danube*, p. 128; Interview with M.A. Rawley, 31 August 2019.
48. 'Maintenance of War Graves in the Soviet Zone', 26 December 1947, TNA, FO 371/64626.
49. 'Air Ministry Report on Royal Air Force and Dominions Air Force Missing Research and Enquiry Service, 1944 to 1949', TNA, AIR 20/9350. Spark, 'British Military War Dead', pp. 211–12.
50. 'Hitler's Men Taken from Town Graves', *Swindon Echo*, 15 March 1963, VDK, A100/975.
51. 'Symptoms and Emotions in Berlin', *The Cologne Post*, 15 November 1921, p. 4. Keith Jeffrey, '"Hut ab," "Promenade with Kamerade for Schokolade," and the *Flying Dutchman*: British Soldiers in the Rhineland, 1918–1929', *Diplomacy & Statecraft*, 16 (2006), pp. 455–73.
52. Christian Kruse (ed.), *In den Mühlen der Geschichte: Russische Kriegsgefangene in Bayern 1914–1921* (Munich: Generaldirektion der Staatlichen Archive Bayerns, 2013), p. 58.
53. Zentral-Nachweiseamt to IWGC, 26 August 1922, CWGC/1/1/7/C/18.
54. Thomas Greig, 'Exhumations at Bayreuth', 7 March 1925, CWGC/1/1/7/C/19.
55. IWGC Land and Legal Adviser, 'Exhumations Bayreuth', 8 April 1925, CWGC/1/1/7/C/19.
56. Elspeth O'Riordan, 'The British Zone of Occupation in the Rhineland', *Diplomacy and Statecraft*, 16 (2005), pp. 439–54, p. 450.
57. Edward Perceval to Fabian Ware, 5 April 1923, CWGC/1/1/7/C/19.
58. Fabian Ware to Edward Perceval, 19 February 1923, CWGC/1/1/7/C/19.
59. Dr Grenzebach, 'Reiseeindrücke einer Revisionsreise auf Veranlassung des Auswärtigen Amtes', 10 July 1962, VDK, A10/93.
60. VDK, 'Tätigkeitsbericht', 7 November 1962, VDK, A10/86; VDK, 'Schlussbericht', 31 May 1963, VDK, A10/93.

61. 'Dornier Do217 U5+GR at Easterside, Hawnby', Aircraft Accidents in Yorkshire: http://www.yorkshire-aircraft.co.uk/aircraft/planes/42/u5gr.html (accessed 15 March 2024).

62. 'The Unwelcome Gravediggers', *Daily Herald*, 26 June 1962, p. 7.

63. Dishforth Parish Council to Home Office, 1 August 1962, TNA, HO 282/21.

64. Mitchell, 'The Missing Research and Enquiry Service'.

65. IWGC, 'Report', 1 July 1924, CWGC/1/1/7/C/20.

66. Torrance, *Danube*, p. 131.

67. VDK, 'Schlussbericht', 31 May 1963, VDK, A10/93.

68. VDK, 'Tätigkeitsbericht', 9 May 1963, VDK, A10/86.

69. 'Note for M.R.E.U Exhumation Officers', TNA, AIR 2/6959.

70. M.J. Moriarty to H.G. Maybury, 1 August 1962, TNA, HO 282/21.

71. VDK, 'Tätigkeitsbericht', 7 November 1962, VDK, A10/86.

72. St Ervan and St Eval Rectory to Diocesan Registrar, 18 July 1961, Cornwall Record Office, P61/2/3/7.

73. Hobohm, 'Report', 16 September 1924, CWGC/1/1/7/C/19.

74. VDK questionnaire, 'St. Eval Churchyard', 8 February 1961, Cornwall Record Office, P61/2/3/11.

75. The Vicarage Potters Bar to Registrar of the Diocese of London, 13 December 1961, London Metropolitan Archive, DL/A/C/02/108/015.

76. VDK, 'Tätigkeitsbericht', 7 June 1962, VDK, A10/86.

77. Hanna Smyth, 'The Material Culture of Remembrance and Identity' (unpublished PhD, University of Oxford, 2019), p. 240.

78. Melton – St Andrews Old Church, Suffolk, Returned from the Front blog, 25 July 2016: http://thereturned.co.uk/crosses/melton-st-andrews-old-church-suffolk/ (accessed 25 January 2023).

79. 'Wooden Crosses being Burned', *Dundee Courier*, 27 November 1926, p. 7.

80. 'War Crosses from British Graves Burnt as Lumber', *Daily Mirror*, 30 November 1926, p. 1.

81. Any remaining British headstones were gradually removed later in the 1920s: Zentralnachweiseamt für Kriegerverluste und Kriegergräber to Minister des Innern, 1 March 1927, Hessisches Staatsarchiv Marburg, 330 Zierenberg, A583.

82. 'Bericht über die Dienstreise von Herrn Seifert nach Großbritannien in der Zeit von 11. bis 19. Juni 1962', VDK, A100/124.

83. VDK, 'Tätigkeitsbericht', 6 September 1962, VDK, A10/86; *East Grinstead Observer*, 11 January 1963, VDK, A100/124.

84. Archaeology Scotland has since reconstructed the memorial: 'Memorial to German Prisoners planned at Hawick to Mark Centenary', *Southern Reporter*, 27 July 2018.

85. 'German War Graves', *Sutton County Herald*, 25 April 1963, VDK, A100/975.

86. 'German POW's Bodies to be Exhumed', *Aberdeen Evening Express*, 27 March 1961, p. 1.

8 Breaking

1. On Eulen, see her obituary in 'Christel Eulen: Ein Leben für den Volksbund', *Kriegsgräberfürsorge*, May 1971, pp. 74–6.

2. VDK, 'Tätigkeitsbericht', 11 April 1963, VDK, A10/86.

3. 'The Bomber that Didn't Return', *Western Independent*, 24 March 1963.

4. VDK, 'Schlussbericht', 31 May 1963, VDK, A10/93.

5. Laqueur, *Work of the Dead*, p. 18.

6. Pierre Nora (ed.), *Realms of Memory: Rethinking the French Past* (New York: Columbia University Press, 1996).

7. Arthur Brown to IWGC Cologne, 24 July 1923, CWGC/1/1/7/C/19.

8. IWGC, 'Minutes of Proceedings', 29 November 1921, CWGC/2/2/1/39.

9. IWGC Enquiries Branch, 24 July 1924, CWGC/8/1/4/1/2/69.

10. H. Simmons, 'The Commonwealth War Graves Commission', March 1961, Wiltshire and Swindon Archives, PR/Sutton Veny, 2351/11.

11. IWGC to Home Office, 16 December 1959, TNA, HO 282/20.

12. Home Office to CWGC, 1960, TNA, HO 282/21.

13. VDK, 'Einzelfragen aus den Besprechungen mit der IWGC', 20 January 1960, VDK, A100/116.

14. Symondsbury Rectory to Diocesan Registry, 12 October 1961; T. Paul to VDK, 13 December 1961, Wiltshire and Swindon Archives, D1/61/111/20.

15. IWGC, 'Graves in German Cemeteries', 11 June 1947, TNA, WO 32/11593.

16. IWGC, 'Draft', 11 June 1947, TNA, WO 32/11593.

17. Graves Registration and Enquiry to Air Ministry, 21 May 1947; IWGC to War Office, 12 March 1947, TNA, WO 32/11593.

18. IWGC Cologne to Arthur Brown, 21 July 1923, CWGC/1/1/7/C/19.

19. IWGC to Mrs Davenport, 15 July 1924, CWGC/8/1/4/1/2/69; VDK, Information Sheet for Families, VDK, A100/975.

20. E.H.R. Stephens to William Hicks, 16 July 1924, CWGC/8/1/4/1/2/69.

21. E.H.R. Stephens to Frederic Wise, 12 September 1924, CWGC/8/1/4/1/2/69.

22. E.H.R. Stephens to IWGC, 6 January 1925, CWGC/8/1/4/1/2/69.

23. ICRC, 'List No. 230 of German Prisoners of War', 34188: https://grandeguerre.icrc.org/en/List/143944/898/34188/ (accessed 18 March 2023).

24. VDK questionnaire, 'St. Andrew Churchyard', 9 February 1961, Worcestershire Archive, 850shelsleywalsh/8499/2/ii.

25. P.H.C. Slocombe to Diocesan Registry, 1 September 1961, Worcestershire Archive, 713-829, 725/1/4043/i. For a similar response in Scotland, see: 'Bilsby's War Graves', *Louth Standard*, 2 September 1960, p. 14.

26. Diocesan Registry to P.H.C. Slocombe, 5 September 1961, Worcestershire Archive, 713-829, 725/1/4043/i.

27. J.H. Ellison to Bishop of Salisbury, 20 March 1962, Wiltshire and Swindon Archives, D1/61/111/20.

28. Diocesan Registrar to CWGC, 31 March 1962, Wiltshire and Swindon Archives, D1/61/111/20.

29. CWGC to Diocesan Registrar, 27 March 1962, Wiltshire and Swindon Archives, D1/61/111/20.

30. Bishop of Salisbury to J.H. Ellison, 22 March 1962, Wiltshire and Swindon Archives, D1/61/111/20.

31. Royal Air Force, Tangmere, 'Memorial Organ Appeal', VDK, C1/1.

32. IWGC Meeting, 'German War Graves', 7 December 1959, National Records of Scotland, HH61/962.

33. '"Duty to Fight but not to Hate"', *Portsmouth Evening News*, 15 December 1959, p. 10.

34. Gilly Carr, 'The Small Things of Life and Death: An Exploration of Value and Material Culture of Nazi Camps', *International Journal of Historical Archaeology*, 22 (2018), pp. 531–52, p. 543.

35. Bishop of Chichester, 'Dedication of Tangmere Organ', 14 December 1959, VDK, C1/1.
36. VDK to IWGC, 10 May 1960, CWGC/7/4/2/10219.
37. F.J. Kenyon, 'Sutton Veney [sic] Churchyard', 3 March 1922, CWGC/7/4/2/12363-1.
38. IWGC, 'Sutton Veny (St. John Churchyard, Wilts.)', 14 October 1954, CWGC/7/4/2/12363-1.
39. VDK to Bailiff Jersey, 22 October 1959, Jersey Archive, B/A/W56/1; Home Office, 7 December 1955, TNA, HO 282/4.
40. On this complex and controversial history, see: Paul Sanders, *The British Channel Islands under German Occupation 1940–1945* (Jersey: Jersey Heritage Trust, 2005).
41. 'Agreement between the Government of the United Kingdom of Great Britain and Northern Ireland and the Government of the Federal Republic of Germany regarding German War Graves in the United Kingdom', 16 October 1959.
42. VDK, 'Schlussbericht', 31 May 1963, VDK, A10/93.
43. Home Office, 'Form of Application for the Removal of Human Remains', 5 November 1959, TNA, HO 282/20.
44. IWGC to Home Office, 21 January 1960, TNA, HO 282/20.
45. 'Hitler's Men Taken from Town Graves', *Swindon Echo*, 15 March 1963.
46. CWGC, 'Park Hall Prisoner of War Cemetery', 5 June 1964, CWGC/7/4/2/7387.
47. Mitchell, 'The Missing Research and Enquiry Service'.
48. For a general discussion of these shortages, see: Johannes-Dieter Steinert, 'Food and the Food Crisis in Post-War Germany, 1945–1948', in Frank Trentmann and Fleming Just (eds), *Food and Conflict in Europe in the Age of the Two World War* (Basingstoke: Palgrave, 2006), pp. 266–88.
49. Richard Bessel, 'The Shadow of Death in Germany at the End of the Second World War', in Alon Confino, Dirk Schumann and Paul Betts (eds), *Between Mass Death and Individual Loss: The Place of the Dead in Twentieth-Century Germany* (Oxford: Berghahn, 2008), pp. 50–68, p. 50; Laura Tradii, '"Everywhere" and "On the Spot": Locality and Attachments to the Fallen "Out of Place" in Contemporary Rural Germany', *History and Anthropology*, 35 (2024), pp. 456–77, p. 457.
50. This was the case when those killed in the Nazis' death marches were exhumed in the 1950s: Christopher Mauriello, *Forced Confrontation: The Politics of Dead Bodies at the End of World War II* (Lanham: Lexington, 2016), p. 175.
51. War Crimes Investigation Team, 23 October 1945, TNA, WO 235/49. More generally: Jennie Gray, '"Nothing Can Excuse Us if We Fail": The British and their Dead Servicemen, North-West Europe, 1944–1951' (unpublished PhD, University of Exeter, 2016), pp. 307–12.
52. Rolf Brinkmann, 'Petition', 23 January 1946; 'Statement by Werner Assmussen', 21 November 1945, TNA, WO 235/49.
53. Margarete Franziska Vordermayer, *Justice for the Enemy? Die Verteidigung deutscher Kriegsverbrecher durch britische Offiziere in Militärgerichtsprozessen nach dem Zweiten Weltkrieg (1945–1949)* (Baden-Baden: Nomos, 2019), pp. 183–7.
54. Hoffmann, *Fliegerlynchjustiz*, p. 370.
55. 'Sie waren noch so jung . . .', *Frankfurter Rundschau*, 21 November 1959.
56. CWGC to Rector of Theberton, 26 April 1963, Suffolk Archives, FC70/N1/2.
57. CWGC to Starston Rectory, 25 April 1963, Norfolk Record Office, PD 119/34.

58. 'Campsie Graves', *The Scotsman*, 23 February 1961, p. 8. For a similar history, see Linstead Parva in Suffolk: M. Ingate to the Superintendent, 17 July 1963, CWGC/7/4/2/7264-1.
59. 'German War Graves to be Moved from Salop', *Border Counties Advertiser*, 20 February 1963, VDK, A100/975.
60. R. Dourass to IWGC, 1 December 1963, CWGC/7/4/2/7264-1.
61. R. Dourass to IWGC, 1 December 1963; R. Dourass to CWGC, 1 January 1964, CWGC/7/4/2/7264-1.
62. 'Five German Bodies to be Exhumed', *Corby Leader*, 18 January 1963.
63. 21 Army Group, 'Besetzungs-Befehl', 14 February 1947, CWGC/7/4/1/RA 41554.
64. Stadtplanungsamt to Stadtrechtsrat Hübner, 18 April 1958, Stadtarchiv Celle, Best. 16 H, Nr. 0073, Bd. 3; To Nieders. Minister des Innern, 8 May 1958, Niedersächsisches Hauptstaatsarchiv Hanover, Nds. 120 Lüneburg, Acc. 103/86, Nr. 98.
65. IWGC, 'Form A', 24 April 1951, CWGC/7/3/2/2/118.
66. IWGC, 'Form A', 25 June 1954, CWGC/7/3/2/2/118.
67. Torrance, *Danube*, p. 124.
68. Report, 'Brit. Militärfriedhof in Sage', Niedersächsisches Landesarchiv Oldenburg, Best. 136, Nr. 20489.
69. P. Haltmair to Gemeinde Dürnbach, 12 June 1949, Staatsarchiv Munich, BezA/LRA, 218572.
70. Torrance, *Danube*, p. 124.
71. P. Haltmair to Gemeinde Dürnbach, 12 June 1949, Staatsarchiv Munich, BezA/LRA, 218572.
72. Niedersächsische Minister des Innern to IWGC, 22 April 1953, Niedersächsisches Landesarchiv Oldenburg, Best. 136, Nr. 20489.
73. Dr Königsdorfer to Regierung von Oberbayern, 20 October 1956, Staatsarchiv Munich, BezA/LRA, 218572.
74. 'Critic of Chase Cemetery Proposal', *Rugeley Times*, 28 January 1961, p. 8.
75. 'Germans to Work on Cannock Chase', *Walsall Observer*, 9 March 1962, p. 9; 'Minutes of the Twelfth Annual General Meeting of the Association of Friends of Cannock Chase', 4 November 1960, Staffordshire Record Office, D4768/2/3.

9 Nationalising

1. 'German War Graves to be Moved from Salop', *Border Counties Advertiser*, 20 February 1963.
2. 'Deutscher Soldatenfriehof Cannock Chase', 24 February 1967, VDK, A100/147.
3. Deutsche Botschaft, 'Bericht über meinen Besuch der Kriegergräber im Friedhof von H. M. Borstal Institution ausserhalb Feltham', 6 July 1927, PA-AA, RZ 407/47918.
4. Brian Feltman, *The Stigma of Surrender: German Prisoners, British Captors, and Manhood in the Great War and Beyond* (Chapel Hill: University of North Carolina Press, 2015), pp. 60–1.
5. Urban District Council of Feltham to Home Office, 26 September 1961, TNA, HO 282/21.
6. On the intensity of memory wars between Germany and Denmark, see: Inge Adriansen, *Demkal und Dynamit: DenkmälerSTREIT im deutsch-dänischen Grenzland* (Neumünster: Wachholtz, 2011), pp. 67–90.

7. David Renton to Mr Stotesbury, 1961, TNA, HO 282/21.
8. Deutsche Botschaft, 'Bericht über meinen Besuch der Kriegergräber im Friedhof von H. M. Borstal Institution ausserhalb Feltham', 6 July 1927, PA-AA, RZ 407/47918.
9. Jean-Marc Dreyfus, 'Renationalizing Bodies? The French Search Mission for the Corpses of Deportees in Germany, 1946–58', in Elisabeth Anstett and Jean-Marc Dreyfus (eds), *Human Remains and Violence: Methodological Approaches* (Manchester: Manchester University Press, 2014), pp. 129–45, p. 140. More generally, see: Benedict Anderson, *Imagined Communities: Reflections on the Origin and Spread of Nationalism* (London: Verso, 1983).
10. Winston Churchill, House of Commons, 4 May 1920, Volume 128, Column 1970.
11. Friedhofsdirektor to J.S. Parker, 19 October 1927, StAHH, 325-1, 221.
12. 'Plans for German Cemetery', *Staffordshire Newsletter*, 10 March 1962, p. 9.
13. Sabine Behrenbeck, *Der Kult um die toten Helden: nationalsozialistische Mythen, Riten und Symbole 1929 bis 1945* (Vierow: SH-Verlag, 1996).
14. Robert Tischler to VDK Vorstand, 23 January 1957, VDK, A10/123. On Tischler and Tobruk, see: Böttcher, *Geschichte der Kriegsgräberfürsorge*, pp. 242–6.
15. Dr Banasch, 'Stellungnahme'; 'Niederschrift über die erste Sitzung des Ausschusses für Gestaltung der Kriegergräberstätten im Ausland', 10 July 1957, VDK, A10/123.
16. 'Deutscher Soldatenfriehof Cannock Chase', 24 February 1967, VDK, A100/147.
17. See for example: 'Kunst als Künderin der neuen Zeit', *Der Führer: Das Haupt Organ der NSDAP Gau Baden*, 23 April 1942, p. 5. On Wimmer's complicated relationship to National Socialism, see: Melanie Wittchow, 'Hans Wimmer', in Karin Althau et al., *Kunst und Leben 1918 bis 1945* (Berlin: Deutscher Kunstverlag, 2022), pp. 252–5.
18. VDK, Abteilung Auftragsbau, 17 November 1964, VDK, A100/975.
19. 'Niederschrift über die Sitzung des Sachverständigen-Beirats in Kassel', 27 January 1961, VDK, A10/183.
20. Philip Longworth, *The Unending Vigil: The History of the Commonwealth War Graves Commission* (Barnsley: Pen & Sword, 2010 [orig. 1967]), p. 36.
21. Chief Horticultural Officer, 'Oppeln Cemetery, Silesia', 8 October 1930, TNA, WO 32/3144.
22. Morris, 'Gardens "For Ever England"', p. 424.
23. IWGC, 'Anglo-German-French Mixed Committee. Minutes of the First Meeting', 8–9 June 1936, CWGC/1/2/D/12/5/10.
24. 'Preliminary Estimate and Reports for Cemetery Construction', 26 August 1952, CWGC/7/3/2/2/114; 'Preliminary Estimate and Reports for Cemetery Construction', 29 September 1950, CWGC/7/3/2/2/109.
25. Garten- und Friedhofsamt, 'Die Gestaltung unsere Ehrenfriedhöfe', Stadtarchiv Münster, Amt 67, Nr. 449.
26. Garten- und Friedhofsamt to Liegenschaftsamt 4 July 1956, Stadtarchiv Münster, Amt 67, Nr. 374. VDK, 'Ehrenfriedhof Lauheide. Besichtigung am 4.9.1957', Stadtarchiv Münster, Amt 67, Nr. 335.
27. David Crane, *Empires of the Dead: How One Man's Vision Led to the Creation of WWI's War Graves* (London: Collins, 2014), p. 241. Fabian Ware, 24 April 1933, cited in Ziino, *Distant Grief*, p. 129.

28. In general terms, see: John Horne and Edward Madigan (eds), *Towards Commemoration: Ireland in War and Revolution 1912–1923* (Dublin: Royal Irish Academy, 2013).

29. On Limburg camp see: Detlef Wild, '90 Jahre irisches Hochkreuz in Dietkirchen, Hessen', *Ireland Journal*, XVIII (2007), pp. 90–5.

30. Arthur Browne to IWGC Cassel, 9 May 1924, CWGC/1/1/7/C/11.

31. British Army of the Rhine, 'Disposal of Indians after Burial', 6 October 1945, TNA, WO 171/3926.

32. Böttcher, *Geschichte der Kriegsgräberfürsorge*, pp. 176–7; Ulrich et al., *Volksbund Deutsche Kriegsgräberfürsorge*, pp. 364–5.

33. 'Gratton Man's Aid to Austrian Family', *Staffordshire Sentinel*, 25 May 1954, p. 7.

34. IWGC to Home Office, 20 September 1954; Foreign Office to IWGC, 16 September 1954, CWGC/1/2/E/5.

35. ICRC, 'List No. 145 of Austrian or Hungarian Prisoners of War', V466: https://grandeguerre.icrc.org/en/List/385346/968/466/ (accessed 7 June 2023).

36. Borough of Sutton and Cheam to Home Office, 11 November 1960, TNA, HO 282/21.

37. VDK to Auswärtiges Amt, 13 July 1961; Bundesministerium für auswärtige Angelegenheiten to Österreichische Schwarze Kreuz, 3 March 1960, PA-AA, B 92-REF.602/IV3/299.

38. IWGC, 'Knutsford Cemetery', 9 April 1948, CWGC/7/4/2/6943-1.

39. Gerald Fleming, *Hitler and the Final Solution* (Berkeley: University of California Press, 1987), pp. 140–1.

40. This oft-repeated phrase is attributed to Winston Churchill: Gillman and Gillman, *'Collar the Lot!'*

41. Simon Dixon, *The Island of Extraordinary Captives: A True Story of an Artist, a Spy and a Wartime Scandal* (London: Sceptre, 2022), p. 144.

42. A slight celebratory overview of Rushen is available: David Wertheim et al., 'Rushen Camp, Isle of Man – Camp W (Women and Children), Camp Y (Married), "Treat them with Kindness"', in Gilly Carr and Rachel Pistol (eds), *British Internment and the Internment of Britons: Second World War Camps, History and Heritage* (London: Bloomsbury, 2023), pp. 101–13.

43. Isle of Man, 'Regional Advisory Committee', 20 March 1942, HO 396/190. On Anna Ortner, see: Manx National Heritage: https://www.imuseum.im/search/collections/people/mnh-agent-105170.html (accessed 7 June 2023).

44. 'Austritte in Frankfurt a. M.', *Neue Jüdische Presse*, 15 April 1921, p. 3. UNRRA, Central Tracing Bureau, 29 June 1946, Arolsen Archives: https://collections.arolsen-archives.org/en/document/86547863 (accessed 7 June 2023).

45. Bernard Seidel record, TNA, HO 396/276.

46. CWGC to VDK, 15 February 1972, CWGC/1/2/A/36.

47. 'A New Birth of an Old Evil', *The Times*, 30 December 1959, p. 7.

48. Peter Reichel, *Vergangenheitsbewältigung in Deutschland: Die Auseinandersetzung mit der NS-Diktatur von 1945 bis heute* (Munich: Beck, 2001), pp. 147–8.

49. Home Office, 15 October 1962, TNA, HO 282/21; Isle of Man Hebrew Congregation to Town Clerk, Douglas, 21 February 1966, Manx National Heritage, MS 10855, Box 4, File 27.

50. Tim Grady, *The German-Jewish Soldiers of the First World War in History and Memory* (Liverpool: Liverpool University Press, 2011), p. 193.

51. Clementine French to Foreign Office, 30 October 1915; Foreign Office to Mrs C.M. French, 3 November 1915, TNA, FO 383/79.
52. 'Equality of treatment' was at the heart of Frederic Kenyon's foundational report: Frederic Kenyon, 'War Graves: How the Cemeteries Abroad will be Designed' (London: His Majesty's Stationery Office, 1918).
53. Victoria de Voss to Rudyard Kipling, 4 March 1919, CWGC/1/1/7/C/12.
54. IWGC London to IWGC Germany, 2 August 1924, CWGC/1/1/7/C/19.
55. On responses to the cut-off dates, see: Megan Kelleher, ' "I will remember it as one more to the list of courtesies I have received": Interactions between the Imperial War Graves Commission and the Bereaved', *British Journal for Military History*, 7 (2021), pp. 83–101.
56. See for example: 'Young Officer Drowned', *The Cologne Post*, 13 September 1919, p. 1.
57. 'The Late Capt. W. T. Ellerker', *The Cologne Post*, 18 December 1921, p. 1. 'British Graves', *Western Morning Post*, 6 May 1927, p. 7.
58. 'Air Lift Plane Down in Flames: 5 Die', *Manchester Evening News*, 16 July 1949, p. 5. On the Berlin blockade more generally, see: Carolyn Eisenberg, *Drawing the Line: The American Decision to Divide Germany* (Cambridge: Cambridge University Press, 1996).
59. IWGC, 'Tour Report Northern Region', 13–21 June 1958, CWGC/7/4/1/RA 41489-3.
60. IWGC Brussels to IWGC, 20 November 1957, CWGC/7/4/1/RA 38024-1.
61. On the role of the British forces, see: Peter Lesniewski, 'Britain and Upper Silesia, 1919–1922' (unpublished PhD, University of Dundee, 2000).
62. 'A Royal Highlander Laid to Rest', *The Cologne Post*, 15 June 1921, p. 1; 'Oppeln Tragedy', *The Cologne Post*, 16 July 1921, p. 1.
63. IWGC Berlin, 6 November 1924, CWGC/1/1/7/C/28; IWGC, 'Oppeln Cemetery', 3 September 1930, TNA, WO 32/3144.
64. On Czech graves, see: Otto Margraf, 'Bericht über die gelegentlich der Reise nach England', 1 February 1952, VDK, A10/81.
65. VDK to Auswärtiges Amt, 17 December 1956; Auswärtiges Amt to VDK, 4 January 1957, PA-AA, B 92-REF.602/IV3/71.
66. Fabian Lemmes, *Arbeiten in Hitlers Europa: die Organisation Todt in Frankreich und Italien 1940–1945* (Cologne: Böhlau, 2021), pp. 81–109; Charles Dick, *Builders of the Third Reich: The Organisation Todt and Nazi Forced Labour* (London: Bloomsbury, 2020), p. 7.
67. IWGC, 'German Burials in United Kingdom 1939-1945', 8 October 1955, FO 369/5163.
68. T.X.H. Pantcheff, *Alderney Fortress Island: The Germans in Alderney, 1940–1945* (Chichester: Phillimore, 1981), pp. 13–14.
69. The spelling varies between Onuchowski, Onukowski and Onnuchowski, see: Caroline Sturdy Colls and Kevin Colls, *Adolf Island: The Nazi Occupation of Alderney* (Manchester: Manchester University Press, 2022), pp. 236, 438.
70. This was the VDK's description from a 1958 tour: 'Bericht über die Besichtigung der deutschen Kriegsgräber auf den Kanalinseln', 6 June 1958, VDK, A11/56.
71. Auswärtiges Amt, 10 August 1961, PA-AA, B 92-REF.602/IV3/299. CWGC to Home Office, 26 September 1961, TNA, HO 282/84.
72. VDK to Bailiff's Chambers, Jersey, 8 August 1961, Jersey Archives, B/A/W56/1. Home Office to Foreign Office, 29 August 1961, TNA, FO 371/160658.

73. 'The German War Cemeteries Disappear', *Jersey Evening Post*, 22 December 1961.

74. CWGC to Home Office, 26 September 1961, TNA, HO 282/84; 'Exhumation of Germans' Remains', *Guernsey Evening Press*, 17 November 1961. More generally: Graham Smyth, 'Denunciation in the German-Occupied Channel Islands, 1940–1945', *Journal of British Studies*, 4 (2020), pp. 291–314.

75. Caroline Sturdy Colls and Kevin Colls suggest several potential gravesites remain on Alderney, for example: Sturdy Colls and Colls, *Adolf Island*, pp. 296, 340–2.

76. ICRC, 'Prisoners of War Admitted into or Discharged from Hospitals During Internment', D127-3: https://grandeguerre.icrc.org/en/List/52820/952/127-3/ (accessed 27 June 2023).

77. Camberwell House to German Embassy, 2 February 1932, VDK, R13.

78. Kate Vigurs, *Mission France: The True History of the Women of SOE* (New Haven and London: Yale University Press, 2021). On occupation deaths, see for example: 'Death of Miss Miles', *The Cologne Post*, 9 March 1921, p. 1.

79. IWGC to Home Office, 5 March 1951, Jersey Archives, D/S/A/13/A440.

80. 'Sunderland Sensation', *Shields Daily News*, 5 October 1914, p. 4.

81. 'A Prison Tragedy', *Woman's Dreadnought*, 31 March 1917, p. 1; 'Ein Nachspiel zum Tode des deutschen Konsuls Ahlers', *Hamburger Nachrichten*, 2 April 1917, p. 4.

82. This is the euphemistic phrase the VDK employs for those left behind: VDK, 'Gräbersuche-Online. Georg Eid': https://www.volksbund.de/erinnern-gedenken/graebersuche-online/detail/713d8a0792cbf3d512fb4a1e4b40272b (accessed 27 June 2023).

83. 'Note of Discussion on Friday 28th September, 1951, Regarding German Graves in the United Kingdom', TNA, FO 371/93573.

84. CWGC to Home Office, 10 October 1960, TNA, HO 282/21.

85. CWGC, 'German Z.A.K. Tablets', 28 May 1965, CWGC/7/4/2/5488.

86. IWGC, 'Concentration in Germany', 15 March 1927, CWGC/1/1/7/C/19. CWGC France to CWGC London, 22 September 1960, CWGC/7/4/1/RA 39236.

87. IWGC, 27 June 1949, CWGC/7/4/1/RA 41520-1.

88. Interview with M.A. Rawley, 31 August 2019.

89. Medical Officer of Health Westmorland to Ministry of Health, 2 July 1962; Ministry of Health to Medical Officer of Health Westmorland, 4 July 1962, TNA, HO 282/21.

90. On the messages with which the IWGC cemeteries were imbued, see: Edwards, 'An Empire of Memory', pp. 255–86.

10 Ritualising

1. Eric Hobsbawm and Terence Ranger (eds), *The Invention of Tradition* (Cambridge: Cambridge University Press, 1983).

2. RAF Mission Germany, 'Operations Record Book', 8 November 1959, 13 November 1960, 12 November 1961, 11 November 1962, TNA, AIR 29/3554.

3. '3000 britische Soldaten ruhen in bayerischer Erde – Gedenkstunde auf dem Friedhof bei Dürnbach', *Miesbacher Merkur*, 12 November 1957, Staatsarchiv München, BezA/LRA, 218572. On wartime narratives of a 'community of fate' in Nazi Germany, see: Jörg Arnold, *The Allied Air War and Urban Memory: The Legacy of Strategic Bombing in Germany* (Cambridge: Cambridge University Press, 2011), pp. 31–3.

4. Böttcher, *Geschichte der Kriegsgräberfürsorge*, pp. 316, 322.

5. 'Germans who Jeered', *The Cologne Post*, 20 November 1920, p. 1.

6. Jeffrey, 'Soldiers in the Rhineland', pp. 455–6.

7. 'Allerheiligen – Allerseelen', *Kölner Lokal-Anzeiger*, 2 November 1929, p.3.

8. British Consulate General to Friedhofsverwaltungsbüro, 25 November 1930, StAHH, 325-1, 221.

9. Some of the ribbons had been removed by unknown vandals: Friedhofsamt to Reichsvereinigung ehem. Kriegsgefangenener Berlin, 15 December 1931, StAHH, 325-1, 221.

10. 'The Brotherhood', *Daily News*, 2 April 1929, p. 9.

11. 'Eine Rechtfertigung des englischen Amateurfußballs', *Kölnische Zeitung*, 30 March 1929, p. 5.

12. 'Der englische Besuch in Köln', *Kölnische Zeitung*, 24 July 1935, p. 9.

13. 'Stahnsdorf', *Teltower Kreisblatt*, 16 July 1935, p. 3.

14. 'Britische Frontkämpfer nach Berlin zurückgekehrt', *Hamburger Nachrichten*, 18 July 1935, p. 5.

15. 'To Meet Mussolini', *Daily Herald*, 12 April 1937, p. 9.

16. 'Ex-Service Men and Germany', *The Times*, 12 June 1935, p. 12.

17. 'Ex-Service Men Home from Germany', *The Times*, 25 July 1935, p. 10.

18. Grady, *German-Jewish Soldiers*, pp. 122–57.

19. Niall Barr, *The Lion and the Poppy: British Veterans, Politics, and Society, 1921–1939* (Westport: Praeger, 2005), pp. 167–9. A confused understanding of Hitler and Nazism pushed the legion and others forward: Detlev Clemens, *Herr Hitler in Germany. Wahrnehmung und Deutungen des Nationalsozialismus in Großbritannien 1920 bis 1939* (Göttingen: Vandenhoeck & Ruprecht, 1996).

20. 'Warm Welcome in Germany', *Leeds Mercury*, 2 April 1937, p. 5; 'Leeds Men Back from Rhine', *Leeds Mercury*, 15 April 1936, p. 5.

21. Niall Barr, '"The Legion that Sailed but Never Went": The British Legion and the Munich Crisis of 1938', in Julia Eichenberg and John Paul Newman (eds), *The Great War and Veterans' Internationalism* (Basingstoke: Palgrave, 2013), pp. 32–52.

22. 'Deutschland braucht und will Frieden', *Völkischer Beobachter*, 12 March 1939, CWGC/7/4/1/RA 38290-1.

23. 'War Graves Services', *Staffordshire Advertiser*, 24 April 1948, p. 3. For the most detailed discussion of the British Legion's relationship to Nazi Germany, see: Barr, *The Lion and the Poppy*, pp. 151–90.

24. IWGC Brussels to Brigadier J. McNair, 19 May 1948, CWGC/1/2/A/517.

25. C.A. Batty to British Embassy Berlin, 16 September 1933, CWGC/1/1/7/C/24.

26. Berta Dreyer to Berlin Intelligence Staff, 5 September 1948, CWGC/1/2/A/517.

27. Berolina, 'Wherefore East Germany?', *The Scotsman*, 29 January 1966, p. 10. The background is discussed in detail in: Stefan Berger and Norman LaPorte, *Friendly Enemies: Britain and the GDR, 1949–1990* (New York: Berghahn, 2010), pp. 76–113.

28. 'Unter Seerosen lauert der Tod', *Neue Berliner Illustrierte*, 2 August 1959, pp. 10–11.

29. British Military Government to British Embassy, 15 October 1959; British Military Government to British Embassy, 4 November 1959, TNA, FO 371/146090. The two airmen were finally identified in 2016 and reburied: BBC News, 'Lost WW2 Bomber Crews Remembered in German Service', 27 April 2016: https://www.bbc.co.uk/news/uk-england-36140400 (accessed 2 March 2024).

30. Alexander David Robin Graham Wilson, 'Oral History', March 2000, IWM, Doc. 20456.

31. BRIXMIS, 'British Military Cemetery (1914–1918) Stahnsdorf UU70', 9 October 1968, CWGC/7/4/1/RA 38290-2. More generally: Richard Aldrich, 'Waiting to be Kissed? NATO, NORTHAG, and Intelligence', in Jan Hoffenaar and Dieter Krüger (eds), *Blueprints for Battle: Planning for War in Central Europe, 1948–1968* (Lexington: University Press of Kentucky, 2012), pp. 55–74.

32. G.O.C. Berlin and Chief BRIXMIS, 'Inspection of Stahnsdorf Cemetery German Democratic Republic', 6 August 1983, TNA, FCO 33/6454.

33. Brigadier J.H. Learmont to British Embassy Berlin, 20 April 1983, TNA, FCO 33/6453.

34. BRIXMIS to FCO London, 14 November 1984, TNA, FCO 33/7269.

35. On the CWGC's attempts to avoid publicity over Stahnsdorf, see for example: BBC Bristol to CWGC, 19 November 1985, TNA, FCO 33/7903. On maintenance more generally, see: Anett Ladegast, 'Der Erste Weltkrieg im Spiegel nationalen Gedenkens – Die drei Soldatenfriedhöfe auf dem Südwestkirchhof Stahnsdorf bei Berlin', *RIHA Journal* (June 2017): http://nbn-resolving.de/urn:nbn:de:101:1-201711132008.

36. Hermann Wentker, *Außenpolitik in engen Grenzen. Die DDR im internationalen System 1949–1989* (Munich: Oldenbourg, 2007), p. 451.

37. Foreign and Commonwealth Office to CWGC, 18 December 1981, TNA, FCO 33/4733.

38. British Embassy, East Berlin to Foreign and Commonwealth Office, 30 August 1985, TNA, FCO 33/7903; British Embassy, East Berlin to CWGC, 8 February 1984, TNA, FCO 33/7267.

39. 'Agreement between the Government of the United Kingdom of Great Britain and Northern Ireland and the Government of the German Democratic Republic Concerning the Treatment of War Graves of Members of the Armed Forces of the United Kingdom of Great Britain and Northern Ireland in the German Democratic Republic', 27 April 1987: https://www.un-ilibrary.org/content/books/9789210595759s002-c003?mlang=en (accessed 15 July 2023). 'Regierungsabkommen mit Großbritannien', *Neues Deutschland*, 28 April 1987, p. 2.

40. British Embassy, East Berlin to Foreign and Commonwealth Office, 16 November 1988, TNA, FCO 33/9571.

41. VDK to VDK Bremen, 18 April 1967, VDK, A100/147.

42. 'Feierstunde zur Einweihung des deutschen Soldatenfriedhofes Cannock-Chase', 10 June 1967; 'Inaugural Speech given by Deacon Walter Trepte', 10 June 1967, VDK, A100/975.

43. The Dresden–Coventry relationship was very similar: Stefan Goebel, 'Commemorative Cosmopolis: Transnational Networks of Remembrance in Post-War Coventry', in Stefan Goebel and Derek Keene (eds), *Cities into Battlefields: Metropolitan Scenarios, Experiences and Commemorations of Total War* (Farnham: Ashgate, 2011), pp. 163–83.

44. Hans Koschnick to Mr Chairman, Mr Mayor, Mr Evans, Staffordshire Record Office, C/C/PR/5/1/4.

45. Peter Berrisford to Hubertus Rogge, 26 June 1967, Staffordshire Record Office, C/C/PR/5/1/4.

46. VDK, 'Bericht über die Dienstreise nach Stafford / England wegen Einweihung des deutschen Soldatenfriedhofes Cannock – Chase', 24 January 1967, VDK, A100/147.

47. VDK to Staffordshire County Council, 12 December 1966, Staffordshire Record Office, C/C/PR/5/1/4.

48. Dedication seating plan, VDK, A100/147.

49. Staffordshire County Council, 'Progress Report', Staffordshire Record Office, C/C/PR/5/1/4; Staffordshire County Council to VDK, 26 May 1967, VDK, A100/147.

50. Alresford Rectory to VDK, 6 February 1963, VDK, A100/147.

51. Staffordshire County Council to the English Electric Company, 13 June 1967, Staffordshire Record Office, C/C/PR/5/1/4.

52. Harold Doffman to VDK, 27 June 1967, CWGC/7/4/2/7264-3.

53. 'A Town and it's [sic] People Condemn War Graves Vandalism', *Lichfield Mercury*, 16 June 1967, p. 14; 'At Long Last . . . Rest in Peace', *Staffordshire Newsletter*, 16 June 1967, p. 21.

54. CWGC to VDK, 30 November 1990, CWGC/7/4/2/10219; 'German War Widow wants English Burial', *Daily Telegraph*, 24 July 1990, p. 4.

55. Julia Rugg and Stephen Holland, 'Respecting Corpses: The Ethics of Grave Re-Use', *Mortality*, 22 (2017), pp. 1–14.

56. Doris Francis, Leonie Kellaher and Georgina Neophytou, 'Sustaining Cemeteries: The User Perspective', *Mortality*, 5 (2000), pp. 34–52.

57. Elsie Cook to IWGC, 12 March 1937; IWGC France to IWGC London, 27 April 1937, CWGC/8/1/4/1/2/433.

58. 'Visit to War Graves in 1926', *The Cornishman*, 10 February 1926, p. 2; 'To Visit War Graves', *Liverpool Echo*, 6 September 1957, p. 15. On the history of cemetery visits, see: Lloyd, *Battlefield Tourism*.

59. Theresa Rapley to CWGC, 18 September 1966; IWGC, 'Becklingen War Cemetery', 3 October 1966, CWGC/7/4/2/19472-2.

60. Kolbe, 'Trauer und Tourismus', p. 76.

61. VDK, 'Reiseprogramme mit uns', 1980, VDK, A100/249. For reflections on tourism and German war memory, see: Alon Confino, 'Traveling as a Culture of Remembrance: Traces of National Socialism in West Germany, 1945–1960', *History & Memory*, 12 (2000), pp. 92–121.

62. 'Kriegsgräberfahrt nach Cannock Chase', 17 March 1980, VDK, A100/249. 'War Burials Report Form', 14 July 1944, CWGC/7/4/2/10041-1.

63. Brunhilde Mai to VDK, 30 June 1980; Adolf Guratzsch to VDK, 2 July 1980, VDK, A100/249.

64. Kolbe, 'Trauer und Tourismus', p. 78.

65. 'Kriegsgräberfahrt nach Cannock Chase', 1 September 1984; VDK, 'Reiseprogramm mit uns', September 1984, VDK, A100/492.

66. CWGC, 'Support Us': https://www.cwgc.org/join-the-foundation/ (accessed 25 August 2023).

67. 'Niederschrift über die erste Sitzung des Ausschusses für Gestaltung der Kriegsgräberstätten im Ausland', 10 July 1957, VDK, A10/123. On the VDK's youth work more generally, see: Böttcher, *Geschichte der Kriegsgräberfürsorge*, pp. 304–28.

68. 'Cannock Chase', *Stimme und Weg*, December 1963, p. 9.

69. Staffordshire County Council, 27 June 1963, Staffordshire Record Office, C/C/PR/5/1/4; 'Begegnung stand an erster Stelle', *Ostbremer Rundschau*, 9 September 1971; VDK Archive, Image Nr. 14763.

70. 'Zum zehnten Mal in Cannock Chase', *Bremer Nachrichten*, 30 August 1971.

71. 'Vale Youth Beaten by Germans', *Staffordshire Sentinel*, 7 August 1965, p. 7.

72. 'Das Ziel wurde erreicht', *Stimme und Weg*, November 1965, p. 11.

73. 'Enthüllung eines Gedenksteines durch seine königliche Hoheit, dem Herzog von Kent, auf dem deutschen Friedhof Cannock-Chase', 16 July 1987, VDK, A100/925/03.

74. Laqueur, *Work of the Dead*, p. 17.

11 Mythologising

1. On the annual *Führertag*, see: Ulrich et al., *Volksbund Deutsche Kriegsgräberfürsorge*, p. 213. The Ostmark was the Nazis' term for Austria: 'Der Bundesführer des Volksbundes Deutsche Kriegsgräberfürsorge', *Kriegsgräberfürsorge*, May 1938, p. 4.

2. James Bjork and Robert Gerwarth, 'The Annaberg as a German-Polish *Lieu de Mémoire*', *German History*, 25 (2007), pp. 372–400, p. 374.

3. Korbinian Böck, ' "Bollwerk des Deutschtums im Osten": Das Freikorpsehrenmal auf dem Annaberg / Oberschlesien', *RIHA Journal* (June 2017): https://journals. ub.uni-heidelberg.de/index.php/rihajournal/article/view/70295 (accessed 18 September 2024).

4. 'Letzter Appell der Toten Freikorpskämpfer auf dem Annaberg in Oberschlesien', *Kriegsgräberfürsorge*, May 1938, p. 76.

5. Bernadette Kester, *Film Front Weimar: Representations of the First World War in German Films from the Weimar Period (1919–1933)* (Amsterdam: Amsterdam University Press, 2003).

6. 'Erinnerungsbilder aus englischer Gefangenschaft', *Der Heimkehrer*, 6 May 1920, p. 3. Some of the earliest POW histories include: Bogenstätter and Zimmermann, *Die Welt hinter Stacheldraht*; Sachsse and Cossmann, *Kriegsgefangen in Skipton*.

7. Reichsvereinigung ehem. Kriegsgefangener to Staatsministerium Oldenburg, 15 November 1922, Niedersächsisches Landesarchiv Oldenburg, Best. 136, Nr. 20482. 'Gräberfürsorge', *Der Heimkehrer*, 15 August 1922, p. 3; 'Gräberfürsorge', *Der Heimkehrer*, 15 September 1922, p. 3.

8. On Lersner and the ReK's development, see: Rainer Pöppinghege, ' "Kriegsteilnehmer zweiter Klasse"? Die Reichsvereinigung ehemaliger Kriegsgefangener 1919–1933', *Militärgeschichtliche Zeitschrift*, 64 (2005), pp. 391–423. On the group's political campaigns, see: Jones, *Violence against Prisoners of War*, p. 343; Feltman, *The Stigma of Surrender*, pp. 176–84.

9. 'Mrs Bugg', *East Anglian Daily Times*, 8 December 1914, p. 2.

10. Among the many communities to dedicate a POW memorial were: Dresden (1926), Bleicherode (1929), Bielefeld and Frankfurt (1930), Bonn (1931), Leipzig, Menden and Darmstadt (1932), Bremen (1934).

11. 'Jahresbericht der R.E.K., Ortsgruppe Brambauer für 1929', 21 January 1930, Stadtarchiv Lünen, 07.32, Nr. 9. On the dedication, see: 'Denkmals- und Fahnenweihe der ehem. Kriegsgefangenen in Lünen-Brambauer' (newspaper cutting), September 1929, Stadtarchiv Lünen, 07.32, Nr. 40.

12. For images and a short overview, see: Hansestadt Lübeck, 'Gedenktafel für Carl Hans Lody': https://www.kunst-im-oeffentlichen-raum-luebeck.de/kunstwerke-details/gedenktafel-fuer-carl-hans-lody.html? (accessed 20 October 2023).

13. 'Lübeck weiht ein Karl Hans Lody-Denkmal', *Hamburger Nachrichten*, 6 November 1934, p. 7.

14. 'Carl Lody', *Blyth News*, 3 November 1938, p. 4. 'Week-End Off', *Daily Express*, 3 October 1938, p. 8.

15. 'Englische Frontkämpfer in Westdeutschland', *Hagener Zeitung*, 27 September 1935, p. 10. ReK, 'Bericht über den Besuch der englischen Frontkämpfer in Grundschöttel', 1935, Stadtarchiv Lünen, 07.32, Nr. 53. 'Ex-British Prisoners of War', *Leeds Mercury*, 30 September 1935, p. 1.

16. Amtsbürgermeister Roxel to Landkreis Münster, 25 September 1945, Stadtarchiv Münster, Roxel II, Nr. 1058. More generally, see: Iris Horstmann, Ulrike Junker, Katrin Klusmann and Bernd Ostendorf (eds), *'Wer seine Geschichte nicht kennt . . .': Nationalsozialismus und Münster* (Münster: Agenda, 1993).

17. Neil Gregor, *Haunted City: Nuremberg and the Nazi Past* (New Haven and London: Yale University Press, 2008), pp. 37–62, p. 168.

18. Friederich Heyenga, 'Sammelbrief Nr. 9', 18 Dezember 1948, Stadtarchiv Lünen, 07.40, Nr. 38.

19. Werner Kießling (ed.), *Zur 25 Jahrfeier vom 10. – 11. Mai 1975. Verband der Heimkehrer K.-V. Aschaffenburg* (Aschaffenburg, 1975).

20. Brigit Schwelling, *Heimkehr – Erinnerung – Integration. Der Verband der Heimkehrer, die ehemaligen Kriegsgefangenen, und die westdeutschen Nachkriegsgesellschaft* (Paderborn: Schöningh, 2010), p. 79.

21. Frank Biess, *Homecomings: Returning POWs and the Legacies of Defeat in Postwar Germany* (Princeton: Princeton University Press, 2006), p. 105.

22. Moeller, *War Stories*, pp. 33–4, fig. 13.

23. Maximilian Mühlbauer, *Verband der Heimkehrer. 50 Jahre Ortsverband Amberg, 1949–1999* (Amberg: Verband der Heimkehrer, 1999), p. 63.

24. For the classic study, see: Frei, *Vergangenheitspolitik*.

25. Schwelling, *Heimkehr*, p. 102.

26. F. Niklowitz, 'Mahnplastik "Gedenkt der Gefangenen"', 26 September 2001, Stadtarchiv Lünen, 09.02, Nr. 149.

27. Ulrich Herbert, 'Liberalisierung als Lernprozeß. Die Bundesrepublik in der deutschen Geschichte – eine Skizze', in Ulrich Herbert (ed.), *Wandlungsprozesse in Westdeutschland: Belastung, Integration, Liberalisierung 1945–1980* (Göttingen: Wallstein, 2002), pp. 7–49.

28. Anna Rosmus, *Against the Stream: Growing Up Where Hitler used to Live* (Columbia: University of South Carolina Press, 2002), pp. 5–13.

29. Fredy Niklowitz and Wilfried Heß, 'Lünen', in Frank Göttmann (ed.), *Historisches Handbuch der jüdischen Gemeinschaften in Westfalen und Lippe* (Münster: Ardey, 2016), pp. 547–58.

30. Christoph Friedrich and Ilse Sponsel (eds), *Juden und Judenpogrom 1938 in Erlangen* (Erlangen: Stadtmuseum Erlangen, 1988), pp. 10–15.

31. 'Ein Tag der Schande', *Nürnberger Nachrichten*, 14 September 2010.

32. Fred Kormis, 'P.O.W. Memorial', 1942–48; London Borough of Brent, 'Programme', 11 May 1969, The Wiener Holocaust Library, Nr. 1032. On Kormis, see: 'Kormis at Ninety', *AJR-Information*, 11 November 1984, p. 2.

33. Interview with Fritz Kormis, The Wiener Holocaust Library, 1032/1/110.

34. *Willesden & Barnet Chronicle*, 9 May 1969, p. 1.

35. 'Desecration Worries', *Huddersfield Daily Examiner*, 29 August 1990, p. 3. For the most complete overview of the Kormis memorial, see: Hazel Starmes, 'The Forgotten Holocaust? Post-War Representations of the Non-Jewish Victims in the

United States of America and the United Kingdom' (unpublished PhD thesis, University of Southampton, 2007), pp. 183–91.

36. Kormis's date of birth is given variously as 1894 and 1897: 'A Nonagenarian Artist', *AJR-Information*, February 1985, p. 3.

37. On the association, see: Clare Makepeace, 'For "ALL Who were Captured"? The Evolution of National Ex-Prisoner of War Associations in Britain after the Second World War', *Journal of War & Culture Studies*, 7 (2014), pp. 253–68.

38. 'For Captives Deserve to Suffer', *The Scotsman*, 21 January 2002, p. 3.

39. *Intrepidus: Journal of the National Ex-Prisoner of War Association* (2007), pp. 6, 8–10, 38–9.

40. David Childs, *Growing Remembrance: The Story of the National Memorial Arboretum* (Barnsley: Pen & Sword, 2008), pp. 1–29.

41. 'Our Memorials', The National Memorial Arboretum: https://www.thenma.org. uk/visit-us/what%27s-here/the-memorials/our-memorials (accessed 15 March 2024). Nataliya Danilova, *The Politics of War Commemoration in the UK and Russia* (Basingstoke: Palgrave Macmillan, 2015), p. 65.

42. Noakes, *War and the British*, p. 37; Hewitt, 'Sceptical Generation', p. 93.

43. Robert Hewison, *The Heritage Industry* (London: Methuen, 1987), p. 29.

44. International Bomber Command Centre, *Recognition, Remembrance, Reconciliation* (Norwich: Jigsaw, 2022); Steve Darlow et al., *Our Story, Your History: The International Bomber Command Centre* (Hitchin: Fighting High, 2018), p. 13.

45. For reflections on the garden, see: Patrick Joyce, *Going to My Father's House: A History of My Times* (London: Verso, 2021), p. 169.

46. For the most comprehensive overview, see: Terri Blom Crocker, *The Christmas Truce: Myth, Memory, and the First World War* (Lexington: University Press of Kentucky, 2015).

47. 'A Speech by the Duke of Cambridge at the Unveiling of the Football Remembers Memorial', 14 December 2014, The Royal Household: https://www.royal.uk/ speech-hrh-duke-cambridge-unveiling-football-remembers-memorial (accessed 28 March 2024).

48. On these echoes of memory, see: Jeffrey Olick, *The Politics of Regret: On Collective Memory and Historical Responsibility* (Abingdon: Routledge, 2007), p. 105.

49. International Auschwitz Committee, 'Ten Years of AfD: Increasingly Radical', 6 February 2023: https://www.auschwitz.info/en/press/press-informations/press-information-single/lesen/ten-years-of-afd-increasingly-radical-2782.html (accessed 28 March 2024).

50. Thomas Schaarschmidt, 'Ein Kunstprojekt macht Geschichte: Gunter Demnigs Stolpersteine', in Frank Bösch et al. (eds), *Public Historians: Zeithistorische Interventionen nach 1945* (Göttingen: Wallstein, 2011), pp. 288–300, p. 291.

51. Wolfgang Wippermann, *Denken statt Denkmalen: Gegen den Denkmalwahn der Deutschen* (Berlin: Rotbuch, 2010), p. 144.

52. Ulrike Jureit and Christian Schneider, *Gefühlte Opfer: Illusionen der Vergangenheitsbewältigung* (Stuttgart: Klett-Cotta, 2010), pp. 7–16. For the counter-argument, see: Aleida Assmann, *Das neue Unbehagen an der Erinnerungskultur* (Munich: Beck, 2013).

53. This is the basis of a debate unleashed by Dirk Moses in 2021: A. Dirk Moses, 'Der Katechismus der Deutschen', *Geschichte der Gegenwart*, 23 May 2021: https://geschichtedergegenwart.ch/der-katechismus-der-deutschen/ (accessed 18 September 2024).

54. Eva Bahl et al. (eds), *Decolonize München: Dokumentation und Debatte* (Münster: Edition Assemblage, 2015). See, in particular, the critical work of Jürgen Zimmerer, 'Deutschlands Tor zur Welt: Weltoffenheit und koloniale Amnesie in Hamburg', in Jürgen Zimmerer and Kim Sebastian Todzi (eds), *Hamburg: Tor zur kolonialen Welt: Erinnerungsorte der (post-)kolonialen Globalisierung* (Göttingen: Wallstein, 2021), pp. 15–28.

55. 'Gedenken an Flieger', *Stadt Spiegel*, 4 September 2018.

56. Reynolds, 'Problem of Narrative', p. 217.

57. 'Welcome to the Battle Proms Picnic Concerts', Battle Proms: https://www.battle proms.com/ (accessed 15 July 2024). On the spread of the Second World War in British public life, see the contributions to: Lucy Noakes and Juliette Pattinson (eds), *British Cultural Memory and the Second World War* (London: Bloomsbury, 2014).

58. 'World War One and World War Two Recreations', The Great Dorset Steam Fair: https://www.gdsf.co.uk/attractions/world-war-1-2-commemorations/ (accessed 28 March 2024).

59. Ibid.

60. CWGC to Diocesan Registry, 25 October 1961, Wiltshire and Swindon Archives, D1/61/111/20.

61. 'Memorial Honours War Fallen', *Wilmslow Guardian*, 30 March 2016, p. 12.

Conclusion: The Ghosts of War

1. Reuters, 'About 600 Square Kilometres of Ukraine's Kherson Region under Water after Dam Destroyed, Says Governor', 8 June 2023: https://www.reuters.com/ world/europe/about-600-sq-km-ukraines-kherson-region-under-water-after-dam-destroyed-governor-2023-06-08/ (accessed 15 November 2023).

2. VDK, 'Volksbund prüft Meldungen über Gebeinfunde am zerstörten Kachowka-Staudamm', 13 June 2023: https://www.volksbund.de/nachrichten/volksbund-prueft-meldungen-ueber-gebeinfunde-am-zerstoerten-kachowka-staudamm (accessed 15 November 2023). In more general terms: Christian Hartmann, *Wehrmacht im Ostkrieg: Front und militärisches Hinterland 1941/42* (Munich: Oldenbourg, 2009), pp. 255–6.

3. Tania Delabarde, Christine Keyser, Antoine Tracqui, Damien Charabidze and Bertrand Ludes, 'The Potential of Forensic Analysis on Human Bones Found in Riverine Environment', *Forensic Science International*, 228 (2023), pp. e1–e5.

4. Ministry of Defence, 'World War 2 Airman Finally Laid to Rest 70 Years after He Gave His Life for His Country', 16 March 2017: https://www.gov.uk/govern ment/news/world-war-2-airman-finally-laid-to-rest-70-years-after-he-gave-his-life-for-his-country (accessed 15 November 2023).

5. 'Wolds Memorial Causes Diplomatic Exchange of Letters', *Hull Daily Mail*, 31 August 1938, p. 1; 'Denkmäler, die beseitigt werden sollten', *Schwäbischer Merkur*, 2 September 1938, p. 1. On depictions of the enemy on memorials such as the one in Yorkshire, see: Loretana de Libero, *Rache und Triumph: Krieg, Gefühle und Gedenken in der Moderne* (Berlin: De Gruyter, 2014), p. 213.

6. Judith Butler, *Precarious Life: The Powers of Mourning and Violence* (London: Verso, 2004), pp. 19–49.

7. For example: Mathias Haeussler, *Helmut Schmidt and British–German Relations: A European Misunderstanding* (Cambridge: Cambridge University Press, 2019);

Jeremy Noakes, Peter Wende and Jonathan Wright (eds), *Britain and Germany in Europe 1949–1990* (Oxford: Oxford University Press, 2002); Bernd-Jürgen Wendt (ed.), *Das britische Deutschlandbild im Wandel des 19. und 20. Jahrhunderts* (Bochum: Brockmeyer, 1984).

8. Buonaiuto, 'Grave Reconciliation'.

9. Laqueur, *Work of the Dead*, p. 8.

10. IWGC, 'Bishop's Stortford New Cemetery', 9 June 1953, CWGC/7/4/2/6887.

11. IWGC, Bishop's Stortford Notes, 19 September 1955; IWGC to German Embassy, 24 April 1958, CWGC/7/4/2/6887.

12. The IWGC's efforts to control the dead has been much discussed, see in particular: Heffernan, 'For Ever England', p. 299.

13. Andrea Bradley, 'Designing and Assuring the UK's Largest Ever Human Remains Reburial Programme', HS2 Learning Legacy, 17 September 2020: https://learn inglegacy.hs2.org.uk/document/designing-and-assuring-the-uks-largest-ever-human-remains-reburial-programme/ (accessed 15 November 2023).

14. Mark Skinner, Djordje Alempijevic and Marija Djuric-Srejic, 'Guidelines for International Forensic Bio-Archaeology Monitors of Mass Grave Exhumations', *Forensic Science International,* 134 (2003), pp. 81–92.

15. IWGC Brussels to IWGC Wooburn Green, 26 June 1952, CWGC/7/4/2/19490-1.

16. VDK, 'Gräbersuche-Online: Paul Löhofer': https://www.volksbund.de/erinnern-gedenken/graebersuche-online/detail/f3b25e18e496ae9332f8dce378313d9d (accessed 28 March 2024).

17. German Embassy, 'Besuch der deutschen Kriegergräber in Greenwich Borough Cemetery', 12 November 1929, VDK, R13. IWGC, 'German Combatant Burials in the United Kingdom', 13 February 1936, CWGC/1/1/8/36.

18. 'The Unwelcome Gravediggers', *Daily Herald,* 26 June 1962, p. 7.

19. 'Airmen's Graves' (newspaper cutting), Suffolk Archives, Ipswich, HD1295/2/33.

20. 'Friedhof Lauheide abgeriegelt', *Westfälische Nachrichten,* 9 November 1996.

21. 'We'll Miss Our Corners of a Foreign Field', *Daily Telegraph,* 2 June 2006.

22. On repatriations, see: Sebastian Nieke, 'Die Trauerfeiern des Afghanistaneinsatzes', *IF: Zeitschrift für Innere Führung,* February 2020, pp. 5–11. On the Bundeswehr memorial, see: Manfred Hettling and Jörg Echternkamp (eds), *Bedingt erin-nerungsbereit: Soldatengedenken in der Bundesrepublik* (Göttingen: Vandenhoeck & Ruprecht, 2008).

23. Michael Griffith, *The Speaking Stone: Stories Cemeteries Tell* (Cincinnati: University of Cincinnati Press, 2021).

24. BBC News, 'Afghanistan's "Graveyard of Foreigners"', 9 June 2012: https://www.bbc.co.uk/news/magazine-18369101 (accessed 22 November 2023).

25. On the repatriations through Wootton Bassett, see: Sandra Walklate, Gabe Mythen and Ross McGarry, 'Witnessing Wootton Bassett: An Exploration in Cultural Victimology', *Crime, Media, Culture,* 7 (2011), pp. 149–65.

26. CWGC, 'Welcome to War Graves Week', May 2023: https://www.cwgc.org/war-graves-week/ (accessed 20 November 2023). CWGC, 'Take Part in First Ever War Graves Week', 17 May 2021: https://www.cwgc.org/our-work/news/take-part-in-first-ever-war-graves-week/ (accessed 20 November 2023).

27. On this point, see: Grady, 'A Dance with Death'.

28. According to the Charity Commission, the NMA's income for 2022 was £5.15 million and the IBCC's £2.1 million: https://register-of-charities.charitycommis sion.gov.uk/charity-search/-/charity-details/1043992/charity-overview (accessed

28 March 2024) and: https://register-of-charities.charitycommission.gov.uk/charity-search/-/charity-details/5021212/charity-overview (accessed 28 March 2024).

29. SeaCity Museum Southampton, 'Civil Defence Training Experience', May 2023: https://seacitymuseum.co.uk/events/civil-defence-training-experience/ (accessed 28 March 2024).

30. Kent & East Sussex Railway, '1940s Weekend', May 2024: https://kesr.org.uk/1940s-weekend (accessed 28 March 2024); Grand Central Railway, '1940s Wartime Weekend', June 2023: https://www.gcrailway.co.uk/special-events/wartime (accessed 28 March 2024).

31. 'Councillors Urged to Act over Bury Nazis', *Jewish Chronicle*, 24 June 2010; 'Bury Re-Enactment: Still There Were Nazis', *Jewish Chronicle*, 2 June 2011.

32. Out of 82 standard gauge heritage railways, 63 have staged wartime-themed days or weekends since 2010.

33. BBC News, 'New French WWI Memorial Focuses on Individuals, Not Nations', 11 November 2014: https://www.bbc.co.uk/news/blogs-eu-29991019 (accessed 20 November 2023). More generally: Sabina Tanović, *Designing Memory: The Architecture of Commemoration, 1914 to the Present* (Cambridge: Cambridge University Press, 2019), pp. 205–13.

BIBLIOGRAPHY

Archival Sources

Archiv der deutschen Jugendbewegung, Witzenhausen

A228   Archiv der Jugendmusikbewegung

Auswärtiges Amt – Politisches Archiv, Berlin (PA-AA)

B 10-ABT.2   Politische Abteilung
B 92-REF.602/IV3   Kirchliche Beziehungen zum Ausland
RZ 407   Wehrpflicht/Arbeitsdienst, Kriegsfolgen

Bundesarchiv, Berlin (BArch Berlin)

R67   Archiv für deutsche Kriegsgefangene des Frankfurter Vereins
                               vom Roten Kreuz und für Kriegsgefangenenforschung
R901   Auswärtiges Amt

Bundesarchiv Militärarchiv, Freiburg

PH2   Preußisches Kriegsministerium

Cheshire Record Office, Chester

NHM/8   Parkside Lunatic Asylum

Commonwealth War Graves Commission Archive, Maidenhead (CWGC)

CWGC/1/1/5   Treatment of Graves and Cemeteries
CWGC/1/1/6   Relations with Foreign Governments
CWGC/1/1/7   Care of Graves and Cemeteries of British and Empire War
                               Casualties
CWGC/1/1/8   Care of Non-British Empire Graves by the Commission

329

CWGC/1/2/A   'A' Files
CWGC/1/2/D   'Add' Files
CWGC/1/2/E   'CM' Files
CWGC/2/2   Commission Meeting Minutes
CWGC/7/3   Cemetery and Memorials Design and Construction
CWGC/7/4/1   RA Files
CWGC/7/4/2   Cemetery Files
CWGC/8/1   Casualty Archive

Cornwall Record Office, Redruth

P61   St Eval Parish Church

East Sussex Record Office, Brighton

SPA/1/1   Wartime Sussex Police Force

Hessisches Staatsarchiv, Marburg

Bestand 165   Preußische Regierung Kassel
Bestand 330   Stadt Zierenberg

Historisches Archiv der Stadt Köln, Cologne

Best. 756, A20   Englischer Friedhof

Imperial War Museum Archive, London (IWM)

HU   Bond of Sacrifice – First World War Portraits Collection
Documents, 9046   Air Ministry's Missing Research and Enquiry Unit

International Bomber Command Centre, Lincoln (IBCC)

Andrew Bain Collection
Peter and Lesley Jenkinson Collection
Ernest Henry Tansley Collection
John Valentine Collection
John Warren Collection

Jersey Archive, St Helier

B/A/W56   Bailiff's Chamber Occupation Files
D/S/A/13   Registration and Identification of Persons

Kendal Oral History Group

0070   Interview with Marie Trapp

London Metropolitan Archive

DL   Diocese of London

BIBLIOGRAPHY

Manx National Heritage, Douglas

M 06104	Camp Reports
MS 10855	Diocesan Deposits

Mass Observation Archive, Brighton

D5205	Diarist
DS409, DS080	Day Respondent Surveys
FR276	Supplementary Reports

The National Archives, Kew (TNA)

AIR 2	Air Ministry: Registered Files
AIR 20	Air Ministry: Air Historical Branch
AIR 29	Air Ministry: Operations Records Books
CAB 128	Cabinet Minutes
FCO 33	Foreign Office: Western European Department
FO 369	Foreign Office: Consular Department
FO 371	Foreign Office: General Correspondence
FO 383	Foreign Office: Prisoners of War and Aliens Department
FO 1006	Foreign Office: Control Commission for Germany
HO 282	Home Office: Burials and Cremation
HO 396	Home Office: Aliens Department
MEPO 2	Metropolitan Police: Correspondence and Papers
WO 32	War Office: Registered Files
WO 171	War Office: Allied Expeditionary Force
WO 235	War Office: Records of the Judge Advocate General
WO 309	War Office: British Army of the Rhine War Crimes Group

National Records of Scotland, Edinburgh

HH61	Local Authority Health Services
SC1	Aberdeen Sheriff Court
SC7	Kilmarnock Sheriff Court

Niedersächsisches Landesarchiv, Hanover

Nds. 120 Lüneburg	Regierungspräsident Lüneburg
Nds. 120 Hannover	Bezirksregierung Hannover

Niedersächsisches Landesarchiv, Oldenburg

Best. 136	Oldenburgisches Innenministerium
Best. 230-12	Verwaltungsamt Friesoythe

Norfolk Record Office, Norwich

PD 108	Parish Records of Kenninghall
PD 119	Parish Records of Starston

BIBLIOGRAPHY

North Devon Record Office, Barnstaple

B723/OHA   Exmoor Oral History Archive Recordings

Oswestry Town Council Archives

OTC/10   Oswestry Cemetery

Staatsarchiv Hamburg (StAHH)

325-1   Friedhofsverwaltung

Staatsarchiv Munich

BezA/LRA   Bezirksamt / Landratsamt Tölz

Stadtarchiv Celle

Best. 16   Kirche und Friedhöfe

Stadtarchiv Lünen

07.32   Reichsvereinigung ehem. Kriegsteilnehmer, Brambauer
07.40   Verband der Heimkehrer, Ortsverband Brambauer
09.02   Denkmäler

Stadtarchiv Münster

Amt 32   Ordnungsamt
Amt 67   Gartenbauamt
Roxel II   Amtsarchiv Roxel

Stadtarchiv Wiesbaden

WI/3   Landeshauptstadt Wiesbaden

Stadtarchiv Worms

005/1   Stadtverwaltung Worms

Staffordshire Record Office, Stafford

D4768   Records of Friends of Cannock Chase
C/C/PR   Staffordshire County Council: Public Relations
CC/B   Staffordshire County Council: Committee Minutes

Suffolk Archives, Ipswich

FC70   Theberton Parish
FC205   Clopton Parish
HD1295   Papers of Stanley Frederick Lindley

BIBLIOGRAPHY

Tower Museum Archive, Derry-Londonderry

DMS 2017   Barr Collection

Unilever Archives, Port Sunlight

GB1752.UNI/BD/2/1/1   William Lever Speeches and Writings

Volksbund Deutsche Kriegsgräberfürsorge, Kassel (VDK)

A10   Geschäftsleitung / Vorstand
A11   Gremien des Vereins
A100   Gesellschaft
C1   Volkstrauertag
R13   Deutsche Botschaft London

The Wiener Holocaust Library, London

1032   Fred Kormis Collection

Wiltshire and Swindon Archives, Chippenham

PR/Sutton Veny   Parish Records of St Leonard and St John the Evangelist
D1   Records of the Bishop of Salisbury
PR132   Parish Records of Fovant St George

Worcestershire Archive, Worcester

850shelsleywalsh Shelsley Walsh Parish Records
713-829   Diocese of Worcester

Newspapers

Aberdeen Evening Express, 1961–1962
Aberdeen Press and Journal, 1916, 1941
AJR-Information, 1984–1985
Army and Navy Gazette, 1922
Belfast News-Letter, 1945
Belfast Telegraph, 1967
Berliner Börsen-Zeitung, 1919
Berliner Tageblatt, 1909
Birmingham Post, 1959
Blyth News, 1938
Bognor Regis Observer, 1918
Bonner Nachrichten, 1942
Border Counties Advertiser, 1963
Bremer Nachrichten, 1971
Bury Free Press, 1946
Cheshire Observer, 1967
Chester Chronicle, 1914

The Cologne Post, 1919–1921
Corby Leader, 1963
The Cornishman, 1926
Coventry Evening Telegraph, 1945
Crawley and District Observer, 1952
Daily Express, 1938
Daily Herald, 1937, 1962
Daily Mirror, 1926, 1928, 1934, 1948
Daily News, 1920, 1929
Daily Telegraph, 1946, 1990, 2006
Derby Daily Telegraph, 1945
The Derbyshire Advertiser, 1915
Derbyshire Times, 1928
Dorset County Chronicle, 1915, 1920
Dortmunder Zeitung, 1914
Dresdner Volkszeitung, 1914
Dundee Courier, 1926, 1941, 1954
Dundee Evening Telegraph, 1915, 1919, 1945
East Anglian Daily Times, 1914
Edinburgh Evening News, 1939
Der Erft-Bote, 1939
Evening Star, 14 June 1983
Flintshire Observer, 1914
Frankfurter Rundschau, 1959
Der Führer: Das Haupt Organ der NSDAP Gau Baden, 1942
General-Anzeiger der Stadt Mannheim und Umgebung, 1909
Gloucester Citizen, 1934
Gloucestershire Echo, 1919
Grange Now, 1999
Guernsey Evening Press, 1961
Hagener Zeitung, 1935
Hakenkreuzbanner, 1934, 1938
Hamburger Nachrichten, 1917, 1933–1935
Der Heimkehrer, 1920, 1922, 1934
Herts and Essex Observer, 1955
Huddersfield Daily Examiner, 1990
Hull Daily Mail, 1914, 1938, 1947
Intrepidus: Journal of the National Ex-Prisoner of War Association, 2007
Isle of Man Examiner, 1914–1916, 1921
Jersey Evening Post, 1961
Jewish Chronicle, 1916, 2010, 2011
John Bull, 1933
Journal of the Chemical Society, 1918
Kölner Lokal-Anzeiger, 1928–1929
Kölnische Zeitung, 1909, 1914, 1929, 1935
Kriegsgräberfürsorge, 1921–1922, 1934, 1938, 1948, 1951–1952, 1955, 1959–1960,
    1971
Lancashire Evening Post, 1916
Leeds Mercury, 1935–1937

Leicester Daily Mercury, 1919, 1939
Leicester Journal, 1919
Lichfield Mercury, 1967
Liverpool Echo, 1956–1957
London Sentinel, 1946
Louth Standard, 1960
Manchester Evening News, 1914, 1918, 1949
Montrose Standard, 1941
Newcastle Journal, 1962
Neue Berliner Illustrierte, 1959
Neue Jüdische Presse, 1921
Neue Mannheimer Zeitung, 1936
Der neue Tag, 1939
Neues Deutschland, 1987
Newcastle Evening Chronicle, 1940
Niederrheinisches Tageblatt, 1916
Norddeutsche Allgemeine Zeitung, 1909
North Devon Journal, 1947
Northern Daily Telegraph, 1914
Nottingham Evening Post, 1919, 1947
Nottingham Journal, 1945
Nürnberger Nachrichten, 2010
Ostbremer Rundschau, 1971
Der Patriot, 1936
Peel City Guardian, 1914
Pester Lloyd, 1936
Portsmouth Evening News, 1959
Rugeley Times, 1955, 1961
Runcorn Guardian, 1914
Runcorn Weekly News, 1956, 1960
Salzburger Volksblatt, 1919
Schwäbischer Merkur, 1938
The Scotsman, 1918, 1937, 1940, 1966, 2002
Sheffield Independent, 1917
Shields Daily News, 1914
Simplicissimus, 1911
The Sketch, 1914
Southern Reporter, 2018
Stadt Spiegel, 2018
Staffordshire Advertiser, 1946–1948
Staffordshire Newsletter, 1946, 1962, 1967
Staffordshire Sentinel, 1954, 1965
Stapleford & Sandiacre News, 1928
Stimme und Weg, 1963, 1965
Stobsiade, 1919
Stuttgarter Neues Tageblatt, 1939
Sunday Express, 1940
Swindon Echo, 1963
Tägliche Rundschau, 1926

BIBLIOGRAPHY

The Tatler, 1914
Teltower Kreisblatt, 1935
The Times, 1914, 1919–1920, 1934–1936, 1939, 1945–1947
Uttoxeter Newsletter, 1987
Völkischer Beobachter, 1944
Volkswille, 1919
Vorwärts, 1919
Walsall Observer, 1928, 1962
Weekly Dispatch, 1934, 1952
Die Welt, 1951
Westfälische Nachrichten, 1996
Westfälische Tageszeitung, 1941
West Middlesex Gazette, 1933
Western Independent, 1963
Westminster Gazette, 1909
Western Mail, 1936, 1946
Western Morning Post, 1927
Willesden & Barnet Chronicle, 1969
Wilmslow Guardian, 2016
Woman's Dreadnought, 1917
Yorkshire Evening Press, 1919, 1945, 1954
Yorkshire Observer, 1936

Oral Histories

Interview between Tim Grady and M.A. Rawley [pseudonym], Norfolk, 31 August
    2019
Imperial War Museum Oral History Recordings: 20456, 4896, 10767, 13573,
    21101, 26527, 27051

Published Primary Sources

Bahl, Eva, et al. (eds), *Decolonize München: Dokumentation und Debatte* (Münster:
    Edition Assemblage, 2015).
Benz, Wolfgang and Angelika Schardt (eds), *Kriegsgefangenschaft: Berichte über das
    Leben in Gefangenenlagern der Alliierten* (Munich: Oldenbourg, 1991).
Bielenberg, Christabel, *The Past is Myself* (London: Chatto & Windus, 1968).
Bielenberg, Peter Heinrich, in Jamie Bulloch (ed.), 'Peter Heinrich Bielenberg: 13
    December 1911–12 March 2001' (Marlborough, 2002).
Bogenstätter, Ludwig, and Heinrich Zimmermann, *Die Welt hinter Stacheldraht: Eine
    Kronik des englischen Kriegsgefangenlagers Handforth bei Manchester* (Munich: Piloty
    & Löhle, 1921).
Buckley, Anne (ed.), *German Prisoners of War in Great Britain: Life in a Yorkshire
    Camp* (Barnsley: Pen & Sword, 2021).
Caine, Hall, *The Woman of Knockaloe: A Parable* (Toronto: Ryerson Press, 1923).
Chesney, George Tomkyns, *The Battle of Dorking* (London: Blackwood's, 1871).
Childers, Erskine, *Riddle of the Sands* (London: Smith, Elder & Co., 1903).
Childs, David, *Growing Remembrance: The Story of the National Memorial Arboretum*
    (Barnsley: Pen & Sword, 2008).

Commonwealth War Graves Commission, 'Report of the Special Committee to Review Historical Inequalities in Commemoration' (Maidenhead, 2021).

'Correspondence with the German Government Respecting the Death by Burning of J.P. Genower, Able Seaman, when Prisoner of War at Brandenburg Camp', Miscellaneous, No. 6. (London: His Majesty's Stationery Office, 1918).

Darlow, Steve, et al., *Our Story, Your History: The International Bomber Command Centre* (Hitchin: Fighting High, 2018).

Deutsche Gartenstadt-Gesellschaft (ed.), *Aus englischen Gartenstädten* (Berlin: Renaissance, 1910).

Deutsches Reichsgesetzblatt (Berlin, 1923).

Eden, Anthony, *The Eden Memoirs: Facing the Dictators* (London: Cassell, 1962).

Gerard, James W., *My Four Years in Germany* (New York: Hodder & Stoughton, 1917).

Government Committee on the Treatment by the Enemy of British Prisoners (ed.), *The Horrors of Wittenberg: Official Report to the British Government* (London: Pearson, 1916).

Hardy, Florence Emily, *The Later Years of Thomas Hardy 1892–1928* (London: Macmillan, 1930).

Hillson, Norman, *I Speak of Germany: A Plea for Anglo-German Friendship* (London: Routledge, 1937).

House of Commons, *Hansard's Parliamentary Debates: The Official Report* (London: Hansard).

International Bomber Command Centre, *Recognition, Remembrance, Reconciliation* (Norwich: Jigsaw, 2022).

IWGC, 'Annual Report of the Imperial War Graves Commission, 1919–1920' (London: His Majesty's Stationery Office, 1920).

IWGC, *Fourth Annual Report of the Imperial War Graves Commission 1922–1923* (London: His Majesty's Stationery Office, 1923).

Johnson, Gaynor (ed.), *Our Man in Berlin: The Diary of Sir Eric Phipps, 1933–1937* (Basingstoke: Palgrave, 2008).

Kenyon, Frederic, 'War Graves: How the Cemeteries Abroad will be Designed' (London: His Majesty's Stationery Office, 1918).

Kießling, Werner (ed.), *Zur 25 Jahrfeier vom 10. – 11. Mai 1975. Verband der Heimkehrer K.-V. Aschaffenburg* (Aschaffenburg, 1975).

Kipling, Rudyard, 'The Graves of the Fallen' (Imperial War Graves Commission, 1919).

Kipling, Rudyard, 'Mary Postgate', in Rudyard Kipling, *A Diversity of Creatures* (London: Macmillan, 1917), pp. 419–41.

Le Queux, William, *The Invasion of 1910* (London: Macmillan, 1906).

McIlraith, Frank, and Roy Connolly, *Invasion from the Air: A Prophetic Novel* (London: Grayson & Grayson, 1934).

Masterman, J.C., *On the Chariot Wheel: An Autobiography* (Oxford: Oxford University Press, 1975).

Ministry of Transport, 'Report on the Collision which occurred on the 17th September, 1947, at the Burton Agnes Level Crossing on the London and North Eastern Railway' (London: His Majesty's Stationery Office, 1947).

Mühlbauer, Maximilian, *Verband der Heimkehrer. 50 Jahre Ortsverband Amberg, 1949–1999* (Amberg: Verband der Heimkehrer, 1999).

Niklowitz, Fredy and Wilfried Heß, 'Lünen', in Frank Göttmann (ed.), *Historisches Handbuch der jüdischen Gemeinschaften in Westfalen und Lippe* (Münster: Ardey, 2016), pp. 547–58.

Powell, Joseph, and Francis Gribble, *The History of Ruhleben: A Record of British Organisation in a Prison Camp in Germany* (London: W. Collins, 1919).

Rosmus, Anna, *Against the Stream: Growing Up Where Hitler Used to Live* (Columbia: University of South Carolina Press, 2002).

Sachsse, Fritz, and Willy Cossmann, *Kriegsgefangen in Skipton: Leben und Geschichte deutscher Kriegsgefangener in einem englischen Lager* (Munich: Reinhardt, 1920).

Schnur, David (ed.), *Tagebücher eines Stadtarchivars. Die Schwäbisch Gmünder. Kriegschronik von Albert Diebele (1939–1945)* (Schwäbisch Gmünd: Stadtarchiv Schwäbisch Gmünd, 2020).

Stampfer, Friedrich, *Erfahrungen und Erkenntnisse* (Cologne: Verlag für Politik und Wissenschaft, 1958).

Taylor, Eric, *Combat Nurse* (London: Robert Hale, 1999).

Torrance, Duncan Leitch, *Desert to Danube* (Berwick: Torrance, 2010).

Vischer, Adolf Lukas, *Die Stacheldraht-Krankheit: Beiträge zur Psychologie des Kriegsgefangenen* (Zürich: 1918).

Wingfield-Stratford, Esmé, 'Before the Lights Went Out', in I.F. Clarke (ed.), *The Great War with Germany, 1890–1914* (Liverpool: Liverpool University Press, 1997), pp. 256–8.

Websites

Aircraft Accidents in Yorkshire: www.yorkshire-aircraft.co.uk

Arolsen Archives: https://collections.arolsen-archives.org

BBC News: https://www.bbc.co.uk/news

BBC Radio 4, 'Desert Island Discs': https://www.bbc.co.uk/programmes/b006qnmr

HS2 Learning Legacy: https://learninglegacy.hs2.org.uk

British Pathé: https://www.britishpathe.com

Charity Commission: https://register-of-charities.charitycommission.gov.uk

Commonwealth War Graves Commission: https://www.cwgc.org

Foreign, Commonwealth and Development Office: https://www.gov.uk/guidance/uk-treaties

Grand Central Railway: https://www.gcrailway.co.uk

The Great Dorset Steam Fair: https://www.gdsf.co.uk

The Guardian: https://www.theguardian.com

International Auschwitz Committee: https://www.auschwitz.info

International Encyclopedia of the First World War: https://encyclopedia.1914-1918-online.net

International Humanitarian Law Databases: https://ihl-databases.icrc.org/en

Kent & East Sussex Railway: https://kesr.org.uk

Kunst im öffentlichen Raum Lübeck: https://www.kunst-im-oeffentlichen-raum-luebeck.de

Manx National Heritage: https://www.imuseum.im

Ministry of Defence: https://www.gov.uk/government/organisations/ministry-of-defence

The National Memorial Arboretum: https://www.thenma.org.uk

Oxford Dictionary of National Biography: https://www.oxforddnb.com/

Prisoners of the First World War, the International Committee of the Red Cross Archives: https://grandeguerre.icrc.org/en
Returned from the Front: http://thereturned.co.uk
Reuters: https://www.reuters.com
Royal Household: https://www.royal.uk
SeaCity Museum Southampton, 'Civil Defence Training Experience', May 2023: https://seacitymuseum.co.uk
Stalag XIC (311) and KZ Bergen-Belsen: http://www.bergenbelsen.co.uk
SWR2: https://www.swr.de
Tripadvisor: https://www.tripadvisor.co.uk
United Kingdom Legislation: https://www.legislation.gov.uk
United Nations Library: https://www.un-ilibrary.org/
Volksbund Deutsche Kriegsgräberfürsorge: https://www.volksbund.de

Secondary Sources

Adam, Thomas, *Transnational Philanthropy: The Mond Family's Support for Public Institutions in Western Europe from 1890 to 1938* (Basingstoke: Palgrave, 2016).

Adriansen, Inge, *Demkal und Dynamit: DenkmälerSTREIT im deutsch-dänischen Grenzland* (Neumünster: Wachholtz, 2011).

Aldrich, Richard, 'Waiting to be Kissed? NATO, NORTHAG, and Intelligence', in Jan Hoffenaar and Dieter Krüger (eds), *Blueprints for Battle: Planning for War in Central Europe, 1948–1968* (Lexington: University Press of Kentucky, 2012), pp. 55–74.

Alexander, Kristen and Kate Ariotti, 'Mourning the Dead of the Great Escape: POWs, Grief, and the Memorial Vault of Stalag Luft III', *Journal of War & Culture Studies*, 16 (2022), pp. 1–22.

Anderson, Benedict, *Imagined Communities: Reflections on the Origin and Spread of Nationalism* (London: Verso, 1983).

Arnold, Jörg, *The Allied Air War and Urban Memory: The Legacy of Strategic Bombing in Germany* (Cambridge: Cambridge University Press, 2011).

Assmann, Aleida, *Das neue Unbehagen an der Erinnerungskultur* (Munich: Beck, 2013).

Audoin-Rouzeau, Stéphane, and Annette Becker, *Understanding the Great War, 14–18* (New York: Hill and Wang, 2002).

Barnes, James, and Patience Barnes, *Nazis in Pre-War London 1930–1939: The Fate and Role of German Party Members and British Sympathizers* (Brighton: Sussex Academic Press, 2005).

Barr, Niall, ' "The Legion that Sailed but Never Went": The British Legion and the Munich Crisis of 1938', in Julia Eichenberg and John Paul Newman (eds), *The Great War and Veterans' Internationalism* (Basingstoke: Palgrave, 2013), pp. 32–52.

Barr, Niall, *The Lion and the Poppy: British Veterans, Politics, and Society, 1921–1939* (Westport: Praeger, 2005).

Barrett, Michèle, 'Subalterns at War: First World War Colonial Forces and the Politics of the Imperial War Graves Commission', *Interventions*, 9 (2007), pp. 451–74.

Bauerkämper, Arnd, *Sicherheit und Humanität im Ersten und Zweiten Weltkrieg*. Band 1: *Erster Weltkrieg* (Oldenbourg: De Gruyter, 2021).

Beckett, Ian, *The Making of the First World War* (New Haven and London: Yale University Press, 2012).

BIBLIOGRAPHY

Behrenbeck, Sabine, *Der Kult um die toten Helden: nationalsozialistische Mythen, Riten und Symbole 1929 bis 1945* (Vierow: SH-Verlag, 1996).

Berger, Stefan, and Norman LaPorte, *Friendly Enemies: Britain and the GDR, 1949–1990* (New York: Berghahn, 2010).

Bessel, Richard, *Germany after the First World War* (Oxford: Oxford University Press, 1993).

Bessel, Richard, 'The Shadow of Death in Germany at the End of the Second World War', in Alon Confino, Dirk Schumann and Paul Betts (eds), *Between Mass Death and Individual Loss: The Place of the Dead in Twentieth-Century Germany* (Oxford: Berghahn, 2008), pp. 50–68.

Biess, Frank, *Homecomings: Returning POWs and the Legacies of Defeat in Postwar Germany* (Princeton: Princeton University Press, 2006).

Bjork, James, and Robert Gerwarth, 'The Annaberg as a German-Polish *Lieu de Mémoire*', *German History*, 25 (2007), pp. 372–400.

Black, Monica, *Death in Berlin: From Weimar to Divided Berlin* (Cambridge: Cambridge University Press, 2010).

Blackbourn, David, '"As dependent on each other as man and wife": Cultural Contacts and Transfers', in Dominik Geppert and Robert Gerwarth (eds), *Wilhelmine Germany and Edwardian Britain: Essays on Cultural Affinity* (Oxford: Oxford University Press, 2008), pp. 15–37.

Böck, Korbinian, '"Bollwerk des Deutschtums im Osten": Das Freikorpsehrenmal auf dem Annaberg / Oberschlesien', *RIHA Journal* (June 2017): https://journals.ub.uni-heidelberg.de/index.php/rihajournal/article/view/70295.

Böhme, Werner, 'Siegfried Emmo Eulen', *Niedersächsische Lebensbilder*, 6 (1969), pp. 143–59.

Böttcher, Jakob, *Zwischen staatlichem Auftrag und gesellschaftlicher Trägerschaft. Eine Geschichte der Kriegsgräberfürsorge in Deutschland im 20. Jahrhundert* (Göttingen: Vandenhoeck & Ruprecht, 2018).

Bourke, Joanna, *Dismembering the Male: Men's Bodies, Britain and the Great War* (London: Reaktion, 1996).

Bulfin, Ailise, 'The International Circulation and Impact of Invasion Literature', *Critical Survey*, 32 (2020), pp. 159–92.

Buonaiuto, Zoe Rose, 'A Grave Reconciliation: The Establishment of German War Cemeteries in Normandy, 1944–1964', *International Journal of Military History and Historiography*, 38 (2018), pp. 170–95.

Butler, Judith, *Frames of War: When is Life Grievable?* (London: Verso, 2010).

Butler, Judith, *Precarious Life: The Powers of Mourning and Violence* (London: Verso, 2004),

Caglioti, Daniela, *War and Citizenship: Enemy Aliens and National Belonging from the French Revolution to the First World War* (Cambridge: Cambridge University Press, 2020).

Calder, Angus, *The Myth of the Blitz* (London: Jonathan Cape, 1991).

Carr, Gilly, 'The Small Things of Life and Death: An Exploration of Value and Material Culture of Nazi Camps', *International Journal of Historical Archaeology*, 22 (2018), pp. 531–52.

Clark, Christopher, *The Sleepwalkers: How Europe Went to War in 1914* (London: Penguin, 2013).

Clemens, Detlev, *Herr Hitler in Germany. Wahrnehmung und Deutungen des Nationalsozialismus in Großbritannien 1920 bis 1939* (Göttingen: Vandenhoeck & Ruprecht, 1996).

BIBLIOGRAPHY

Cohen, J.M., *The Life of Ludwig Mond* (London: Methuen, 1956).

Confino, Alon, 'Traveling as a Culture of Remembrance: Traces of National Socialism in West Germany, 1945–1960', *History & Memory*, 12 (2000), pp. 92–121.

Coontz, Stephanie, *Marriage, a History: How Love Conquered Marriage* (London: Penguin, 2005).

Crane, David, *Empires of the Dead: How One Man's Vision Led to the Creation of WWI's War Graves* (London: Collins, 2014).

Crocker, Terri Blom, *The Christmas Truce: Myth, Memory, and the First World War* (Lexington: University Press of Kentucky, 2015).

Custodis, Johann, 'Employing the Enemy: The Contribution of German and Italian Prisoners of War to British Agriculture during and after the Second World War', *Agricultural History Review*, 60 (2012), pp. 243–65.

Daalen, Marjolijn van, 'An Aquatic Decomposition Scoring Method to Potentially Predict the Postmortem Submersion Interval of Bodies Recovered from the North Sea', *Journal of Forensic Sciences*, 62 (2) (2017), pp. 369–73.

Danilova, Nataliya, *The Politics of War Commemoration in the UK and Russia* (Basingstoke: Palgrave Macmillan, 2015).

Das, Santanu, *Touch and Intimacy in First World War Literature* (Cambridge: Cambridge University Press, 2006).

David, Rob, ' "Once a German always a German": Attitudes to People of German and Austrian Extraction in Cumbria During the First World War', *Transactions of the Cumberland & Westmorland Antiquarian & Archaeological Society*, 16 (2016), pp. 73–93.

Delabarde, Tania, Christine Keyser, Antoine Tracqui, Damien Charabidze and Bertrand Ludes, 'The Potential of Forensic Analysis on Human Bones Found in Riverine Environment', *Forensic Science International*, 228 (2023), pp. e1–e5.

Dendooven, Dominiek, ' "Bringing the Dead Home": Repatriation, Illegal Repatriation and Expatriation of British Bodies during and after the First World War', in Paul Cornish and Nicholas Saunders (eds) *Bodies in Conflict: Corporeality, Materiality and Transformation* (New York: Routledge, 2014), pp. 66–79.

Dick, Charles, *Builders of the Third Reich: The Organisation Todt and Nazi Forced Labour* (London: Bloomsbury, 2020).

Dixon, Simon, *The Island of Extraordinary Captives: A True Story of an Artist, a Spy and a Wartime Scandal* (London: Sceptre, 2022).

Dreyfus, Jean-Marc, 'Renationalizing Bodies? The French Search Mission for the Corpses of Deportees in Germany, 1946–58', in Elisabeth Anstett and Jean-Marc Dreyfus (eds), *Human Remains and Violence: Methodological Approaches* (Manchester: Manchester University Press, 2014), pp. 129–45.

Dziuban, Zuzanna (ed.), *Mapping the 'Forensic Turn': Engagements with Materialities of Mass Death in Holocaust Studies and Beyond* (Vienna: New Academic Press, 2017).

Edwards, Sam, 'An Empire of Memory: Overseas British War Cemeteries, 1917–1983', *International Journal of Military History and Historiography*, 38 (2018), pp. 255–86.

Eisenberg, Carolyn, *Drawing the Line: The American Decision to Divide Germany* (Cambridge: Cambridge University Press, 1996).

Eley, Geoff, 'Finding the People's War: Film, British Collective Memory, and World War II', *American Historical Review*, 106 (3) (2001), pp. 818–38.

Emden, Richard van, *The Quick and the Dead: Fallen Soldiers and the Families in the Great War* (London: Bloomsbury, 2011).

Fell, Alison, 'Far from Home? Perceptions and Experiences of the First World War Nurses and Their Patients', in Alan Beyerchen and Emre Sencer (eds), *Expeditionary Forces in the First World War* (Basingstoke: Palgrave, 2019), pp. 57–78.

Fell, Alison, 'Nursing the Enemy in the First World War', *European Journal for Nursing History and Ethics* (2022), pp. 1–23.

Fell, Alison, and Susan Grayzel, 'Women's Movements, War and the Body', in Ingrid Sharp and Matthew Stibbe (eds), *Women Activists between War and Peace: Europe 1918–1923* (London: Bloomsbury, 2017), pp. 221–49.

Feltman, Brian, *The Stigma of Surrender: German Prisoners, British Captors, and Manhood in the Great War and Beyond* (Chapel Hill: University of North Carolina Press, 2015).

Fleming, Gerald, *Hitler and the Final Solution* (Berkeley: University of California Press, 1987).

Forwick, Helmuth, 'Zur Behandlung alliierter Kriegsgefangener im Zweiten Weltkrieg', *Militärgeschichtliche Mitteilungen*, 2 (1967), pp. 119–34.

Foschepoth, Josef, 'Westintegration statt Wiedervereinigung: Adenauers Deutschlandpolitik 1949–1955', in Josef Foschepoth (ed.), *Adenauer und die deutsche Frage* (Göttingen: Vandenhoeck & Ruprecht, 1988), pp. 29–60.

Foster, Ann-Marie, 'The Bureaucratization of Death: The First World War, Families, and the State', *Twentieth Century British History*, 33 (2022), pp. 475–97.

Fowler, Corinne, *Green Unpleasant Land: Creative Responses to Rural England's Colonial Connections* (Leeds: Peepal, 2020).

Francis, Doris, Leonie Kellaher and Georgina Neophytou, 'Sustaining Cemeteries: The User Perspective', *Mortality*, 5 (2000), pp. 34–52.

Francis, Martin, *The Flyer: British Culture and the Royal Airforce, 1939–1945* (Oxford: Oxford University Press, 2008).

Frei, Norbert, *1945 und wir: Das Dritte Reich im Bewußtsein der Deutschen* (Munich: Beck, 2005).

Frei, Norbert, *Vergangenheitspolitik: Die Anfänge der Bundesrepublik und die NS-Vergangenheit* (Munich: Beck, 1996).

Frevert, Ute, *Emotions in History – Lost and Found* (Budapest: Central European University Press, 2011).

Friedrich, Christoph, and Ilse Sponsel (eds), *Juden und Judenpogrom 1938 in Erlangen* (Erlangen: Stadtmuseum Erlangen, 1988).

Fritzsche, Peter, *A Nation of Fliers: German Aviation and the Popular Imagination* (Cambridge, MA: Harvard University Press, 1992).

Fry, Helen, *The London Cage: The Secret History of Britain's World War II Interrogation Centre* (New Haven and London: Yale University Press, 2017).

Gillman, Peter, and Leni Gillman, *'Collar the Lot!' How Britain Interned and Expelled its Wartime Refugees* (London: Quartet, 1980).

Gilroy, Paul, *Postcolonial Melancholia* (New York: Columbia University Press, 2005).

Goebel, Stefan, 'Commemorative Cosmopolis: Transnational Networks of Remembrance in Post-War Coventry', in Stefan Goebel and Derek Keene (eds), *Cities into Battlefields: Metropolitan Scenarios, Experiences and Commemorations of Total War* (Farnham: Ashgate, 2011), pp. 163–83.

Goldstein, Erik, 'Great Britain: The Home Front', in Manfred Boemeke, Gerald Feldman and Elisabeth Glaser (eds), *The Treaty of Versailles: A Reassessment after 75 Years* (Cambridge: Cambridge University Press, 1998), pp. 147–66.

Gough, Paul, 'Corporations and Commemoration: First World War Remembrance, Lloyds TSB and the National Memorial Arboretum', *International Journal of Heritage Studies*, 10 (2004), pp. 435–55.

Grady, Tim, 'A Dance with Death: The Imperial War Graves Commission and Nazi Germany', *The English Historical Review*, 138 (2023), pp. 1307–36.

Grady, Tim, 'Dying with the Enemy: Prisoners of War Deaths in First World War Britain', in Holly Furneaux and Matilda Greig (eds), *Enemy Encounters in Modern Warfare* (Basingstoke: Palgrave, 2024), pp. 173–93.

Grady, Tim, *The German-Jewish Soldiers of the First World War in History and Memory* (Liverpool: Liverpool University Press, 2011).

Gray, Jennie, '"Nothing Can Excuse Us if We Fail": The British and their Dead Servicemen, North-West Europe, 1944–1951' (unpublished PhD, University of Exeter, 2016).

Gregor, Neil, *Haunted City: Nuremberg and the Nazi Past* (New Haven and London: Yale University Press, 2008).

Gregor, Neil, '"Is he still alive, or long since dead?": Loss, Absence and Remembrance in Nuremberg, 1945–1956', *German History*, 21 (2003), pp. 183–203.

Gregory, Adrian, *The Last Great War: British Society and the First World War* (Cambridge: Cambridge University Press, 2008).

Green, Jennifer, and Michael Green, *Dealing with Death: A Handbook of Practices, Procedures and Law* (London: Jessica Kingsley, 2006).

Griffith, Michael, *The Speaking Stone: Stories Cemeteries Tell* (Cincinnati: University of Cincinnati Press, 2021).

Grimm, Barbara, 'Lynchmorde an alliierten Fliegern im Zweiten Weltkrieg', in Dietmar Süß (ed.), *Deutschland im Luftkrieg: Geschichte und Erinnerung* (Munich: Oldenbourg, 2007), pp. 71–84.

Hadaway, Stuart, *Missing Believed Killed: Casualty Policy and the Missing Research and Enquiry Service 1939–1952* (Barnsley: Pen & Sword, 2008).

Haeussler, Mathias, *Helmut Schmidt and British–German Relations: A European Misunderstanding* (Cambridge: Cambridge University Press, 2019).

Hainmüller, Bernd, *Tod am Schauinsland. Das 'Engländerunglück' am 17. April 1936 und seine Folgen* (Freiburg: Rombach, 2021).

Hall, Kevin, *Terror Flyers: The Lynching of American Airmen in Nazi Germany* (Bloomington: Indiana University Press, 2021).

Hartmann, Christian, *Wehrmacht im Ostkrieg: Front und militärisches Hinterland 1941/42* (Munich: Oldenbourg, 2009).

Hasch, Wolfgang, 'Gräberfelder und Denkmäler für Opfer und Teilnehmer von Kriegen', in Ralf-Quirin Heinz and Gerold Bönnen (eds), *100 Jahre Hauptfriedhof Hochheimer Höhe Worms 1902–2002* (Worms: Stadt Worms, 2002), pp. 57–64.

Hase, Karl-Günther von, 'Aus der Geschichte der Deutschen Botschaft in London', in Wilhelm Reissmueller, *Der Diplomat: Eine Festschrift zum 70. Geburtstag Hans von Herwarth* (Ingolstadt: Donau Courier, 1974), pp. 103–14.

Heffernan, Michael, 'For Ever England: The Western Front and the Politics of Remembrance in Britain', *Ecumene*, 2 (3), pp. 293–323.

Held, Renate, *Deutsche Kriegsgefangenschaft in Großbritannien: Deutsche Soldaten des Zweiten Weltkriegs in britischem Gewahrsam* (Munich: Oldenbourg, 2008).

Helmcke, Hans, Klaus Lubbers and Renate Schmidt von Bardeleben (eds), *Literatur und Sprache der Vereinigten Staaten: Aufsätze zu Ehren von Hans Galinsky* (Heidelberg: Carl Winter, 1969).

Herbert, Ulrich, 'Liberalisierung als Lernprozeß. Die Bundesrepublik in der deutschen Geschichte – eine Skizze', in Ulrich Herbert (ed.), *Wandlungsprozesse in Westdeutschland: Belastung, Integration, Liberalisierung 1945–1980* (Göttingen: Wallstein, 2002), pp. 7–49.

Hettling, Manfred, and Jörg Echternkamp (eds), *Bedingt erinnerungsbereit: Soldatengedenken in der Bundesrepublik* (Göttingen: Vandenhoeck & Ruprecht, 2008).

Hettling, Manfred, and Jörg Echternkamp, 'Deutschland: Heroisierung und Opferstilisierung Grundelemente des Gefallenengedenkens von 1813 bis heute', in Manfred Hettling and Jörg Echternkamp (eds), *Gefallenengedenken im globalen Vergleich: Nationale Tradition, politische Legitimation und Individualisierung der Erinnerung* (Munich: Oldenbourg, 2013), pp. 123–58.

Hewison, Robert, *The Heritage Industry* (London: Methuen, 1987).

Hewitt, Nick, 'A Sceptical Generation? War Memorials and the Collective Memory of the Second World War in Britain, 1945–2000', in Dominik Geppert (ed.), *The Postwar Challenge: Cultural, Social, and Political Change in Western Europe, 1945–1958* (Oxford: Oxford University Press, 2003), pp. 81–97.

Hilger, Andreas, *Deutsche Kriegsgefangene in der Sowjetunion, 1941–1956: Kriegsgefangenschaft, Lageralltag und Erinnerung* (Essen: Klartext, 2000).

Hinz, Uta, *Gefangen im Großen Krieg: Kriegsgefangenschaft in Deutschland 1914–1921* (Essen: Klartext, 2006).

Hobsbawm, Eric, and Terence Ranger (eds), *The Invention of Tradition* (Cambridge: Cambridge University Press, 1983).

Hoffmann, Georg, *Fliegerlynchjustiz: Gewalt gegen abgeschossene alliierte Flugzeugbesatzungen 1943–1945* (Paderborn: Ferdinand Schöningh, 2015).

Holman, Brett, *The Next War in the Air: Britain's Fear of the Bomber, 1908–1941* (Farnham: Ashgate, 2014).

Höpp, Gerhard, *Muslime in der Mark: Als Kriegsgefangene und Internierte in Wünsdorf und Zossen* (Berlin: Das Arabische Buch, 1997).

Horne, John, and Alan Kramer, *German Atrocities, 1914: A History of Denial* (New Haven and London: Yale University Press, 2001).

Horne, John, and Edward Madigan (eds), *Towards Commemoration: Ireland in War and Revolution 1912–1923* (Dublin: Royal Irish Academy, 2013).

Horstmann, Iris, Ulrike Junker, Katrin Klusmann and Bernd Ostendorf (eds), *"Wer seine Geschichte nicht kennt . . .": Nationalsozialismus und Münster* (Münster: Agenda, 1993).

Hugill, Peter, 'German Great Power Relations in the Pages of "Simplicissimus", 1816–1914', 98 (2008), pp. 1–23.

Jacobsen, Hans-Adolf, and Arthur Smith, *The Nazi Party and the German Foreign Office* (London: Routledge, 2007).

Jalland, Pat, *Death in War and Peace: Loss and Grief in England, 1914–1970* (Oxford: Oxford University Press, 2010).

Janz, Nina, 'Deutsche Soldatengräber des Zweiten Weltkrieges zwischen Heldenverherrlichung und Zeichen der Versöhnung' (unpublished PhD, Universität Hamburg, 2018).

Jeffrey, Keith, ' "Hut ab," "Promenade with Kamerade for Schokolade," and the *Flying Dutchman*: British Soldiers in the Rhineland, 1918–1929', *Diplomacy & Statecraft*, 16 (2006), pp. 455–73.

Jones, Heather, *Violence against Prisoners of War in the First World War: Britain, France and Germany, 1914–1920* (Cambridge: Cambridge University Press, 2011).

Joyce, Patrick, *Going to My Father's House: A History of My Times* (London: Verso, 2021).

Jureit, Ulrike, and Christian Schneider, *Gefühlte Opfer: Illusionen der Vergangenheitsbewältigung* (Stuttgart: Klett-Cotta, 2010).

Kellehear, Allan, *A Social History of Dying* (Cambridge: Cambridge University Press, 2007).

Kelleher, Megan, ' "I will remember it as one more to the list of courtesies I have received": Interactions between the Imperial War Graves Commission and the Bereaved', *British Journal for Military History*, 7 (2021), pp. 83–101.

Kennedy, Paul, *The Rise of the Anglo-German Antagonism, 1860–1914* (London: Allen & Unwin, 1980).

Kent, Susan Kingsley, *The Influenza Pandemic of 1918–1919* (Boston: Bedford/St Martin's, 2013).

Kershaw, Ian, *Hitler. 1936–45: Nemesis* (London: Allen Lane, 2000).

Kester, Bernadette, *Film Front Weimar: Representations of the First World War in German Films from the Weimar Period (1919–1933)* (Amsterdam: Amsterdam University Press, 2003).

Kochavi, Arieh, *Confronting Captivity: Britain and the United States and their POWs in Nazi Germany* (Chapel Hill: University of North Carolina Press, 2005).

Kolbe, Wiebke, 'Trauer und Tourismus: Reisen des Volksbundes Deutsche Kriegsgräberfürsorge 1950–2010', *Zeithistorische Forschungen*, 14 (2017), pp. 68–92.

Kramer, Alan, *Dynamic of Destruction: Culture and Mass Killing in the First World War* (Oxford: Oxford University Press, 2009).

Kruse, Christian (ed.), *In den Mühlen der Geschichte: Russische Kriegsgefangene in Bayern 1914–1921* (Munich: Generaldirektion der Staatlichen Archive Bayerns, 2013).

Kushner, Tony, 'Clubland, Cricket Tests and Alien Internment, 1939–40', in David Cesarani and Tony Kushner (eds), *The Internment of Aliens in Twentieth Century Britain* (New York: Routledge, 1993), pp. 79–101.

Kushner, Tony, 'One of Us? Contesting Disraeli's Jewishness and Englishness in the Twentieth Century', in Tony Kushner and Todd Endelman (eds), *Disraeli's Jewishness* (London: Vallentine Mitchell, 2002), pp. 201–62.

Ladegast, Anett, 'Der Erste Weltkrieg im Spiegel nationalen Gedenkens – Die drei Soldatenfriedhöfe auf dem Südwestkirchhof Stahnsdorf bei Berlin', *RIHA Journal* (June 2017): http://nbn-resolving.de/urn:nbn:de:101:1-201711132008.

Langhamer, Claire, Lucy Noakes and Claudia Siebrecht (eds), Total War: An Emotional History (Oxford: Oxford University Press, 2020).

Laqueur, Thomas, *The Work of the Dead: A Cultural History of Human Remains* (Princeton: Princeton University Press, 2015).

Lattek, Christine, 'Bergen-Belsen: From "Privileged" Camp to Death Camp', in Jo Reilly et al. (eds), *Belsen in History and Memory* (London: Frank Cass, 1997), pp. 37–71.

Lawrence, Jon, 'Forging a Peaceable Kingdom: War, Violence, and Fear of Brutalization in Post-First World War Britain', *Journal of Modern History*, 75 (2003), pp. 557–89.

Lemmes, Fabian, *Arbeiten in Hitlers Europa: die Organisation Todt in Frankreich und Italien 1940–1945* (Cologne: Böhlau, 2021).

Leonhard, Jörn, *Die Büchse der Pandora: Geschichte des Ersten Weltkrieges* (Munich: Beck, 2014).

Lesniewski, Peter, 'Britain and Upper Silesia, 1919–1922' (unpublished PhD, University of Dundee, 2000).

Libero, Loretana de, *Rache und Triumph: Krieg, Gefühle und Gedenken in der Moderne* (Berlin: De Gruyter, 2014).

Lindner, Ulrike, 'Imperialism and Globalization: Entanglements and Interactions between the British and German Colonial Empires in Africa before the First World War', *German Historical Institute London Bulletin*, 32 (2010), pp. 4–28.

Lloyd, David, *Battlefield Tourism: Pilgrimage and Commemoration of the Great War in Britain, Australia and Canada, 1919–1939* (Oxford: Berg, 1998).

Longworth, Philip, *The Unending Vigil: The History of the Commonwealth War Graves Commission* (Barnsley: Pen & Sword, 2010 [orig. 1967]).

MacKenzie, S.P., *The Colditz Myth: British and Commonwealth Prisoners in Nazi Germany* (Oxford: Oxford University Press, 2006).

McCartney, Innes, *Scapa 1919: The Archaeology of a Scuttled Fleet* (Oxford: Osprey, 2019).

Makepeace, Clare, *Captives of War: British Prisoners of War in Europe in the Second World War* (Cambridge: Cambridge University Press, 2017).

Makepeace, Clare, 'For "ALL Who were Captured"? The Evolution of National Ex-Prisoner of War Associations in Britain after the Second World War', *Journal of War & Culture Studies*, 7 (2014), pp. 253–68.

Manz, Stefan, and Panikos Panayi, *Enemies in the Empire: Civilian Internment in the British Empire during the First World War* (Oxford: Oxford University Press, 2020).

Manz, Stefan, Panikos Panayi and Matthew Stibbe, 'Internment during the First World War: A Mass Global Phenomenon', in Stefan Manz, Panikos Panayi and Matthew Stibbe (eds), *Internment during the First World War: A Mass Global Phenomenon* (Abingdon: Routledge, 2019), pp. 1–18.

Mauriello, Christopher, *Forced Confrontation: The Politics of Dead Bodies at the End of World War II* (Lanham: Lexington, 2016).

Miehe, Lutz, 'Zu den Gräbern der Kriegsgefangenen des Ersten Weltkrieges auf dem Gebiet des heutigen Landes Sachsen-Anhalt', in John Palatini (ed.), *'Gäste des Kaisers'. Die Kriegsgefangenenlager des Ersten Weltkrieges auf dem Gebiet Sachsen-Anhalts Teil I* (Halle: Landesheimatbund Sachsen-Anhalt, 2018), pp. 119–43.

Moeller, Robert, *War Stories: The Search for a Useable Past in the Federal Republic of Germany* (Berkeley: University of California Press, 2003).

Morris, Mandy, 'Gardens "For Ever England": Landscape, Identity and the First World War British Cemeteries on the Western Front', *Ecumene*, 4 (1997), pp. 410–34.

Moses, A. Dirk, 'Der Katechismus der Deutschen', *Geschichte der Gegenwart*, 23 May 2021: https://geschichtedergegenwart.ch/der-katechismus-der-deutschen/.

Mosse, George, *Fallen Soldiers: Reshaping the Memory of the World Wars* (Oxford: Oxford University Press, 1990).

Müller, Ringo, *'Feindliche Ausländer' im deutschen Reich während des Ersten Weltkrieges* (Göttingen: Vandenhoeck & Ruprecht, 2021).

Nachtigal, Reinhard, 'The Repatriation and Reception of Returning Prisoners of War, 1918–22', *Immigrants & Minorities*, 26 (2008), pp. 157–84.

Nicholls, Anthony, 'Always Good Neighbours – Never Good Friends? Anglo-German Relations 1949–2001', Annual Lecture (London: German Historical Institute London, 2004).

Nieke, Sebastian, 'Die Trauerfeiern des Afghanistaneinsatzes', *IF: Zeitschrift für Innere Führung*, February 2020, pp. 5–11.

Noakes, Jeremy, Peter Wende and Jonathan Wright (eds), *Britain and Germany in Europe 1949–1990* (Oxford: Oxford University Press, 2002).

Noakes, Lucy, *Dying for the Nation: Death, Grief and Bereavement in Second World War Britain* (Manchester: Manchester University Press, 2020).

Noakes, Lucy, 'Valuing the Dead: Death, Burial, and the Body in Second World War Britain', *Critical Military Studies*, 6 (2020), pp. 224–42.

Noakes, Lucy, *War and the British: Gender and National Identity, 1939–91* (London: I.B. Tauris, 1998).

Noakes, Lucy, and Juliette Pattinson (eds), *British Cultural Memory and the Second World War* (London: Bloomsbury, 2014).

Nora, Pierre (ed.), *Realms of Memory: Rethinking the French Past* (New York: Columbia University Press, 1996).

Noyes, Ann, 'Memorials and Landscape', *Surrey History*, 7 (2005), pp. 3–13.

Olick, Jeffrey, *The Politics of Regret: On Collective Memory and Historical Responsibility* (Abingdon: Routledge, 2007).

O'Riordan, Elspeth, 'The British Zone of Occupation in the Rhineland', *Diplomacy and Statecraft*, 16 (2005), pp. 439–54.

Ortsgemeinde Dirmstein (ed.), ' "Dirmstein erinnert sich". Tage des Gedenkens an die Opfer des Nationalsozialismus' (Dirmstein, 2009).

Page, Norman, 'What Happens in "Mary Postgate"?', *English Literature in Transition 1880–1920*, 29 (1986), pp. 41–7.

Palatini, John, ' "A German Horror" – Das Kriegsgefangenenlager Kleinwittenberg in der englischen Propaganda', in John Palatini (ed.), *'Gäste des Kaisers'. Die Kriegsgefangenenlager des Ersten Weltkrieges auf dem Gebiet Sachsen-Anhalts Teil I* (Halle: Landesheimatbund Sachsen-Anhalt, 2018), pp. 83–96.

Panayi, Panikos, *The Enemy in Our Midst: Germans in Britain during the First World War* (Oxford: Berg, 1991).

Panayi, Panikos, *German Immigrants in Britain during the 19th Century, 1815–1914* (Oxford: Berg, 1995).

Panayi, Panikos, *Prisoners of Britain: German Civilian and Combat Internees during the First World War* (Manchester: Manchester University Press, 2012).

Pantcheff, T.X.H., *Alderney Fortress Island: The Germans in Alderney, 1940–1945* (Chichester: Phillimore, 1981).

Pennell, Catriona, *A Kingdom United: Popular Responses to the Outbreak of the First World War in Britain and Ireland* (Oxford: Oxford University Press, 2014).

Pistol, Rachel, *Internment during the Second World War: A Comparative Study of Great Britain and the USA* (London: Bloomsbury, 2017).

Pope, Rex, 'British Demobilization after the Second World War', *Journal of Contemporary History*, 30 (1995), pp. 65–81.

Pöppinghege, Rainer, ' "Kriegsteilnehmer zweiter Klasse"? Die Reichsvereinigung ehemaliger Kriegsgefangener 1919–1933', *Militärgeschichtliche Zeitschrift*, 64 (2005), pp. 391–423.

Range, Matthias, *British Royal and State Funerals: Music and Ceremonial since Elizabeth I* (Woodbridge: Boydell, 2016).

Reichel, Peter, *Vergangenheitsbewältigung in Deutschland: Die Auseinandersetzung mit der NS-Diktatur von 1945 bis heute* (Munich: Beck, 2001).

Renshaw, Layla, 'Anzac Anxieties: Rupture, Continuity, and Authenticity in the Commemoration of Australian War Dead at Fromelles', *Journal of War and Culture Studies*, 10 (2017), pp. 324–39.

Reynolds, David, 'Britain, the Two World Wars, and the Problem of Narrative', *The Historical Journal*, 60 (2017), pp. 197–231.

Rietz, Simon, 'Deutsche Soldatenfriedhöfe des Ersten Weltkrieges und der Weimarer Republik. Ein Beitrag zur Professionsgeschichte der Landschaftsarchitektur' (PhD, Leibniz Universität Hannover, 2015).

Robin, Ron, ' "A Foothold in Europe": The Aesthetics and Politics of American War Cemeteries in Western Europe', *Journal of American Studies*, 29 (1995), pp. 55–72.

Roche, Helen, *The Third Reich's Elite Schools: A History of the Napolas* (Oxford: Oxford University Press, 2021).

Rothberg, Michael, *Multidirectional Memory: Remembering the Holocaust in the Age of Decolonization* (Stanford: Stanford University Press, 2009).

Rüger, Jan, *Heligoland: Britain, Germany, and the Struggle for the North Sea* (Oxford: Oxford University Press, 2017).

Rüger, Jan, 'Revisiting the Anglo-German Antagonism', *Journal of Modern History*, 83 (2011), pp. 579–617.

Rugg, Julia, and Stephen Holland, 'Respecting Corpses: The Ethics of Grave Re-Use', *Mortality*, 22 (2017), pp. 1–14.

Sanders, Paul, *The British Channel Islands under German Occupation 1940–1945* (Jersey: Jersey Heritage Trust, 2005).

Saunders, Andy, *Finding the Foe: Outstanding Luftwaffe Mysteries of the Battle of Britain and Beyond Investigated and Solved* (London: Grub Street, 2010).

Schaarschmidt, Thomas, 'Ein Kunstprojekt macht Geschichte: Gunter Demnigs Stolpersteine', in Frank Bösch et al. (eds), *Public Historians: Zeithistorische Interventionen nach 1945* (Göttingen: Wallstein, 2011), pp. 288–300.

Scheck, Raffael, *Love between Enemies: Western Prisoners of War and German Women in World War II* (Cambridge: Cambridge University Press, 2021).

Schrafstetter, Susanna, ' "Gentlemen the Cheese is All Gone!" British POWs, the "Great Escape" and the Anglo-German Agreement for Compensation to Victims of Nazism', *Contemporary European History*, 17 (2008), pp. 23–43.

Schramm, Martin, *Das Deutschlandbild in der britischen Presse 1912–1919* (Berlin: Akademie, 2007).

Schwelling, Brigit, *Heimkehr – Erinnerung – Integration. Der Verband der Heimkehrer, die ehemaligen Kriegsgefangenen, und die westdeutschen Nachkriegsgesellschaft* (Paderborn: Schöningh, 2010).

Scotland, A.P., *The London Cage* (London: Evans Brothers, 1957).

Sellers, Leonard, *Shot in the Tower: The Story of the Spies Executed in the Tower of London during the First World War* (Barnsley: Pen & Sword, 1997).

Sharples, Caroline, 'Burying the Past? The Post-Execution History of Nazi War Criminals', in Richard Ward (ed.), *A Global History of Execution and the Criminal Corpse* (Basingstoke: Palgrave, 2015), pp. 249–71.

Sharples, Caroline, 'A Legend of the London Landscape: Giro the "Nazi" Dog' (unpublished paper, 2014).

Sharples, Caroline, ' "Where Exactly is Auschwitz?" British Confrontation with the Holocaust through the Medium of the 1945 "Belsen" Trial', in Tom Lawson and Andy Pearce (eds), *The Palgrave Handbook of Britain and the Holocaust* (Basingstoke: Palgrave, 2021), pp. 181–200.

Skinner, Mark, Djordje Alempijevic and Marija Djuric-Srejic, 'Guidelines for International Forensic Bio-Archaeology Monitors of Mass Grave Exhumations', *Forensic Science International*, 134 (2003), pp. 81–92.

Skrine, Peter, 'Hall Caine's *The Woman of Knockaloe*: An Anglo-German War Novel from the Isle of Man', in Susanne Stark (ed.), *The Novel in Anglo-German Context* (Amsterdam: Rodopi, 2000), pp. 263–76.

Smith, Malcolm, *Britain 1940: History, Myth and Popular Memory* (London: Routledge, 2000).

Smyth, Graham, 'Denunciation in the German-Occupied Channel Islands, 1940–1945', *Journal of British Studies*, 4 (2020), pp. 291–314.

Smyth, Hanna, 'The Material Culture of Remembrance and Identity' (unpublished PhD, University of Oxford, 2019).

Spark, Seumas, 'The Treatment of the British Military War Dead of the Second World War' (unpublished PhD, University of Edinburgh, 2009).

Stargardt, Nicholas, *The German War: A Nation under Arms, 1939–45* (London: Bodley Head, 2015).

Starmes, Hazel, 'The Forgotten Holocaust? Post-War Representations of the Non-Jewish Victims in the United States of America and the United Kingdom' (unpublished PhD, University of Southampton, 2007).

Steinert, Johannes-Dieter, 'Food and the Food Crisis in Post-War Germany, 1945–1948', in Frank Trentmann and Fleming Just (eds), *Food and Conflict in Europe in the Age of the Two World War* (Basingstoke: Palgrave, 2006), pp. 266–88.

Stibbe, Matthew, *British Civilian Internees in Germany: The Ruhleben Camp, 1914–18* (Manchester: Manchester University Press, 2008).

Stibbe, Matthew, *Civilian Internment during the First World War: A European and Global History, 1914–1920* (Basingstoke: Palgrave, 2019).

Stibbe, Matthew, *German Anglophobia and the Great War, 1914–1918* (Cambridge: Cambridge University Press, 2001).

Stibbe, Matthew, 'A Question of Retaliation? The Internment of British Civilians in Germany in November 1914', *Immigrants & Minorities*, 23 (2005), pp. 1–29.

Stone, Dan, *Responses to Nazism in Britain 1933–1939: Before War and Holocaust* (Basingstoke: Palgrave, 2012).

Storer, Colin, *Britain and the Weimar Republic: A History of a Cultural Relationship* (London: I.B. Tauris, 2010).

Strobl, Gerwin, *The Germanic Isle: Nazi Perceptions of Britain* (Cambridge: Cambridge University Press, 2000).

Sturdy Colls, Caroline, and Kevin Colls, *Adolf Island: The Nazi Occupation of Alderney* (Manchester: Manchester University Press, 2022).

Sulzbach, Herbert, *With the German Guns: Four Years on the Western Front* (Barnsley: Pen & Sword, 1998).

Tanović, Sabina, *Designing Memory: The Architecture of Commemoration, 1914 to the Present* (Cambridge: Cambridge University Press, 2019).

Tradii, Laura, 'Conflicted Afterlives: Managing Wehrmacht Fallen Soldiers in the Soviet Occupation Zone and GDR', *Journal of Contemporary History*, 58 (2023), pp. 267–86.

Tradii, Laura, '"Everywhere" and "On the Spot": Locality and Attachments to the Fallen "Out of Place" in Contemporary Rural Germany', *History and Anthropology*, 35 (2024), pp. 456–77.

Tradii, Laura, '"Their Dear Remains Belong to Us Alone": Soldiers' Bodies, Commemoration, and Cultural Responses to Exhumations after the Great War', *First World War Studies*, 10 (2019), pp. 245–61.

Ugolini, Wendy, '"When Are You Going Back?" Memory, Ethnicity and the British Home Front', in Lucy Noakes and Juliette Pattinson (eds), *British Cultural Memory and the Second World War* (London: Bloomsbury, 2014), pp. 89–110.

Ulrich, Bernd, et al., *Volksbund Deutsche Kriegsgräberfürsorge: Entwicklungslinien und Probleme* (Berlin: be.bra Verlag, 2019).

Urbach, Karina, '"England is pro-Hitler": German Popular Opinion during the Czechoslovakian Crisis, 1938', in Julie Gottlieb, Daniel Hucker and Richard Toye (eds), *The Munich Crisis, Politics and the People: International, Transnational and Comparative Perspectives* (Manchester: Manchester University Press, 2021), pp. 171–91.

Urmson, Birgit, *German and United States Second World War Military Cemeteries in Italy* (Bern: Peter Lang, 2018).

Verdery, Katherine, *The Political Lives of Dead Bodies: Reburial and Postsocialist Change* (New York: Columbia University Press, 1999).

Vigurs, Kate, *Mission France: The True History of the Women of SOE* (New Haven and London: Yale University Press, 2021).

Vordermayer, Margarete Franziska, *Justice for the Enemy? Die Verteidigung deutscher Kriegsverbrecher durch britische Offiziere in Militärgerichtsprozessen nach dem Zweiten Weltkrieg (1945–1949)* (Baden-Baden: Nomos, 2019).

Vourkoutiotis, Vasilis, *Prisoners of War and the German High Command: The British and American Experiences* (Basingstoke: Palgrave Macmillan, 2003).

Walklate, Sandra, Gabe Mythen and Ross McGarry, 'Witnessing Wootton Bassett: An Exploration in Cultural Victimology', *Crime, Media, Culture*, 7 (2011), pp. 149–65.

Walter, Tony, *On Bereavement: The Culture of Grief* (Buckingham: Open University Press, 1999).

Watson, Alexander, *Ring of Steel: Germany and Austria-Hungary at War, 1914–1918* (London: Allen Lane, 2014).

Weber, Thomas, '"Cosmopolitan Nationalists": German Students in Britain – British Students in Germany', in Dominik Geppert and Robert Gerwarth (eds), *Wilhelmine Germany and Edwardian Britain: Essays on Cultural Affinity* (Oxford: Oxford University Press, 2008), pp. 249–70.

Wendt, Bernd-Jürgen (ed.), *Das britische Deutschlandbild im Wandel des 19. und 20. Jahrhunderts* (Bochum: Brockmeyer, 1984).

Wentker, Hermann, *Außenpolitik in engen Grenzen. Die DDR im internationalen System 1949–1989* (Munich: Oldenbourg, 2007).

Wertheim, David, et al., 'Rushen Camp, Isle of Man – Camp W (Women and Children), Camp Y (Married), "Treat them with Kindness"', in Gilly Carr and Rachel Pistol (eds), *British Internment and the Internment of Britons: Second World War Camps, History and Heritage* (London: Bloomsbury, 2023), pp. 101–13.

Wild, Detlef, '90 Jahre irisches Hochkreuz in Dietkirchen, Hessen', *Irland Journal*, XVIII (3 July 2007), pp. 90–5.

Wilkinson, Oliver, *British Prisoners of War in First World War Germany* (Cambridge: Cambridge University Press, 2017).

Winkler, Heinrich August, *Der lange Weg nach Westen – Deutsche Geschichte I: Vom Ende des Alten Reiches bis zum Untergang der Weimarer Republik* (Munich: Beck, 2020 [orig. 2000]).

350

Winter, Jay, *Sites of Memory, Sites of Mourning: The Great War in European Cultural History* (Cambridge: Cambridge University Press, 1995).

Winter, Jay, and Antoine Prost, *The Great War in History: Debates and Controversies, 1914 to the Present* (Cambridge: Cambridge University Press, 2020).

Wippermann, Wolfgang, *Denken statt Denkmalen: Gegen den Denkmalwahn der Deutschen* (Berlin: Rotbuch, 2010).

Wittchow, Melanie, 'Hans Wimmer', in Karin Althau et al., *Kunst und Leben 1918 bis 1945* (Berlin: Deutscher Kunstverlag, 2022), pp. 252–5.

Wright, Patrick, *On Living in an Old Country: The National Past in Contemporary Britain* (London: Verso, 1985).

Wylie, Neville, *Barbed Wire Diplomacy: Britain, Germany and Politics of Prisoners of War, 1939–1945* (Oxford: Oxford University Press, 2010).

Ziemann, Benjamin, *War Experiences in Rural Germany 1914–1923* (Oxford: Berg, 2007).

Ziino, Bart, *A Distant Grief: Australians, War Graves and the Great War* (Crawley: University of Western Australia Press, 2007).

Zilien, Johann, 'Der "Volksbund Deutsche Kriegsgräberfürsorge e.V." in der Weimarer Republik', *Archiv für Kulturgeschichte*, 75 (1993), pp. 445–78.

Zimmerer, Jürgen, 'Deutschlands Tor zur Welt: Weltoffenheit und koloniale Amnesie in Hamburg', in Jürgen Zimmerer and Kim Sebastian Todzi (eds), *Hamburg: Tor zur kolonialen Welt: Erinnerungsorte der (post-)kolonialen Globalisierung* (Göttingen: Wallstein, 2021), pp. 15–28.

INDEX